Waldwick

Waldwick...Little Spirit

Kenneth Linde

Waldwick Books

www.Waldwickbooks.com

McHenry, Illinois

Waldwick...Little Spirit

Waldwick Partners, Inc.
dba Waldwick Books
www.WaldwickBooks.com

April 11, 2018

Second Printing: June 2024

Printed in Wisconsin, United States of America

Registration Number: TXu-2-120-149

Library of Congress Control Number: 2019900114

ISBN: 979-8-9852613-4-**9**

$19.95
ISBN 979-8-9852613-4-9
51995>

9 798985 261349

Graduation: Here I am a senior in Journalism at the University of Wisconsin in Madison. Four years of booze, broads and Badgers in a major that is a dinosaur. Journalism! What was I thinking? Newspapers don't want you. The professors "forgot" to tell us newspapers lost two-thirds of their revenue in fourteen years. Now, I'm not a math major, but this indicates to me it's not a very lucrative place to find gainful employment, especially when you're just getting out of college.

How about magazines? Are you kidding me? Nobody reads magazines. They even took the naked ladies out of Playboy! The Internet? It's all nonsense. Write books? Try to find a publisher or worse yet, an agent. That's like trying to find a virgin senior at the UW. I ain't pretty enough to make it on local TV, let alone the networks and I'm a farm kid from outside Mineral Point, Wisconsin who thought he could change the world, rearrange the world. Geez! I sound like Crosby, Stills, Nash and Young.

My old man was right. Stick to farming! Come home and milk 250 cows a day. Marry my high school sweetheart, whoever she was, and help spread cow manure and forget about all that you know.

SHIT! It ain't gonna happen! I need one more story! One more article! One more writing fix and then I'm done! I'll get my degree in Journalism and get a job waiting tables or doing something, anything but standing ankle deep in cow shit every day. My brother can have the farm. I have zero and I mean zero interest in all there is about farming. Now don't get me wrong. My old man has done all right for himself and there is something about the tranquility, but it's just not for me.

My dad said he had a graduation present for me. I can imagine. What a new John Deere? I just need one more article, one more paper and I'm done. I rack my brain trying to think of something to write about ...anything. My roommates and I live on Doty Street, five blocks from the Capitol. It's cool. Lots of mixers...kids who have graduated and found jobs in the city, too old or too broke for grad. school. Man, college is expensive. Then there's the hanger's…too young or too immature to leave Mad City, who are caught in the transitional zone.

One night, my roommates and I concluded that we needed some excitement. To be honest, we've gotten stoned, been laid, gone to all the Badger football and basketball games and gone crazy. Madison is a big small town. It's great and yet, what is there to do when you're twenty-one, besides drink and screw? At 41%, the city has the highest percentage of unmarried male 20-somethings in the United States. At the same time, 32% of the females are in the same boat. Well you get the picture!

We all agreed we needed something to take our minds off finals and the decision was made to go out to Ho-Chunk and gamble. BINGO! Get drunk and be oblivious. Not too expensive, because we're all broke…like student broke…and yet at Ho-Chunk, we can act like fools with the locals. Duh!

Now being a college student means some degree of irreverence and even an extremely high level of periodic stupidity, without total insanity and so a designated driver is needed. The infamous paper-scissors-rock game is played and I lose. Little did I know that losing two rounds of one innocuous game would completely change my life!

Round one, I chose paper…all fingers open. Roommate, Tony from Cleveland chose scissors! Bang scissor cuts paper, I lose! Loser's meet in battle, I offer a closed fist, representing rock. Rick loses to Charlie, whose roommate number two. Rick chooses paper that covers rock! I lose again! No drinking for me. I get to bring three drunken roommates home. It's part of being 21! We climb into my fifteen-year-old Jeep and head out highway 18&51 and scoot past the interstate. It's seven o'clock and the casino parking lot is full. What in hell is going on?

We go in and I can't believe it. I think every redneck in Dane County is there. I actually saw a mullet. A guy with a mullet! Incredible! Shit! I've never seen so many tank tops and hairy armpits in my life and that's on the women...just kidding. The women are proud of their tattoos as they waddle down the aisles, beer in hand, looking for their next big thrill. There are hundreds of cars in the lot and most of the facility's 1,100 slot machines are in use. Row after row of players are participating in a grand income redistribution scheme, parting with their money in hopes of making more. It is a pursuit that has only one sure winner....the house.

My boys sidle up to the bar and begin doing shooters...three-dollar shots of whatever. You can't be 21 and play bingo sober. I stand and watch. Holy shit do they look stupid. I'm laughing my ass off at them. I take all five dollars I have to my name, (heh I'm a big-time gambler, you know)...and head for the quarter slots. At twenty-five cents a pull, it doesn't last long. Shit! I could have had one and two-thirds drinks. Instead I watch the wheels spin to financial oblivion!

Now, I'm bored. What to do for a couple of hours. I peruse the entire scene and see this really big and I mean, really BIG Indian guy standing with his enormous arms crossed. Security! He had to be. Earphone in one ear, arms crossed like two huge Sequoia logs. Jet black hair in a pony tail! Jesus, Mary and Joseph, I'm glad he's not pissed at me.

I watch the three idiots getting hammered as they saunter into the bingo hall and realize there might be a story in there for me, something, anything, to keep the grim reaper, Doctor Pettersen off my ass. One more paper! One more story! One more chance to show him that farm boys can write. That's all I need! Three townies in the bingo hall! What it's like to get drunk and try to slur the word BINGO! They get lost in a sea of blue haired old ladies where two-hundred-pound "runners" peddle bingo cards, check numbers and offer free drinks. I head for the big man!

"Heh, how, ya doin?" I ask in my best Cheese Head accent. When you get it right....it comes out as one word... howyadoin? Then the locals know that you're from around these parts, heh.

"I'm fine, thank you for asking" he responds.

What-the-heck, polite and intelligent! What a surprise!

"Been here long?" I inquire.

"Started work two hours ago" he replies without ever taking his eyes off the casino floor.

"Sorry, I meant, have you been working here long?" Round one goes to the big guy and that's certainly not me.

"Three years" he responds.

"Wow. Bet you've seen some real shit in this place." I reply.

"Ahh it's not that bad. People are just out trying to have some fun." He politely replies.

He actually seems like a nice guy.

"Do you go to the University?" I dig, trying to reach some common ground. "No, I went out east to school" he replies still looking at the growing crowd.

"And you came back to Madison?"

"Sure, I love it here. The lakes, the city! It's young and alive and right now it really satisfies my needs".

"Where are you from?" I inquire.

"Black River Falls". He answers, never taking his eyes off the casino floor.

"By Tomah, right?"

"Yup."

"Where the "'I' divides" I proudly state as if I was an expert on Wisconsin geography. "You got it!"

"Where'd you go to school?"

"I got my bachelors from Cornell University and an MBA at Carnegie Mellon" he politely answers, but I could tell the game of twenty questions was getting old.

"Wow."

"My dad went to Cornell." He replied in a still-polite, but now official, manner. "Really? Did you play football?"

"No, I played rugby" he responds, now getting somewhat short in his answers. I was beginning to feel like a news reporter.

"What did you major in?"

"Analytics!" he responded with a frown upon his face.

"What?"

"Analytics…"

"OK…now you got me," I respond.

His eyes leave the floor and he looks at me like I'm sort of dolt, which I readily admit that I am. "Analytics uses mathematics and statistics to create predictive models from data. You then take the empirical information to recommend action or guide decisions in business. If you enjoy math, it can be really cool to look at numbers and see where they are taking you."

"As an example, in gambling, by using analytics, we can determine what our profit margins will be and what the risk factors are not only for the games, but also the bar, everything, even down to the probability of when and or where there will be problems. By using the data, we can be better prepared and more efficient with our resource allocation. As an example, if you're playing blackjack and the dealer is showing a five, there is a 40.6% chance that he will bust!"

"Shit!"

"If my data serves me well, this being a Thursday night, we can expect 1.2 altercations that will require our intervention. We can also determine what our typical net revenue should be, alcohol consumption, even how often we need to clean the bathrooms. In using analytics, we have been able to improve our bottom line without detrimentally affecting the entertainment experience we are trying to provide."

"If you don't mind me asking, and don't take this the wrong way, I thought you were the bouncer". I retort.

"I am, for now. We all start at the bottom and work our way up. Because of my math skills, I needed to learn more about people, and trust me this is giving me a great education when it comes to that."

"What kind of future do you have here?" I asked, again, pretending to be the reporter.

He was either softening or getting ready to walk me out the door. "Pretty good, if I work hard and prove to the CEO that I am people-oriented, my next step will either be in casino operations or corporate. Casino operations mean managing one of the facilities someday. Corporate means moving back to Black River Falls and working in the overall operations including finance, risk management, operations and marketing."

"Who's the CEO?" I asked.

"My dad." he replies, now getting mildly perturbed.

"You own this place?"

"My family and 600 other families". He replies with a shy grin on his face.

"Holy shit." I respond. (As you can tell, I'm quite the conversationalist.)

A wry smile came across his face. Was it boredom, frustration or simply joy in talking to someone?

"Do you ever have any problems?"

"Our share of drunks, punks and sore losers" he said as he stared at the growing crowd. "Some get drunk and get pushy. Others get pissed because they lose their money to a bunch of Indians."

"You mean Native Americans," I interjected in a feeble attempt at political correctness. "Whatever!" He responds, without emotion. He was cool!

"Right now, there's a guy in the casino who has lost all his money. He is getting belligerent and beginning to upset some of the other guests. In three minutes, I'll need to excuse myself and assist the gentleman out the door."

The big guy's badge said his name was Rodney. Now that seemed like a funny name for an Indian, but when the guy's arms are bigger than your legs and it's his place...along with 600 others...I'm certainly not going to challenge it.

The ice broke…."You go to the U?" He asks without looking at me.

"Three more weeks and I'm done," I respond.

"Then what?"

"Try to find a job"

"What's your major?"

"Journalism."

He laughed. "I thought analytics was bad,"

I'm beginning to think he's happy to have someone to talk to.

I was embarrassed. Another laugher! I might just as well have said French literature.

"What are you going to do with that?"

"It beats milking 250 cows twice a day"

"Maybe"

"You a farm boy?"

"Yup! Born and raised."

"Where?"

A little town southwest of here."

"Which one?"

"You probably never heard of it."

"Try me."

"Waldwick".

"Outside Mineral Point on Highway 23 towards Darlington," he replied.

"How in hell, have your ever heard of Waldwick?"

"My great-great-great-great-great grandfather sold some land down there."

"Was he a farmer?"

"No. He was an Indian like me." He laughs.

"What's your name?" Now, he was becoming the reporter.

"My name is George but everyone calls me 'Q'."

"Q"? That's worse than being called Rodney". He chortled.

"I'm George Terrill the fourth and so instead of George the fourth, I became Quad and that became "Q"."

Now Rodney was smiling and nodding his head "Q" that's cool. What happened to the second and the third?

"The second was my great-great grandfather and the third was my great grandfather. They were both pretty cool when they were my age, from what I have heard, but I really don't know much about them."

The two of us were bonding. God only knows why, but it was cool, like we had known each other for a long time.

One thing about a degree in journalism is that you need to read a lot. It's where ideas come from. It's much easier to steal ideas than create your own! It's not plagiarism if you only take a thought and then create your own ideas from that. In journalism school, you spend a lot of time reading great news reports or articles that show you how to compose a story and hopefully learn the trade of telling another story!

Every now and then I would read about people coming along that really piqued another person's interest. I read about love at first sight. I read about people meeting in bars, on planes or on vacations who became life-long friends. While this certainly wasn't any sort of physical thing, for some reason, I was already beginning to like this guy, especially if I ever got in a fight and he was around. He could scare the shit out of anybody else.

In a matter of minutes, the barriers were coming down and the warmth of his smile and his laughing at my smart-ass remarks were making this become a really cool encounter. Now I'm neither a loner, nor weird…well not too weird, but all my friends consist of those from high school and college. With my hopeful…and I mean, really hopeful… college graduation only a few weeks away, my roommates would be gone and the entire generation of people who I had hung out with for the past four years would have departed.

My roommates had been my buddies ever since our freshman year in Witte Hall. We had been together and poof, it was about to be over. Perhaps that was it! Perhaps I was afraid of being alone, but for some reason it seemed like Rodney and my conversation was so much more. I was really enjoying talking to this guy and felt like he was enjoying talking to me…just two guys hanging out in a casino, where one could kick the shit out of anybody In the place and get away with it and the other having barely enough strength to pull down the lever on a slot machine.

He kept his eyes on the casino floor and we talked for about an hour. We talked about Madison girls, Madison women, Madison old ladies trying to look 20-30-40 years younger; Madison's college girls versus Cornell girls; Badger football; Badger basketball; Badger hockey; the Brewers and of course the Packers and all the other stuff guys talk about. Did I mention that we talked about women? Yup! I guess I did. The more we talked, the more we laughed and, for some reason even the mundane stuff was interesting and I really felt like we had known each other for a long, long time. This was spooky!

Based on his responses, I was beginning to believe that he felt the same way. This wasn't about a bouncer and a patron, or even a random meeting. This was about two guys who met and began talking and laughing, who were enjoying each other's company. There was a sense that this was meant to be and this was fate for the two of us that could end up is a real friendship.

Rodney looked down at the casino carpet and I could tell he was thinking a deep thought.

"Heh man, I don't know what's going on, but I feel like I've known you for a long time".

"I've got the same feeling!" I replied.

"You've never been here before?"

"Nope!"

"You ever been in the post office?" I asked.

"Sure! Why?" he responded.

"Because my picture is in every one of them and I'm not the president!"

Ooops! Probably the wrong thing to say to a guy in charge of security in a casino full of cash!

The big guy just looked at me and laughed a deep belly laugh that made me giggle. He understood that, other than the President, the only other pictures were of the ten most wanted criminals in America.

Rodney shook his head and quietly said…"I don't have a lot of friends outside of this place because all I seem to do is work. I can't tell you the last time I talked to a person about anything but here!" He shook his head again and there was a strange smile on his face. I could tell he was pondering something and I already knew this was one really smart guy!

"Journalism?" Again, he shook his head.

"Tell me Q what do you know about my family?" Rodney asked as his stare went from the casino floor and into my eyes.

"Just that your ancestors got royally screwed." I replied.

There was a pause as if he was reluctant to say something. "Hold that thought." As his finger pointed up towards the ceiling in exclamation!

Rodney had an earphone in his right ear. "I'm on my way," he spoke into the microphone that was on his sleeve.

"Stay here." Rodney smiled and excused himself. "Time for a diplomatic ejection!"

I obliged and watched as some clown in a white undershirt rant and rave because "the Indians took all his money and stopped giving him free drinks."

I stood and watched as this giant of a man carefully made his way through the crowd and addressed the drunk. Few words were spoken and it was realized that protocol meant a taxi ride to wherever for the obstinate guest and a free ride back in the morning to pick up his car. Two more security guys helped the man out. In about five minutes Rodney returned.

"Part of the job! He won't remember he made an ass out of himself in the morning, wonder where his car is, find the card in his pocket and come back and get his car and brag about how much he won last night."

"1.2 times per Thursday night?" I laughed.

"Might be more tonight, there are three drunk clowns in the bingo hall making asses out of themselves"

I cringed.

Rodney resumed his position with lumber arms crossed and his focus went back on anything and everything.

"Journalism?"

"Yup"

"Are you a good writer?"

"I think so! I'm still young and naïve and believe in telling the truth."

"Boy, you are new!" Rodney responded.

I could tell there was something he wanted to say, but was reluctant.

"A good writer?" he asked again.

"I think so and so do most of my professors!"

"My dad and I were talking about finding someone outside the nation who could write about what it's like to be an Indian. We don't want any bullshit, just someone who could tell it like it is before too many of the elders are gone."

Holy shit!

"As a journalist, do you think you could write an article about what it is was and will always be like to be an Indian, Native American, Indigenous Person…whatever you want to call us?"

Wow! I came out to get drunk and play bingo and I might get the chance to write my last article for the Grim Reaper!

"Yeah! Sure"! I said with false bravado!

"If you really think you can do it, I can talk to my dad and see if I can get you the information so that you can see what we are really like."

"Man, that would be incredible and it would help me graduate!"

"One requirement…"

"What's that?"

"You tell it like it is and none of the whitewashed crap we get all the time."

"How about, you approving every word I write?"

"That's not enough! My old man gets final say."

"Sure, why not?"

"You don't understand…he's a tight ass."

"You never met mine."

With his finger raised in anticipation, Rodney listened to his earpiece.

"Three in the bingo hall, are they your friends?"

"Yup!"

"Time for them to go home."

"I'll get them. No need to scare the shit out of them."

Rodney laughed as he looked at me with his deep dark eyes and we shook hands. God he was big! His hands almost crushed mine!

"You're serious about the article, right?" he asked.

"Hell, yes! I need one more article to pass my last class and this would be great."

"Let me talk to my dad and see if he was serious and then, if he was, when he can see you. When do you need to write this paper?"

"Couple of weeks" I said.

"Cool. Go take care of your friends. They're making asses out of themselves right now."

"So, what else is new?"

We exchanged phone numbers as we mutually tapped them into our cellphones and I thanked him. The boys had lost and I had won. I just didn't know or realize how well this would work out until much, much later. God they were drunk!

The Phone Call: A couple days went by and the night at the casino was beginning to fade. I came back from classes and had a text.

"Heh Q, you still want to meet the chief? Rod."

"Hell yes. When and where?" I texted back.

"Black River Falls next Tuesday at 8:00 am."

"Shit. Black River Falls at 8:00 in the morning?" I responded.

"That's the old man. If you want it, you have to work for it."

"I'm in. I need the address." I replied with fingers shaking in excitement.

"I'll pick you up at 5:30. Give me your address."

"551 West Doty apartment 4B." I answered.

"I'll be out front." Rodney replied and added.

"For sure?"

"Guaranteed. Farm boys are used to getting up early".

Tuesday morning at exactly 5:30 AM, a black Mercedes CLS550 AMG Racer pulls up with me standing by the front door.

"Nice wheels!"

"Bought it used when it came in off lease. I can't drive it in the winter because it's rear wheel drive, so I've got a truck as well."

I jumped in and we head up I-90 past the Dells. Rodney points out that the Ho-Chunk Casino in the Dells is the number one grossing center because it's a class two and not class three like Madison, which means that Madison is just slots and bingo.

We get to where the 'I divides'…and Rodney head towards Eau Claire. Man, I love the wheels! What a wonderful ride. Rodney is cool. Jeans, boots and a Badger tee shirt. We bullshit about anything and everything, except being an Indian and a white guy. I'm cool. He's cool. Two dudes driving north. One really big guy and one little shit…namely, me!

Just past Tomah, the subject of his dad comes up. "He's really pretty cool, but he's also running a big-time business that has a lot of people depending on him. If he is short, don't take it personal. He just got a lot going on right now. He means well and is pretty shy. Let him do the talking. He will tell you what he wants to say. Ask questions and he will shut up. Cool?"

"Cool."

"The old man thinks I'm becoming too white and so, if he's a little defensive, hang loose, he'll come around. My mom gets after him all the time about being a racist and judging everyone before he gets to know them. I take after my mom."

We pull up to a nondescript office building. I wasn't expecting a teepee, but really didn't know what to think. Rodney had the coolest car in the lot mainly because everyone else in the office drove pick-up trucks. We went inside and I looked at the photographs of all the casinos on the wall along with a black and white photo of a small trailer.

I stopped and looked and Rodney offered, "that's where my uncle started everything in the Dells in 1982 when he started selling tax-free tobacco from a used trailer. The State tried to stop him but he had the balls to fight and went to court and won the case that we are truly a separate nation. The next year, on the same site, the tribe opened a bingo hall and the ball began rolling." Rodney responded with a smile.

We wait in the lobby. At precisely 8:00 AM the door opens and a very distinguished gentleman in a tailored light gray suit opens the office door. Mid-fifties, trim, salt-and-pepper hair, beautiful necktie. The only acquiescence were his lizard skin boots, polished to such a sheen that I really do believe you could use them to look up a girl's dress.

"Come on in" Rodney's dad said in a soft pleasant voice.

"Thank you sir" I replied. Mom and dad taught me a long time ago that the words sir and mam go a long way towards showing respect. We went through the pleasantries, but I could tell that this man was all business.

He stared out the window. "Journalism?"

"Yes, sir"

"Waldwick?"

"Yes, sir" I thought I was the reporter.

Any relation to the Harris'?

"Yes, sir" I assumed we were because every family in Mineral Point who had been there over 100 years was related somehow.

"I bought horses from a gentleman named Harris about 30 years ago." "That was probably Parmley Harris," I replied.

Rodney's dad smiled. "You got it. I knew he had a strange first name. One heck of a salesman that Parmley Harris, I think he could have sold me anything."

His mind seemed to wander as he looked out the window…"Good people. Mineral Point! Always loved that little town! Love the dog statue on the building. Is it still there?"

"Yes, sir" I replied.

"No better place for Cornish Pasty except maybe Myles Teddywedgers in Madison.

"You know about Teddywedgers?" I asked, quite surprised.

"Whenever I come to Madison, I stay at the Edgewater and walk over and get a Teddywedger."

"So cool." (I thought).

"I live a few blocks from Teddywedgers and get them for dinner" I replied.

"Rodney said you want to write a story about our casinos?"

"No sir."

"You don't?"

"No, I want to write a story about your nation and all that you have accomplished."

"Where do you want to begin?"

"At the beginning." I replied.

"You don't want to write an article, you want to write a book?"

"I want to write the truth. If it's an article or a book doesn't matter, I just know I want to write the truth."

"That's a unique perspective for someone in your profession."

"Consider me to be a rookie idealist."

Rodney's dad smiled and continued. "I remember how it used to be. My people were impoverished, like most of the nation's Native American tribes. Unemployment was rampant. There were no tribal businesses and tribal debt stirred talk of bankruptcy. The tribe subsisted wholly on federal and state programs and was, for all practical purposes, a welfare state. All that is different today! We now operate a network of six gaming facilities with 175,000 square feet of floor space, 5,000 slot machines and about 100 tables for games including blackjack, poker and roulette."

"Gambling has provided tribal members with jobs, opportunity and income. It has allowed the nation to build its infrastructure and create programs for its roughly 7,400 members as we try to preserve the Ho-Chunk way of life. In the course of less than 35 years, we've changed a complete society, and for the better. Gambling has allowed us to capitalize on what is otherwise our greatest drawback, which is our land holdings that are mostly small and scattered in more than a dozen Wisconsin counties."

"While many Nations have reservations, having scattered lands in key places is an advantage if your goal is to make money." But, he added, "if your goal is to preserve your people, your culture, your language, it's the worst thing on Earth. Our families have been ripped apart, our communities have been disenfranchised, our stories have been lost, and our villages are no longer," the Chief said wistfully as he looked out the window.

"We are the largest employer in both Sauk and Jackson counties, where the Dells and Black River Falls casinos are located. Our casinos and convention space draw in visitors, and the nation works cooperatively with non-native businesses, like small hotels to help them grow. We have a philosophy of giving back to the community. Last year, we donated $25,000 to help build an amphitheater at Mirror Lake State Park," the Chief said proudly. "Perhaps, most importantly, it has created jobs for our members. We employ 3,500 people of which 2300 work in the casinos or affiliated business of which 28 percent are tribal members."

He continued, "Each of our nation's 7,400 enrolled members receive around $12,000 a year in per capita payments from gambling revenues, in quarterly installments. That comes to nearly $90 million. Payments to young people are held in trust until they turn 18 — or 25, for those who don't graduate from high school or get a GED diploma, with many receiving $200,000 in one lump sum. We also have an annual operating budget of roughly $ 50 million which funds a range of programs, including housing assistance, college scholarships, health and dental coverage and elder care and we give about $1 million a year to charity."

I could tell that The Chief was proud of what had been accomplished and rightfully so. He turned from looking out the window and said: "Tell you what. How about giving you complete access to the Madison facility? It's a class three but you will get an idea of what happens and all that goes on. Then, when you've got the present covered for your paper, I would like to have you see where the profits go."

"I'd like that." I replied.

"Then, if I like what you have written, I would like you to meet with my grandfather and learn about our heritage."

Rodney had a smile on his face. His dad had never allowed anyone, other than employees and the government, to have a complete look at the casino. With that, Rodney's dad stood and I got the hint that our twenty-minute meeting was over. Four hours up from Madison to Black River Falls and it all happened for 20 minutes. Time to head back to MadCity!

We jumped in the MB and headed down the highway and were about 20 miles out of Black River Falls. We were cruising and not going any faster than traffic flow. I mentioned to Rodney that it felt like we were doing 40 when he had the cruise control set at 74.

"Shit!" Rodney exclaimed.

"What?"

"Cop!" As red lights behind us appeared.

Rodney began to slow and pull over to the shoulder with the patrol car behind him. He reached for his phone and hit speed dial and the speaker phone.

"Dad...they did it again!"

"How fast were you going?" His dad asked.

"Cruise was set at 74."

"Play it cool and leave the phone on. I'll call Charlie."

I learned later that Charlie was Charlie Birdsong, the tribal lawyer. Charlie was educated at Harvard law school and was no dummy.

The cop came up to the window. He had to be my age and was a skinny, little shit. His hat was too big and hung over his ears like Barney Fife and his badge was too shiny.

We all knew cops are as nervous as you are when they approach your vehicle. Its best to keep your hands on the wheel and in plain sight.

"License and registration" the officer demanded.

"What's the problem, Officer?" Rodney asked in a polite way.

"You know what problem is." The officer responded.

Rodney was irritated, but he knew better.

"Speeding." The officer announced.

I responded..."That's crazy, he had the cruise control set at 74 and we were discussing how everyone was passing us."

The cop looked at me with a sinister gaze. "Who asked for your opinion?"

Rodney turned and looked at me and his eyes told me to shut up.

"How can a guy like you afford a car like this? Selling drugs?"

Rodney responded. "Officer, I neither use nor sell drugs; it is against my religion".

"And why should I believe you? Tell you what, you sit here. I'm calling for back up and we will get a search warrant."

With that the officer took Rodney's license and registration and began walking back to his squad.

Rodney looked at me and said..."Welcome to our world!"

Now, most the policemen I ever met were good guys...just trying to do their job and keep things safe. I'd been stopped enough to know that they mean well and if you treat them with the respect they deserve, they're going to treat you the same. It's a tough job. This one, though! Man, I felt like kicking the shit out him.

Rodney's dad came on. "Where are you son?"

Rodney gave him the location near Mile Marker 136.

"Charlie's on his way. Just be calm and delay as long as possible. Don't confront the cop! Don't get out of the car! Don't shut off the phone, we're recording everything."

Jesus! I couldn't believe all this for being four miles over the speed limit.

We sat there for twenty minutes when another cruiser pulled up. This cop looked younger and had his gun out of his holster.

Now I was getting scared.

"Dad! A second cop just arrived and unbuckled his gun."

"Be calm, Edna called Ed Thomas. Rod, Charlie's only a couple miles away!" I learned that Ed Thomas was the Jackson County Sheriff and a friend of Rodney's dad.

The first cop came back to the MB and Rodney ignored him.

"Roll down the window!" the cop commanded.

Rodney continued looking forward pretending not to hear him.

"I SAID ROLL DOWN THE WINDOW!"

"Do it son"! Rodney's dad interjected.

Rodney was filled with anger and hurt and simply shook his head as he pushed the window button.

"Listen, when I tell you to roll down the window, I mean it."

Now the anger was really in Rodney's eyes and I began to understand. College educated, affluent, intelligent. However, because he was Native American, this cop thought Rodney was a piece of shit.

"Get out of the car!"

Rodney looked at him with disdain.

I said get out of the car or this will be your last ride!"

You could cut the tension with a knife. Rodney sat looking forward when a black Chevy Silverado pulled up in front of the MB. It was Charlie who opened his door and came up to the officer.

Wearing a navy-blue pinstripe suit with white shirt and red tie, Charlie offered. "My name is Charles Birdsong. I am this gentleman's attorney. What seems to be the problem?"

"Wow what are we having here, a pow wow? Why don't you get back to the reservation? This doesn't concern you."

Charlie looked at the kid and held his tongue. The little son-of-a-bitch didn't realize that he was not only being recorded but the Jackson County sheriff was listening in. "Officer, this car has been equipped with a black box that indicates time, location and speed at all times. I can download the data and show you that you're in error if you like"

"Heh, Chief, you want to go to jail too? Get back in your truck and get the hell out of here."

Charlie looked down at the ground and then at the officer. "Once again, I'm informing you that I am representing my client and if you decide to give him a ticket, please do so. We would like this matter resolved".

"Again, you don't seem to understand. I am the law here and I suspect that these two clowns are transporting illegal drugs."

Charlie looked at the kid and responded... "Predicated on what? You are required to have due cause and traveling, with traffic, at 74 miles per hour at ten o'clock in the morning, in a vehicle that meets all state laws regarding safety, emissions, insurance and registration, leads me to believe that you have targeted this young man based only on his race."

The cop shook his head. "Get out of here or there will be two dead Indians. ... understand?"

With that the second officer approached. "Dwayne, Sheriff's on the radio and wants to talk to you now!"

The kid looked at the second officer and then at Charlie and then Rodney.

"Dwayne, Chief says I'm supposed to take your weapon."

The kid looked in disbelief.

"What?"

"Give me your weapon!"

The kid froze when he saw the second officer was serious and noticed a Wisconsin Highway Patrol vehicle streaming across the median with its lights on.

"This will show you, these perps have drugs!" Dwayne responded.

The Highway Patrol car pulled in front of Charlie's truck and the officer put on his Smokey hat. He was about 50 and a seasoned vet. You could tell because there wasn't the furor of emotion that was enveloping the two county guys. He walked up and shook hands with Charlie as he spoke, "Officer your weapon, please", looking right in the eyes of Barney. And you" pointing at the second officer, "take your buddy here in to see Sheriff Thomas."

"Sorry Rodney!" The State Trooper said leaning in the window. "We've had several complaints about this guy, but no one could prove anything. I want to apologize for all you've gone through."

With that, Rodney's dad spoke. "Frank, it's Charles! Thank you!"

"No problem, sir. How's Rose?" which I learned later was Rodney's mother.

"She's doing fine, just wishes her son wouldn't drive such a fancy car."

Finally, the drama was over and I could clean out my pants.

"Sorry Rodney that you had to go through all this." The State Patrol officer lamented "we've had other complaints on this guy before and finally, I think we've got enough on him to put him behind a desk and into so sort of social awareness program. I don't know where in hell we get these kids, but put a badge and a gun on them and they think they can rule the world."

With that Charlie got in his truck and the trooper turned his vehicle around as we headed south. In the window, I saw the empty squad car and shook my head. My God, just because we were in a nice car and some idiot didn't think Rodney deserved it.

The phone was still on. "All ok, son?"

"All ok, dad."

"Tell George welcome to the nation!"

We were cruising along for several minutes of deafening silence when Rodney finally spoke. "Well, how did it feel?"

"Like shit! I was scared to death."

"Welcome to our world! We are either made fun of, talked down to or hated simply because we are different. We can't be intelligent! We can't be successful and God forbid, we better not try and live like the white man as it's simply not allowed. I get called Chief and boy more than my name."

We made it past "where the 'I' divides" and the Dells and started experiencing what has become Madison's urban sprawl all up and down the Interstate. Few words were spoken. I think we both needed time to get our blood pressure back to normal.

"Do you really have a black box in the car?" I asked. Rodney simply smiled.

We made it to Doty Street a little after four.

"Heh dude, totally cool…lots to write about!" I offered in my collegiate vernacular.

"When are you coming for the tour? Any time except on the weekend as its crazy then." Rodney replied.

"I do want to see all that happens."

"Thursday nights are fine except when drunken college kids show up." Rodney responded.

"That's cool, I don't have classes on Friday."

"Typical senior," Rodney responded as he shook his head.

"I've got enough for the paper just from today, but now I want to write either a magazine series or a book."

"Cool. How about eleven next Thursday night?" Rodney replied.

"See you then and thanks for the day".

I went in the house and took the day's events and wrote the paper I felt Dr. Pettersen wanted. I told it like it was and filled it with all the anger and frustration that I felt simply by witnessing the prejudice I had seen because of the color of one's skin and their heritage.

When you are a white boy from an all-white town, you never really understand. Through my college years, I had several African-American friends and thought I sensed what it was like, but really had no idea, no concept, and no inclination that simply because you drove a nice car and belonged to the Nation of the Ho-Chunk, your life could be endangered. My God! I can only imagine what it's like when the have's take on the have -not's and could only fear what it was like when those closest to the edge feel threatened and ostracized.

Here's the paper I handed in…my last bit of collegiate journalistic pleasure…

"The Brave Man"…

How can I explain what it is like to be a Native American? How can I share the turmoil, the diffidence and stares that come when one belongs to a different race? I am a white man in a rainbow world. I believe that my friends are of all races and all creeds. They worship God and respect life in a different way and yet, because I am what I am, I look differently on them and they do me.

No matter how wide I spread my arms to welcome them, there is and will probably always be reservation. In experiencing first-hand the throes of prejudice, my thoughts turned inward to determine what it was like to be part of the minority, a segment thought less of simply for what I was instead of who I was.

In 1961 John Howard Griffin wrote a non-fiction book entitled "Black Like Me" where Griffin, a white man, underwent transformation to temporarily take on the appearance of a black man in the deep south. During Griffin's trip, he never changed his name or his demeanor, only the color of his skin. The result was quickly learned when he would get the "hate stare" as he called it from whites. Wherever he went in the Deep South, Griffin met with pre-judgment, social ostracizing and segregation.

On a bus trip, Griffin rose to give his seat to a white woman, but disapproving looks from black passengers stopped him as the hatred and distrust went both ways. Griffin thought he had a momentary breakthrough with the woman, but she insulted him and began talking with other white passengers about how impudent the blacks were becoming.

During the early 1960's Reverend Martin Luther King and his peaceful movement brought attention to African Americans and those who never knew of the hatred they saw on television as it was broadcast live in black and white into their living rooms and they began to feel what it was like to be black in the south. Today, thank God, things are better and yet, sadly, beneath the surface, the distrust resides... smoldering... permeating... infiltrating thoughts and deeds, friendships and associations where demarcations begin and end with the adjective that describes the color of one's skin.

Tragically, Native Americans have never had a Doctor King to stand on the steps of freedom and preach "I have a dream". Native American activist Russell Charles Means stood for the rights of Native American people and became a prominent member of the American Indian Movement (AIM) after joining the organization in 1968 that attracted national and international media coverage, but there was never the response to what African Americans were able to achieve. His celebrity led him out of South Dakota and into Hollywood where he became an actor.

While today America appears closer to the adage..."Liberty and justice for all," the silence of prejudice continues amongst all peoples...White, Black, Native American, Hispanic and Asian, while society seems deaf to the insipient clamor that should rattle the bells of democracy.

We all move asunder from the toils and turmoil of indifference until one day it reaches up and slaps us across the face, reminding us that prejudice remains. I am proud of my friends and my ability to look past their heritage and inside the person. I met a man who is becoming my friend who is Native American. Through events and circumstances, we are getting to know each other and my hope is that the adjectives...White and Indian, will someday be gone between us as we share laughter and dreams based on three critical elements...mutual trust, mutual respect and mutual growth.

Less than 20 years ago, Native Americans continued to be relegated to reservations...land that was allotted to their nations as compensation for all that had been taken by our government, by our people and by those who simply did not respect the integrity of the American indigenous people. Much like concentration camps without guards, these reservations represented nothing more than long term death sentences filled with high unemployment, high alcoholism rates and little, if no, hope. A way of life was sequestered and with it came the squalor of poverty and injustice based simply on what these people were and not who they had become.

While the German's would never think to include the photo of Adolph Hitler on their Deutschmarks, American's today continue to see fit to include the image of Andrew Jackson on their $20.00 bills. Andrew Jackson...author of and signor of a presidential decree allowing for ethnic cleansing in America! Andrew Jackson...the president who moved millions of Native Americans from their land and forced them to land no one wanted. Andrew Jackson...slave holder, whose purpose was the enhancement of the slavery of one race of people through the destruction of another. Incarceration and oppression in the name of commerce and who remains on our $20.00 bill.

In the past two decades, Native Americans have been given the right to form businesses around the premise that, as independent nations, they can enter into enterprises such as gambling that are not afforded other American citizens. In so doing, these people are beginning to rebuild their society, while hoping to sustain their culture and the dignity and pride to which they have been without for so many generations. These people never wanted to have their hands out. All they have ever wanted was the American dream or that which we afford to any conquered nation.

My friend is one of these people. He is intelligent, educated, articulate, hardworking and above all else, honest...to himself, to his Ho-Chunk nation and to the United States of America. Through ability, desire and dedication he is achieving what we all want...a better life for himself and for his family. In so doing, he is achieving it by dedicating his life to his job and to his people so that they too can learn the meaning of the word dignity. Along the way, he is measuring his own achievements the way all Americans do, through the acquisition of milestones that remind him of how far he has come. Be it a car or a home or even clothes, with each step forward, we all measure our distance traveled.

Working 70 hours per week, my friend has acquired the resources to have one of the things he always wanted…a German luxury car. While many people would only dream of his reality, his ownership is such that he is criticized and ridiculed and has become the target of those who believe that, because of the color of his skin, he does not deserve such luxury. Being with him and witnessing the vitriolic nature of those who are jealous has shown me what it is like to walk in his moccasins where he is called…'boy, chief, Indian and Brave' in a time and place where all he wants to be called is a man.

After "Black Like Me" was published, Griffin received many letters of support. However, he also encountered hostility and threats to himself and his family in his hometown of Mansfield, Texas to the point that he and his family moved to Mexico for a number of years, simply for safety.

I am an American. I have a friend who is an American who I trust and respect and only hope and pray that, the burdens of prejudice that he has encountered are such that they someday go away. When America is right, when its people are honest and sincere, then the message…."We hold these truths to be self-evident, that all men are created equal with certain unalienable rights including life, liberty and the pursuit of happiness" will focus on the word "All" regardless of race, religion or heritage and we will all have reached our dream.

My new friend Rodney read what I wrote and I saw tears in his eyes. He looked at me and nodded. "Nice paper" I nodded back and we shook hands. He grabbed me and gave me a big hug. "You need to meet Great Grandfather."

"Cool" Was all this great conversationalist and boy of many words could say as I got an "A" with a comment…'nice' written by Pettersen, which was more than this professor of journalism had noted on anything I'd ever written before.

Job Hunting: It's amazing what happens when school is out. Those who were your roommates disperse. One to Chicago. One to Denver. One home to Milwaukee. Finally, me. My options were quite simple. I could head home to Waldwick and cows and milk and cow shit or find a job. My dad gave me until September to find reality and then I was on my own. My girlfriend was moving to Cleveland and we weren't that close and so it was the tearful goodbye and promises to keep in touch, which meant adios amigo.

All of a sudden, my world was shrinking. I was becoming a tweener. Between college and reality. Journalism majors weren't in big demand. I could postpone the eventuality and go to grad school or start looking around. People with Master's degrees in what I learned had no more pedigree than those who were in my shoes. Either you can write or you can't. I didn't want to make it look like I wasted the old man's hundred grand and so I hit the pavement with all my stories, articles and everything in place.

First, I hit the TV stations...Channels 15, 27 and 3 and never made it past the receptionist. Guys with real talent were lined up outside the door. Nobody wants to leave Madison. Next, it was the Madison newspapers. Shit, no way Jose. The incredible shrinking medium was certainly not looking to add writers. They were looking for ways to have them go away. My crazy ass ideas included ad agencies and so I spent two weeks digging through all the locals and got nowhere. The cows were looking prettier each day.

I decided I needed a break and a cheap drunk. "Rodney! Rodney! Can I get blasted? Heh buddy, I'm down and out and need something, anything, to boost my spirits." I thought. The rent was paid through the end of August. Welcome to the world of college rental. You pay even though you were leaving unless, of course, you could find someone to sub-rent the apartment and that was as probable as me having sex with a Badger cheerleader. Out to the Casino I went. Big brother was there.

"Heh dude," I called as I sidled up to the big man.

"Where you been little brother?" My friendly giant responded.

"Graduation and reality." I replied.

"And?"

"Got an 'A' on the paper, thank you, but job hunting…Zero, zip, zilch, nada, nix." I replied.

"Want to work for the nation?" Big brother asked.

"Doing what?" I asked.

"My dad liked the article," Rodney responded. "Part time working here, doing whatever, and part time writing our story. Consider it like marketing."

Are you kidding me?"

"The Chief wants 2000 words per week. 100,000 total words and so you've got a yearlong gig, if you want it."

I almost wet my pants. I was going to be legitimate.

"Hell, yes! When do I start?"

"Training first and then reality."

I had a big shit-eating grin on my face.

"If you want to impress the chief, write about what we do here and where the money goes and then the nation."

My head tilted back and big brother knew there was joy in my heart. "When?"

"Tomorrow morning at 6:30."

I didn't remember there was a time called 6:30 in the morning.

"No partying. I'm going home and to bed." I left and went back to Doty Street. Holy shit! I had a job and started in the morning. Incredible!

I awoke at five and was at the casino at 6:15. First job...cleaning the bathrooms and mopping up the puke from the drunks. Four years of college, but it was a start. I was in show business. My pencils and note pads would have to wait; brushes and mops would pay the bills. I whistled while I worked for four straight weeks. This was the test, during which time I read everything I could about the Ho-Chunk nation. I hadn't seen Rodney and yet I knew he and the chief were watching. Humility is a wonderful way to begin adult life; you've got no way to go but up.

At the end of the fourth week, I was called in and told I had made it through probation and was asked whether I would prefer to continue cleaning toilets or becoming a runner in the bingo hall. I had seen enough puke and pee to kill a horse and hollered BINGO.

Rodney asked for the first 2000 words and I pulled it from my case. A deal is a deal. It wasn't very good, but better than bullshit. Rodney didn't like his name and so I began calling him Big Brother. He thought it was totally cool and so he started calling me Little Brother. After my "promotion", he came to me and said it was time to learn the business. The Chief, as Rodney called his dad, said I didn't know shit and it showed. In a matter of minutes, I went from toilet cleaner and puke scraper to inside man. Finally, I would get to see the operation.

I quickly learned that gambling is all about analytics. Rodney was so right on. The first lesson was how the games were played. While Vegas casinos see you playing against the house. The Ho-Chunk casinos have you playing against other guests, with the house taking a percentage of the winnings, just like horse racing. Slots and bingo were the things that kept the Madison casino going.

The next thing I know, I'm driving to the Dells and learning all about craps, roulette and black jack and what the odds were. Analytics! I wondered if the word anal came from it or the other way around. It didn't matter.

The next phase was cheating. How people tried to cheat the house...shaved dice, card counting, you name it. The odds were against them. The art of cheating is always defeated by the science of business and my big buddy knew all the tricks and how and when it was going down and what to do about it.

With each week, I was gradually being allowed deeper into the inner sanctum as I earned management's trust. I quickly learned the psychology of gambling and casinos. Make the players feel like they had a chance. Make sure you broadcast the big winners. Always console the losers and make them feel appreciated. Always, and I mean always, make everyone feel like they were having fun and losing money could be exciting and even sexy. I saw the entire spectrum of society.

At the end of my second month, Rodney got me into the counting room. This fortified, windowless, armada had cameras everywhere and was designed for the ultimate in security. At any one time there could be a half million in cash lying on the table. Runners would bring the money to the outer door and then a second runner would go between the doors where a video camera would determine he was alone. They would place their hand on a screen that would read their fingerprints. If they were alone, they would be allowed into the interior, with double doors locked and no way in or out. Lead us not into temptation.

Next the sorters would begin. Singles, fives, tens, twenties, fifties and hundreds. Dreams. Rent money. Groceries. While twenties would seem like they should be the tallest pile, in the counting room, this was not the case. In fact, it was the shortest. I sat and watched people speed through the piles with the flick of their fingers. Faster than my eyes could keep track, they were sorting the cash and looking for counterfeit. In a matter of minutes, they took the cash and placed it in the counting machines. Zoom. Zoom. Zoom. The cash was counted. Not by denomination but by bulk. 300 of this, 735 of that. This was all about value as much as about bulk. Each pile went through two different machines and the numbers correlated. Any discrepancy meant a hand count.

Big brother had me watch as the tally increased. The vault was behind me and was double locked with a time release and a separate set of release codes that were sent every night from Black River Falls that no one in Madison knew.

At precisely 11:00 PM screens from all five counting rooms lit up. You could see the organized structure. Rodney called to each of the casinos asking for discrepancies. This night there were none.

"Everyone on target?" Rodney asked.

There was a unanimous affirmative.

"Ok, shredders please."

I watched as the cameras focused on each counting room.

"One for our ancestors." Rodney announced as a twenty-dollar bill was fed into the shredder.

"One for the other nations." Rodney reiterated as another twenty went through the machine.

"One for the reservations." he said as the act was repeated.

"One for our success." as another went through the machine.

"One for our children's, children, children."

I was shocked. $500 shredded with the confetti placed in an urn and set ablaze.

"How often does this happen?" I asked.

"Every night at eleven."

"Why?"

With my inquiry, the counting room stopped. They were incredulous. I could tell by their expressions they were insulted by my ignorance.

"Who is on a twenty?"

"Andrew Jackson" I replied, then remembering what I had written.

Rodney asked if I knew anything else about the eighth president of the United States.

Even though I had included it in my paper, I shook my head. "No".

"Before you can come into the counting room again, you need to know your history. My grandmother won't touch a twenty. Imagine, America honoring the son-of-a-bitch."

I was embarrassed. I looked in Rodney's deep dark eyes and apologized for not knowing more.

"Heh, Little Brother. You're not alone. America honors the guy and we have to be reminded every day about what he did to our ancestors, our way of life and all we stood for. I don't blame Americans. Most of them don't even know. What makes me upset is that those who do know, do nothing about it. Are we that weak as a people, as a Nation, as a country?"

I didn't know if he meant the Ho-Chunk nation or the United States. I had a new purpose. My God what an incredible hook to my story!

Another week and another 2000 words. I was getting into it.

One morning, I was scheduled at 8:00 AM, which, after my months on the cleaning detail, taught me was a weird time in the world of casinos. I walked in and you could cut the tension with a knife. Rodney was there in dress jeans and looked like something big was going down.

"The Chief is here," he whispered.

"Shit!" I looked like a pauper.

There was a high roller room with a private door and the Chief used it as his office when he was in town.

Rodney approached..."The Chief wants a meeting."

I almost peed in my pants. Our twenty-minute meeting in Black River Falls was one thing, but I was working for the guy. I swallowed hard and followed Rodney into the card room.

I stood waiting to be recognized. There was soft smile on the Chief's face. "Your college article was really good, but what you have submitted since then is pure horseshit. It's not because you can't write, it's because you don't know what you're writing about." So much for beating around the bush.

"Rodney says that you work hard and that everything you do, is being done to the best of your ability." I had become an expert in toilet 101, puke dissemination and all the other wonderful things you find in bathrooms.

Whew!

"I think you are wasting your time in the casino. We want you to work in our marketing department full time."

I was shocked. I thought I was being canned and the Chief wanted me to stop cleaning toilets and hollering bingo. "OK" I replied, not knowing what it meant, but realizing I was one giant step closer to the inside. A white, farm boy from Waldwick Wisconsin in the Ho-Chunk marketing department, Holy shit!

"Do you think you can write a book on our history?"

"Yes sir." I said with false bravado.

"I do too!" the Chief replied. "We need someone outside the nation to tell our story before it's too late."

Wow! I was going to be a professional writer. My old man was going to have a cow that he would never get to milk and mom would get to tell him "told you so".

Rodney had a shit-eating grin from ear-to-ear. "Does this mean he gets to meet Great Grandfather?" Rodney inquired.

There was a nod from the chief, "but first I want him to see our nation...all of it."

"Yes sir." Rodney responded.

The chief nodded and I knew it was time to get out of the hoity toity room.

"I'm on high alert while the Chief is here. I'll fill you in tomorrow," Rodney whispered as he escorted me out. I could never play poker because I can't keep a straight face and I know that every employee in the casino could see the shit-eating grin on my face, which made Rodney's look like a frown.

It was just past eleven and I was out in the sunlight. It's only about 20 minutes from the casino to downtown and so as I was driving home, I thought, what the hell...a Teddywedger for lunch! Then I thought, shit, the Chief said he liked them. I parked the car in the Mifflin Street cul-de-sac next to the little restaurant and went in and ordered three...one for big brother, the Chief and me. Now if you never had pasty you have no idea what you are missing...meat and potatoes baked in a pie crust. I paid and asked the clerk for a marker writing "thank you" on the foil. I zipped back out to the casino with the wonderful smell of home infiltrating my nostrils. God, I missed my mom's cooking.

I slid Into the vestlbule by the front door and told Ike the doorman that I had a delivery for the Chief and would be right out. I quickly walked back to the card room where the Chief was sitting talking to Rodney. Quietly, I wrapped on the door, slipped in, handed them the bag and paper plates and was gone. I wanted no recognition.

I reached the front door and Ike opened it and I slid behind the wheel of the Jeep when I got a text from Rodney consisting of one smiley face.

"You're welcome," I whispered to myself as I headed for home. "You're welcome."

Party Hardy: I had the weekend off as my parents had a graduation party scheduled for me. They waited until August because there were so many vacations, weddings and graduation parties in June. Besides, August is a slow time on Wisconsin farms. Finally, I would find out what my dad had for me.

Saturday morning, I got up and headed down Highway 18&151 past Verona, Mount Horeb, Blue Mounds, Ridgeway, Barneveld and then Dodgeville, where I flipped the obligatory bird. Mineral Pointers never forgot or forgave Dodgeville for taking the county seat away and then the hospital. When we played them in football, it was always the same. We went to kick their asses and they ours. They usually won at football, but we always kicked their butts in wrestling. Farm boys are tough.

The bypass around Mineral Point had sucked a lot of life out of our little town and the drive down Shake Rag street was quiet. I turned left towards Darlington past my great, great Grand Mother's limestone house she built herself. Now, there's a story I should write someday.

As I hit the Waldwick turn, life and living began slowing down as peace and tranquility slithered through my soul. Like a pair of old jeans, I was regaining my comfort zone where so many memories were stored in special compartments of "firsts" that were too many to reflect on in a short period of time, but contained a closet full of smiles, all hanging, waiting for me to pull them out and enjoy and put back for yet another day. I reached our drive and the pace slowed even more. There truly is no greater place than a farm. I hope my writing success can be such that I can live and write in the country where the only noise is that of the soft, summer breeze whispering tranquility.

Mom saw me coming and was at the front door. She was one of the only women other than grandma that still wore an apron when she worked in the kitchen. I guess some things never are given up. I always came in through the mud room and so I guess my position had transcended into that of a guest, instead of family. Mom gave me a hug as if it had been months or years instead of weeks since we saw each other.

"Where's dad?" I asked, even though I knew where he was.

"He's in town." Which meant that he was in Mineral Point? "He'll be home soon".

Everything was as it was and had always been as long as I could remember. Nothing moved except the hands on the clock and they seemed to move slower here than in Madison. There was the Amelia Barr poem, "The Farmer," hanging on the wall

The king may rule o'er land and sea,

The lord may live right royally,
The soldier ride in pomp and pride,
The sailor roam o'er ocean wide;
But this or that, whate'er befall,

The farmer he must feed them all.
The writer thinks, the poet sings,
The craftsmen fashion wondrous things,

The doctor heals, the lawyer pleads,
The miner follows the precious leads;
But this or that, whate'er befall,
The farmer he must feed them all.

The merchant he may buy and sell,
The teacher do his duty well;
But men may toil through busy days,
Or men may stroll through pleasant ways;
From king to beggar, whate'er befall,

The farmer he must feed them all.
The farmer's trade is one of worth;
He's partner with the sky and earth,
He's partner with the sun and rain,

And no man loses for his gain;
And men may rise, or men may fall,
But the farmer he must feed them all.

God bless the man who sows the wheat,
Who finds us milk and fruit and meat;
May his purse be heavy, his heart be light,
His cattle and corn and all go right;

God bless the seeds his hands let fall,
For the farmer, he must feed us all.

"Where's Tommie?" I asked, already knowing that my brother would be with dad.

"He went with dad". Mom replied.

Tommie and dad were as close as close could be. Mom and I were buddies. It just worked out that way.

After a little chitchat, watching mom fixing enough food for an army, I told her I was going to take a walk. She knew where I was going. My favorite spot on earth! A place so revered, that every time I went, I had tears in my eyes. She nodded. The party was in four hours and so all was cool.

"Where's Jake?" I asked. Jake was my third brother, except he had four legs and was a Border Collie. Mom just nodded and I knew that he was in town, too. All you had to do was pick up your keys and Jake would go crazy and shoot for dad's truck. It meant town and a stop at the Dairy Delight for an ice cream cone.

I put on my boots and began the walk to Skunk Hollow and the ancient oaks. I passed the family cemetery... surrounded by a limestone fence that warmed the souls of so many people I never knew. It was over a mile to my destination through the shoulder high corn and ancient apple trees and down into the valley. I could feel the spirits welcome me as I walked through the tall grass of memories and headed for the trees.

Nowhere else had ever filled me with the peace that I felt in the forest. I walked among my wooden friends and looked up at their majestic branches. This was my holy ground. I peered at the wild flowers growing in the shadows as the majesty of my second mother...Mother Earth, stood before me and I felt at home. I closed my eyes and breathed the warm, rich scent of peace. How could I not want to be here forever?

Our lives are measured in minutes, hours and days. My beloved trees measured time in centuries. I quietly walked amongst my friends to the clearing where the stone foundation of my Grandfather's school remained. I paused imagining what it was like walking each day to and from school when I was always in such a hurry to simply get to my Jeep.

I stopped and closed my eyes and felt the warm summer sun on my back and thanked God for all that I had. Today was to be my day and yet, it was for mom and dad, as they made it all possible. I vowed that I would make certain that they knew how much I appreciated all that they sacrificed for me. I didn't stay long, but then I never did. Only a few minutes respite replenished my heart and soul and washed away all the frustration and stress that was within me. I always want to stay longer. Someday. Someday. Someday!

The walk back from my arbor friends took me past the old apple trees and the orchard and brought me back to Waldwick reality where the first sight of the Chevy let me know that Tommie, dad and Jake were home. I was 100 yards from the house when I saw Jake hurtling towards me. Within a few steps, I knew that I would have forty pounds of excitement launched into my arms, tail wagging, and tongue slurping wet kisses of hello. God, I love that dog. He's my buddy, my pal, my loyal friend. As a pup, he was to be a farm dog. The first night he was with us, I felt sorry for him and snuck him into my room. That night was the last night with that "farm dog" assignment. I went to college and Jake moved in mom and dad's room. Son number three...spoiled rotten, and worth every bit of it.

I hugged my pal and knelt before him to allow his joy to wane. He was happy to see "Q" and God I was happy to see him. He led the way back to the house as if to show mom and dad what he found. Tail wagging, tongue slurping, my little buddy was in puppy heaven.

Tommie gave me the honored, big brother hug. He was younger but bigger than me and had farm hands…tough, strong, powerful. He went to State in wrestling. Some kid from up by Fond du Lac beat him and went on to be the state champion in their weight class.

"Heh, brother, how are the heifers?" I asked, which was brother farm talk for who are you dating?

"Not bad." He replied, filling me in on a girl named Heather from down by Belmont.

"She coming today?" I asked.

"Too soon." was his response.

"Aw, come on Tommie, are you afraid that little brother, with all his big city charm, is going to sweep her away from you?"

"Just the opposite." Tommie replied." I'm afraid she will think I'm like you and never go out with me again."

Touché! Tommie wins round-one of what will be good natured harassment all weekend long.

"You go down to the forest?" Tommie asked already knowing that I was there.

"You know, if I had my way, I'd cut those trees down and sell the lumber. We could put 10 acres of corn down there". His taunts were getting serious as he knew my love for the ancient forest.

"Peace." I responded as their demise was one of my worst nightmares.

It wasn't long before the guests began to arrive. Christ! You forget how many there are ...aunts, uncles, cousins, neighbors, friends. Half the time, you have no idea who they are. All smiling, some wishing they were anywhere else. Food! We could feed an army. Mom made my favorite…peanut squares! Small cubes of angel food cake, rolled in frosting and covered with crumbled peanuts! I got one before they were all snarfed up! Dad had the field ready for softball and the horseshoe posts were in place. There would be a lot of laughing, drinking, joking and good - natured fun. As always there would be talk about the Brewers, Badgers and Packers. My heart was warm with the smiles of love. I had rehearsed my answers regarding the fact that I had graduated and wanted to be a writer. There were to be no surprise questions.

I watched as mom organized and controlled all the food and dad made sure that each set of demographics had something to see and do to be entertained and amused. The wagon was set for the obligatory hay ride for the little ones and everything was timed to make sure everyone got fed, entertained and yet home for evening milking, including Tommie and dad.

After lunch and all the games, everyone was gathered round and dad served as master of ceremonies. The invite said no gifts and most adhered. It was time for the unveiling of what had been promised. Dad had me come forward and there was a box on the picnic table that was wrapped. I opened the card and it said it was from my great-great-great-great-great grandfather. I didn't understand but continued on. As I opened the box, I found a leather-bound book of hand-written pages…written by someone so long ago. The cover was embossed with one word…. Waldwick.

Tears streamed from my face. I knew this was our history and I was being entrusted to sustain the legacy. I asked Tommie to come up and join me as it was his heritage as well. Dad informed me that the book had been scanned and Tommie had a copy.

"You, my son, the writer, must keep our family alive through your words and deeds" as dad shared with everyone what was in the book and all that transpired. "I have marked three special spots and ask that you read two of them out loud for everyone to hear. For those of you who do not know. "Q's" great-great-great-great -great grandfather George Terrill, kept a journal on his life and how all that we have before us came to be. We found the journal when we were taking down the old house. It had been kept in the root cellar and was almost buried forever. I cannot tell you how honored we all were to find it and to share parts of it with you today. Waldwick is about yesterday. Waldwick is about today. Waldwick is about tomorrow and the dreams we have that create our reality."

There was a hushed silence where the only sound was the summer breeze and the redwing blackbirds chirping in the trees as I opened the ancient book to where the first red marker was placed and looked down upon the faded pages. I had tears in my eyes and a lump in my throat. My heart felt like it weighed a ton and even Jake sat at attention, waiting to hear what dad asked me to read…"Elizabeth and I knew our land and what we had. We understood what was good for farming and what was fallow. It was this knowledge that allowed us to succeed where other miners often failed. On the southwest corner, we had a glen of ancient oak trees in which we saw a mother skunk with her babies. We called it skunk hollow."

We had been there many times before, but this journey was different. We were alone and we were together, bonded in unison as one. I watched as Elizabeth walked on, stopping here and there to look at what God had brought forth. The oak trees had to be 200 years old…a time before even Blackhawk's family had nurtured what God had given them. From the old wood came an ancient melancholy that was somehow soothing to us and much, much better than the harsh insentience of the outer world that now permeated our lives.

Perhaps it was the solitude. Perhaps the silence pierced our souls. There was no noise lest the rustling of the leaves as the gentle breeze trussed against my mind and permeated my heart. Even today, so many years later, I have a fondness for that day, the moment, that memory. Even with the changes that have taken place, we have endured. I have always loved the inwardness of that remnant of the forest and the unspeaking reticence of those old trees. They have always been a place where I could come and think... a very power of silence, and yet a vital presence.

As those ancient trees saw the land around them turn from forest to grassy plain and then to field after field after field, I oft-times wondered if they too were waiting for the end; to simply be cut down, cleared away, marking the end of the forest, and for them the end of all things. This was not to be. This was our parish. This was our enclave of solitude where nothing else mattered except the silence, the tranquility and the trees.

As years passed, I have often wondered why this spot has meant so much to me. Perhaps it was the trees and their strong and aristocratic silence, perhaps it was because it reminded me of my Elizabeth and the beauty, tranquility, dignity and balance she had given me...the silence of these strong trees, has always meant something else, it meant my love for my wife.

Life is not just about here and now, but also about tomorrow. What the eye does not see and the mind does not know simply does not exist. Yet with each day, there is so much more to see and to know and this meant opening the world to those around us."

There wasn't a dry eye anywhere, including mine. My great-great -great-great-great grandfather's words gave meaning to me, allowing me to reach back and touch something I loved. I now knew why that sacred spot was so special to me. It was where my ancestors are calling out to me, healing me, welcoming me to tranquility.

Dad's one of the strong, silent types and when our eyes met, his eyes were covered with the joy that only a father can know when he is truly proud of his son and it was an instance that burrowed into my heart and will remain with me forever. Dad nodded and I found the second red marker. I breathed deep…

"Education is a privilege. It allows you to look beyond here and now and to learn about the world in which we live. Every family needed to teach their children that learning was important and that knowledge meant sacrifice regardless of the time, inclination or the Wisconsin weather. There was to be no shirking. In the winter, the children faced the west wind across a high field and sometimes when they reached school they would have rosy cheeks or a red nose. From this, they learned about nature and about safety and what to look out for. While it was a challenge that took dedication, we never let it get too dangerous for it opened the world to them and gave them joy."

My great-great-great-great-great grandfather….(oh heck, let's just call him George the First from now on)…exclaimed one of my father's intrinsic values and allowed him to speak to me. Our family and friends sat in awe for they were hearing first hand why my parents had sacrificed so much for my education.

Dad stood beside me, hugged me and shook my hand. He looked at Tommie and asked him to come forth. Now Tommie and I are about as different as night and day, with me totally comfortable talking to groups of people and Tommie the quiet one like my dad.

Tommie didn't go to college, but that didn't mean he couldn't have. It's just that he found all he needed on the farm. Tommie picked up the book and turned the page to the white marker. He took a deep sigh and looked up at the sky and closed his eyes. He had been practicing what he was about to read and the fear of family was overtaken as he elicited a poem from the book as well…

Today will be yesterday, tomorrow.
And with it,
Will go another bit of our future,
Slowly slipping into the past.

I cannot remember each today,
And some I wish I could forget.
I only know that all today's must turn to yesterdays,

And slip slowly into the past.
Yesterdays … Once so near, slowly slip beneath our today's
That were once tomorrow's,
Before they too
Slipped slowly into the past.

Soon, all of our tomorrow's become yesterdays.
Making today's today and tomorrow's today's,
Only nothing more than yesterday.

"Written by George Terrill our George the First in 1871 for us to share nearly 150 years later," Tommie lamented. "Congratulations, 'Q'!" as he gave me a great big hug to the applause of those who had gathered with us that day.

Then the fun began. Hay rides, horseshoes and lots and lots and lots of talk and laughter. My God, everyone was laughing about this story or that and what fools we had made of ourselves in one way or another. It was all in good jest. It was all what it should have been…people getting together to share life, to share love and to share each other's happiness. This is what family is all about.

Dad knew that inquisitive friends and neighbors would put the book at risk and so Tommie's copy was placed on the table for all to see, along with a family tree, where a copy of the yellowed pages and faded ink reached out and pulled us all in. My extended family stood in awe as they touched our history. We promised to put a copy up on a website for everyone to read. Yet, Tommie and I were the lucky ones as there is no gift that could have been given that could have meant more to me. My family! My heritage! My story! My God was I blessed!

After everyone left, clean up completed and the chores done, it was just the four of us and as we sat out on the screen porch with Jake at our side, lightly panting to the cricket's cadence. I thanked mom and dad for the party and for the book. I asked if it could be put in a vault for safekeeping and asked if it was all right to make a copy. Tommie smiled and tossed me a thumb drive. He knew that I wouldn't want to risk something so precious and would honor the dignity of our family by always knowing that Waldwick, the book, belonged to both of us.

Church: Sunday morning meant church where my ancestors had gone. We went up to the Mineral Point cemetery and looked at all those who couldn't be buried at home, as it was against the law. We went to the Red Rooster for breakfast and then it was time to head back to Madison. I jumped in the Jeep and for 52 miles my mind replayed all that transpired and I thought of my brother and how truly lucky he was. He knew what he wanted out of life and it stood beneath his feet. He could reach down and feel its warmth and know where it came from and why the land was so special to us all.

The apartment seemed cold and lonely and so very, very quiet. I put the thumb drive in and began reading. For six hours I read and laughed and cried and, like a caterpillar into a butterfly, I changed from a boy into a man. I learned of love and hate and diligence and sacrifice and for the first time, I had meaning to all that I was. I tasted oppression and realized that it was still all around me, not as direct, but obtuse looks and stares, ideas and opinions forever challenging humanity and decency.

My current existence now seemed so trite. What I thought was cool now seemed so juvenile. As I read about Red Bird and Blackhawk, Big George and Clara, in the journal, my mind became filled with the reality of how blessed I was and all that transpired. I also knew that my employment was meant to be and I was committed to doing my very best to tell the story, one more time, with hope that no more people would have to endure injustice simply because of the color of their skin. God had reached down and put this in my hand as George the First had wished and I was charged with its reality.

The Reservation: Rodney and I set a day to go visit one of the predominant Ho-Chunk communities. Rodney explained that, unlike many Native American nations, the Ho-Chunk land was dispersed over a myriad of counties and therefore there was no "reservation". In the period of three hours, I learned more about American Indians than I thought possible. I took all kinds of notes and so what follows isn't what Rodney actually told me but what I am writing from those notes.

Rodney and I got in what I began calling the Batmobile and headed north on I94. Normal chitchat about all that was going on at the casino lasted until we were to the rest stop just south of the Wisconsin River. Everything from business to fellow workers to hot babes included.

"Heh, why don't you drive?" Rodney asked.

"You kidding me?" I responded in excitement.

"Why not?" He replied.

"Cool." This was just about as good as driving a John Deere 7020.

We pulled into the rest area just south of the Wisconsin River and both got out. There used to be a great view here, but a three-lane bridge on both sides now obstructed it. So much for progress! Rodney went in to pee and I jokingly asked him if he was going to Tea Pee.

"Ha. Ha." He snickered.

"No tee, hee." I replied, which got a mischievous grin out of him.

I looked at his marvelous machine and imagined me behind the wheel. I had never driven a sports car in my life and was about to be the captain of a rocket ship.

He came out and tossed me the key. "Remember, this thing is really fast and it doesn't seem like it."

The warning was registered as this little kid slid behind the wheel and began adjusting the seat. That's when I realized just how big this dude was. I slid the seat forward and then the steering wheel down and lowered the motorized headrest and pulled the mirror down as well. God, he was huge.

As I turned on the engine, I heard the purr. 502 horses! Shit! Slowly I backed out of the parking spot and made certain that no one was coming. The last thing I wanted was to be creamed by some idiot who had to take a pee.

I pulled out onto the rest area ramp and gave the Batmobile some gas. It pushed me back against the seat and the speedometer read 82 before I even merged back onto I-94.

Rodney chuckled. "Hold on little man or it will get away from you." By the bridge over the Wisconsin River I hit triple digits and let off the gas. Holy shit! I had no idea!

"How fast will it go?" I asked.

"They say, 205, but the tires are only rated at 160 so I've never had it above that." I checked the tach and at 80 it was only reading 1600 RPM. My God, what a beast! No wonder Rodney loved it.

"You ever take any anthropology?" Rodney inquired.

"Never" I replied.

"Know anything about the land bridge?"

I didn't have a clue what he was talking about.

"Around 20,000 years ago, a small asteroid smashed into earth and the skies clouded. In a period of a few hundred years, the mean temperature of the earth dropped ten degrees."

"Doesn't sound like much" I responded.

"Enough to begin a glacial period that saw the creation that took all the topsoil from northern Wisconsin and shoved it into Illinois, while it scraped out the Great Lakes and lowered sea levels by around three-hundred feet."

"Wow". I politely exclaimed with my eyes glued to the road.

Rodney continued, "This was a slow process. Not like somebody pulling the plug in a bathtub. As the water level went down, it created the land bridge called Beringia from Siberia to Alaska and about 13,000 years ago my ancestors began emigrating from Mongolia. These were the first humans in North America. If it hadn't been for the mixing of cultures and races, it would probably have resulted in different species just like dogs and horses are from the same evolutionary chain. With each generation, my ancestors spread further and further until the indigenous reached from coast-to-coast and into South America."

I was sort of listening but not really paying attention. You know the thrill of the road and all. I blame it on testosterone.

"Even though DNA indicates that Native Americans split from those in Mongolia about 25,000 years before Beringia, we still have many common traits including the melanin in our skin that creates skin color, our eyelids, teeth, flat feet, little facial hair and of course hair color and texture."

I was listening, but wondering where Rodney was going with this.

"What do you know about neurochemistry?" he asked. Again, I knew little and scrunched up my shoulders, realizing I was about to get a lesson in the subject.

"The brain regulates all your body's functions and enables you to interpret and respond to everything you experience while it shapes your thoughts, emotions and desires. This all happens because the brain makes chemical cocktails at a rate of about 100,000 per minute."

"I'll bet the Chief wishes our bartenders could work that fast." I included, trying to put a little levity in the conversation only to get the evil stare of the big guy. He was being serious and so I shut up.

"What you ingest through eating, drinking or even breathing affects what chemicals the brain makes and what degree it makes them, not by the substance themselves, but by the chemicals within the substance. Drugs are obviously nothing more than composites of chemicals mixed together that, when ingested, tap into the brain's communication system and interfere with the way neurons normally send, receive or process information. Some drugs, like marijuana and heroin, activate neurons because their chemical structure mimics that of a neural transmitter. This fools the receptors, allowing the drugs to attach to and activate the neurons. While it could be beneficial if they activated the neurons in the same way, they don't and end up sending crazy messages through the entire network. Other drugs, like speed and coke, can cause the neurons to release abnormal amounts of natural neurotransmitters while preventing the recycling of brain chemicals. This makes the brain function like a radio turned up too loud so that there is all kinds of distortion."

I was keeping my eyes on the road and still didn't have a clue where Rodney was going with all this, but it was his car and I sincerely loved the ride as he added, "Obviously, we all crave pleasure. It's part of our inherent need and our brains are wired to ensure that we repeat life-sustaining activities by associating them with pleasure or reward. Whenever the reward or pleasure circuits turn on, they're like search lights in the sky, indicating that something important is happening that we need to remember and the brain subconsciously teaches us to keep repeating the activity without even thinking about it."

"OK,"

I said as Rodney got the hint that I wasn't catching his drift and continued, "Let me explain. Because narcotics can stimulate the same circuits, you can see what happens. The brain says I like that, do it again and drugs become abused. Most drugs that are abused ...nicotine, caffeine, cocaine, heroin and alcohol directly or indirectly target the brain's reward system by flooding it with a neurotransmitter called dopamine. When the dopamine level increases, it affects movement, emotions and feelings of pleasure. When there is a normal level, dopamine rewards our natural behaviors but to a lesser degree. When too much dopamine is produced, it creates a level of euphoria that the body wants repeated; just like throwing a ball for a dog...over and over and over."

"OK," I said, nodding to indicate I understood as Rodney added, "While the body naturally produces dopamine from the foods we ingest, street drugs release up to ten times the amount we normally get from food. In some cases, like smoking or injections, the high is almost immediate because it's in the blood stream and affects the receptors in the brain. Alcohol takes longer as it needs to be ingested, digested and transferred into the blood stream. Either way, the results on the brain's pleasure circuits dwarf those produced naturally."

"Something like me standing next to you?" I responded.

Rodney chuckled. It was good to hear him laugh. "The pleasure reward is such a powerful motivator that it takes some people and motivates them to do it again and again and again. While every now and then might be OK, consistency allows the brain to adjust to the higher levels of dopamine by producing less naturally or by reducing the number of receptors that can receive the signals. As a result, naturally produced dopamine's impact on the reward circuit of the brain can become low and a person's ability to experience pleasure is reduced. This is why there are so many sad alcoholics because alcohol is a depressant." he continued. "With acute alcoholism so prevalent amongst Native Americans, I took the time to study alcoholism and addiction and learned that there appears to be a biological basis."

"About half of the nearly 20 million alcoholics in the United States seem to be free of cognitive impairments. In the remaining half, or 10 million people, however, neuropsychological difficulties can range from mild-to-severe. For example, up to 2 million alcoholics, develop permanent and debilitating conditions that require lifetime custodial care. Examples of such conditions include alcohol–induced persistent amnesic disorder and dementia, which seriously affect many mental functions such as memory, language, reasoning, and problem-solving abilities."

Rodney was staring out the front window. I could tell that he was deep in thought and it was time for me to get serious as he continued, "Alcohol can change the activity of neurotransmitters and cause neurons to respond through excitation or interfere with responding inhibition while different amounts of alcohol can affect the functioning of different neurotransmitters."

"Over periods of days and weeks, receptors adjust to chemical and environmental circumstances. Changes that occur with chronic alcohol consumption create imbalances in the action of neurotransmitters which can result in seizures, sedation, depression, agitation, and other mood and behavior disorders. An addicted person's impaired ability to stop using drugs or alcohol has to do with variances in the function of the pre-frontal cortex of the brain and this can be associated with genetics, making a person or even a race of people much more susceptible to addiction."

This was like listening to some doctor giving a speech, but I knew, what he was saying was important to him and leading up to something.

Rodney explained…"The pre-frontal cortex, which is located right behind your forehead, is the part of the brain responsible for problem solving, self-monitoring, emotion, creating the ability to delay rewards and integrate different messages to create reasoning and even the pleasure center."

Damn, this dude was smart! We were near the Dells exit as Rodney continued explaining that the lateral prefrontal cortex seems to help us choose a course of behavior by letting us assess the various alternatives. It is considered the brain's "executive", like our father's…or in my case, my mother (sorry dad, but we all know she's the boss). Rodney added that it is necessary for planning and regulating behavior, inhibiting the occurrence of unnecessary or unwanted behaviors, and supporting adaptive "executive control" skills such as goal–directed behaviors, good judgment and problem–solving abilities.

Rodney added. "Disruptions of the normal inhibitory functions of prefrontal networks often have the interesting effect of releasing previously inhibited behaviors. As a result, a person may behave impulsively and inappropriately, which may contribute to excessive drinking and seems to let us defer certain immediate gratifications and emotions in order to obtain greater long-term benefits."

Rodney went on. "When you look at Native American's, you normally find people who are kind, gentle, introspective and quite amiable. This does not mean that their brains are smaller, nor are their intellectual skills any less. It just appears that some of the brain circuits in the pre-frontal cortex aren't as developed as those of Caucasians. Does this make them less human? Does this make them less intelligent? No! It just makes the race more susceptible and particularly vulnerable to all sorts of emotional, behavioral and chemical issues that affect the ability of a person of Mongolian heritage to modify their behavior."

"This affects all people, regardless of race when they are young. Because the pre -frontal cortex is the last to develop, all young people are really susceptible to the challenges of immaturity including decision making and addiction. While being young is a real challenge, add in the socialization factors that our Indian nations have been subjected to in terms of greater exposure to those who are addicted and a pervading sense of social and economic hopelessness and one can quickly see where the issues we face can come into play."

We were nearing Camp Douglas and Rodney continued. "Addiction has been shown to be essentially a form of 'learning'. After all, if the brain is wired to form new connections in response to the environment and potent psychoactive drugs suddenly enter that environment, those substances are tapping into a much more robust habit-forming ability that adolescents have, compared to adults. Sadly, once addiction sets in, it's incredibly difficult to counter the urges. While many try, the emotional response, when an addict is deprived of the drug or alcohol, is usually an extremely negative emotion. This is a reaction to the fact that the chemical need is 'hard-wired' in the brain to the point that any type of strong association intensifies the craving for the substance. Just one more drink...one more snort...one more hit...one more pull on the slot machine. Locations, events and circumstances can take a recovering alcoholic or addict right off the wagon again."

"Addicted people try, but the deck is stacked against them because the brain releases a flood of intensely intoxicating neurotransmitters, like dopamine, norepinephrine and serotonin that are important in mood regulation, which, during drug or alcohol use, create the physical pleasure the drinker has experienced. This is called the 'reward pathway' where repeated abuse makes the brain relatively insensitive to 'normal' sources of pleasure, making it focus all of its attention on obtaining the rush created by addictive substances."

There were pauses to allow me to digest the information and Rodney continued..."For those already addicted, most of those with some form of impairment, will show some improvement in brain structure and functioning within a year of abstinence, but some people take much longer. Unfortunately, little is known about the rate and extent to which people recover structural and functional processes after they stop drinking."

I was in awe of this guy's intelligence and passion for knowledge. "And so, the cycle begins. At first, the user feels flat, lifeless and depressed and unable to enjoy things that were previously pleasurable. Now the person needs to keep taking drugs just to try and bring their dopamine levels back to anything close to normal and from there it only gets worse as they become addicted and need more and more and more to overcome their tolerance. Once addiction begins, the cycle becomes profoundly difficult to stop as other areas of the brain become affected, impeding everything from the ability to learn, to concentration and loss of memory."

"One critical area is in the formation of habits and non-conscious memory systems that can actually trigger craving for drugs. 'I need a cigarette' is a classic example of someone who has an uncontrollable craving for nicotine, even years after they quit smoking."

"Now what's on the other side? People who can have the pleasure without becoming addicted?" Without waiting for my innocuous answer, he responded. "For some it's social and legal pressure. For others, it's simply genetics. Those who can control it and live near the edge are the lucky ones. For others, even taking one small step leads down the path to catastrophe. As I noted, Asians and Indians share a lot of physical similarities because we share many of the same genes and this includes low alcohol tolerance and high levels of addiction caused by a naturally low level of dopamine in our system."

I put one and one together and could see that this was where the social factors came in as Big Brother continued. "In Asia, laws and social pressure are such that you don't have the drug and alcohol problems we do, but seem to have a larger gambling problem. Historically, Native Americans have been susceptible to alcohol, since they were offered it by the French and English to the point that it was used to get concessions from my ancestors and is the biggest problem facing my, and all Indian nations today. However, I guess we got even, we introduced tobacco to the white man."

"It's not the white man's fault. Historically, we have always had an extremely difficult time with the use of alcohol. Today, 12% of the deaths of the Native American nation are alcohol related. While that's a tragic number, alcoholism isn't as wide-spread as the media paints it out to be. Use of alcohol varies by age, gender and tribe. Indian women, and older Indian women in particular, are the least likely to be regular drinkers. In fact, they are more likely to abstain entirely from alcohol than the general US population. Some of this is due to the fact that many people of Asian descent are allergic to alcohol. While everyone talks about the drunken Indians, the frequency of use among Native Americans is generally less than the general population. However, when Indigenous people do drink, the quantity they consume and the level of intoxication is generally much greater than the norm and this is where the real problem comes in."

Rodney had a sad look in his eyes as he continued. "Our elders asked the US Department of Health, Education and Welfare if there were any statistics concerning death amongst Native Americans attributed to alcohol. They responded that a survey of death certificates over a four-year period showed that the per-capita deaths among Native Americans due to alcohol are about four times greater than the general US population and are often caused by traffic accidents and liver disease with homicide, suicide, and falls also contributing."

"Today, approximately 40% of children on reservations are under the poverty level. Housing conditions are poor and unstable, and there isn't enough food. Jobs are scarce and college graduates are only around 11%. Native Americans definitely need support and aid. Sadly, our youth are far more likely to experiment with alcohol than other youth with 80% alcohol use reported. We are now teaching children in all grades that alcohol and drug abuse by Native Americans puts them at a tremendous risk and has been shown to be associated with development of hearing and vision, kidney and bladder problems, head injuries, pneumonia, tuberculosis, dental and liver problems and pancreatitis. Sadly, alcohol abuse is carried on to the next generation because our rate of fetal alcohol spectrum disorder runs as high as 1.5 to 2.5 per 1000 live births, or more than seven times the national average."

"It's a vicious cycle. Our people start drinking because they are bored or unemployed and want a little escape. Soon the drugs and alcohol get the best of them. They are no longer reliable and no one will hire them, even in our own casinos. They become more addicted and then even the basics are violated and dignity and respect become secondary to that next hit, that next drink, that next fix."

As we zoomed closer to the Black River Falls exit, we passed the infamous "stopping point" of our first journey and I thought of that shit-head cop and hoped that he was in hot water. We were still heading north when Rodney directed me to the next exit. "We're almost there. Better let me drive from here". With that we went up the exit ramp and pulled over on the shoulder and traded places. He slid the seat down and back and pulled the steering wheel back, raised the head rest and adjusted the mirror and just shook his head with a wry smile on his face. I know what he was thinking, "Little shit".

About five miles down the road he found a rutted, gravel road and turned in. Rodney said..."I hope you understand what I have been trying to explain. You really need to learn before you pass judgment on my family, my friends and my nation."

We slowly drove past run-down houses and trailers. I couldn't believe anyone could be living in such deplorable conditions. It made our apartment on Doty Street look great, even in the worst of times or the best of parties. After a pause Rodney interjected..."When the nation first started making money, the elders elected to provide a stipend to each person. It was a major mistake. Instead of improving life, it destroyed some even further as they had the resources to buy booze and drugs and go deeper down the rabbit hole as I call it."

"This was the first phase, HUD houses and cash. I'm taking you to where my aunt lived, my mother's sister who died a couple months ago so that you can see for yourself what we are up against and why I vowed a long time ago never to drink or do drugs."

As we made our way, the stench of hopelessness wafted up my nose. Wherever I looked there were signs, not printed, but constant reminders of sadness, desperation and a total lack of commitment to any form of self-respect. Trash littered virtually every yard. Abandoned cars and tires sat as broken tokens towards the despair I was about to see. When unemployment ranged from 50%-85% one could understand poverty, but the profound loss of dignity was simply overwhelming. Death was everywhere…in the society, in the culture and even in life itself. So many had simply given up, waiting for the grim reaper to come and end their misery…starting each day with the sun shining, ending each day in a drunken abyss from which there was no escape. How tragic. How true.

Rodney noted that it wasn't just the men who were dying. Young Native American women were also experiencing accelerating rates of premature death over the past decade. Not in the cities, but in rural areas and worst of all for those in the lower middle class and those considered in poverty.

While the stipend from the Ho-Chunk nation was intended to lift them out of the doldrums of abject poverty, it only provided the necessary funds needed to sustain their habits of doing every possible thing, every single day to escape their own social and emotional demise. Rodney informed me that drug and alcohol over-dose rates for working-age American Indian women had quadrupled and suicides were up by as much as 50 percent in the past twenty years.

We approached what I thought was an abandoned house. It was not. It was the former residence of Rodney's Aunt Grace. We parked in front and unclipped our seat belts. Rodney sucked in his last deep breath of dignity as I was about to learn the meaning of sadness.

We walked up to the front door and Rodney knocked. As the door slowly opened, a girl about my age who looked as if she was in her 50's opened the door. Her black hair was matted and the clothes she wore had been hanging on her skeleton for many days. A faint smile of her yellowed teeth quickly told me that she had not taken advantage of the dental clinic and there was more on her mind than living. We walked into a cluttered room where she, her kids and boyfriend had been waiting for us and where all of them needed something.

The girl's name was Rhonda. She had two children…her eight-year-old daughter who wanted dinner and a disabled three-year-old daughter. Rhonda lamented that the three -year-old should have gone to another doctor's appointment in Madison that day but didn't go because the father of her children, Chad, needed the car to run errands, if he could sober up enough to drive. Rhonda was supposed to be working at one of the gas stations owned by the Nation, but kept forgetting to show up. Her brother, Anthony needed money for rent. Then there was the house itself, which HUD had provided and the Nation remodeled. The Nation's plan had been to clean the place up and make it livable. Nation funds were provided, but that was two years ago and the place was a disaster, with faulty electricity, a broken shower and no door for the bathroom.

I looked at the mess and wondered how anyone could possibly live this way. What were the children learning and what would they ever expect out of life? Within a few minutes, I concluded that all goals had receded into the distance while reality stretched on for day after day after exhausting day, until it was only natural to desire very little beyond themselves. Perhaps it was just some mindless TV program on the new big screen that moaned in the corner or time on the antique computer, both of which had been provided with last year's stipend. Perhaps a sleeping pill to ease one through the night so that they could begin again. Maybe a prescription narcotic from the Ho-Chunk clinic to numb the physical and psychological pain or a trip to the casino that they couldn't really afford but did anyway, as it was "their casino," they justified. Perhaps some marijuana, or meth, or the drug that had run strongest on both sides of her family for three generations and counting…alcohol.

Chad was blasted as he sat on the couch, legs spread wide, shaking his head as he looked with disdain at the white man who stood before him. Rhonda drank a quick shot and sat down next to Chad on the filthy living room couch. Rhonda began talking about her mother. She reported that she and Chad had gotten drunk with Rhonda's mother dozens of times and it was almost always fun. Rhonda proudly said that Grace was a happy drinker who made for good company around a fire with fun stories and a throaty laugh. After she was diagnosed with cirrhosis in 2012, doctors said her prognosis was good if she stopped drinking. Her liver had a few years left. She would be eligible for a transplant that the Nation would pay for. For a few months she managed to quit, but reality often left her depressed. Her husband was long gone and her boyfriend was dead. A few of her nephews were arrested for using drugs and she thought society was against her. She filed for bankruptcy, pledging her Nation stipend to keep her out of jail. She had worked at the casino but kept drinking until she was too sick and too unreliable to work.

"I would be mean to her sometimes," Rhonda said, sitting in the living room staring off into darkness. "I kept saying to her, 'You're killing yourself."

"You were just trying to pull her out of the spiral," Chad said with slurred speech, as if that same trail was not the one upon which he tread.

They all had gone through spirals of their own. Chad had been arrested for driving under the influence three times in the two years after his own mother's death before straightening himself out enough to take care of the children and getting hooked on meth. Rhonda had sometimes gone to work so hung-over that she would need to come home. When she became pregnant with the three-year-old, she went nine months without a beer or cigarette. She looked at her handicapped daughter "I wasn't going to make my problems, my kid's problem and look what I got". Even after all she said they had been through, there was still hope that her children would have it easier with the education program that the Nation was providing.

Rhonda lit up a tax-free Winston she bought at the casino and blew the smoke into the already stale, damp air. Now she was talking to no one..."Don't you want to see what your grandchildren become?" Rhonda spoke as if her mother was still there. "Don't you want to be here for them?" Rhonda continued on, telling us that Grace loved her granddaughters and babysat for them, and even admired the way Rhonda and Chad cared for them. Rhonda was proud that Grace bought them whatever she could. Sadly, she could never give them what they really needed and that was hope...hope for a better tomorrow without the drugs, without the alcohol and oppression that came from a realized eventuality.

Rhonda outlined that Grace had quit drinking and then started again, quit and then started. She fell down the outside stairs and broke her leg and had to use a wheelchair but they couldn't afford a ramp out of the house. She lost her car and then her driver's license. She stayed in her living room and watched TV for hours at a time until the emotionless emotions numbed her, dumbed her and made her nothing more than a receptacle for any form of escape. Rhonda continued that Grace had been gone for nearly two months. "I don't understand why it wasn't enough. I mean she had me and Chad and the kids right here." Rhonda pleaded. "She just didn't want to live no more".

With Grace gone, it was now just Chad and Rhonda and the kids left in their "home". With bed sheets blocking the windows and her mother's medications still stacked on the counter, care and consideration was not something that penetrated their concept of existence. Chad's eyes drooped as he reached for yet another half-filled bottle and took a gulp. He chased it with water and then drank again. "Last day," he said. "Tomorrow it's detox, getting a job, all that."

The day before had also been the last day, and so had the weekend before that. Now it was two weeks until $200 in rent came due on the land where the HUD house sat. He had no money of his own and nowhere else to go. For the past five years he had been living with Rhonda's mother and surviving on her annual Nation stipend and $197 a month in food stamps. Grace had supported the two of them and they had been her caretaker, lifting her out of bed in the mornings and pushing her wheelchair up the hill to a shelter whenever it was too cold or a storm hit. They had monitored her medications, washed her jaundiced skin, and dealt with her diapers. They even tried to keep her from drinking, just as the doctors insisted. But Chad was buying vodka with Grace's money and drinking it in front of her, and she would yell and beg and then threaten to withhold her cash so he couldn't drink himself. Eventually he decided to compromise by rationing her liquor. Sometimes he would pass out on the couch or go to the bathroom and when he came back, the line in the bottle between sobriety and sadness looked lower than before.

"Do you blame us?" he asked anyone in general.

"You did the best you could," Rhonda told him.

"There's no sense obsessing over it." Chad slurred as he sipped again from the bottle. He lay back on the couch, and reported that lately he had been having a recurring dream where he was sitting in the living room with Grace, a woman not yet 55 and already dead, who had some color back in her cheeks and her jet -black hair in a braid with a white feather in it. He wanted to be honest with her, to tell her she was dying, and finally he blurted it out: "You're dying." he said, but she didn't look back at him. "You're dying", he said again. "You are dying". But the TV was blaring, the bottle was in her hands, her eyes were glazed over, and she was too far gone to hear him. She turned away from him and when she turned around Grace's face was gone and in its place was his. His head shook as his blurry eyes looked into mine, "I'm dying too. I dying!" he said as his eyes closed, his shoulders shrugged and took another gulp.

It was time to go. I had seen enough. My heart was heavy, my sadness profound. After we left, Rodney pointed out that the clothes strewn across the living room were Grace's, and it was probably her microwave jambalaya leftovers in the sink along with her empty $8.75 liter of Heaven Hill Vodka pushed against the couch. The ride back to the Dells was in total silence.

As we passed the sign for the Ho-Chunk Casino, Rodney finally spoke. "We know what the problems are. The challenge is separating the children from the adults and providing them with both awareness and hope. The kids need to know and understand that our people are profoundly susceptible to alcohol and drug abuse, just as my ancestors were susceptible to disease. Yet we hope that they can rise up and become something of themselves based on one thing…pride…pride of being who they are, what they are and above all else what they can be. We know it will not be easy. We know that there will be many failures for each success. Yet we also know that if we don't strive to reach our goals, their lives and our lives and our way of life, will have no meaning and will disappear forever. You can own all the casinos in the world. You can have all the money you could ever want or need. However, without pride and hope there is nothing."

I sat in total silence. I had no idea. I could see the honor and dignity in the man who sat beside me in his car and with it came a new level of respect. He was willing to dedicate his life to the betterment of his people, the maintenance of his heritage and, above all else, the belief that things would be better for those who followed in his footsteps. I did something I had never done to another man before. I put my hand on his right shoulder and looked him in the eyes. "I am honored to be your friend." I spoke as tears moistened my lids. He placed his hand upon my knee, if only for a second…"and you mine, little brother and you mine."

As we rode along, I asked Rodney what it was like to be a minority. In my attempt to learn more about my friend, I mixed the words race and ethnicity together. Little did I know that there was a difference. Rodney, polite as always, took it upon himself to outline the differences between the two. He so adroitly noted…"The traditional definitions of race and ethnicity are related to biological and sociological factors. Race refers to a person's physical characteristics, such as bone structure, skin, hair, or eye color. Ethnicity, however, refers to cultural differences, including nationality, regional culture, ancestry, and language. An example of race is brown, white, or black skin, while an example of ethnicity is German or Spanish regardless of race."

Rodney looked at me with great sincerity and added, "While one doesn't need to be of a different race to have a unique ethnic background, people of a different race, such as Native Americans, could also have a different ethnic background, which is what caused so many problems when the first white settlers arrived. Not only were American Indians a different race, they also had a different ethnic background and culture that included all kinds of different languages, religions and traditions that continue today. Because I look different and have a different set of ancestors and lineal language, I am automatically considered different and to many, subservient. I believe America has come a long way in terms of reducing racial prejudice, but I don't know if we will ever get to the point where we eliminate ethnic prejudice."

Holy cow, I thought to myself as Rodney continued. "What's crazy is that modern data is confirming many of the 19th century views that races differ markedly in such things as maturation rate, brain size, bone density, susceptibility to disease, and perhaps even personality. While skin color is the first hint, races differ in skin color because of different levels of melanin production. All races have approximately the same number of melanocytes, or melanin-making cells, but they differ in how actively the cells make melanin. Skin color does have one physiological effect: three and a half times as much ultraviolet light from the sun passes through your skin than through blacks, and we are somewhere in between. Light skin is beneficial in the northern regions where whites evolved, since ultraviolet light converts ergosterol in the body into vitamin D, while dark skin protects against the tropical sun."

"Remember evolution has taken thousands upon thousands of years and there are several racial characteristics that are obviously adaptations to the climates in which the different races evolved. As an example, many East African peoples have elongated limbs and bodies that easily dissipate heat and also make them very good at running. My people, on the other hand, evolved in a cold climate. Our bodies are not as elongated as most Caucasians. We have thick, dark hair, and an epicanthic fold that creates our almond-shaped eyes, which is thought to have reduced glare from snow and ice, until of course, Mr. Ray Ban came along and invented sunglasses. At the same time, my flat nose is less exposed to cold than yours and my absence of facial hair not only means that I can't grow a beard, but probably evolved so that condensation from my breath would not freeze my beard and chill my face."

"For whatever reasons, races also don't smell the same and by that I don't mean with their noses. Blacks and whites have strong but differing smells and many Asians have scarcely any smell. Koreans often have no odor -producing glands in their arm-pits at all and Japanese have very few. Indians from India have a completely different scent. It's funny that early Japanese found Europeans so foul-smelling that even today, a common Japanese expression for anything Western means "stinking of butter.""

What doesn't this guy know? Most people just move from day -to-day and accept what happens for what it is. Rodney had taken the time to learn about life and where he fit in. I should be so lucky!

"Recent Immigrants from Mexico and Central America are going through the same process of racial and ethnic bias we do. As generations pass, if groups assimilate like the Irish, Germans…whoever did, they will be more attuned to the social mainstream simply because they can "blend in" better than I can. African Americans, for the most part have ethnically blended. Where they have trouble is that they are immediately racially categorized. While it's certainly better than it was during my grandfather's time, it's still challenging when you are described by an adjective…black, white, Mexican, Indian, instead of just being a man. We all do it. It's part of our nature when we are amongst our own ethnic or racial group, just like you see different types of ducks always with their own kind…Mallards, Wood Ducks, Merganser. How do they know what they are? What's sad is when barriers are established simply because of these criteria. Dr. King certainly had it right, but I don't know if things are really any better now in terms of subjective acceptance where one person doesn't question the other simply because of what they are ethnically instead of who they are."

We were past the Lodi exit and over the Wisconsin River and once again, I was the student and he was the teacher. I told him I hoped he didn't consider me adjectival and he said "no". He thought we were beyond that. I asked him what he called me amongst members of his nation and he said "asshole", to which we both laughed. It was a short laugh but still good to see him laugh as it had been a rough day.

"While we are all grouped 'together,'" he said as he quickly held two fingers up each hand to create exclamation marks, "identity is a sensitive issue amongst our nations that can be complicated by issues related to tribal recognition and tribal membership or enrollment. Tribes have diverse stances on how to determine membership and enrollment. This issue can be politically, emotionally and financially challenging."

"Initially, when no one wanted to admit they were Native American because there was little value to it, tribal membership was determined through systems of kinship, clan, and even adoption. The members of the communities accepted those who belonged to their tribe through their language, behavior, and cultural expressions. Whether the result of warfare, orphaning or marriage, individuals could be raised in one Indian Nation and be married to someone in a different nation. We are Ho-Chunk and yet my great-great-great-great grandfather was Sauk. I have cousins who identify with the Fox because of who their parents married. Back in the olden days, many tribes were matrilineal, where the women ran the show."

"You mean like being a white guy today" I interjected.

"Matrilineal tribes passed the clan and source of belonging through the mother. Patri-lineal tribes passed the clan and source of belonging through the father. In some cases, this meant a child would belong as a member in two tribes – that of his mother and that of his father, if they were of differently organized tribes. Again, this is what happened in our family. My ancestor was Sauk and they were patrilineal. Great, great grandmother was Winnebago as we were called back then and so my great grandfather belonged to both nations. Even after contact, unions between tribal members and settlers occurred to build alliances and coalitions, similar to how and why they had been occurring between tribes. There were no set ways, just like some of the laws of Canada and the United States and those of Mexico are all quite different. Native American's traditional ways of determining membership were quite diverse and reflected the values of the community."

"One of the most common ways is called blood quantum which is used to describe an individual by the "blood" contributions of their parents, where one half from each parent considered is then divided based on their heritage, consisting of fractions ranging from 4/4 where both parents are totally American Indian out to 1/1024 where great grandma or grandpa took a tumble in the hay with someone of a different race."

"Today, each nation sets its own rules but the federal government and several states also maintain their own various definitions of who is an Indian and therefore eligible for certain services, such as the historical allotment process of the Dawes Act or separate tribal schools. Further, enrollment within the tribe is used for determining eligibility for other federal services. While in the past it was mostly about government assistance, today it's all about money…a lot of it…that is flowing in from the various businesses. Native American nations receive a whole set of federal benefits that are being set up by the different nations and people who would never have admitted their heritage before, are lining up to prove they belong.

"What's crazy is that there are 26 states named after Native Americans. Some are named after a tribe, such as Alabama (Alibamu tribe, meaning "clears the thicket"). Others are named after Native American languages, such as Massachusetts (means "about the big hill") while Wisconsin's original name was 'Miskous', which was an Indian word that means 'river that meanders through something red'. This probably referred to the sandstone bluffs of the Wisconsin Dells. Miskous was first recorded in 1673 by Father Jaques Marquette, and mis-read by his traveling companion Louis Joliet as 'Misconsing'. The name was then further mis-read the following year by the French explorer La Salle, who read it as 'Ouisconsing'- from here, it became adapted and mutated to the current name of Wisconsin."

"Cheese heads are mutants?" I joked as Rodney continued.

"The context of tribal membership has changed over time for a variety of reasons, including our political status and clout. It's amazing what a few million dollars per year in political donations can do to change the way the government acts towards us. As you will learn from my Great Grandfather or my dad, enrollment in American Indian nations sets up particular rights and responsibilities of the citizen that may or may not require regular participation in tribal activities or even residence on tribal lands. The context of tribal enrollment also involves the distinct political status of the American Indian. People forget that all 526 recognized tribes are sovereign nations and are mentioned as such in the US Constitution."

"The Constitution doesn't say anything about dirt farmers from Wisconsin," I interjected as another feeble attempt at humor.

"No, but you do have a line in the Declaration of Independence" that was never offered to us….'We hold these truths to be self-evident that all men are created equal, with certain unalienable rights to life, liberty and the pursuit of happiness". So much for my humor.

Rodney added. "Thank God, my dad's generation stood up and fought for the true intent of the Constitution or I would be living in one of those HUD houses we visited today."

I swallowed hard at the thought and thanked God that was not the case. We pulled up to the apartment on Doty Street. Big Brother got out of the car and came around and shook my hand and, as has become the common act amongst men, gave me a one-handed bear hug.

"Thanks for coming," he said.

"Thanks for sharing your life with me," I replied.

As I turned to go into the apartment, he called. "I hope you got another 2,000 words today the Chief is expecting them". In my mind I had more than 2,000 words. I had 10,000 thoughts and hundreds of memories that kept flashing before my eyes like bright neon lights.

Sleep did not come easily that night as I outlined what I was going to write about. How does one talk about dignity and degradation in the same paragraph? How does one share integrity and futility in another one? How does one go about expressing the thoughts and, more importantly, the emotions that I felt in a few hours…laughter, excitement, profound sadness and wonder all wrapped up in a single day? How can I speak of what left me speechless?

The Bypass: I awoke early and my body ached as my mind raced. I knew that the only place to find peace would be in the forest. I had the day off and dad and Tommie would be farming. Mom would be at work…lousy pay, but group health insurance, even with a $5,000 per person deductible. Jake would be lying on the screen porch waiting for someone, anyone, to come home. I jumped in the Jeep and headed south, my mind asunder in all that I had seen and experienced the day before.

As I slipped past Dodgeville and gave the Pointer salute, I got careless and my wheels hit the shoulder and I lost control of the Jeep. I remember watching as it tumbled into the ditch. I was rolling, rolling, rolling, dirt, rocks, glass, plastic, the taste of blood, the aches that come from knowing immediately that something was seriously wrong.

The next thing I remember were bright white lights and beep, beep, beep. I was in Madison in intensive care. I learned later that I was airlifted and mom and dad were told it didn't look good. Two broken legs, a ruptured spleen, broken jaw, fractured skull, three missing teeth and four broken ribs that punctured my right lung. I lay there not knowing where I was or when it was. All I knew was ,it was serious…really fucking serious. A doctor came in and asked how I felt. He was a little Asian guy, but you could tell one of those really smart guys. Being the smart ass that I am I said…"and how do you think I am? I feel like shit".

"You are one very lucky guy. Another few feet and you would have hit a tree. In addition, a physician was on his way home from the Dodgeville hospital and administered first aid or you probably would have bled to death."

Shit....

"Because you are young and in good shape, you're probably going to make it. We've got to watch your vitals and you have to do everything we say when we tell you to or you could still check out. You're going to be here at least a month and then in rehab for another two or three months after that."

Holy Shit!

"Your parents are out in the hall, they've been here all week and they would like to see you."

"Sorry." I whispered as they walked in. My head was clearing a little bit.

"Water." I asked for and the doctor shook his head in the negative.

"Ice chips," he noted. With that mom placed a cold chip on my swollen lips and I let it melt dribbling down upon my gown.

"How long have I been here?" I lisped.

"A week," mom replied.

I took a deep breath and tried to shake my head but it hurt like hell.

"Insurance?" I whispered trying to raise my arm.

"Don't worry about that now," Dad responded.

I knew how much hospitals cost and also knew that insurance premiums for farmers and their kids were astronomical and mom and dad could only afford basic insurance.

By day three of my awakening, the clouds were beginning to clear and the doctor decided I could move from beep, beep, beep, land to a regular room. I was wheeled down the hall, IV's and all and placed in an elevator. I was given a private room and told to rest. The days became routines...blood work, blood pressure, measuring my pee, pokes and prods until any sense of modesty was totally gone.

A week had gone by and I saw a very large man walking down the hall...Big Brother was coming.

"Heh little brother." Rodney whispered as he entered my room. "Did you think you were driving the Batmobile?"

I tried to shake my head but it hurt too much.

"How did you find me?" I lisped through my missing front teeth.

"When you didn't show up at work, I was worried. When I called your phone for three straight days and no one answered, I drove down to Mineral Point and asked around and they told me you had been in a major car accident. I went out to your farm and talked to your brother. He filled me in and I asked him to call me when you were well enough for guests."

"You're not a guest. You're my big brother."

This brought a big, shy, grin to his face and there was a twinkle in his eyes. "The chief says that he will let you slide until you're better, but then he needs those 2000 words."

Needless to say, when you got tubes coming out of everywhere, eating nothing but pudding and Jell-O and shitting in a pan, 2000 words was not on the top of my list of considerations.

"Tell him, I'm sorry". I replied. "As soon as I can I'll get back to work".

"He knows that and wanted me to tell you that you're still on the payroll. In fact, I've got your last paycheck here."

"He doesn't need to do that". I weakly replied.

"Heh man, you're family and now an honorary member of the Ho-Chunk nation."

I cocked my head a little bit and smiled. "Thank you and please thank the Chief."

"How long are you going to be here?" Rodney asked.

"I don't know. It's going to be a few weeks and then to rehab."

"Can I come see you?"

"Hell yes! Tell me when so I can make certain all the pretty nurses are on duty. In my daze I think I even saw one who might meet your requirements."

"An Indian?"

"Yup."

"And not a Mahatma, from India?"

"Nope."

"Shit." Rodney was grinning from ear-to-ear.

"Married?"

"Didn't see any ring?"

"What tribe?"

"How in hell do I know? You all look the same to me." I cackled.

"Ha, ha." was his retort as I smiled. It felt good to smile, even with all the missing teeth.

"Good looking?"

"Other than the crossed eyes and buck teeth, not bad. But then for you, only the best". Actually, she was gorgeous. I was afraid I was setting big brother up for disappointment as she had to be dating someone.

He had a shy smile on his face.

"I'll try and find out if she's involved before you come again. Now get out of here unless you want to change my bedpan."

The next day, she walked in. Her dark black hair was simply gorgeous as were her perfectly white teeth. Her name tag came into focus and it read Ms. Ann Wolf.

"Good afternoon Nurse Wolf" I said in the most pleasant of slur you could possibly imagine. "Good afternoon Mr. Terrill. How are you feeling today?"

"Much better thank you."

Even though the beep, beep, beep machine was on, she said…"Let me take your pulse."

I watched as she held my wrist. I was certain that it jumped twenty points when I looked at her face and I was afraid that all the beeps would ruin the moment. She pressed a button on her I-Pad and made some notes and scanned my wrist band.

As she was about to leave, I spoke. "Could I please have an ice chip?" I wanted her to stop.

She reached into the little refrigerator and pulled one from the freezer. As she was about to place it in my mouth, I thought it was time to ask but backed away, only noticing that there was no ring on her left hand.

The thing with hospitals is that it's all routines. I was in my room for about five days and could look at the clock and tell you what or who was coming next and what was going on. After Ms.

Wolf had done her duties for several days, I finally got up the courage to ask.

"I know that this is probably being too forward, Ms. Wolf but does the Ms. stand for miss or missus?"

"It's miss."

Whew! "Well, Miss Wolf, the next question is the tough one".

I think she thought I was hitting on her.

"Which nation are you a citizen of?"

This caught her totally off guard.

"The United States."

"And?" I persisted.

"And"?

"Ho-Chunk, Fox, Sauk, Ojibwa, Potawatomi"? I pursued.

Her head bent down and I thought she was going to be offended.

"Potawatomi" she replied.

"Cool!" I lisped.

"My best friend is a member of the Ho-Chunk nation and I work for them as a writer."

She had a look that spelled out "bull shit" in her eyes.

"Seriously. I just graduated and they hired me to write a story from their side."

Her demeanor quickly changed as she smiled.

"About time. I've got to do my rounds. I'll see you tomorrow."

I checked my watch, which consisted of a cheap wall clock. It was 2:15. I knew what time big brother needed to be visiting tomorrow. All I needed to do was get hold of him. Problem was that his number was in my cell phone that was probably crunched in what was left of the Jeep. Who remembers telephone numbers today?

I tried to breathe deep…."OUCH."

My logic came back to me. I thought Rodney called mom and dad and so they would probably have his phone number. I squeezed the call button on the bed and a CNA came in, all sweet and preppy in her uniform. "I need to give my mom a message, can you call her for me?"

"Sure."

She picked up the phone and I gave her our house number. As the phone was ringing little Miss Preppy put it to my ear. "Mom. Its 'Q', have you got Rodney's phone number?"

She told me that Rodney hadn't called our house, but drove down to the farm to see what had happened. I was still unconscious and she and dad were with me. Tommie talked to him. Tommie told mom, he saw tears in big brother's eyes. Big Brother excused himself and came back to Madison and to the hospital. Mom said that when I was being transferred out of intensive care, I was supposed to go into a shared room and Rodney found out, called his dad called and arrangements were made for me to have a private room. Now I had tears in my eyes.

"Mom, can you call out to the factory"...mom didn't like me telling people I worked in a casino and so we called it the money factory...and ask for Rodney. If he isn't there, please tell them that he has a very important meeting tomorrow at 2:15 in my new office. He'll understand."

Of course, mothers being mothers, she wanted all the details. I told her, I would tell her the next time she and dad came to see me as I was getting tired and I also had this little girl holding the phone and I didn't want people to know that tomorrow's meeting was anything more than accidental.

About a half hour later the phone rang and rang and rang and finally another CNA came in and lifted it. She looked at me and reported that Rodney had gotten the message and would follow my instructions. I think she must have thought I was some big shot or something as I fell asleep with a smile on my fractured face.

I awoke at 6:00 AM to the normal hospital clatter. God, I needed to go somewhere and get some rest. The hours wore on with visits from doctors and therapists and social workers and even a minister and then a reconstructive dentist. I ate my lunch of soft food and watched the noon hour slip by. Around 2:00 the friendly giant walked into my room. "Heh little brother. A meeting? What's going on?

I had a sly smile on my face. "Wait about 15 minutes and you'll see."

We had our normal chit-chat about all the goings on at the "factory" and how everyone wanted to know how I was doing. At exactly 2:15 PM, Nurse Wolf walked in and Rodney's world changed. Nurse Wolf looked at him and Big Brother at her and if there was ever a thing call love at first sight, this was it. She was all smiles and Big Brother had a goofy grin on his face.

"Rodney Whitehorse, I would like to introduce you to Nurse Ann Wolf. Miss Wolf, this is my big brother Rodney Whitehorse."

Time was of the essence as she was making her final rounds of the day. As she took my pulse and looked in my eyes, I could see the smile in hers.

"Gee, I'm sorry, but I'm just finishing my final rounds of the day and need to have everything done by 3:00, when I get off work."

Even dumb me got the hint, but not Rodney. Nurse Wolf walked out with Rodney standing love struck, but unable to move.

"Heh dummy." I whispered as Rodney looked out the door.

"Yes you". I inferred.

Big Brother turned and looked at me.

"Are you so naïve that you didn't get the hints?"

He had a perplexed look on his face.

"Rodney…3:00 o'clock. Needed to finish her rounds when she got off work. Go after her and ask her if she would like to have a cup of coffee when she gets done. Even with all the pain meds going through me, I got that message." What a ding-dong! No wonder he was still single, I thought as I tried to shake my still pain-filled head.

"Really?"

"Yes, really."

"Go before she gets too far away and then come back and fill me in."

Rodney walked down the hall until he saw her in with a patient and waited until she came out of their room. A few minutes later he came back with a huge smile on his face. "Coffee downstairs at 3:30" He was in pig heaven.

"How do I look?"

"Ugly." I chortled.

"Seriously."

"Like I said…uuuugly." as I tried to laugh.

"Should I get her flowers or anything?"

"No. You're getting her coffee and talking. Don't push it. Be cool. Let it be natural." God he was excited.

"Don't blow it. And above all else, be yourself."

He went in my bathroom and looked in the mirror making certain that each strand of his thick black hair was in place, his shirt was straight. I watched as he rubbed the tops of his boots on the back of his jeans to give them a polish and laughed an excited boyish laugh.

"Call me tomorrow and tell me how it went. Now go down there and please…be yourself."

I lay back with a smile on my face. All my pain was forgotten by the joy in my heart. The next morning the phone rang and for the first time, I could pick it up. Hooray. Progress…painful, but progress.

"Heh little brother. Thank you."

"What happened?"

"We talked for about a half hour and then she said she needed to get away from prying eyes. I asked her out for dinner and she said yes."

"When?"

"Last night."

"You two had dinner last night?"

Yup! She went home and I went and got cleaned up and went and picked her up at her apartment by West Towne. We went to Fitzgerald's and had dinner and talked for four hours."

"It went well?"

"No, it went fantastic. We talked and talked and talked and laughed and have so much in common. Man, I can't thank you enough."

"You just did by the smile in your voice. When are you seeing her again?" "Tomorrow. She's off and we're going out on Lake Mendota sailing."

"Sailing? You know how to sail?"

"No, but she does."

"Cool."

More therapists came in and so I had to cut it short. "Call me after you make a fool out of yourself tomorrow. I want all the details."

At precisely 2:15 PM, Nurse Ann Wolf walked into my room. There was a huge smile on her face and a radiance that you only see when people are truly happy.

"How is Mr. Terrill today?"

"Please call me 'Q'" I replied.

"Q?"

"Yeth, my name is George Terrill the fourth and so I had my choice of "F" for fourth which would have gotten me into too many fights or "Q" for Quad and so everybody, including my mother calls me "Q".

"OK 'Q'. How is 'Q' doing today?"

"Superb…Simply superb." I lisped.

"And how is Nurse Wolf, today?" I asked with a bit of lilt in my voice.

"Likewise." she smiled. "Likewise!"

God had me wreck my car so that two people could meet. God asked me to put happiness in their lives and, through fate, I was doing his work. There was a deep, joyous feeling in my heart that only comes when you can share the joy of others.

"He doesn't know a damn thing about sailing." I whispered.

"I know. That's why we're going." she whispered back.

I had a big toothless, shit-eating grin on my face as she walked out.

The next day was the first time they had me out of bed. Ouch, but I toughed it out without crying. I had to sit up, but the pain was worth the trouble. My mind kept going to Rodney and Ann and sailing. It was a beautiful late-August day and there was a slight breeze. Perfect weather for sailing on Lake Mendota.

After dinner, the big man showed up, with a wide grin on his face. "Big Brother…how ya doin?" I asked, but already knew the answer.

He just smiled.

"That good?"

He just smiled.

"Not so fast my friend". I warned.

"I know, but what a great day and what a wonderful person. Kind, considerate, intelligent and what a body!"

"Gee, I hadn't noticed" I lied. "How was the sailing?"

"It was cool. I only tipped the boat over twice and drank half of Lake Mendota."

"The Memorial Union was packed with students, but she's able to rent boats because she's in grad school. She wants to become a Physician's Assistant in Pediatrics. A couple of the regulars from the factory were there and I think they were surprised to see me in a sailboat. They probably thought we should be in a birch bark canoe," he giggled.

"How are you doing little brother? He asked as he got serious for a moment.

"As well as can be expected". Vampira Jones was in today to take more blood and Rodentia Johnson, the physical therapist came in to torture me."

"Are those really their names?" Rodney asked.

"No, but the names are my way of getting back at them for the pain they are putting me through."

"When are you two going out again?" I asked.

"Sunday, we're going to Milwaukee to the zoo. She loves animals."

"No wonder she's attracted to you." I smart-assed back. "Bet her favorite animal is the gorilla."

That got a chuckle out of him as he got serious and sincerely said. "Thank you, little brother."

"What are friends for?"

He carefully shook my left hand as the right ribs couldn't take the motion.

"You are my friend. You certainly are." he replied.

"What did she think of the Batmobile?" I asked.

"I took the truck." Rodney replied. "I didn't want her to think I was showing off".

"I hope you took all the dead fish out of it before you picked her up."

"She likes to fish."

"Really?"

"Yup, she said her family went deep sea fishing in the Caribbean and also fishing on Lake Michigan."

"Did you ask her if she liked to ice fish?"

"Not on the first date. You have to wait until you're married to make a woman go ice fishing."

"Is that an old native American custom?"

"No. Common sense."

With that, the big man was out the door and silence enveloped me in thoughts of one happy guy. I couldn't wait until 2:15 the next day to see what her reaction was.

As the clock ticked, I waited and waited and waited. No Ms. Wolf. I rang the buzzer and the CNA came in. "Where's the nurse?" I asked.

"She's running late. She had a meeting today."

Oh, the agony of waiting even when there's absolutely nowhere you could possibly go.

About 4:00 in walks Ms. Wolf all polite and professional. The wrist goes out and the fingers press against it. At first, it's a gentle touch and then they dig into my wrist. "Holy Shit."

"You…what am I going to do with you Mr. Terrill?"

Now I'm scared.

"You set me up with this big, handsome, intelligent, kind, generous, native American man that my parents are going to fall in love with. You! I've got so much school in front of me and now all I can think about is some guy whose friend is one of my patient's. Thanks."

I didn't know if she was serious or not.

"Regrets?" I asked.

"Are you kidding me? If you tell him how wonderful the day was, I'll never forgive you. He needs to get a new truck though or at least one that doesn't smell like fish, but we had a great time."

I played dumb, which for me isn't that difficult, and made a note to tell Rodney to either clean the truck or fess-up and take the Batmobile. "You going out with him again?" I asked, playing dumb, which comes quite naturally.

"We're going to Milwaukee to the zoo." she replied.

"You're not going to trade him in for one of the gorillas, are you?" I said with a straight, but still badly bruised, face. "I don't think he will fit in one of their cages."

She burst out laughing. "Mr. Terrill, you are certainly quick of wit. Now it's time for your wonderful dinner."

She punched her I-Pad and was out the door.

Saturday was the first home Badger game of the season and the first one I was going to miss in four years. It was on TV. At least, I was sober and knew what happened. Mom and Dad and Tommie came to visit along with some of the Pointer Brothers after the game. They were all dressed in typical red-and-white

Badger garb and it was good to see my hometown buddies still half buzzed in their red-and-white bib overalls with the obligatory right strap undone. It's a Badger thing, so don't worry about it. Mom said I was looking better. Tommie said, better than what? Dad added better than looking like he just got hit by a truck, which was almost the truth.

Whoa, I guess I really had a close one. I'm not ready to meet my ancestors quite yet.

I spent five weeks in Meriter and then it was off to the rehab center, which I immediately called the half-way house. I wanted to go in a car, but they said it had to be by ambulance. I asked them if they could put the siren on for me. They ignored my request.

Big Brother came to visit at least once each week to fill me in on the factory and all that was going on and, of course, I got to know more about Ann as she came to visit when she had the time. When you're sitting in a senior citizen center, you don't realize how "close" these two were getting when they're on the outside and you're within.

The half-way house was just like Meriter without as much noise and a lot more, old people. I was told I would be there for two or three months and then head back to Waldwick. Mom and dad came to visit and brought Jake. My God it was good to see him. All the old folks thought he was cool and he seemed to understand he was there to make everyone happy. I guess that's why God spelled backwards is dog. They have a way of making any day seem better.

When you are institutionalized, the one thing you seem to forget is time and the meter running all the time. It's like being drunk and riding in a taxi. It's taking you somewhere, but you forget the meter keeps going and going and going. It was the week before Christmas and my good doctor came to visit me and thought that I was healed enough to go home. Badger football and Thanksgiving were long over. Damn! Maybe next year we will win the BIG championship. I was able to walk on my own again with a walker and felt like I was 90, but it was better than looking up from the brown side of the earth. My Christmas present was getting out of the asylum.

I don't know who was happier, me or the staff. Something about the loony one in room 304. I guess my youthful exuberance was a bit much for them.

It was Christmas Eve day and time to check out. I got my celebratory ride to the accounting department in a wheelchair. I thought I would shit my pants when I saw what three months-worth of hospital and half-way house bills looked like. The invoice they shoved in front of me was about three inches thick. Procedure this. Medicine that. Room costs. I could have stayed in a suite in Vegas for less than what they were charging. They almost had to take me to the cardiac ward. Dad looked at the pile and I could see mom was running numbers through her head and it wasn't good. There goes the farm!

I gingerly plucked at the pages until I got the very last one. The total bill was over a million dollars. I sucked in a deep breath and looked at my balance....$238.15. Huh? I looked at the lady behind the counter but didn't have to say a word. "You work at Ho-Chunk, right?"

"Yes" I replied.

"You're covered, like all employees with their insurance. You owe the $100 deductible and then $138.15 for the phone."

You could have knocked me over with a feather. I closed my eyes and there were tears of relief and gratitude. My second "family" had taken care of everything. I shook my head. My mom shook hers too and even the tough guy…dad…had tears in his eyes. We all just sat there for a moment in shock…deep profound shock…one of disbelief…one of incredible gratitude. These people for whom I had only worked a few weeks had taken care of everything.

My dad took out his checkbook…(yes, some people, especially farmers, still do have checkbooks)…and wrote the check…hands and head shaking to the point that even the Holsteins printed on the check seemed to be smiling. The nice lady stamped the last page "paid in full" and we walked out of the facility…actually mom and dad walked and I was in the iron maiden as I called it. We got to the truck and all three of us took deep breaths of fresh winter's air. My God, generosity is a wonderful thing.

As we began the trek towards Waldwick, I called Rodney. "Thank you." I said in my most sincere voice and through my new screwed in teeth. "Thank you very much."

"Heh, little brother, you're an employee. We don't pay as well as a lot of other places, but we do take care of our family." Rodney couldn't see the tears in my eyes or hear the sobs of my mother. I knew that the tough guy was also choked up, but he was driving and my 'big brother' knew that it was coming from the heart.

Tell the Chief, I will never, ever forget this." I said "He knows" Rodney replied and "Merry Christmas." "Thank you, Big Brother. Thank you."

I hung up and forgot to wish him a Merry Christmas back. I waited about 20 minutes and then called back.

"Merry Christmas." I whispered as he picked up the phone.

"Just a minute, somebody wants to say hello."

Ann came on the phone. Sweet, sweet Ann.

"Hi, Merry Christmas." I offered.

"What are you doing next September 9th"? She asked

"If it's a Saturday, probably Badger football, why?"

"We want you to be in our wedding."

Holy shit! I could feel the love and excitement coming through the phone. Rodney had just proposed and she had said yes. Now I was really happy. My jaw ached from the width of my smile as my head tilted back. This was the best Christmas EVER.

"What's going on?" Mom said.

"Rodney and Ann just got engaged." I replied.

Mom giggled in her girly way and even the tough guy had a smile on his face.

"Next September 9th and they want me to be in the wedding." I said as my head rocked from side-to-side and tried to keep up with my ever-increasing smile. "I hope I have my new teeth by then."

"Life is good." I said to mom.

"Life is good." she replied, as it was her favorite saying.

The truck pulled into our driveway and dad helped me into the house. Jake was waiting with tail wagging and lots of wet, slurpy kisses. He knew something was wrong with me and so he didn't go bonkers, but he was sure glad to see me. Dogs really are totally cool.

Mom and dad, Jake and I sat in the living room on Christmas Eve and simply looked at each other. Tommie was at Heather's house. God it was good to be home. So very, very good!

The Forest: Dad helped me up the stairs and into my bedroom. It was so quiet and peaceful and packed with memories. As I lay there in the dark, I thanked God for all that he had done for me and my family and for Rodney and Ann. The door opened just a crack and 50 pounds of puppy came and crawled onto the bed next to me. I petted him and he gave me a kiss. "Merry Christmas." I whispered as he lay beside me as I began to fall asleep. "Merry Christmas."

Christmas morning meant church in Mineral Point…the same church George the First wrote about. After services, we went over to my cousin's house. Everyone made me feel welcome. For the first time ever, I really appreciated their company. The day was long and I was tired and yet, I asked for only one thing for Christmas and that was a ride into my forest. I needed to go back and have my soul cleansed, as it would give closure to the entire accident and escapade.

Christmas night saw a full moon and the silent sky speckled with stars as if God had turned on a flashlight for me. Dad got out the snowmobile and attached a little sled behind it from when we were kids. He wanted to take me and I said I needed to be alone. Mom insisted that I take my cell phone in case I had any problems. I took it. No more crazy things.

The cold winter's air was clean and fresh. It was nearly zero and the snow crunched beneath my feet. Jake wanted to go too, but I needed time alone to thank God for all that had transpired. We had been to church in the morning. Now I needed to go to my sanctuary.

I got into my snowmobile suit and realized it was now a size too big. I lost 20 pounds in the hospital and half-way house. I put on my gloves and helmet and made my way on the Arctic Cat. It was only a mile and I took my time as each bump reminded me of the day in September when I was coming to this very spot. As I neared my majestic oaks, I slowed even more. The trees were welcoming me home…dark fingers glistening in the moonlight, bringing me back to my favorite glen where Mother Earth and I collided in tranquility. God, I love these woods.

I shut off the Cat and slowly walked deeper into the woods to the spot where the school house once stood in Skunk Hollow. My right leg was killing me, but my majestic friends beckoned. As I walked to the clearing, I could sense them welcoming me home. I was surrounded by silence, enveloped in the peace that only comes with harmony. I took a deep breath of the crisp winter air, feeling it cascade within my lungs. I was at peace and peace was with me. I stood amongst the trees and looked at each of them as I would a piece of nature's art...So tall! So strong! So silent! I didn't know why this spot meant so much to me and yet, I really didn't care. This was MY spot where nothing else mattered.

I stood frozen in solitude and listened to nothing. My God, peace can be narcotizing! Through the trees, I saw him and he saw me...a buck who had escaped man's tyranny. We stood looking at each other, his big brown eyes focused on me, my heart focused on him. Nary a word was said and emotion became motionless, like the trees. I was home.

We stood at attention, he and I, pondering each other, wondering what the other was thinking, feeling, doing. I was afraid my slightest motion would scare him away and yet, there was no fear in him as he came closer than I had ever seen a deer come before. For what seemed like a lifetime, we stared at each other, sharing, caring, rendering an instant that seemed to last forever. I closed my eyes and opened my ears and there was nothing but the sounds of silence. He seemed to understand that we were both within the grasp of unity.

I stood motionless as did he and then his head nodded up and down and moved on...quietly, gracefully, permanently, gone from my instant. My soul was rejuvenated and the peace that I had sought was within me. I turned and gingerly walked back to the Cat, sat upon the seat and smiled. My forest...my primeval forest…God how I love this place where no man has ever stamped his signature…so clean, so clear, so pristine.

I started the Cat and headed home. What I had wanted, what I had dreamed about, what had motivated me for nearly four months met fruition. It was time to return to reality. Mom asked how my trip was and I shared with her my encounter and made her promise that Tommie and dad would let whoever and whatever lived in the forest simply live in peace and harmony.

Back-To-Work: January meant back to work. Mom volunteered to drive me both ways as my right leg was still stiff and sore. I said "no". I drove mom's car, made it to the "factory", and everyone greeted me. Nothing had changed except my perspective on life.

Big Brother came out with a huge grin on his face. "Welcome back, little brother." he offered.

"2000 words?" Rodney asked.

"2000 words." I replied smiling through my all-new ceramic teeth.

"The Chief thinks it's time for you to meet my Great Grandfather."

"OK" I offered.

He was one happy dude. I just smiled and saw the joy in his eyes knowing it was for Ann and not me.

"When can I get back to work?"

"You're here, do you want to clean toilets or wash dishes?

I just looked at Big Brother and my expression must have said it all as he just roared in laughter.

"Great Grandfather is in an assisted living facility we have in the Dells."

"No problem" I replied. Boy was I being talkative. "When?"

"Let me see when Great Grandfather can see you"

With that Rodney got on the phone and called the Chief. They talked a little bit and he asked me if Thursday would work.

I said, "sure".

Rodney knew that my apartment was long gone and I had intended on commuting from Waldwick until I found a place to live. The problem was that Madison's rents are crazy, especially living alone.

"Why don't you stay with Ann and I?" Rodney asked.

"Really?"

"We talked it over and she is OK with it."

"How long you two been living together?" I asked.

"Since Thanksgiving," Rodney said.

"You work fast."

"We both knew it was right the moment we met. Something in my heart just tingled liked nothing ever before."

"Are you sure?" I asked again. "I don't want to intrude."

"Little brother, without you, there would not be an 'us'". Rodney replied. "I have a three-bedroom house on Lake Waubesa and there's plenty of room and the guest bedroom never gets used. There is a big, three-season, glass porch where you can write while looking out at the lake."

"I don't have to eat Indian food, do I?" I joked.

"No, Ann doesn't like porcupine and rattle snake either."

My eyes must have gotten pretty big with the response because Rodney just laughed. "Seriously, what do you think we eat?"

"I don't know."

"Half the vegetables you eat, my ancestors domesticated."

"Duh." I never thought of that.

I drove home to Waldwick and let mom and dad know what was going on. I think mom was a little disappointed that I wasn't staying longer. I knew that Jake was going to be pissed that his bunk mate was leaving and he would be back sleeping on the floor in mom and dad's bedroom, but I needed to be closer to Madison and work.

That weekend, mom and dad helped me get all my things in the truck and followed me to the Lake Waubesa house. I don't know what I was expecting, but it was a real surprise to see a beautiful cottage that had been converted into a year-round house. The house was old and had wood paneling, but was simply immaculate. Wherever I looked I could see the pride of family and accomplishment and could sense the love that was filling each room. There were family photos and then, of course, photos of Rodney and Ann. On one shelf, I saw a photo of

Rodney and me from the previous summer and that put a smile on my face.

Rodney outlined which was my bedroom and it had an adjacent bathroom. The bedroom was small, but tidy and would work out until I could find some different roommates, even though living on a lake in Madison is just about as good as it can get.

We put the stuff in my closet and set up the room. After it was all put away, dad asked if I wanted to go to Paisan's for pizza. God yes! It had been four months since I had any pizza and Paisan's was my favorite. We drove separate so that afterwards they could go out John Nolen Drive, get on the Beltline and head for home. We sat in the fireplace room and had my favorite Paisan's pizza…thin-crust, pineapple and shrimp. No alcohol. It had been four months and my leg still wasn't 100% and I didn't want to risk anything.

The first couple days were what I would call "polite" times with Rodney and Ann where we were still getting accustomed to having each other around. I truly enjoyed the company and with each day, got to learn more about both of these wonderful people. Rodney, the big lug. Totally in love. Incredibly intelligent. Extremely generous. Ann, the sweetheart…kind, considerate, compassionate and also in love. I watched as they would light up when the other came home. I watched as their soft touches melted into each other like butter on pancakes. Rodney and my schedule at the factory were different and between working, going to grad school and studying, Ann was hardly ever there.

Thursday crept up on me and yet, I knew it was going to be a big day on Rodney's calendar. He was taking the Batmobile and I was riding shotgun. Shooting up I-94 to the Dells from Madison is a breeze. As we rode, we talked about anything and everything…the weather, the factory, you name it. Rodney pointed out his Great Grandfather was 94 years old and blind. He warned me not to think less of him because of his age or his inabilities.

"Only if he won't think less of me" I responded.

I asked Rodney about his grandfather as he was never mentioned and watched as Rodney's eyes focused on the road ahead with an intense stare.

Without looking at me, Rodney noted: "He died a long time ago."

"I'm sorry to hear that."

"My dad never met him."

"Geez, that's too bad" I wanted to know more. I wanted to put another piece in the puzzle.

"If you don't mind me asking, what happened?"

Rodney was still looking out the front window as he drove. "He died in Viet Nam."

"Sorry to hear that." I replied.

There was a serious and somewhat bitter tone to my friend that I had rarely heard. "He threw himself on a land mine and saved the lives of his platoon members"

"Wow." I responded. "A war hero."

"I guess. They called him 'chief' and made all kinds of remarks about his heritage and yet he was the one brave enough to sacrifice his life for them."

I had a lump in my throat.

"They brought him home and he's buried up in Black River Falls. At first it was just another dead soldier. Being Native American, no one thought anymore about it. One day, one of the elders read about a white guy who had given his life whose family was receiving the Congressional Medal of Honor. For my grandfather, there had been nothing. The elders contacted the military and asked why my grandfather had not received some recognition. After two years of working with one of the US Senators, my grandfather was awarded the Congressional Medal of Honor that my dad has in a display case in his office. There have been eight Native American recipients and one of them was him."

Dad and I went to visit the Viet Nam War Memorial in Washington when I was in high school. Like a lot of people, I took a piece of paper and a pencil and rubbed it over his name and brought it home. My mom had a frame made that matches the Medal of Honor frame and it also hangs in my dad's office. I guess my grandpa was pretty cool and tolerated all the bullshit back then without getting too angry and frustrated with how he was being treated. All he ever wanted to be was a man…Not an Indian. Not a Redskin. Nothing more than a man."

"You know, I see you that way." I said. "But more than that, I see you as my friend for whom I would do anything. You have taught me friendship, you have taught me loyalty and above all else, you have taught me dignity and I will always be grateful."

Now we both had I lumps in our throats.

Great Grand Father: In the Dells, we hit the Highway 12 exit. However, instead of heading south to the casino, we headed north past the water slides to the edge of town to what looked like an apartment complex with empty flower boxes outside waiting for spring and a front vestibule that allowed people to get out of their cars without getting wet.

We parked the Batmobile and went inside. There was a huge Christmas wreath still hanging over the fireplace. The lady at the front desk stood as we entered and a broad smile spread across her face. She knew Rodney and why he had come.

"He's been asking for you" she announced.

We walked down the hall to room 113 and quietly entered. The room was small, but tidy. There were family photos on the dresser and my mind wondered what a blind man needed pictures for until I realized that he did have a family who came to see him along with many others. On one wall there was a special shelf that held two white eagle feathers proudly mounted in a glass display case.

Rodney explained that a feather symbolizes trust, honor, strength, wisdom, power, freedom and many more things. To be given one of these is to be hand-picked by of the rest of the men in the tribe. If given a Bald Eagle feather it is one of the most rewarding items that can ever be awarded as Indians believe that eagles have a special connection with the heavens since they fly so close to the sun. Many Indians believe that if they are given this feather, it is a symbol from above. They also believe that the eagle is the leader of all birds, because it flies as high as it does and sees better than all other birds.

Rodney said: "Once an Indian receives a feather he must take care of it, and put it out for everyone to see. This will be a constant reminder of how to behave. An eagle feather is a lot like the American flag. It must be handled with care and can never be dropped on the ground."

Great Grandfather was still the actual chief and would be until he went to meet those who came before him. Sitting in the winter's sun in an oversized rocking chair with a hand-made quilt over his legs sat a tiny old man. His eyes were open and I could see the empty stare caused by nerve damage that had made him blind.

We were only two feet inside the door and a smile creased his face…"Rodney, you are here." He whispered in a voice so soft and gentle it sounded like it came from a kitten. We hadn't said a word and the carpeted floor muffled any sound of footsteps.

"I feel the joy in your heart. Is she a good woman?" Great Grandfather inquired.

"Yes, Great Grandfather. She is a good woman." Rodney had a bashful grin on his face.

"Ho-Chunk?" Great Grandfather asked.

"Potawatomi" Rodney responded.

"Good people." Great Grandfather replied. "I knew many of their members and they were always honorable."

"Who is with you?" Great Grandfather asked. "I feel his spirit and it is strong."

I stood amazed as not a word had been said.

"He is my friend," Rodney replied.

"I feel your bond and your love for each other and it is good." Great Grandfather replied.

With his hands still resting on the arm rests, the old man curled his fingers and beckoned me closer. I took a few steps inward and his facial expressions changed and in it there was a sense of awe. "I know your spirit." Great Grandfather professed. "I feel your goodness and that of many others. Come closer."

I did as instructed and stood before this blind man as his white eyes looked up towards my face. "I cannot see with my eyes, but I can with my heart."

Again, he beckoned me closer, reaching out his hand.

"Let me shake your hand"

Instead of having his one hand vertical, both of his palms were outstretched. I looked at Rodney for guidance and he nodded. I placed my hands in his Great Grandfathers. They were soft and boney. As his fingers wrapped around mine, a smile came across his face. "Your spirit has come to me from a forest where you find great peace"

I was starting to get goose bumps.

"It is a special place in your heart as it should be, for the trees shelter you and hold the mysteries of life and that of your family."

How in hell did he know about the forest? No one knew what was in the book I received for graduation except mom, dad and Tommie and how much the forest meant to me. I was getting scared.

The old man smiled. "Your spirit and that of ours are woven as one and that is why you and my great grandson are so close…like brothers."

I didn't understand, as I stared at this little old man with a quilt on his lap who held my hands.

"Many years ago, in that forest, your ancestors came upon an Indian girl and saved her life. That Indian girl was my great grandmother. Had your ancestors not saved her, I would not exist, my son would never have saved the lives of others, my grandson would not be saving our people and Rodney would not be your brother. On that day, so long ago, our spirits and your spirit became one, forever joined. This is why you have been chosen to write about our people. This is why you are here today and will come many more times before I join the spirits for eternity."

I stood shaking with tears in my eyes. This little old man knew of George the First and how he and his sons had saved the Indian girl, which was Rodney's great, great grandmother. I began to understand why the forest was my enclave of tranquility.

The spirit of life resided there and when I walked amongst the trees, they were whispering to me…peace, peace, peace.

"Did running deer come to meet you when you were there the last time?" great grandfather inquired.

Now I was really getting the chills as the only person I had mentioned the deer to was my mom.

"Yes sir."

"That is good. The spirit is strong. Did your eyes meet?"

"Yes sir." I responded.

"Then all that has been shared with me is true. This makes me very happy. The spirits have sent you."

Tears trickled down my cheeks as I looked at Rodney and he at me. One day, one time, one instant so long, long ago the spirits predetermined that we would meet and that all would transpire…our friendship, Ann, everything. My God! I was excited, humbled, aroused and afraid all at once. A maelstrom of emotions exuded my soul as I quivered before this old man.

"Do not be afraid my son" Great Grandfather said. "The spirits are there and will always await your return. You have been chosen by the great one to share a story seldom told…a story that will allow our spirits to finally find the peace that they have been seeking for so many lifetimes. I am told to call you 'Little Spirit' and so it is. "Little Spirit" you are."

"Rodney, please tell your father that Little Spirit and I must walk together through the past before I meet with those who came before me. Little Spirit's words will be my words and those of many who came before. Do not be afraid Rodney for Little Spirit is kind of heart and full of joy and he will tell the truth. I am an old man and now I must rest. I will await your return Little Spirit as we have much to talk about."

With that Great Grandfather released my hands. My mouth was agape. In a few minutes so much had been learned and so many questions answered and yet the challenge put before me seemed almost insurmountable. I was excited, relieved and yet filled with trepidation. Rodney nodded, indicating it was time to go. I looked at the little old man in the rocking chair with awe and wonder. His eyes were closed, as he was already in a deep sleep, perhaps transcending to tell the others of his visitor… "Little Spirit".

We walked out into the bright, winter's light and I took a deep breath. "Holy shit." was all I could say.

We got into the car and Rodney started the engine and turned down the radio.

I shook my head…"How did he know all that about the forest and your great, great grandmother? It's in the book but we've never told anyone."

Rodney looked at me. "Do you really think we are alone?"

I closed my eyes and shrugged my shoulders. "Wow. Do I get a headdress, too?"

"Yeah, they sell them at the gift shops down on Main Street here in the Dells. They're made in China." So much for the spiritual feeling.

Running Bear: As the days began to blend back into normalcy, the routine was set and the words flowed. It was time for my first solo visit to see Great Grandfather. I drove up to the Dells and went to the assisted living center. I smiled at the receptionist and signed in, telling her that I was there to see Great Grandfather as everyone called him.

Quietly, I walked down the hall and peered into his room. He was asleep as if I had just left him, alone, covered with the shawl in his rocking chair near the window. For an instant, I stood watching this once noble man and a smile came across my face. With that, Great Grandfather awakened as if I had pulled upon his shoulder. A smile came across his face and he looked towards the door. "Little Spirit, is that you?"

"Yes, Great Grandfather, it's me."

"Come in and hold my hands," as he outstretched his hands as he had the time before.

"Pull up the cedar chest at the end of my bed, as we might be here for a while."

With that, I pulled the old, somewhat battered chest in front of him, turned on my recorder and took his hands in mine.

"Your spirit is strong today and I can feel your joy. My ancestors have spoken to me many times since you and Rodney visited and asked me to share with you our story. What we share, you will always remember. It will be with you forever."

Once again, the goose bumps rose on my arms as Great Grandfather began a soft chant. What I write are the sounds and not words and I apologize if they are incorrect... hoiyayaya... hoiyayaya. Over and over he whispered. After a few moments his eyes opened wide and a different voice began to speak.

"I am Running Bear, Chief of the Siouan. It is my task to tell the story of why we left our land so far away. For many seasons we lived in peace within the mountains and valleys of a place now called Virginia. We raised our children and wanted nothing more than to be accepted by the spirits for who we were...just visitors of their land. We raised our children and taught them the language of the land…the whisper of the wind, the roar of the sun, the shutter of the trees and the joy of all of the creatures who lived in harmony. We named our land after "the world and everything in it" which we called "Pamahsawuh".

"When the Jamestown settlers arrived in Virginia in 1607, there were already thousands of my people in different clans wanting nothing more than to simply live. Forests covered most of the land and there were many different Indian nations. We lived, for the most part, together even though each tribe spoke with a different tongue and held different beliefs, traditions, and customs. Yet, there was enough land and food for all of us to live our lives in peace".

"While we had heard stories of the great water that you could not drink, most of our people had never seen it or heard its great roar, as the spirits warned us of the danger within. I had been there and could not understand how so much water could be in one place and what would happen if you went to its end. While many tribes lived near the great water, our people lived within the peaks where Mother Earth's fingers reach towards the heavens above. Life was not always good and yet, for many generations we had always been able to count on the land for food, shelter and life."

"The seasons came and went and with it so did our lives. In the winter, we hunted deer, black bear, turkey, fish and other animals. In the spring, we ate fish, berries, nuts, wild plants and roots. In the summer and fall, we grew and harvested our "three sisters:" corn, squash, and beans that we dried or smoked and used for food during the winter months. While our villages were surrounded by a palisade of wooden poles, we were scattered based on our clans. Even though we were apart, one thing always remained the same…our villages were near water for fish and drinking."

"As I told you Little Spirit, we lived, for the most part, in peace, yet we were enemies of the Algonquian and the Iroquoian and it was this never-ending anger that forced us to leave our homes and find a new place. We were honorable people who only wanted to live in harmony and yet, I am told that Chief Powhatan of the Algonquin warned a Captain John Smith that we were unfriendly and would not allow the settlers into our land. This was not true. However, Chief Powhatan had the trust of the great Captain and we were strangers to the strangers."

"As more settlers came, Chief Powhatan and his council decided that our nation and his could no longer exist side-by-side, even though there was much land and many valleys between us. One day, he and his braves came to attack our villages. Not just our braves, but the women and children and even the elderly and this was wrong. For us, the great God looked down upon us as we tried to escape. We left all that we had and headed towards the setting sun. When we reached Cedar Creek and did not have a way to cross, we prayed for the Great Spirit to protect us and a Natural Bridge appeared, allowing our women and children to cross the creek safely. While there were many warriors against us, my braves and I stood at Cedar Creek and defeated the Powhatan."

"There was joy in our victory. However, we also knew that the Powhatan had many more warriors than our nation and it would not be long before they would come again. Our council of elders chose not to fight another war and continued to find a new place away from the siege that was upon us where we could live in peace away from the Powhatan and the white man. For many seasons our nation traveled until we came to another great water which had no salt. There were many tribes already here and no white men and so we believed we could live in peace as we had done before."

"With each passing day, we continued to search for a place like Pamahsawuh where we could hunt, fish and grow our three sisters. One day, one of our scouts returned and told stories of such a place in the land of the red river on the banks of the great water that was so fresh and clean that all could drink from it. We believed that the white men we had seen were gone forever and we could live our lives in peace.

"Little did we know that what we saw was only the beginning of our tomorrow. Little did we realize that our peace would never be. Little did we understand that peace would never come again. All we wanted was to live in peace. All we wanted was to share our lives and our future. We did not want to leave Pamahsawuh and yet, we knew that the crow could not fly again, as it had before."

Great Grandfather's voice softened and his white eyes turned down. He was exhausted and yet relieved. I hoped my recorder had everything stored on the disc and in my memory and my soul. Great Grandfather spoke…"Running Bear was a great and brave leader. He moved his entire nation from what is Virginia to Wisconsin with only one wish, to live in peace, but then isn't that what we all want? Simply to live in peace?"

"I must rest now, Little Spirit" Great Grandfather whispered as his grip on my hands loosened and I knew it was time for me to go.

"Come again, soon," he whispered. "Come again soon."

I nodded my head and could see what Great Grandfather had shared had taken his strength away. "I will leave you now, Great Grandfather. I will come again soon." I whispered.

The old man took my hands in his again and stared into my eyes. "Go home. Go soon. The spirits are restless. They need you."

I had no idea what Great Grandfather meant, yet there was so much concern on his face that I knew I needed to go home.

As I was about to head back to Madison, I called home. "Mom. It's 'Q'. What's going on?" I asked.

"Why?" she inquired.

"I have a strange feeling I need to come home. I need to know what's happening." I responded.

"There's nothing happening that I know of" mom replied. "It's February and it's cold, but other than that, there's nothing going on."

I was relieved and yet, what grandfather had said made me nervous.

I took the cut off down Highway 151 past MATC and towards Stoughton. As I turned in the driveway, I saw both cars and thought it was weird to have both Rodney and Ann home at the same time, especially in the afternoon.

As I walked in the house, I could see the tension in Ann's eyes. At first, I thought the two of them had a fight, but then I knew better.

"What's going on?" I asked.

Ann began to cry. I'd never seen anything but stoic dignity from her. Her tears became my tears. Her sadness, my sadness! Her anger, my anger!

"Some son-of-a-bitch at the hospital insulted and groped Ann." Rodney said, with anger boiling in each and every word.

"What?" I inquired incredulously.

Rodney reiterated, "Some son-of-a-bitch told the head nurse that he didn't want a squaw taking care of him. That he raped squaws and shot them like he was deer hunting. As Ann was taking care of him, he grabbed her breasts."

Now I was getting all riled up and said. "Give me a gun. I'll go shoot him."

Now Ann was beginning to see I was getting really agitated and attempted to appease me. "Calm down 'Q'. I should be able to take it. He's coming down through detox. He and his girlfriend are junkies. He didn't know what he was doing or saying."

"No Ann. Not this time. You don't have to take that shit from anybody. You are my family." I responded. "No one insults my family…Not my mom. Not my dad. Not my brother. Not Rodney and especially not you. Is he on the floor I was on?"

Ann nodded in the affirmative. "He's in your old room. No insurance of course and he expects that we treat him like a king."

"What happened to him?"

"He was stoned and fell off a ledge and broke his hip" Ann outlined. "Don't worry, they won't keep him long."

"Jerk!" I reiterated. Skinny old me, still all crippled and beat up and itching for a fight. A good old Minnie Point ass whipping and I wanted it.

"What does he look like?" I asked.

Ann remained quiet.

"Ann, tell me or I'll go and try and try to kick the shit out of everybody on the floor."

"Late 20's. Long brown, greasy hair, ink on his neck, yellow teeth and about your size."

"You mean a little shit?" which got a nervous laugh out of the two of them.

"Rodney. You better call the chief and tell him I might need to borrow some bail money."

Rodney tried to stop me. "This is my fight." He said. "She's my fiancée."

"Yes, but a skinny white boy will get in a hell of a lot less trouble than some giant Indian on the warpath," I responded. "Trust me, I'll teach the asshole a lesson and he will learn not to mess with any of us again."

Boy was I riled up. I guess all those months of being banged up had taken the old testosterone levels up to a new high. I headed out the door, back towards the hospital. I was speeding and zooming through right-on-red as I was really getting amped up. I knew the way to Meriter and knew I was really pissed. I parked the car in the hospital lot and walked in the front door. I slammed my finger into the elevator button for the sixth floor and when the door opened, there were smiles all around as the staff who had taken care of me thought I had come to visit. It wasn't long before the scowl on my face let everyone know that I wasn't there on a social call.

"Where is he?" I inquired to no one, everyone.

"Where is who?" Sandy, the clerk behind the desk asked.

"The jerk with the ink on his neck."

"What's going on?"

"That asshole called Ann Wolf a squaw, said he wanted to rape her, shoot her like a deer and grabbed her breasts. Ann's home crying right now and I came because I knew if Rodney responded, there would be one dead doper on sixth floor."

Sandy had never seen good old 'Q' riled up as she reached for the phone.

I raised my hand and pointed my index finger at her. "Two minutes…two minutes. Nothing physical, I give you my word. If I'm not out of there in three minutes call E.R. because you're going to need it."

I walked into the room and saw this skanky, sleaze-ball lying in bed with his wench of a girlfriend sitting next to him.

I pointed to her and jerked my thumb back. "Out." I said. She looked up like she didn't understand. "I said, get out of this room **now**."

She was about to speak when I looked at her one more time. "I'm telling you to leave before I really hurt your boyfriend. Understand?"

Now the clown in the bed…my old bed…looked at me with a stupid grin on his face.

"Wipe that smile off your face or I'm going to shove your good foot all the way up your ass."

The smile evaporated.

"Listen! You made a big mistake today. I mean a big mistake."

The smirk was back.

I reached over the end of the bed and moved his leg.

He winced in pain.

"You decided to insult one of the finest people in this hospital. You piece of garbage, decided you didn't want an intelligent, dedicated, woman to care for you and then you insulted her and groped her.

He flipped me the bird as his reply.

"OK!" I said. I couldn't hit him, but I knew what to do as I started pressing the button that started raising the foot of his bed beneath his knees. "You have no idea who or what you are messing with. You have no idea how lucky you are that I came and simply warned you that if you EVER insult that nurse or any of the nurses again, the pain you are in right now will seem like nothing. Do you understand?"

He was starting to take the hint as the bend in the bottom of the bed contorted his leg and hip. "I came here to save my friend...not his fiancée...but my friend. You see, if he came, you would be dead. Do you understand? I came to save your worthless life."

He sat there as the pain morphed into his soul, obliterating whatever medicine he was on. He reached for the call button but I grabbed it out of his hands. "Not this time. No one to hide behind. No one to take advantage of. Just you and me and it's about time you learn a little lesson called life."

With that I pushed the other button that started raising the head of his bed. I could see the incredible pain that was beginning to overcome his body as he was being folded in two.

"Squaw?"

"Rape her?"

"Deer hunting?"

"Groping her?"

"Who do you think you are?"

He was now bent nearly in half. "Feel the pain? This will be the BEGINNING when I am done with you if you EVER insult her again. Do you understand?"

He was beginning to convulse in pain. "Do you understand?"

My anger was at its boiling point when security came in. "Eddie." I said with a smile as my phony pleasantries returned.

Eddie responded back. "What's going on?"

"Seems I needed to have a discussion with this young man about social tolerance, when he asked me to raise his bed. I replied "You know Eddie, it's been a while and I forgot which button to push.""

The idiot in the bed was writhing in pain.

"We better put him down," Eddie responded.

By now, the entire nursing staff, who knew what had happened earlier in the day, was standing in the doorway.

"Get him out of here," the jerk demanded.

I looked at him and he could tell by the anger in my eyes that I wasn't messing around.

"Do you understand?" I asked one last time.

There was no response. "If you ever insult any of these nurses again, I will be back and I won't be alone. Remember the pain! Remember the pain!" I said as I pointed my index finger at him. With that I walked past the nurses and watched as one of them winked at me. I had done what they could not do.

"Who was that," the doper asked.

I heard Eddie respond. "I don't know, I thought he was a friend of yours"

His girlfriend was in the hallway and looked at me.

"Fucker!" she screamed as I walked by and she flipped me the bird.

I spun on my heels and came face-to-face with her. "Let me tell you something…bitch. Your little boyfriend in there is a loser. Your little boyfriend not only insulted, but sexually assaulted a nurse this afternoon. Your little boyfriend is lucky that it was me who came and not the police or the nurse's fiancée. Had it been either one of them your little boyfriend would either be handcuffed to the bed or been in a whole hell of a lot worse shape than what just happened. Tonight, was a warning. A warning that you don't offend good people regardless of who they are. I have no idea who you are or where you came from and I will probably never see you again, but I'm going to give you some advice…stay away from this loser. Life is too short to be around people who are willing to hurt others."

She sat there dumbfounded. She could see my anger. She could sense my frustration. She was beginning to see that her life-choice was a loser. I felt sorry for her and yet, I had so much disdain for people like him and her, leaching off society, taking advantage of everyone and everything…taking, taking, taking…never giving anything back. Filthy body, filthy mind and filthy spirit! God, what is wrong with my generation?

I stared one more time at her blank face memorizing the dark eyes, fallow cheeks and purple lips, marking the spot in place and time when I met with death before it happened, knowing deep within my heart that she would not, could not, ever change. She was an addict and had begun the death spiral much like what I had seen when I went to visit Rodney's family.

Dark eyes, empty hearts, wasting away with needles in their arms, racing towards oblivion and only wanting one more thing…that next great high…the next profound rush…that next trip to fantasyland where all was numb and their innocuous laughter made a few hours, a few minutes, a few seconds make it all seem worthwhile. Gone was any sense of decency. Gone was any sense of decorum. Gone was any sense of propriety. Like vicious animals, they had absolved any association with society and reality, subjecting themselves to the fact that they did not belong to a world filled with love and laughter and death stood just around the corner.

As I left the hospital, I wondered what her childhood was like. Was it filled with fairy tales and dreams of princes? Were there dolls and happiness and thoughts of love? Only she would know and yet, she no longer knew. Her dreams had become nightmares. Her future had become the past. She was living only for now and the next needle in her arm, regardless of who or how it hurt those around her.

I walked to my car in the cold winter night and stood for a moment and asked for God's forgiveness. Then I shook my head and whispered to myself…"No one, and I mean no one, would ever demean, degrade or insult my family as long as I had any say in it."

I drove back to the cottage and the lights were still on. I parked the car and walked up the stairs. Rodney opened the door and gave me a big hug. Someone from the hospital called and said that one of the patients claimed that some stranger raised the legs and then the head of his bed and threatened him. The staff thought it must have been a hallucination because no one had seen anyone on the floor and the security cameras were blank.

Ann came and gave me a hug. "Thank you," she whispered.

"For what?" I asked. "For standing up for my family? For making certain that no one would have to tolerate shit if I could help it? For protecting the two of you?" I shook my head and they understood…we were family.

"Little Spirit". I was one of them and I hoped this was what Great Grandfather meant about restless spirits.

I went to my room, yet sleep was simply not there. Too much adrenaline was flowing through my veins. I needed to write. I needed to express myself. I decided to turn on the recorder and listen to what Great Grandfather had said. I pressed the play button and there was nothing. I examined the recorder and the indicator reflected 45 minutes had gone by and yet there was just the silence that comes from spirits who enter your mind through your heart and not through your ears. Again, the goose bumps arose. My God, where was I? What was going on? How could this all be happening?

2000 Words: The days were sliding by and soon the ice would be off the lake. It had grown gray and pocked by spots where sunlight had drilled holes waiting, waiting, waiting for summer's warmth to once again arrive. This was a dangerous time. The ice was not safe. Jake loved to run on the ice in the winter and then slide on his butt. Spring was when even he knew it was no longer safe to play on the lake.

With the ice slowly receding, it was wonderful to see the birds beginning to return and feel the warmth of the early spring. What a difference a few days could make! Gone would be the silence of winter, replaced by the chirping of robins calling to each other, letting them announce that life was good and the warmth of the sun was upon them. Dad would be anxious to get out in the fields and get the plowing done. "Cows need to eat in the winter" he would always say! It meant sixteen-hour days, but I knew Dad and Tommie loved it. Wisconsin winters can be long and tedious and, for the first time in five years, there was no spring break to Florida for me to go crazy for a few days.

2000 words doesn't sound like much until you get a writer's block and then they can be really tough. Thank God for computers or I would have shredded a few hundred messed-up pages along the way. The ideas weren't coming as I had hoped and so, it was time for something different. I visited the Wisconsin Historical Society building to see if they could help. They showed me a lot of pictures and a few artifacts, but nothing got my mind going until I saw an old map of where the Winnebago, as they were called back then, lived and I began to realize all that had happened.

The mental block was still there and so I told myself it was time to go home and into the forest. Perhaps the peace would clear my mind and let me see where I needed to be. The drive home was normal except around Dodgeville, where I saw the "spot" and slowed down. Shaking my head, saying to myself, "God I was lucky".

I got home and was viciously attacked by none other than Jake who was all over me with wet, slurpy kisses. Dad and Tommie were in Janesville at some auction and left Jake home alone. Mom was at work in Spring Green, so Jake had run of the house. I knew he had been up on my, or mom and dad's bed and was all excited about seeing me.

"Come Jake, let's go for a walk." Now he was going crazy with his tail wagging and whining with excitement. We went out to the barn and got the ATV with the cart and Jake jumped in. He had ridden in it a hundred times and loved the ride.

The ground was still firm and so there was still a trade-off between sloppy mud and a bumpy ride. After six months, every bone in my body that had been mangled in my carelessness reminded me that I needed to slow down and be careful. Jake and I headed out to the forest and I felt the warm spring air on my face. This was my first true love. The forest was clean and calm and the air scented with nothing but freshness. I shut off the engine and there was no noise, just the sound of the spring breezes caressing the buds, welcoming them to the world. The mosquitoes and flies had yet to arrive and there was freshness in the air and no summer humidity, so the air was still pristine.

Jake and I walked to the foundation where Skunk Hollow School had been and I thought about all those who had come before me and learned so much about life. The school had been torn down in 1956 and yet it was still filled with memories. I drove an ATV and they used to walk every single day, regardless of the weather. My God, we are spoiled.

As we walked back into the forest, I saw him again. The giant buck I had seen in December. His antlers were beginning to grow and were covered in soft velvet to protect them during their developing stage. There was no noise and no motion. I looked at him and he looked at me. I thought Jake would bark, but he too was frozen in silence as three living beings stood in respect, looking each other in the eye, recognizing each other's existence as part of our wonderful world. After what seemed like an eternity, he quietly turned and walked away. He did not run. He simply walked away when the spell was broken. Was it really true what grandfather said that it was "Running Deer" looking after me?

Jake and I headed up the path to the creek where George the First had interceded and saved the young girl and a chill went through my body. Were there really spirits and why were my emotions so strong where I stood? Jake stopped for just a moment, as he too must have felt something and then ran ahead to where the water gurgled out from beneath the limestone rocks and lapped the clean, clear water. I followed and cupped my hands. I closed my eyes and took a long, cool drink of the freshest, purist water there is. Like life springing forth, the waters came clean and pure only to meander until they were filled with the refuse of reality, melded into a cornucopia of elsewhere, admonished in purity, before making its way to the mighty Mississippi and finally the sea.

We walked back to the ATV and both of us knew it was time to head for home. Jake jumped in the back cart and I turned the ignition and headed for home. The air and tranquility had washed away all the dirt and filth of the clown in the hospital. My mind had been cleansed and it was time to begin again.

Even with the ground frozen, there was mud and so Jake knew that it meant going into the barn where there was a shallow pan to get his feet washed. He didn't like it, but also realized that going from barn dog to house dog meant some sacrifices and wet feet that were hand dried and sleeping on a bed was a lot better than straw in the barn. I washed his feet and dried them and he gave me a slurp. He was my buddy and it was his way of saying thanks for a day away from solitary.

We went into the quiet house and I wrote mom a note telling her that I had been there but needed to get back to Madison. An hour later would have meant dinner which would have meant another couple of hours and I wanted to get "home" as my mind was clearing and I wanted to prepare for my next meeting with Great Grandfather.

Koan-Kaw: It was Thursday and time to meet with Great Grandfather again. The time had been set for 10:00 am, as always. I knew he would be in his chair with the blanket over him. The trip up the interstate was becoming a snap and going alone was also becoming more comfortable. I arrived at the assisted living center a little before 10:00 and out of respect waited until the precise moment to enter Great Grandfather's room. I quietly knocked on the jamb of the door and Great Grandfather's head tilted back and a slight smile came across his face.

"Little Spirit, you have come." he whispered. "I can feel your presence and it is good."

I didn't know if Great Grandfather knew about what happened at home and decided to let sleeping dogs lie.

"She's a good woman." Great Grandfather whispered.

"Who?" I inquired.

"Why Rodney's Ann, of course!" he replied.

"Did they come to visit?" I asked.

"No, not yet, but the spirits tell me she is a good person, full of love and kindness!"

"I agree." I responded.

"What you did was a noble deed, Little Spirit. The sign of a great warrior! To protect and defend a woman's honor is a noble act."

How did he know? "Great Grandfather, how did you know?"

"I know many things that are not spoken. The spirits tell me. You and your dog went into the forest to clear your mind. Your dog was not afraid of Running Deer and he saw kindness in his eyes. You have a great friend in your dog and he loves you. What is his name?"

"It's Jake," I responded.

"A Border Collie?"

"Yes sir." Now I was getting goose bumps again.

"Very intelligent dogs. I wish people could be like them. Kind, honest, sincere. Don't you?"

"Yes, Great Grandfather."

"You are like your dog and that is good. Come closer and hold my hands, someone would like to speak with you."

I turned on my recorder and pulled up the cedar chest and put my hands in Great Grandfather's. The slow, quiet chant began as it had before and I saw his eye's slowly move upward, at which time, a different voice came through.

"My name is Koan-Kaw. I am a Winnebago chief from the past and I am here to tell the story of our nation from long ago."

Once again, I sat mesmerized.

"For as long as anyone can remember, my nation...the Winnebago, lived near the green bay by the mighty water. We were the most powerful tribe and it was our nation whose strength provided peace along the mighty water's shore. Our families wanted nothing more than to grow our crops and hunt for the food we ate and live our lives in harmony with the spirits. For many seasons, there was peace and all was good."

"Our people were proud of who they were. We stood taller than those we came in contact with and lived a different life than they. We built our houses of wood and made our canoes of the stumps of trees...strong, sturdy and dependable, like our warriors. What happened to my people was not caused by us, for we wanted nothing more than to live in peace. Unfortunately, the white man came across the great water and traveled down the great river in search of fur. These men, who at first came from France, began trading with other nations, providing them with fire sticks and arrows with heads of steel in trade for beaver, muskrat, mink and fox. At first, this did not affect us. Sadly, as more and more of the hides were taken, nations who traded with the French had to move beyond where they lived for many seasons and into the lands of others. With fire sticks and pointed arrows, those who had lived in peace...the Cheyenne, Suita, Menominee and Arapaho... in the land called Michigan began to seek a different home. The Cheyenne, Suita and Arapaho continued beyond the land of the Winnebago, while the Menominee became our allies and friends, sharing with us the threats to our peace."

"With so many new people, the land could not bring forth the food and hides that we needed to survive and so, our elders elected to move away. Sadly, our nation moved into the lands of what was called the Illinois Confederation of many nations who pledged to protect the land that was theirs. Within our nation, there was a great deal of anger and fear and many people began to leave our nation with the Iowa, Missouri and Otoe moving beyond where the sun sets across the mighty river. Now in much smaller numbers, we faced threats from above from the Ojibwe and below from the Illini where the birds flock for winter."

"The peace that we had enjoyed was gone. The sense of security disappeared like smoke into the sky. Our nation and its leaders did not know what they could do to make sure we lived in peace. Like many nations, the French had never heard of the Winnebago until the year 1620 when we were spoken of by the Ottawa. We were not there, but believe that, because the Ottawa were allies with the Ojibwe, who were our enemies, what they heard about the Winnebago nation was not good."

"Our land had been ours and no one else since the beginning of time and when the Ottawa and Huron joined with the Ojibwe and wanted to trap on our land, we refused. For the first time, we saw the wrath of the fire sticks, knives and steel pointed arrows that made us realize that our way of life was about to end. The combined nations prepared for war against the Winnebago in the year 1634 and our elders and braves were willing to give their lives for the land they loved."

"Instead, the French sent a man named Nicollet to the red banks of the green bay and this strange looking man was the first any of us had ever seen that did not look as we did. He was a man who was soft spoken and talked of his one God who died for him. We could feel the peace within his heart and our elders listened to this man who spoke of prosperity and change.

In the end, the Winnebago nation agreed that working with the Huron and Ottawa in trading pelts for fire sticks and knives and arrows was better than sacrificing warriors in a war we could not win. Nicollet came to our villages again at what he called La Baye after five seasons. His visit was short but his message was the same…live in peace. He would be the first and last white man I would ever see as it would be many, many seasons until one would come again and I would be with the spirits forever."

Grandfather's voice trailed off and he went into a deep sleep. I quietly arose and pulled his blanket up over his hands. I walked out into the bright early spring sunshine and shivered. My God, what was going on? Why had I been chosen to be the messenger? Where would this all end? My mind was going in a million different directions at one time.

How incredibly difficult to return to "reality" when a few minutes prior you were immersed in something surreal? How could he know about Jake and the forest? How could he change his voice like that? God, this is unreal and I'm in the middle of it. And Great Grandfather? Last time the 'voice' tells me they were from Virginia and now this voice says they have been in Wisconsin forever. What in hell is going on? Two voices from the same old man and they can't even get their bullshit straight. I know white men cheated the Indians, but why do they have to mess with me?

I took a deep breath and wanted nothing more than reality. But what is reality…What you think? What you feel? What you believe? Do I go to the cottage? The house? The farm? The forest? Not the forest, it was giving me the creeps. God, I loved the place but not when I think everything I see, think and feel, is being recorded. Ghosts! Were they ghosts? Were they really spirits? All I want is peace and serenity, not some people from 400 years ago looking over my shoulder wondering what I am doing there. And the deer? God what happens if someone shoots him? Are they killing a person? And poor Jake? What in hell is he thinking with a big deer staring him down and me wandering off? Christ. What a mess. Sorry book, but I'm confused, scared and yet excited by all that is happening…I think!

I wanted to go home, but knew better than to drive and had no money and so I headed for the Tanger Outlet mall. Why was it called Tanger? A city in Morocco? Named after some brightly colored male birds? Shit. At least I knew I wouldn't be mentally challenged as the canned music made me blind to my thoughts and emotions. I wandered through the outlets looking at everything and nothing, waiting for my heart to stop pounding.

Thirty minutes, and then across the street to Mickey D's. Got my order through the drive through and wondered if anyone ever went inside and sat on plastic chairs at plastic tables and ate food laced with the sugar they put in their buns, ketchup, Big Mac sauce, French fries and even some of their meats like sausage patties and chicken McNuggets that you eat with plastic forks from plastic containers and cardboard cups. Dashboard diner for me baby. $7.37 of my money invested in whatever it was that filled me up.

I needed to hit Madcity. As I cruised south, I flashed back on Rodney and Black River Falls, the accident, George the First. My assignment…no my commitment, was to tell the story…the true story of all that had happened to people who were becoming my friends and their ancestors. I thought of old and I mean really old episodes of Dragnet, "the truth and nothing but the truth" bang! Bang! Bang! as the sweaty hand hits the sledge hammer into the steel. Badge 714. Heh that was how many home runs Babe Ruth hit. I love it, when I figure something out that makes me feel smart, at least for a couple of seconds. The first thing they teach you in journalism school is to be objective…don't let your emotions get in the way. Oh yeah. Try it when all that has happened, has happened. Shit!

I zoomed south past Madison and 18/151…passed the "factory" whose parking lot was packed at 2:00 in the afternoon and kept on going to Highway "N" and the Stoughton exit to the house I shared with a friendly giant and the woman I introduced him to. I had forgotten about all the road construction and yet it brought me back to reality. It seems that fifty years ago someone thought they could save money and design the system from Rockford to Madison to always be two lanes in each direction. Whoops. Madcity had exploded, along with all the small towns and the Interstate was way too congested. Instead of a few hundred million to add another lane, they needed to re -do all the bridges and the overpasses and the underpasses and everything else. What should have taken a couple of years was going to take a decade, if not more. Brilliance. Absolute brilliance. Closing lanes each night. What a mess. At least I got to calm down as we muddled along at an astronomically fast 30 MPH.

The house was quiet and it seemed like I had been gone forever. I listened to the tick tock of the small clock on the fireplace mantel and watched as the Waubesa waves made their way from the remaining ice flow to the shore, lapping at the rocks that delineated earth from water…solid from liquid, wondering if I had been in a liquid world where solids did not exist…only dreams and nightmares…thoughts and emotions…concepts and reality. I needed to write. I needed to write. I needed to write. Click went the button on the recorder. Hiss went the sound of empty tape. Nothing again! Simply nothing! Yet, I remembered everything. My God what was happening? Did I share this with Rodney? How about Ann? Call my Dad? No way, he would never understand. How about mom? Tommie? He would only laugh. Was this the beginning of insanity? Had I hit my head in the accident? Was all this a dream?

I sat blankly staring at the lake when the door opened. It was Ann. I looked at her and she at me and she knew right away that I was abuzz.

"Are you OK?" she asked.

I looked at her and really didn't know what to say, which, for me, was quite a unique experience. "Í went to see Great Grandfather today."

"And?"

"We had another séance with a chief from the 1600's." I answered.

"And?"

There was no shock. No trepidation on Ann's part. It was like it was just another conversation.

"And?" I replied "And it was weird. Great Grandfather's eyes rolled back and this strange voice came out of him who told the story about the first time this guy had ever seen a white man."

"And?"

"I was cool the first time, but this guy's story was different than the first guys."

"I'll bet the first one talked about Virginia and this one talked about Wisconsin as if they had been here forever." She said with a smile.

"Yeah, how did you know?"

"Because one part of the Winnebago's came from Virginia and blended in with the indigenous settlers who had been here for hundreds of years. That's why."

"You know all this stuff?"

And looked at me with a somewhat incredulous look on her face and noted. "This is part of my heritage."

"But you're not Winnebago."

"Remember what Rodney told you about how we claim our citizenship? My family claims Potawatomi but is a mixture of virtually all of the nations who ever resided in Wisconsin. Rodney claims Ho-Chunk, but he's also part Sauk. Over the years almost all of the indigenous people married others from different tribes, just like Germans marrying Norwegians or Italians or French. The nations and the clans were too small and there would have been incest and so a lot of my heritage is from the Sauk and Winnebago. It's more about race than about tribes. In the end, we are all just Native Americans, some with more defined histories than others."

Ann sat down next to me at the kitchen table and I could sense her earnestness. When you live with someone, you forget their features…hair, smile, intensity of their eyes, delicacy of their fingers as Ann offered, "Let me see if I can't clear things up for you. In the early 1600's the Winnebago tribe was decimated by disease and the Beaver Wars and there were only a few hundred left when a group of similar background who spoke virtually the same Siouan language showed up. The tribes blended, as did the Winnebago with virtually all the Wisconsin tribes."

It was beginning to make sense. I wondered if I dare tell her about the blank tapes and decided not to.

"What do you mean the Beaver Wars?" My mind was going in a different direction and I almost slapped my own face.

Ann added…"The Beaver Wars started in 1628 when the Iroquois began a war to reclaim their territory on the upper St. Lawrence River from the Algonkin, Montagnais and Huron. The Iroquois were five nations who had joined as one by the tribal leader Hiawatha to suppress internal strife and provide strength against the French. Initially, they were the Mohawk, Oneida, Onondaga, Cayuga and Seneca nations. The fighting quickly spread west to other tribes. Having exhausted the beaver in their homelands, Ottawa, Neutral, and Tionontati warriors equipped with guns, knives and other steel weapons invaded lower Michigan to seize hunting territory from the Algonquin living there. The people living in Michigan had to get out and came west."

"Refugees?" I asked.

"The first refugees from these wars to arrive in Wisconsin were a group of Potawatomi who attempted to settle near Green Bay in 1641. The Winnebago wanted nothing to do with the Potawatomi and pushed them further north into what is now the

UP. The remaining Potawatomi soon joined the early arrivals followed by other tribes from lower Michigan and they all united against the Winnebago."

"So, your ancestors were enemies of Rodney's?"

"At first yes, and finally no! Like our government policy, an enemy of an enemy can be your friend. While the ancestors will say they were all peace-loving, most Winnebago decided on war and to concentrate on the Fox nation. It was a huge mistake and disaster was immediate. Crossing Lake Winnebago in canoes to attack the Fox, the Winnebago were caught in a storm and 500 warriors drowned. The three largest Winnebago bands then drew together into a single village, which turned out to be a death camp. There were 12,000 people confined to a small space which created perfect conditions for epidemics which accompanied the refugees to Wisconsin. Thousands died from small pox and probably yellow fever because our ancestors said they were feverish and turned the people yellow."

"Within months there were less than 1,500 Winnebago warriors and a total of only 4,500 people alive. Nearly two-thirds had perished and those who survived were starving since the war and epidemic made it impossible to harvest their crops. While the war between the Winnebago and the Illinois had gone on for years, the Illinois sent 500 warriors with food to help the Winnebago which proved to be yet another serious mistake. At first, the Winnebago welcomed and held a feast for the Illinois, but in the midst of the celebration, the Winnebago cut their bowstrings to appease the spirits of their warriors killed earlier by the Illinois and assassinated those who came to save them."

"Nice going." I interjected.

"It took the Illinois time to learn what happened. In the meantime, the Winnebago anticipated retaliation and retreated to an island which is now called Doty Island in the middle of Lake Winnebago, where they built a fort. The Illinois waited a year to take revenge and when the lake was frozen, a war party crossed over the ice to attack the village only to find the Winnebago were absent on their winter hunt. After a six-day pursuit, they caught up with the Winnebago and, during the slaughter which followed, annihilated almost all of them."

"A few Winnebago escaped to find refuge with the Menominee and about 200 Winnebago prisoners were taken back as slaves to the Illinois villages. After several years of hard labor, the captives were released and returned to Wisconsin. Less than 500 Winnebago survived to provide a future for their people, but their near -extermination was a serious mistake made by the Illinois. Despite the circumstances which had caused it, the Winnebago never forgave or forgot what had happened"

"Is this why people from Wisconsin call people from Illinois FIBS?" I added in a very weak attempt at humor.

Ann continued without responding to my feeble attempt at humor. "In the east, the Beaver Wars threatened the French fur trade. The climax came in the early Spring of 1649 when the Iroquois overran and destroyed the Huron. Other French allies fell victim during the next few years, while the Iroquois moved into the Ottawa Valley and cut French access to the Great Lakes. The Iroquois then invaded lower Michigan, expelling the remaining Algonquin. When this happened, 20,000 refugees fled to Wisconsin, producing a tide of people which the Menominee and Winnebago could not stop.

"And so, the white settlers weren't the first group to invade the territory?" I added trying to sound intelligent.

"Even the Illinois were forced to surrender territory in southern Wisconsin. So far as known, the Winnebago made only one attempt at resistance during this period when they managed to keep the Mascouten from locating near Green Bay in 1655. However, this success proved temporary and made the Winnebago hated by the refugees. Within three years the Mascouten had allied with the Kickapoo and Miami and settled where they pleased. Only Iroquois attacks in the area during 1660 forced them inland to a safer location at the Fox Portage."

Wow. Ann really knew her stuff.

"The Iroquois victory over the Huron in 1649 virtually destroyed the French trade, but the French traders managed to continue on a limited basis by inviting tribes to bring their furs to Montreal. This was only possible for large, heavily-armed canoe fleets able to fight their way past the Iroquois on the Ottawa River. Having become dependent on French goods, only the Ottawa and Huron were willing to try to break the blockade. They were supported by Ojibwe warriors who fought their way to and from Montreal. In this manner, French goods continued to reach the western Great Lakes in limited amounts. Unfortunately, it also brought Iroquois war parties to Wisconsin to stop the trade at its source."

"The French made separate peace with the Iroquois in 1645, but this collapsed in 1658. Six years of raids and harassment followed before the French got serious and sent a regiment of soldiers to Quebec to deal with the Iroquois. Their attacks on the Iroquois homeland produced an alliance between the British and Iroquois and marked the beginning of the British-French struggle for control of North America. So now you know how the entire war of independence. It wasn't about what white people thought and 'no taxation without representation. It was about the fur trade and nothing more than to keep rich Europeans warm in winter."

Ann continued. "The French resumed travel to the western Great Lakes. In 1665 fur trader Nicholas Perrot, Jesuit Claude-Jean Allouez, and four other Frenchmen accompanied 400 Huron-Ottawa warriors on their return to Wisconsin. After fighting their way past the Iroquois along the Ottawa River, they reached Green Bay. What they found was a disaster: War, disease, and starvation had decimated the Winnebago and only 500 remained."

"French attacks on the Iroquois homeland produced a lasting peace in 1667. For the first time, it extended to French allies and trading partners to those residing in the western Great Lakes. This allowed the French to resume their fur trade, but they first needed to bring some order to the area and end the warfare. Using the threat of withholding trade, they began mediating intertribal disputes, a role which eventually evolved into the relationship of Onontio (the French governor of Canada) and his 'Indian children'. For the first time, a white man was making all the rules."

I shook my head as I knew what was coming.

"Although the French fur trade had been at the root of the Beaver Wars, which almost destroyed the Winnebago, it also saved them from extinction. As peace was restored, the Winnebago accepted the Algonquin refugees in Wisconsin and began to intermarry, adapting parts of their culture in the process and this is why you have two stories about the beginning of the Winnebago."

"The peace lasted thirteen years, until the Beaver War started again in 1680 between the Iroquois and Illinois when Seneca war parties struck the Illinois. During 1684, the Iroquois failed to take Fort St. Louis on the upper Illinois River after which the tide turned. The French responded by strengthening their forts and providing guns to their allies as they developed an alliance to fight the Iroquois. By 1690 the Iroquois were on the defensive and retreating back towards New York."

"If there hadn't been enough war and bloodshed, King William's War of 1688-97 between Britain and France continued until a peace was signed in 1700, which left the French and their allies in control of the Great Lakes. This really helped the Winnebago. With the Iroquois defeated, refugees began leaving Wisconsin relieving overcrowding and competition for food resources. After 60-years, the Winnebago regained most of their homeland."

"While all this was happening, the French fur trade continued and was incredibly successful to the point that by the 1690s there was a glut of fur on the European market which destabilized the entire region once again. The resulting price drop finally motivated the French monarchy to listen to protests from Jesuit missionaries about the corruption the fur trade was creating among my ancestors. In1696 all licenses were revoked and trade was suspended in the western Great Lakes."

"Since the French alliance was based on trade, this was a terrible decision. Even while they were going down in defeat, the Iroquois sensed French vulnerability and began to offer French allies' access to British traders at Albany. Suspecting the French would make their own peace with the Iroquois, the alliance began to unravel, and the French had great difficulty getting their allies to agree to the peace signed with the Iroquois in 1701. Urgent appeals were sent to Paris from Canada asking for a resumption of trade in the Great Lakes, but this only brought limited relief. In 1701 Antoine Cadillac was allowed to build Fort Pontchartrain at Detroit to trade with the Great Lakes tribes. Cadillac quickly invited just about every tribe in the region to move to Detroit. The result was overcrowding and warfare between former allies. Rather than solving the problem, it further strained what remained of the French alliance and by 1712 all the hostilities came to a head with the First Fox War that lasted for four years."

Ann went to the refrigerator and got one of Rodney's bottles of FIJI water and took a sip.

"You really know your stuff." I offered.

"When you are a minority, you need to hang onto what you can to develop some form of identity. So many Caucasians have such a blended European history they don't know who they are. When you have been adjectivized your entire life, you need to know where you came from."

I must have wrinkled my nose at the word adjectivized….

"I'm never that girl or that woman. I'm always that Indian or Native American girl. Rodney is never 'that man' but that Indian man…that's adjectivization. We do it all the time to describe people of a different race, religion or origin. Things like, that black guy, that fat girl, you name it, we all do it."

"I really dislike the terms black and white," Ann continued. "They are opposites and that automatically begins conflict. In reality, we are all simply shades of brown…light brown to dark brown. Wouldn't it be better if you called an African American a dark brown person and they called you a light brown person? Now we are just different shades of the same color instead of opposites."

She, of course, made sense. But then she always did as she continued, "It's all about economics…the haves versus the have-nots. The words "middle class" today represent the working poor…those who play by the rules and pay six different types of taxes, plus eight different types of insurances so that those who are rich and those too poor, don't pay anything. After paying income taxes, sales taxes, excise taxes, social security taxes, Medicare taxes and property taxes, you have to take what's left to pay health insurance, life insurance, dental insurance, optical insurance, prescription insurance, home owner's insurance, car insurance and liability insurance to protect yourself from those who have none. If you're poor, why have insurance when you have no assets when, many times, it's cheaper to simply file bankruptcy than to do what's right. I see it every day at the hospital."

"Some of those on the lower end of the spectrum either really don't care or understand to do anything but blame everyone else for their inadequacies. The world has changed and they have not. They have been left behind believing that we owe them something which was the opportunity to get an education that they squandered. The real secret to America is still the silent majority who are sick and tired of all the favoritism at their expense. America used to be like a Dromedary camel with one big middle-class hump. With all that has happened, we are like a Bactrian camel...two humps, rich and poor who keep squeezing the middle until it finally broke. Those on the front end of the camel, hire people who figure out how not to pay their fair share of taxes while those on the other end don't have insurance and so those in the middle have to pay both."

"It's a crazy system. One-in-seven drivers in Wisconsin ride around with no car insurance. Why? Because it's cheaper, even when you get caught. The fine is something like $375.00. If you're in an accident, what happens? You live in an apartment and have no money in the bank so your net worth is zero. If the damage is great enough, you scrape up $500 and file personal bankruptcy. They can't throw you out of your apartment and you have no assets. So, each year, you risk a grand total of $875 IF you have a ticket or get in an accident verses $125 per month for car insurance that, you have to fight over if you have an accident."

"Health insurance is just as bad. Look at what it would have cost your parents had you not been working for the Nation. Look at their premiums every month. It can be over $2000 per month for a family. Everyone thinks it's easy when they get on Medicare and then they find out that the system is rigged against them as well. Sure, you get basic coverage, but it only covers 80% of your costs. You think it's going to be free because you've been paying into it all your life. Instead, if you're still working, they make you pay Medicare on your earnings and then they charge you more for even the basic coverage. Then you need an additional premium and that can cost another $300-$400 per month and that's just medical. Next, you still need dental insurance. Finally, you need prescription insurance and those premiums can cost another $100 or so per month. All of a sudden your 'free' Medicare is costing $500-$1000 per month, per person."

"I have married friends who work and their husbands work as well. All they want is a decent house and some security and a better life for their kids. One husband works 80-100 hours per week just to make ends meet. The other husband not only teaches full time, but works two part-time jobs to make ends meet. They are the working poor. Trying to do it right and realizing that, even with dual incomes, it's tough."

"The system is broken. 'Life, Liberty and the Pursuit of Happiness'? How can there be life when your medical costs are so high you can't do anything else? How can there be liberty when property taxes are so high that if you miss paying them by one day, they charge you 20% penalty and can eventually foreclose on your property? How can one pursue happiness when all they have time to do is worry about all the costs that go into living in America…land of the free?"

I looked at her and for the first time I saw her social passion and was totally impressed. "What can we do?" I asked.

"It's simple", she responded. "I think we should create a national health care system that is structured like Medicare and offer it to every American citizen for free. Everyone would have a basic health plan and the protection they needed. Add to it, a prescription program that would cover the cost of basic drugs and medications. This would serve as a floor upon which people could then build the type of coverage they felt they needed and could afford. Similar to Medicare, people would be given options and make their own choices for additional coverage. The insurance companies would then compete for the business."

"Socialized medicine?"

"Not really, that's where the program options come in. Everyone would be protected and yet everyone would have costs involved and decisions to make."

"Wouldn't that all be expensive?" I asked.

"Not as expensive as the premiums people are paying now. Do you know what dunning rates are?" Ann asked.

I shook my head no.

"Dunning rates are the percentages of uncollected bills a company endures every year. Most hospital emergency rooms, cannot deny health care and so anyone can walk in for any reason and be treated. While it is noble, this is just one crack in the system. People know this and so they go there for the slightest reason with no intent to pay. Today, the dunning rates are astronomical. With my system, gone would be dunning rates of 30%-40%-50% and higher at hospitals that are then shoved onto those who have insurance."

"To fund the program, I suggest a federal sales or Value Added Tax like those in every other major country in the world. If there was a 3%-5% VAT, I believe it would cover the entire program for everyone regardless of income, race or anything. People think it would be unfair to the poor because they would also be paying it. But in actuality, it wouldn't be unfair simply because those who earn less buy less and therefore would be paying less. The current system is broke, and those trying to fix it just keep adding gasoline to the fire. Let's hope someone somewhere is brave enough to fight the battle for all of us."

Ann glanced at the clock and I could tell that the history and sociology lessons were over for the day. My God! What an incredible, passionate person. War after war after war, I needed to try and make sense of it all and write about the wars between the Indians and also the social war going on in America. I also needed to take all that had happened in a few hours and put it to paper or whatever you call the icons on the screen. Ann recognized my lesson-ending nervous ticks and excused herself. She wasn't home long and then back to the 'stacks'. Studying for some was better in solitude, where distractions were few and thoughts focused.

Old City Cemetery: I looked out at the water and wondered how and why I got into this. I needed to find out why all this was happening to me. I vowed I was doing it for a purpose. I wanted to go home to the forest and clear my head, but knew I didn't have time. I decided to go to the "factory" and have a chat with Big Brother and jumped in Jeepers Creepers the Second, and headed for 18&151. The sign said that $23 million had been won year-to-date. I wondered how much had been "invested" to have that much winning.

I parked in the employee lot, which was set up to make the place look busy even when it wasn't. Ahhh…marketing 101! As I walked through the front door, smiles were everywhere. My fellow employees always made me feel welcome. Big Brother was in his normal location and so I made my way over to him. He smiled. I smiled. You would never know that we lived in the same house. "Heh, little brother, what are you doing here?"

"I needed a break. Ann just filled me in on the Beaver and Indian Wars of the 1600's. Man, did they ever not fight?" I asked.

"Every now and then, but only to make babies," Rodney giggled.

"I didn't know you were part Sauk." I shared.

"Yup, my great-great-great-great grandfather was Sauk." Rodney offered.

"Anyone who is going to be talking to me?" I asked.

"His name was Khay-rah-tshoan-saip-kaw" Rodney replied, with the name sliding off his tongue like it was Michael or Robert.

"Oh! Ok!" I said as I shrugged my shoulders.

I was about to say something profound when the big guy's wrist went to his mouth and he was speaking into the microphone beneath his sleeve. "I'll be back," was all Rodney said as he stepped forward. "Watch the door."

Like me, the little scrawny shit who walked with a limp, talked with a lisp and ached and pained from being in a car accident that almost killed him, was going to intimidate anyone.

Baam! Rodney was gone and I saw the mêlée begin. Some drunk idiot decided he had enough of another guy and they were going to duke it out in the middle of the casino. With that, two of the uniformed security guards took the guy out the front door. A taxi had already been called and the boys had his address.

The argument was quickly over and the good guys won. People can really act stupid when they are drunk. Within a few minutes everything was back to "normal" at the factory. I wondered if the topic would come up in our weekly marketing meeting.

We stood together and I felt tough, especially when so many people smiled and nodded at Rodney. He had handled it properly. No one got hurt. The idiot was gone and patrons had something to talk about. Glad Big Brother is my buddy.

The week flew by and 2000 words were punched into the keyboard. My "weekend" was Sunday and Monday and so Sunday morning, I decided to head home to Waldwick via Mineral Point. I got up early and called mom and told her I would meet them at church. I hoped we could have breakfast at the Red Rooster. It had been three years to the day, since my Grandma passed away. I knew that my coming home meant a lot to mom. It was also getting neat to go home and be with them. I guess I was growing up. I knew that Jake would be in the truck and when church was over, he would ride with me regardless of where we were going.

If you've never been around agriculture in Wisconsin, you wouldn't know that March is a crazy time when you're a farmer. Sometimes it's too cold and the snow is too deep to do anything. Other times, it can be warm and there will be mud everywhere, which was the way it was this year. I wanted to go into the forest but the mud was too bad and, while I hoped I was putting on a good act, there was still a lot of pain from the broken bones and all. The doctor said up to a year and I thought "suuuure." but those darn doctors really knew what they were talking about and I didn't want to risk anything by jumping on an ATV and slopping through the mud. By April it would be dry and I could go visit my friends, the trees.

I met mom and dad in church, making it just before services began. Mom was happy to see me. Dad was a little upset because I was in jeans and a Wisconsin sweatshirt. To him, church always meant his Sunday best and was the only time he wore a necktie.

March was when grandma died and I cried the hardest in my life. We used to come into town and pick her up and take her to church with us and then either go to the Red Rooster or her house where she would make Sunday brunch. I remember her. I remember the smells and the smiles and above all else, I remember the love. God, I missed her and her dignity…such a profoundly good, honest, sincere, humble woman.

We went to the Rooster and had pancakes or "flapjacks" as grandma called them. I saved some of my "belly buster" for Jake, which was his reward for being a "good boy". When breakfast was over, Jake switched from the truck to my Jeep and I told mom and dad, I would see them in a little while. They knew where I was going, as I had gone every year since Grandma died. I was going to the cemetery.

This year was different. I would visit grandma and grandpa's graves. However, after what George the First had written and all that Rodney's Great Grandfather, or whoever it was behind the curtain telling me stories about the past, I also wanted to visit all my other relatives buried in Mineral Point. I wanted to look down upon the grave stones and put all the pieces together. My heart was as open as was my mind. Perhaps, it would make sense if what was going on followed in George the First's footsteps. Then, if I could make sense of what Great Grandfather was talking about, I could possibly write something I could leave for those who followed in my footsteps, IF that was, I could find a girl and fall in love and have kids and do all the stuff that you're supposed to do. Geez. Way too many ifs!

Even in a tiny town like Mineral Point, that only has 2700 residents while thinking you know everything, there is still a lot to learn. I read about the Old City Cemetery, which is just a few blocks off High Street in George the First's journal. I had never really "been" there and so I felt I needed to go and look at all of the old tombstones. I got out of the Jeep and told Jake to stay.

I walked through the gate and down the cinder path. I really didn't know where to look or who to look for, but I was there, alone on a cool March day, warmed by memories of those who had lived before me, who's being allowed me to exist. Off the path, the ground was soft and mushy, but I didn't care. Jake was in the Jeep and away from the mud and my boots were made for washing. (Sorry Nancy. I couldn't resist).

I read the historical marker and knew that some of the people interred dated back to 1838 and the last one in 1908. The standing stones were weathered and yet you could still read whose name was inscribed, detailing whence they begun and when they had ended. Mom told me that some really good people were taking it upon themselves to restore the markers and make the place special again. How sad that headstones, like memories, fade until all that is left is yesterday. Tears had dried, leaves had fallen, the cold snow of forever had taken its toll and beneath lie human remains as nothing more than flecks of what had been. Story has it that the good folks wanted to restore 250 markers. Some had been broken and covered with dirt and they were trying to resurrect them. They took a pole with a metal rod on the end and stuck it in the ground. If nothing came up, they moved on. If they heard a thud, they knew a tombstone probably was buried beneath the shallow dirt and they would start digging.

A lot of people get the heebie jeebies when they go to a cemetery. For me, it's a sacred place to reflect and wonder about those who died. How did they live? Why and when did they die?

Were people sad to see them go? What stories could they share that George the First alluded to? I found a headstone for an eighteen-month-old baby girl who died in 1853. I can only imagine the pain her family suffered when she died. Back then, there was a lot more death among children than there is now and I wonder if the little girl's demise was accepted as nothing more than the consequence of life.

How sad. How truly sad! Yet, today, I wonder if we value life any more. Today it seems that journalists amplify each story and make all of us aware, so aware of the challenges of life. I thought about the Indians and realized that our emotions were their emotions…our fears were their fears…our joys were their joys. It was just that their spirits were not our spirits, their customs, not our customs, their beliefs, not our beliefs and so there were very few places for them to go to remember those who had come before. Every now and then, you would hear about, read about and sometimes even feel about a sacred place where something, someone, somehow had been of such a degree as to simply be remembered. Pearl Harbor. The World Trade Center. For the Indians, there were few and yet, the more time I spent with my new family, the less they seemed different to me and this made me smile.

Jake was barking as he didn't like to be unable to run around, but dogs weren't allowed in the cemetery. God, I had a lot of relatives in the Old City Cemetery…Terrill's, Harris's, Fitzsimons, Huxtable's, they were all part of the family tree in one way or another. Even though we had the family plot out on the farm, they were still there.

As I headed west on High Street, towards the water tower, I stopped and looked up at Mineral Point's famous statue and best loved dog, after Jake of course. It's a statue of a dog, affixed to the side of a building. The dog stands up high so that he can see and be seen from both ends of the street who is named Pointer and made of zinc from our own mines.

Everyone who is anyone who lives in Mineral Point knows about Pointer. We learned in grade school that Pointer originally took his stand to promote a large and elegant local department store called 'Gundry and Gray' and was placed in his prominent spot in 1892. Both Gundry and Gray were from Cornwall and it was a British custom to help identify stores by using statues of animals in much the same way that cigar stores were once identified by wooden Indians. Anyway, Pointer still stands tall and it's always good to see him and, with my new friendships, I'm sure glad there isn't a wooden Indian there.

It's incredible how much of Mineral Point's history he's seen. Good times. Bad times. Happy times. Sad times. He saw boys march off to war and the sadness when they came home to be buried where I had just been or where I was about to go. Pointer had watched people come and go, live their lives and move on, either to different cities or different forms of existence. From tomorrow to yesterday, the zinc dog had seen the people of Mineral Point live their lives in earnest and dignity, forever aware that he was there, watching, watching, watching, looking down upon them, reminding them that life is good. Pointer has always been one of my favorites. I guess I'm not alone as everyone has made it known, on several occasions, that this dog is special and was not to be tampered with or removed. There's not much in Mineral Point other than the Packers and the Badgers, that everyone agrees on, but Pointer is one for them.

I climbed back into the Jeep and Jake knew where we were going…to the west end of town, across old Highway 18&51 to Graceland Cemetery. It's the "new" cemetery in Mineral Point and much bigger than the "Old" City Cemetery.

There are a lot of people buried in both. In the olden days, farm families kept having lots of kids, who had lots of kids, who had even more kids and then they all died and were buried side-by-side. Some were spread out, while other families bought family plots so they could all be together.

To the south, there is pasture and the fairgrounds to the west. I guess that made sense. Mineral Point is a farm town and what better place to go forever than next to a pasture?

Learning to be a journalist meant I needed to learn how to "get the facts". In so doing, I learned that Wisconsin historically regulated cemetery operations to ensure proper management and public health and the Wisconsin Department of Safety and Professional Services notes that the state's statutes do not define or set limitations specifically on private family cemeteries. However, they do reference Wisconsin Statute § 157.065, which outlines who may operate a cemetery, including municipalities, religious organizations, and cemetery associations which I guess means that family cemeteries can't exist.

While this meant that Wisconsin's state law doesn't prohibit family burial plots on private land, once a burial site is established, it must be preserved and cannot be disturbed without proper authorization and families had to figure out who was going to take care the cemetery after they were buried there. This resulted is most folks simply elected to bury their loved ones in one of the two cemeteries in town.

Mineral Point is mostly common folks and so the graves are also pretty common with small granite markers reflecting when the people were born and when they died. No stories are told about what they died from or who they loved and I've always found it interesting to check the difference between when a husband and wife died and wondered what those people did to cure their loneliness when they were but one.

I could only imagine what it is like to lay in bed, alone, for the first time in perhaps 50-60-70 years and feel the cold reality of no one lying beside me. Dreams wash away and all that's left is yesterday. Silence shouts its singularity as the concept of one permeates what had been and sadness darkens the room and pulls down the shades on tomorrow. I wonder if when it came time for the second one to go, they were happy that life was over. Simply birth-death and solitude.

I drove down the gravel path to the south end of the plots, turned east and went to the "new" section where I parked the Jeep and walked to my grandparent's grave. My grandma had been old for as long as I could remember. Grandpa was gone before I arrived. She lived alone in a little white house behind Jerusalem Park on South Street. She wasn't much into television and was born and raised on a farm outside Mineral Point. She liked to sew and loved to laugh and actually darned socks. At night, I would stay with her and keep her company and listen to all the stories about growing up on the farm.

Grandma was old school and had a huge garden. In the basement of her little house was a root cellar where she kept all the food she had raised and canned. You can keep the stuff they sell in the stores, even the food at the Farmer's Market in Madison doesn't taste nearly as good as home-grown vegetables that were planted, weeded, watered and picked by your grandma.

Grandma and I would listen to the Milwaukee Brewers in the summer time and she knew all the players and the batting order. She didn't have much money and would make rugs out of old neckties that she sold at the church bazaar. I think mom and dad were always helping her out in one way or another. That's what farm folks do. What grandma did have was a lot of pride, in what she did and what she was…good, honest, sincere, religious and dedicated to her family and her friends. She used to tell me, "No one elects to be born. All we can do is make the most of what we've got and be satisfied when we have done our best." I am absolutely certain she would have liked to talk with Great Grandfather.

Grandpa had been a salesman. He sold John Deere tractors at Harker, Mahr and Gordon. I guess he knew every farmer for fifty miles around and they all knew him. He died when he was young and the farmers came from all around to pay their respects.

I always liked to go to grandma's house when I was little and play with some antique metal cars that had belonged to my cousin. Grandma kept them in an old-fashioned wooden bus that someone made and I thought that was pretty cool. The bus was painted and the paint had worn off from the countless times one little boy or another had opened the top and his imagination. There was a musty smell to the cars and to the bus that I guess was just the scent of memories of all the little boys with all the little toys who had wandered away from here and now, into their own little worlds of make believe.

The brown area rug in grandma's living room had a pattern to it that went around the outside edge and I used it as a road for the antique cars. It went all the way around the room and intersected with the space heater in the living room, next to an over-stuffed rocker that had been Grandpa's. Grandma placed a slip cover over the leather chair and I would sit in the rocker and imagine that he was there. Grandpa smoked a pipe and the scent of the tobacco still permeated the leather and made it seem as if he had just left the room and that's why I think Grandma never got rid of it.

Grandma had two bedrooms on the first floor along with the living room and the kitchen. The "back bedroom" as she called it, had a white, wrought iron bed in it and that was where I would sleep. In the winter there was a down comforter for the cold, as grandma never heated the house at night. There was a small dresser with a really old light on it that you turned on and off that had a little crank instead of a switch. The window shade was dark green and had holes in it. At night, when the leaves were off the butternut trees the light from the street light in Jerusalem park would reflect off the green shade with little holes that made it look like a million little stars were shining in through the window, telling you to go to sleep.

Grandma's house had a great big back porch that had all been enclosed but was not insulated. When it rained you could sit out there and listen to the symphony of raindrops on the roof as their pitter-patter beat out a tune. Before I was born, there was an outhouse. They converted a small pantry off the kitchen into a bathroom that only had a toilet and sink in it and so grandma would use the kitchen sink to bathe or a plastic fold-up bath tub that was out on the back porch. She never wanted anything more.

Grandma had two space heaters…one in the living room and one in the kitchen. She was a tough cookie and said the cold never bothered her. She had a down comforter for her bed and that was all she needed. At night, you could hear the tick-tock of the clock in the living room that kept cadence to your heart beat. The stairs to the attic were steep and had a crook in them. If you were more than five feet tall and didn't duck, you would bump your head. At Christmas, Grandma always had a small tree on a little table with one strand of old-fashioned lights on it. They were hot and all you had to do was touch them once to learn never to touch them again. If one burned out, they all went out. Dad bought her another new set, but she said that Grandpa had given her the old ones and they were her way of knowing that he was waiting for her and wishing her a Merry Christmas.

My favorite spot of all in grandma's house was her front porch. There were 23 steps from the ground to the landing. 23 steps! She and I would sit out there in the summertime on antique rockers with fancy engraving and look down on Jerusalem Park. She would make popcorn and lemonade and we would listen to the Brewers. She said she never forgave the Milwaukee Braves for moving to Atlanta in 1966. That was way before my time. As Simon and Garfunkel said, "A time of innocence…a time of confidences. Time it was, time it was. Oh, what a time it was!" I still miss her and always will.

Mineral Point was home to some famous people. Daniel Bedford Moore is buried in Graceland. Mr. Moore was the first man in Wisconsin to earn the Congressional Medal of Honor for saving the life of an officer in a battle at Fort Blakely, Alabama in 1865. He lived nearly 50 years knowing he saved the life of another man and was remembered for his bravery. Back then you went to war, they pinned a medal on your chest and you went home. You weren't a hero or celebrity, just a man who did his job.

Probably the most famous person buried in Graceland is Allen Ludden who grew up in Mineral Point, moved to Texas, became a TV celebrity and died of cancer at age 64 in 1961. When he was near death, he said he wanted to come "home to Wisconsin". Those of us born in Wisconsin know the feeling. No matter where you go and where you live, when someone asks where you're from, you always, always, say "Wisconsin".

I visited my grandparent's graves and then my great grandparents. They are all there. Resting, hopefully in peace. Someday mom and dad will be there and Tommie and me. We already "own" the land for our family plot. I just shake my head. I want to be cremated and have my ashes spread around Camp Randall stadium so that I will always be there when the Badgers are playing football. Mom cringes when she hears that. When you're twenty-three, death seems a long, long way away.

My mind wandered when I heard the barking. Jake wanted out. He had to pee. You don't let anyone pee in a cemetery and so we went a few blocks west to the fairgrounds. I parked in the parking lot next to the barns and let him out so that he could get his sniffer in gear and smell all kinds of different smells than what he gets around the farm. It was fun to watch him "explore" with his nose. The horse barn and then the sheep, goats and chickens and every other type of farm animal there was and Jake had to smell each one of them. It had been eight months since the Iowa

County Fair and yet the sights and sounds and smells, for the two of us, were still as distinct as if the fair had been yesterday.

I always loved coming to the fair. In July it's hot and since I was about 13, I was always on the lookout for the prettiest girls that I could try and put the moves on. Tommie would always tease me and call them moooves and bellow like a cow. The girls were always looking for the handsomest guys and so, most of the time, I spent my hours in the cow barn with one of my heifers who had four legs. We took home our share of ribbons and would sleep in the hay. It was the only time, other than Grandma's house, when I didn't sleep at home. Farmers rarely took vacations. It was a fun time and county fairs are when it's really a great time to be a farm kid.

One of my funniest memories from the fair was dad buying us ride tickets and Tommie and I going on all the rides together. The tilt-a-whirl was fun at age seven and the roller coaster at nine. The atomic bomb, which was a free fall, scared the crap out of me at 11, but the one I will never forget is the scrambler. It was made out of stainless steel and you sat in seats and were locked in. There were three different sets of chairs on three different axis. As you spun around your axis, the entire ride also spun so that you would veer in towards the center pole and then head out again. One year, I had some extra money and had eaten a hot dog and cotton candy and I think even a funnel cake. Wrong thing to do! As we got going, I started getting dizzy and then sick and, you guessed it...all over Tommie went the somewhat undigested hot dog, cotton candy and funnel cake. God was he pissed. I was too sick to apologize and mom had to take us home to get cleaned up. I thought dad was going to wet his pants laughing so hard at seeing one sick kid, who was as white as a ghost, and one covered in puke. We rode home in the back of the truck and when I was feeling better, dad made me hose out the bed. Tommie got hosed by mom and had to take his clothes off outside which is not something a thirteen-year-old boy wants to do in front of his mother. I've never been on the scrambler since and don't think I ever want to go again.

Jake and I wandered around the fairgrounds and then headed back to Waldwick. I didn't make it to St. Mary's, St. Paul or Willow Spring Cemeteries as it was getting late and mom would have some humongous meal waiting for us. As we were driving through town, I remembered that it always seemed strange to me that just because someone went to a different church, they had to be buried in a different cemetery. When we were in junior high, one of our friends got killed in a farm accident and we went to the funeral and the Catholic cemetery. So sad! So strange! Aren't we all God's children? You know, I think there are more people buried in Mineral Point than live there.

It was great sleeping in my own bed with my best buddy sleeping next to me, happy that I was home and eating yet another huge farm meal. Tommie and dad had been up since dawn milking cows and doing farm stuff. I was useless and they knew it. Mom and I talked about the "factory" and how the book was going. 20,000 words and counting, I told her. I was afraid to tell her about the voices and all that was happening and so I let it slide. Around noon, I headed back towards the cottage and the challenge of 2,000 words. It was the last week of the month and that meant they were due and there would be a marketing "meeting" in Black River Falls on Friday. Thursdays had become the day I would go and see Great Grandfather and so I had Tuesday and Wednesday to smooth out the gibberish and make it presentable to the Chief. They don't tell you about deadlines in Journalism School. If they did, I wonder how many of those with stars in their eyes, would have selected it as a major.

Earthmaker: The word gods were with me and 2,000 words popped out of the end of my fingers and onto the screen by Wednesday night. The day and time were the same, 10:00 AM, Thursday in the Dells. From Highway "N" to the dells was an easy 70 minutes at most, but I learned to allocate a little extra time, just in case and left at 8:30. I missed the east side interstate traffic, zipped past Deforest and even Highway 19 that took you over to Sauk City and kept rolling. Crossing the bridge on the Wisconsin River, I thought of Rodney and how he let me drive the Batmobile from the rest area. The Baraboo bluffs were still brown, as spring had yet to arrive. I spliced the intersection where you have your choice, Wausau or Tomah "where the 'I' divides." In a few minutes, I was past Highway 33 and the Baraboo exit and knew the next exit would be mine. I also knew Great Grandfather would be waiting, sitting in his rocking chair with his crochet blanket upon his lap, ready for our next session.

The water parks and all the other Dells stuff slapped my face with commercialism, enticing me to join in the whirlwind fun sliding down the water rapids and watching people water ski while standing on each other's shoulders. I pulled past Mickey "D's" and down the street to the assisted living center. I was 15 minutes early and sat in the parking lot until 9:57 when I walked in and said hello to Barbra, the receptionist. After all my visits, she knew me and I knew her and the pleasant smile and nod of the head was all she needed to assure that my visit was with the same intent. Small town folks are that way you know. They assume the best and never imagine the worst.

Quietly, I made my way down the hall to Great Grandfather's room. As expected, he was sitting in his rocker with the comforter on his lap. As soon as I reached the door, he perked up. "Little Spirit, you have arrived," he said with a soft smile upon his face. His eyes were closed and yet his smile was wide.

"Yes, Great Grandfather, I am here." I replied.

"Come, sit with me." he beckoned with his small, bony hand. With that, I pulled up the cedar chest that I had done so many times before.

"Your grandmother wants to know if you still have the old wooden bus and metal cars that were your cousin's." Great Grandfather inquired.

Again, I got the heebie jeebies.

"Yes, Great Grandfather, I do".

"She said she was honored that you came to see her and so many of your ancestors."

Gulp.

"Thank you, Great Grandfather," I responded, not knowing who I was talking to.

"It is good and wise to visit those who have come before you, for their spirits need your comfort. In order for them to rest in peace, they must appreciate that all they lived for, all they sacrificed and all they died for, was not in vain."

"Yes, Great Grandfather."

"Your Grandmother thinks that when you come again, you should let Jake out of the Jeep so that she can feel his spirit too."

Now I was really getting weirded out.

There was a gentle smile on Great Grandfather's face. "Your spirits are strong and they bring great joy to your family. What had been is no more. Your family and our family live together in harmony. Each family understands who and what they meant to each other and why we are here and they are happy. Unfortunately, they speak of dark clouds on the horizon that you, and only you, can blow away. Do not fear Little Spirit, you are the chosen one."

Once again, I was totally confused and had no idea what Great Grandfather was talking about. The chosen one? Dark clouds? My God, where was this going?

Great Grandfather began his ritual chant and soon his milk-white eyes began their gradual roll up into his soul. With each verse, his shoulders lurched further and further until he was rocking in his chair. His hands came forth and, as had been the times before, I placed mine in his. I didn't even turn on the recorder as I knew an hour of hiss would mean nothing at all.

Great Grandfather's grip became stronger than ever before to the point my hands were being squeezed tighter and tighter and tighter. My God, what was going on?

A deep voice rose from within the frail old man. It was not a voice of peace or even of restraint, but one filled with vitriolic anger. Great Grandfather's eyes opened and through the milk-white lenses I saw hate…deep, dark, hate and it scared me. "I am Earthmaker, leader of the Winnebago. Like all members of my nation, I too fasted between the ages of nine and eleven to acquire a bond with my guardian spirit upon whom I could call in any critical situation throughout my life. Without a guardian spirit, any man is completely unanchored and at the mercy of all events in their crudest and most cruel forms. I have always paid homage to my guardian spirit and provide proper offerings to obtain protection and specific powers from many others."

"In time of conflict, no warrior can go to battle unless we have prayed to one of the gods who control our success in war and bestow upon us the power to defeat our enemy. To our gods we provide gifts of paint, feathers, flutes, bones and so forth. However, when the enemy is not a man and not a spirit, we do not know who or what to pray for. Many times, I stood alone on the high rock and asked our gods. 'Why did the white man come to our land? Why did they bring greed and corruption? Why did they bring disease that killed my people and took away our dignity? We did not ask them. We did not invite them. We did not want them to come and change our way of life and yet they came."

"We could fight as warriors against those who were like us. Brave men who fought for their way of life. Brave men who only wanted to defend their people and their families. We fought many battles against the Algonquin and Illinois, but it was warrior-against-warrior and not against the old and young and not our women and children. Our warriors were brave men, but we could not battle against the diseases the white man brought to our land. We could not defeat the greed that came from the rifles and knives that were traded for pelts from the muskrat, beaver and mink with whom God had allowed us to live. We could not stop the flow of the river of white men who came into our land and took what they wanted, whenever they wanted, from all of us."

"For many generations, we lived in peace with our nature and our gods and yet, it was not good enough for the white man. He had to bring not only his way of life but his gods into our land and tell us that what we believed was wrong. How can one man tell another that he is wrong when for so many seasons he lived in peace and harmony with all that he wanted? How can one man, tell another to change, simply because it was the way that he had been taught? How can there be peace when all around there is war?"

"As had been the case since the beginning of time, we continued our rituals to bring peace and prosperity to our people. While each sunrise would bring a new day, the only one that mattered was our War Bundle Feast as it was our glorification of war. Little Spirit, you are the chosen one. You must understand our way. You must carry on our War Bundle ceremony and divide it into two parts. The first will be presided over by the Thunderbird spirits and the second by the Night-spirits. You must do this!"

I was getting uncomfortable. Up until now, they had only spoken of the past. Now, I was being given directions. I shook my head as I didn't know the reason. I wasn't a soldier. I couldn't declare war on anyone.

"You must learn that all the great spirits of our people had their place in the War bundle Feast and, to all, offerings were made. The Thunderbird, Night, Sun, Morning Star, Evening Star, Disease -giver, eagle and black hawk were held in highest esteem to protect our nation and its warriors from harm. As Earthmaker, my goal was peace and yet I failed. Earth, Moon and Water were my allies, and, at times, even the Turtle and Hare were asked to give their strength so that we could be victorious. You, Little Spirit must not fail."

"The war bundle is made from a deerskin in which was wrapped an assortment of objects to glorify our bravery...the body of a black hawk, eagle and snake, a weasel skin, a number of eagle feathers, a deer-tail head-dress, two wolf tails, a buffalo tail, a war-club, three flutes and various kinds of 'paint-medicine'. The black hawk body was to enable its possessor to fly when leading a war party; the wolf tails would give him the power of running; the buffalo tail, fleetness; the snake and weasel skins, the gift of dodging and wiggling; the paint, when smeared over the body, would make him invisible and prevent fatigue; and the flutes, when blown during a fight, would paralyze the running powers of the enemy and make them easy victims."

"As Earthmaker, my war bundle was the most prized of all my Winnebago possessions. It was carefully concealed and guarded not only because of its sacredness, but because dangerous emanations flowed from it which could destroy those who approached it. Little Spirit, to be a successful Winnebago warrior is the highest ideal and it is in the war bundle rites that this ideal receives its greatest glorification."

"It was with the protection of the war bundle that our nation fought the Algonquin in the white man's year of 1638 and yet it was not the arrows that brought us to our knees. It was the disease called small pox. At first, it was but a small cough amongst a few. Then the sight of blisters on many, told us that lives would be lost and innocent would die while those who survived would no longer see. When we were strong, there were 2000 warriors. When the small pox had taken its victims, there were less than 500. We had gone from a nation of strength to one of futility...weak, ravaged, unable to defend ourselves from the anger of our enemies and the disease that the white man brought to my people."

"Today, there is peace. In my time, the Illinois and the Winnebago had been enemies since the beginning of time. As the sun and moon fought forever, so had our people. We were sick and we were weak and our council voted to protect ourselves by taking our nation to an island in the middle of the large lake where we could watch for invaders. We knew nothing of disease and how it would spread. We did not understand that putting so many people together would only result in more death and yet, that is what we did. When we were weak, the Illinois sent a party to help our people and yet, this delegation was not about peace, but about domination. Their overtures were not about unification, but about capitulation. We were to surrender to them and their way of life."

"We, the Winnebago, did not accept their terms and so they came across the frozen water when we were at our weakest and took many braves and made them slaves. Our nation was depleted. Our nation was destroyed. Our nation met its darkest hour when few survived the battles of the white man and the Illini. Yet, those of us who did survive realized that our Gods had saved us for tomorrow and not for today. We lived through the maelstrom of disease and the Illini and from the smallest acorn, the mighty oak of the Winnebago nation began to grow again."

"I lived my life as it had been meant to be, in concert with the land, which our great fathers had provided and it was my time to meet with my ancestors and move to the great nation beyond. We could not fight and yet we did not lose. Our lives were thrown asunder and yet, our nation, our people, our beliefs continued on."

Great Grandfather's hands grew limp. The emotions! The passion! The energy it took had once again taken all of Great Grandfather's strength and spewed it forth for me to hear. I slowly pulled back as Great Grandfather's head nodded. The session had been short and yet profoundly intense. I sensed anger and yet bewilderment. I sensed pride and yet regret. I sensed incredible sadness and yet intense dignity as I sensed before and was certain I would sense again. All that Ann told me was verified. She had been factual. Earthmaker had been emotional, punctuating life with his misery.

"Come again soon, Little Spirit." Great Grandfather whispered as his chin fell upon his chest.

As I was about to pull back the cedar chest, his head raised and his white eyes pierced mine. "There are dark clouds on the horizon and you must clear them away."

"Yes, Great Grandfather." I acknowledged having absolutely no idea what he meant. "Dark clouds." he whispered. "Dark clouds."

Once again, his head drooped into his chest and he was asleep. I closed my eyes and took a deep, deep breath. Whoever had been talking to me had taken every ounce of energy from Great Grandfather and channeled it into me. I quietly put the cedar chest against the bed and headed for the door.

"Dark clouds." he whispered again. "Dark clouds."

Quietly, I walked towards the reception desk and Barbra's eyes caught mine.

"You Ok?" she asked. "You look like you've seen a ghost."

I just shrugged my shoulders and closed my eyes if only for an instant. I had seen a ghost and heard a ghost and the ghost had filled my heart and soul with so much more than ever before. I took a deep breath and headed for the Jeep. The spring sun had been replaced by gray clouds. Was this an omen? What clouds were on the horizon? I checked the clock on the dash and realized that my time with Great Grandfather had been almost an hour. What had seemed like an instant had been drawn out and strung along, filling my mind with thoughts that would not quickly go away. My God, what was going on?

I honestly don't remember the ride home. You get caught up in your thoughts and everything seems so automatic. I walked into the house and went to my historic Ho-Chunk timeline. Reality! I craved reality! Anything that would put my feet back on the ground!

Marketing 101: Friday was my first-ever, professional marketing meeting. I had taken marketing courses in school and remembered the infamous P-D-P-D-P that stood for product development, promotion, distribution and pricing. I didn't know how a casino fit into this but was ready to learn.

The Chief rotated the quarterly meetings between the different facilities so that it became a field trip for those who were locked into Black River Falls and the corporate world and the "locals" as we were called. This quarter's meeting was in the Dells. Rodney was invited as he was in training for a different position and so we got in the Batmobile and headed out. The Chief was always punctual and 9:00 AM meant 9:00 AM, not 9:01 and certainly not 8:59 AM. One of the high roller meeting rooms was closed to the public and everything was set with an overhead projector and an agenda. Every topic on the agenda had a name next to it regarding who was responsible for that segment and what time the segment was to start and end. Needless to say, I was a bit overwhelmed, especially when I saw my name George Terrill IV and 10 minutes.

The two ladies who handled most of the advertising strategy and internal marketing were there and I learned that at 1:00 PM the advertising agency from Milwaukee would discuss the next six months positioning and promotional plans. Right away, I felt inadequate. There was logic to the entire meeting starting from the inside and going out from there.

First up was internal marketing that dealt with the facilities in terms of theme, signage and security. Grace headed up this presentation as I learned that she had a degree in environmental psychology, which I had never even heard of. Because I was the new kid on the block, she took the time to explain her role and then I went home and learned more. As Rodney said, in analytics, nothing is left to chance. Although it's an involved field, the field of environmental psychology can be best summarized as a science that focuses on the interplay between human beings and their surrounding environment, both at the micro or macro levels, encompassing a number of areas, including such disciplines as architectural and ecological psychology, environmental design, sociology and social ecology.

Grace's background included anthropology, architecture, political science, psychology, and interior design. The goal was to create an environment for each casino and all properties owned by the Nation that met the demographics of the target customer. In the casinos, everything from the color and design of the carpeting to the type and color of the felt on the tables, signs, lighting and even the design of the slot machines was tested to appeal to a specific target market. Beyond that there were daily measurements of noise and oxygen levels and even the uniforms worn by the workers to create an environment that is more attractive and appealing to the target customer. In the gas stations, it meant everything from product placement to the location of the bathrooms. At Great Grandfather's assisted living center, it meant noise limitations and temperature control, along with creating a sense of dignity. Because this was a casino meeting, Grace outlined that each facility was "staged" to maximize its appeal and why the Dells looked different than Madison and both looked different than Black River Falls. I just shook my head in amazement. I thought you opened the door and people came in and yet everything and I mean everything, was measured and controlled to ensure optimum appeal to the target customer.

The round-table discussion was about allowing smoking at each property. While it was against the law to smoke indoors in most facilities in Wisconsin, it wasn't in casinos. Different properties were trying different concepts ranging from no-smoking rooms to outdoor smoking only.

With Madison having the highest socio-economic measurement and also the highest negative response to an all-smoking environment, discussions had already taken place to determine the cost/benefit ratio between making the entire casino non-smoking and keeping it as it was. The Nation had spent over $50,000 in research to determine what the consequence would be and learned that there would be an estimated 8% increase in attendance yet a 7% decline in serious gaming and therefore drinking, if no smoking was allowed.

The question then became, should Madison be a test market to see if the numbers held up, allowing it to position itself as Wisconsin's first totally non-smoking casino, thereby differentiating itself from the Casinos in Milwaukee and the Chicago market. Discussions took place regarding cost factors to have the entire place professionally cleaned and disinfected to eliminate the smoking smell and it was learned that it would cost nearly $65,000 to have the casino completely cleaned with a copy of the cleaning bids presented on the overhead.

Discussions took place concerning when the next scheduled cleaning was planned and whether the timing should be then instead of half-way through the cleaning cycle. Grace's time was up and the Chief opened the floor to discussion. It was time for a vote. All parties, except me voted. The Chief looked at me and indicated that as a member of the marketing team, I had an equal vote. I raised my hand in favor of the test as I found cigarette smell to be really unappealing. The vote was four yes and one no with the Chief not voting.

It was ten o'clock and time to discuss positioning, which I thought was what made one brand different than the next. Here again, the professionals had been hard at work with Anna taking the floor and it was time for good old "Q" to get yet another lesson.

I know they were being kind to me and so Anna took time to outline that positioning is a marketing concept that outlines what a business should do to sell its product or service to its customers. It does so by creating an image for the casinos based on their intended audience through the use of promotions, placement and advertising, which are all somewhat limited by state and federal regulations.

Anna was sharp with a degree from UW Eau Claire. She had been with the "company" for six years and had helped elevate the marketing efforts of the Nation to help the guests move from a basic level of awareness of the casino, to their first visit and then taking infrequent guests and converting them into regulars which she called conversion factors.

Anna spent her first year gaining a thorough knowledge of the target customer in each different market. With a good idea of the wants, needs and interests of each casino's target market, she then developed individual positioning statements to help reach as much of the target market as possible.

Anna also served as the liaison with the advertising agency to make certain that the created message was efficient with the market in which it was being presented. Madison's message was different than the Dells and both were different than that of Black River Falls with each message based on demographics. Beyond the message, Anna worked with the advertising agency to make certain that the right channels were selected to get the message across. With advertising so expensive, it needed to be as close to the target demographic as possible. She explained that this was the reason why Ho-Chunk advertised at Camp Randall and the Kohl Center during Badger football and basketball games. Anna explained that the rationale was that those in attendance consisted of a high market-density of educated individuals who had or would someday have more discretionary entertainment dollars to spend. The goal was always to create a positive message by positioning the casinos as a place for fun and excitement that were also a parallel entertainment venue that was willing to give back to the community.

Anna added that, while there are penny slots at the Madison casino, the cost of gambling is never mentioned in the advertising and the price of entertainment not recognized. Anna looked at me and said "simply put…the price of an item tells the buyer more about the item than most realize. Many associate a higher price with higher quality and the opposite with a lower price. Additionally, if a product is positioned as a good alternative to high-priced brands, the marketing department must price it in the middle of the market to avoid comparison to the cheapest end of the spectrum." I guess Big Brother must have told her how we met.

The discussion was whether Wittenberg and Nekoosa needed to re-evaluate their positioning and what level of investment was needed to re-establish their position in the marketplace. Adding 'destination reasons' such as hotels, entertainment and dining were traditional methods and the challenge was that these marketplaces were small and generating a return-on-investment always made things difficult.

The Chief understood the difference between primary and secondary markets and where to invest his dollars. Metro Madison, with over a million people and the Dells, with its high turnover of vacationers, were and would always be the hot spots. However, by minimizing discretionary expenditures, there could be a good return-on-investment. I think he really wanted to see if he could convince the legislators to allow for full scale operation instead of just slot machines and bingo in Madison.

I looked at my watch, as there are never any clocks in casinos, and realized that I was up next. Holy Shit! Ten minutes to fill! After Grace and Anna, I seemed and felt like an absolute amateur. The Chief noted the time and that I had been allocated…10 minutes. He then took about five of those minutes to outline my background and how it all began. The issue on the table was not my writing the history of the Ho-Chunk Nation, but in what style. Did I write it as a non-fiction piece or as something with some emotion in it? The vote was unanimous that, in order to get the message out, don't write a dry piece of history, but to include my own thoughts and emotions…the white boy, learning about what had happened in their world.

I asked for a compromise…a journal of all that was happening with the hope that it would reflect both the past and present and share with those who read the story all that was happening from my perspective. I guess everyone in marketing thought it was a pretty cool idea because the vote was unanimous…write it in the first person and tell it like it was. There was a smile on my face as we broke for lunch and headed to the dining room. Menus were presented and we could order whatever we wanted. Needless to say, with the Chief at the head of the table service was incredible.

I sat to the Chief's left and Rodney to his right. I felt honored. This was social dynamics and the Chief's way of letting the entire team know that this wasn't a kiss-ass job and what I was doing was important…or so I had hoped. Speaking of kiss-ass, I didn't realize how little the Chief thought of the ad agency until the subject came up at lunch when he called them the Ass Kissers. He had never spoken negatively about anyone, even the jerk cop. It seemed that he saw through all the bullshit and only wanted them to give it to him straight. Namely, where were they investing the Nation's money and why? There were two primary goals. First, maximize the casino census on a daily basis. Second, position the Ho-Chunk nation in a positive light in front of all citizens and legislators. These were plain and simple objectives, like nothing more than driving from Madison to Black River Falls. The responsibility of the Ass Kissers was to determine the most effective way to get there.

The ad agency showed up early and the Chief made them wait. One o'clock meant one o'clock and it was his way of showing them that he was the client. They went through their entire spiel including reach-and -frequency analysis and how many impressions they were generating per day, per market and to the target demographics. I yawned. The creative aspect seemed juvenile to me and yet, it wasn't my role, responsibility or right to interject my opinion to the group. When you have positive momentum, everyone looks like heroes, even ass kissers. It's when things slow down and the going gets rough, true talent shows through.

The agency had been allocated an hour and they were done in 45 minutes. The Chief knew they were on an hourly billable and so, he opened the floor to questions. The ass kissers weren't prepared for the onslaught that came forth. First and foremost, Anna's evaluation of the creative was almost to the point of being vicious. How does one defend garbage? Second, Rodney pointed out that the asset allocation seemed out of touch with revenue generation. The cost per thousand in the secondary markets was four times that of the primary markets, meaning that the potential return on investment was upside down. Third, Grace noted that, with two primary objectives, it didn't appear as if there was a concise message being communicated that positioned the casinos as an entertainment destination and not as a place to gamble. There was also no mention of what the Ho-Chunk Nation was giving back to the general community.

Everyone turned to me and asked my opinion. Shit!

Anna, Grace and Rodney had addressed the key salient points. No one wants a grandmother survey. "Well in my opinion". I looked at the duo standing at the front of the room and took a deep breath and replied "I'm new to the team and so, I would like to state that my observations are limited to those of an outsider and not those who have the extensive knowledge or background of those present." There was a sigh from the ass kissers. "However, I think your advertising is very amateurish and does not reflect a positive message of either the entertainment value or the dignity of the Ho-Chunk Nation." They almost shit their pants. "Impressions are one thing, but positive impressions are more critical and what you have shown today and what I personally have experienced over the past five years does not seem to reflect the entertainment value or the community spirit of the Ho-Chunk Nation."

"First and foremost, your media buy talks only of print and broadcast and I saw nothing of social media. It could be that this wasn't part of today's agenda. However ongoing replenishment of a customer base has to look at where the potential customers are most informed and it's not outdoor and newspapers. As Anna noted, people come to the casinos to have fun and excitement and it doesn't show in your ads. Second, there is no reference whatsoever, to the other entities of the Nation including the gas stations and the assisted living centers. These are stand-alone businesses that require awareness that must compete against established multi-national companies and you expect them to thrive based on no investments whatsoever. Finally, these people are providing jobs, creating scholarships for non-indigenous people and supporting communities in ways that no one knows about and yet all you have shown are thematic tag lines as if they will change the perception of the Nation and their investments."

I could see the anger in the eyes of the agency folks as I continued. "I'm not here to be a critic. I'm here only to share with you, ideas and thoughts that might point you in a broader direction. I apologize if I have been too blunt. However, in the past several months I have come to appreciate and recognize the honor, integrity and diligence of a people who are trying to do good and, as a team, including you, we hope that we can all improve the outcome."

The Chief had been standing on the side of the room and I watched his normal tacit demeanor evolve into one that included a gleam of enthusiasm and optimism. I hoped it was because I had spoken from the heart and what I said made sense. God was I in over my head! The Chief looked at his watch.

"It's two o'clock. We have other agenda items. Thank you for your time today" he directed at the agency, as he politely told them to leave without response or recourse.

As the advertising duo left the room, the agenda indicated a fifteen-minute break time. Instead, we momentarily remained in the room and the Chief spoke. "I thank all of you for speaking today and for speaking from the heart. Q, I want to thank you for opening our eyes to our inadequacies. Everything is changing and we are living somewhat in the past when it comes to advertising and promotion and we do need change."

"Rodney, can you please see if the agency has departed? I want them to think about what was just said and not give them time to redirect back at any of us. There is no greater motivator than fear, except perhaps love."

Rodney stood and walked into the casino. He went to the front door and asked the greeter who indicated that the duo had left the building. After our break, Charlie gave a somewhat dry overview of the legal aspects and the challenges of promotion in a highly regulated industry and, as liaison to the politicians, what his feelings were regarding our relative position in the governmental marketplace. Discussions were held regarding potential expansion into different markets and the consequences of those expansions in terms of not only the effects they would have on the existing properties, but relationships with fellow Nations and their territories. The topic of a management company was briefly addressed as, yet another Vegas group had visited Black River Falls with grand plans of how they could dramatically increase revenue. From the tone of the conversation, these folks had about as much chance of winning the contract as snowing on the fourth of July.

The meeting was scheduled to end at 4:00 PM and at precisely 4:00 PM, the meeting ended. There were handshakes and hugs all around and the BRF (Black River Falls) contingent left the building leaving Rodney and I alone as he said…"Great job little brother."

"Thanks, I hope I wasn't too open or wrong."

Wrong? You opened the eyes of the Chief and showed him that we need to look beyond here and now and you did it in a manner that not only informed him, but showed that adding you to the marketing team was the right decision. Do you know much about social media?"

"We studied it extensively in school, why?

"Not a gambling man, but a dime against a dollar, you'll be heading up that segment by Monday."

Gulp.

I'm glad I didn't bet because, sure enough, the Chief announced on Monday that I was involved with social media. The ladies probably weren't too happy that some smart-ass kid was showing them up.

While I think I'm a writer, when it comes to developing websites like Facebook and Twitter, amongst others, my technical expertise is close to zero and yet, I had ideas. The challenge was to determine whether they were legal or not. The gaming industry is REALLY regulated and when you throw alcohol on top of it, it really gets complicated. You can have all the greatest ideas in the world in terms of happy hours and free chips until you look at the laws and realize that none of them can get past the regulators.

Humility: The week was flying by and it was already Wednesday night. When you get used to the pace of daily life, the thought of driving to the Dells and talking to a 94-year-old blind man wasn't very exciting and yet, I was learning so much and beginning to truly appreciate the challenges my adopted family had gone through. My God, did they get the royal shaft!

Great Grandfather and I had a standing appointment at 10:00 AM every Thursday. It takes 70 minutes from the cottage to the front door but I always left with a few minutes to spare. This Thursday, time got away from me and I ended up 20 minutes late. Shit!

I slithered in the center's front door and walked to Great Grandfather's room. The normal peaceful, tranquil, man that I had met so many times before was agitated. "Hello grandfather," I announced as I walked into his room.

There was silence from the old man in the rocking chair.

"I'm sorry I'm late."

More silence as I came closer.

"You're late."

"Yes, Great Grandfather, I am and I am sorry."

"Do you have a reason?"

"Time got away from me."

"That's not a reason, that's an excuse."

He was pissed.

"You're right, Great Grandfather."

"Don't you believe that what we are doing is important?"

"Yes sir."

"Do you think that because I am an old, blind Indian, I don't deserve respect?"

"No, Great Grandfather."

"Don't you have a telephone?"

"Yes, Great Grandfather, I do"

"Yet, you didn't think enough to call and say that you would be late?"

"I'm sorry, Great Grandfather."

"Being late is a sign of disrespect…It says that you don't think that my time and my energy are important"

"You're right Great Grandfather. I won't ever let it happen again."

"Your generation! What are you called? Millennial? Whatever that means? For some reason you feel entitled. I think you have had it too good. I hear of this thing called texting and people not speaking to each other, even in the same room. How can this be? How can people become so distant that they cannot look into each other's eyes or hear each other's voice or feel each other's warmth? I am glad my time will soon come."

He was pissed.

"Little Spirit, one of the great characteristics of being a man is humility. I read many of the white man's books and one author that I always enjoyed was named Ernest Hemingway. Have you ever read any of his books?

"Yes sir."

"You should read him again." Hemingway once said 'There is nothing noble in being superior to your fellow man; true nobility is being superior to your former self. Humility is the quality of being humble. To be humble is to recognize gratefully our dependence on others—to understand that we have constant need for their support.'"

My head was bowed as Great Grandfather continued. "Little Spirit, humility is an acknowledgment that our talents and abilities are gifts from the Great Spirits. Humility is not a sign of weakness, timidity, or fear; it is an indication that we know where our true strength lies. We can be both humble and fearless. We can be both humble and courageous. What Hemingway said and what I also believe… you should never accept what you have done as the best you can do and when you accomplish something, keep it to yourself and don't announce it to the world."

"When the day comes that you are a man, you will understand humility. Until then, you are still a little boy who doesn't think an old, blind man's time is worthwhile. You have a great book that speaks many times of humility, it is called the Bible. I have read this book many times and you should too. You can leave now. I am too tired to meet with you today. I will see you next Thursday at 10:00 o'clock…and not ten-twenty."

"Yes sir."

With that I tucked my tail between my legs and walked out of Great Grandfather's room. Marge was at the front desk and smiled. She knew that Great Grandfather had given me a lesson.

"He doesn't like it when people are late."

"I can see. Lesson learned."

"Hopefully, more than one." Marge said as I walked out the front door.

I got in the Jeep and headed back to Madison. How could I hit 2,000 words if my lack of interview was my fault? Great Grandfather was right! I was taking him for granted. The ride home was a lot longer than the ride to the Dells and taught me a great lesson. Be on time or communicate that you are late. Not doing so is truly a sign of disrespect and, as I was quickly learning, within all Native Americans, respect of the earth and of each other are critical components in their social fabric.

When I got home, Big Brother's car was in the driveway.

"Heard you were late today."

"Yup."

"Heard Great Grandfather reamed you a new one."

"Yup."

"Be thankful he is old and it wasn't the Chief or you wouldn't be sitting for a week."

"Ouch." Lesson learned.

"You need to realize that in our culture, lack of respect is a critical thing and being late for any appointment or meeting makes the person feel that you really don't respect them. Great

Grandfather was teaching you a lesson. Not about punctuality, but about respect. Respect a man and expect that he will respect you back. Be indifferent and they too will be indifferent towards you."

"But he spoke of humility," I replied.

"That's because you're still a boy." Rodney responded.

I don't know whose words cut the deepest, Great Grandfather's or Rodney's, but I knew that it would never happen again.

The day dragged on with nothing on the screen. I sat and thought until I looked at the clock and it was nearly two AM. As had been the case since my first meeting with Great Grandfather, sleep would not come. I crawled beneath the covers and tried. God, I tried to sleep! Instead my mind went in circles until I got up and began writing.

"Let me begin where it cannot end. How do I describe sleep? How can I share with anyone the darkness of my mind when all else ceases to matter? The realm! The insistence that permeates my body and soul taking me beyond where I am, to where I want, think and yet, fear to be. My God how can so much be happening to me? I want nothing more than peace and tranquility. All I want is to be and yet here I am, caught up in a maelstrom, a whirling dervish that spins me like a top around and around and around until I know not where it all began or where it all will end. So much! So much has happened. So much has happened to take me from boy-to-man. Is this my transition? How can this be and why me? I want nothing more than sleep...sleep so deep to bury my thoughts and emotions, sleep so deep to allow me nothing more than to erase any and all and replace my world with the delicate that only happens in peace. I seek simplicity. Nothing that is abject or obtuse. Nothing that is profound and rational. Nothing more than the purity of the absolute! Nothing more than yes and no, black and white, good and bad. Dreams, frantic dreams! Go away and let me be. Please, I beg you, I implore you. Peace!

To awaken to scribbles upon a page that expose so much from deep within can be quite troubling. Where is this winding path leading? I feel as if I can take my hand and slide it through reality and touch another side where people from the past reside. What about tomorrow? Will I touch them too? If yes, will I be there?

Oh my God where does this stop? When does this stop? How will it stop? Is insanity just around the corner? Will reality ever return? But then what is real? What is in my head? Who knows reality? Am I here or there? Where is there, or here for that matter? Why am I? Darkness has been at my doorstep and yet bright light beckons me and I came back. Help. Help. Help. I am pulled into two worlds...three planes that allow me to see beyond here and now and for what reason besides insanity? The abyss, the incredible abyss, where one wanders for what seems like forever...hunting, searching, feeling their way into tomorrow! Oh my God is this insanity?

They say that one is the loneliest number and yet how can one worry about others when they have to worry about themselves so much? I envy mom and dad and Rodney and Ann and yet wonder how they can possibly survive when so much, oh so much, resides within their minds. Sleep, elusive sleep. Now I lay me down to sleep. I pray the lord my soul to keep. Close my eyes. Close my eyes. Shut my mind and let me go asunder. Please. Please. Please I beg! My birthday is next week. 23! So many and yet so few! How can one remember those besides the happy ones and the sad ones? I will be alone...singular...defined as one, with no one to share hopes and dreams and memories. No one to say "you shouldn't have" when it meant so much. My God. I hate being alone."

Great Grandfather was right. So right! I am still a boy in a man's world. I need to grow up and yet I know not how to begin.

Is it something that just happens? What is maturity? I cannot, will not and do not want this to happen. To have reality slap your face, cold, stark, absolute reality! Twenty minutes. Twenty minutes. And yet in the space and time so much, so very, very much was conceived. Reality is such an intense place to be where pretend does not exist. There were no more wannabes. I was there at the cusp. Grow up little boy! Realize that nothing and I mean absolutely nothing is owed. It is all earned like stalactites and stalagmites one drop at a time. No more smart-ass punk! No more, maybe tomorrow. Grow up, you little shit and realize that reality is around you…enveloping you, succumbing you, drowning you in responsibility. Were they…all of them, harboring me, allowing me to be less than them? How could I? When could I? Be a man? This was a whole lot tougher than I thought it would be! Do you get to have fun when you are a man? Can you laugh? Everyone seems so sad. The futility of exuberance, eradicated by the consequence of maturity! Oh my God, the sheets are wet with my sweat. Sadness! Gladness! Madness! They all prevail as my mind wanders from here-to-there and everywhere. Drop, drop, drop, drop insanity, profanity, calamity. Sleep. All I want is sleep.

Humility! Great Grandfather had spoken of humility. How does one find it? How does one acquire it? How can I, the smart - ass punk, who has survived on juvenile arrogance, succumb to reality and let down his guard? I am but a little boy whose shield is nothing more than his wit. I am but a frightened child who has reached the cusp and must strip himself naked…alone, singular so that all that Great Grandfather said penetrates deep within me, curing the raw emotion, tanning the thick skin, skewering me and making me a man, a noble man, capable, so capable of the onslaughts of reality.

How does one vow? How does one promise? How does one create a covenant with themselves? To lie alone in a borrowed bed! To succumb to singularity! Oh, the insanity of youth. So, wasted on the young!

The sun is rising across the lake. The first vestiges of tomorrow address my today. God, please let me be a better person. Please let me understand and accept the challenges of being a man. I hope. I pray for a better day.

What happens when I am old? Will I regret everything? Will I be bitter? Will I look back on yesterday and wonder "Why me?" Oh my God, an intersection...one of those days, those events, those circumstances that take today and alter tomorrow changing it, rearranging it altering it, so that what was is no more and what is can be."

I was at the bottom and felt I could go no lower. My eyes opened to the waking dawn and I walked out to the deck and took a shower in the pink light of sunrise. My head tilted back as the still-cold breeze wafted across the lake and pressed against my heart. I stood in solitude, sequestered from all but my reality when I heard footsteps behind me. It was Ann, beautiful, wonderful Ann. She looked at the disheveled me, wiped clean of my boyish grin and knew that the chill in my heart was not that from the air. My normal being eradicated itself, evaporating in a cloud of reality. "Do you want to talk about it?" she asked.

Our eyes met and the sadness, madness, stupefying singularity of my eyes pierced hers. She knew that I was but a wounded dove floundering upon the ground, in shock about all that was, was no more. I wanted to hug her and cry upon her shoulder but knew that to do so might open a chasm so deep of emotional distrust with Big Brother that any act would be wrong. They were my friends...my very best friends and I am and must remain an emotional outsider...a spectator to their love. One cannot imagine the feeling of one when you live with two who are in love.

Ann looked at me and asked why I looked so forlorn. I told her about Great Grandfather and being late. She lamented that I needed to understand that Great Grandfather had been the chief and commanded respect from everyone. She noted that those who once had power and authority find respect to be the very last thing they ever want to give up. "Power is a narcotic" she said and it can be addictive. She took a slow, quiet sip of her coffee and continued that with each generation, the distance between the power and powerless became less and less until those who were before feel threatened by those who came after. Elders don't understand how our generation could usurp the caveat of humility.

God she was right...so right. She asked when I was meeting again with Great Grandfather and I told her that it would be the following Thursday. She implored me not to be late. Guidance was not needed. I had learned my lesson.

Ann left for another grueling day of reality. I walked onto the porch and sat down and looked at the keys beneath my fingertips... glancing at the shore and then the waves. 2000 words! 2000 words! It could be 20 and it wouldn't make any difference, they were simply not there. I pressed hard upon a key...any key and there was no feeling. Nothing! Simply nothing!

Humility! Does humility take away aggression in a society, culture and existence predicated on competition? Without aggression where would I fit in? Just another cog in the social wheel? Would my dreams, goals and aspirations be smashed upon the shore so that what I wanted would not, could not be? Was there a point of balance? Don't all winners lose at something?

My temples throbbed as I watched one White Crane circle the water looking for its mate. Was this to be me, circling the water, alone, singular, abject to the space below, searching for nothing more than the happiness that comes from feeling wanted needed and loved?

My mind was blank. The screen was blank. My heart was blank. I stood and stretched and realized that the solitude of singularity and its pervading silence was pressing on my mind, squeezing it to mush. I walked back out onto the deck and took a deep breath. If you have never smelled the scent of fresh lake water on a spring morning, you can't understand that its aroma is different...a cross between clean and clear, distinct and yet uncommon. I filled my lungs with hope that my expression would be the poison that had been in my heart.

I stood and listened to the solitude. I stood for an hour doing, thinking, being nothing. I peered at the water and it looked back until the silence was sliced by the gradual sound of an engine, not upon the lake but somewhere.

Silence! I needed silence. Yet the sound grew louder. A truck! In the driveway?

Who?

What?

I walked around the side of the house and there stood a big, brown, beast. UPS! I saw no one and then the door opened and this girl stepped out in her brown, obligatory uniform. My heart skipped a beat as a beguiling young woman appeared before me.

"Are you Rodney Whitehorse?" She asked.

"No, I'm his roommate," I resounded.

She was in a hurry, but then UPS drivers always were. "I need a signature."

I took the pad and was about to sign when I paused for a moment to view the scenery. Five foot six. Almond color skin. Bright, white teeth. Small gold stud earrings. Light brown hair up under her cap. She was already in shorts that would have been too short in July and yet it was only May and sixty degrees. Nice legs with great muscles. Loved the sculpted calves. I looked for missing teeth, but found none...missing that is. Her eyebrows were sculpted and then her eyes met mine. Oh, my God! Deep brown eyes that accentuated her angular face.

"Do I sign my name or his?" I nervously asked.

"Either will do."

Time to be bold! Come on weak-one, be a man. "New to the route?" I asked.

"I'm a temp. Ran out of money for school and got this job. Great pay, but a real killer."

"A trucker?"

She giggled. I memorized the laugh, holding it deep within my brain to savor like a fine wine.

"Heh, I normally don't do this but if I don't, I think I'll regret it the rest of my life."

She looked at me and frowned.

"Are you dating anyone who could beat me up?"

There was a slight guffaw. I knew what she was thinking. She didn't date midgets or little boys and they were the only ones who couldn't probably beat me up, yet, even some of them probably could too as she replied, "No, I just came back from school and I'm not dating anyone."

I knew that her time was measured. "Look I know big brother is watching and you have to go. If you would like to go out some time, here is my email address."

I wrote it on her pad and smiled. Her smile caught me off guard. It was more, so much more than I expected.

I watched and admired her butt as she climbed back into her brown behemoth, turned and waved. Oh my God! One little gesture burned into my heart. I was smitten as I took the small UPS package in the house and put it to my nose to see if her soul was wrapped inside. It wasn't and I was sad. I put it on the table.

The tide had turned. Feelings came back to my fingers. 2000 words flowed quickly. The Chief would get his due.

For two days I checked my email every hour and there was nothing. On Monday, as I sat on the porch, I heard the truck again. My heart skipped a beat. Did I wait or go out to the driveway? Vanity had never been part of my make-up and so, trying to act so cool, I sashayed out to the driveway only to find some old guy sitting in the UPS truck who said, "Got an envelope for you."

I took it and looked at the address. It was addressed to "Silly Guy" and then the house address. As the driver left, I opened the envelope. No one ever would call Rodney "Silly Guy." The note read, "Sorry, I don't have an email address yet because I don't have a computer. If you want to meet, I'll be at the Nitty Gritty Wednesday night. Hope to see you then." I thought my cheeks were going to burst from my smile.

She didn't say what time or give me her name and I had no way to know. Shit! I thought seven, eight or nine. I'd sleep in the corner of the bar if I had to. The Nitty Gritty was famous on campus. I could sit there all night. I got there at five and sat at the bar. It gave me a view of the tables and the corner entrance. About eight she walked in with another girl. Safety in numbers you know. She walked over to me and I stood up. We smiled and her spell on me began again. She was in jeans, a tee-shirt and a dark blue baseball cap with her hair all bundled up beneath. Her friend was wearing whatever, my mind was lost.

"Hi," I said.

"Hi," she responded. Nodding to her right was this really tall, really big girl. "This is my partner Jasmine."

Shit a lesbian. 'My luck!' I thought. And Jasmine, her partner, was a big one at that. Probably six feet tall and arms as thick as my calves. She could beat the ever-loving crap out of me.

"You know I don't even know your name" I responded.

"Amy" was the response. Oh my God. Her name burrowed into my heart.

"Like in Amanda?"

"Like Amelia."

"Is your name Amelia?" I incredulously asked as my eyes went wide and my already tenor voice went up an octave.

"Yes."

"Oh my God, you're named after one of my most favorite people and you have one of my favorite names" I knew she thought I was bullshitting.

"Seriously, I think Amelia Earhart was one of the neatest people ever. She didn't let anything stand in her way. She wanted to fly around the world and almost made it. I've read every book and every article about her."

Still thinking that Amy thought it was bullshit, I proceeded to explain…"Amelia Earhart was born in Atchison, Kansas, in 1897 and began flying in 1921, when she was 24 years old and was one of the earliest female aviators. Her first plane was a Kinner Airster, which was a small biplane. Later she bought a Lockheed Vega 5 and created many records including the first female to fly solo across the Atlantic Ocean."

"On her trip around the world, Amelia flew a specially designed Lockheed Model 10E where the "E" stood for Electra. Lockheed had models from 10A to 10E that were for commercial use. Amelia's plane was powered by dual Pratt & Whitney R-1340 Wasp engines that were designed as radial nine-cylinder models that displaced 1344 cubic inches each. The fuselage was modified to add two rows of fuel tanks, from bulkhead to bulkhead so that the plane could handle 1150 gallons of fuel or enough for 20 hours of flight at a normal flying speed of 194 miles per hour with standard wind resistance. Amelia and her navigator, Fred Noonan were reported missing near Howland Island in the Pacific on July 2, 1937 and the mystery of what happened to them has never really been solved. Some think she lived and was captured by the Japanese and died in prison. I hope not, free spirits need to roam. I made a model of her plane when I was a kid and still have it."

Whew. Where did that come from?

Amy had a smile on her face and Jasmine looked astonished. Here was some guy expounding on a dead woman while they stood in a bar on the University of Wisconsin campus. This clown was excited about a model airplane he admitted building. That's **not** what cool guys normally talk about! I looked at Jasmine and tried to figure out who was the pitcher and who was the catcher. Lesbians! My luck!

"Want a drink?" I asked.

They both wanted beer. I ordered bottles of PBR. Something about a woman drinking out of a beer bottle that turned me on. Something about phallic symbols I guess.

After Amelia Earhart and my enthusiastic biography, the small talk centered around UPS and what I did. I was afraid to ask what Jasmine did. Professional wrestler, perhaps! Bouncer? Former Olympic weight lifter. Yiikes!

I did most of the talking. Nerves I guess. They thought being a writer was glamorous. Not! I watched for clues as Amy and Jasmine stood side-by-side then Amy's hand grasped Jasmines. Shit! My luck!

They clinked bottles and looked in each other's eyes. Amy leaned forward and when their lips were about to touch, Amy stopped and they both looked at me and giggled. "Gotcha."

"This is my friend Samantha and we decided to see if we could pull it off."

"You're not gay?" I asked.

"Would it have mattered?"

"Somewhat" I responded in my most liberal Madisonian manner which got a frown. "Competing against guys is one thing but doubling the odds. WOW, that would be tough."

Samantha had been the insurance to make sure I wasn't some creep. I guess it's a girl thing… public bar, two-against-one. We tried talking, but it was too loud.

"What's your name?" Amy asked and so I went through the whole spiel…George Terrill the Fourth, but everyone calls me "Q". From their expressions, I think they believed it was pretty lame. When you've been called something since you were a little kid, you don't think it's that bad and so I had to explain the name.

"You guys hungry?" I asked.

They both nodded yes.

"Paisan's?"

"Great!"

We jumped in the Jeep and drove to West Wilson Street and walked in the front door.

"Heh Amy. How are you doing?" One of the hostesses called.

"I worked here last summer" Amy offered.

"UPS pays a whole lot more than waiting tables," as I thought and lets you wear sexy brown short shorts to work.

The hostess took us into the Lakeview room with a table overlooking Lake Monona. I love the view! Sitting in the fancy room you can see everything from the Elvehem Art Center...somewhat designed by Frank Lloyd Wright...to across the lake. The three of us spent the next two hours filling each other in on school and where we were from and who we knew and didn't know. In 120 minutes, my heart was mended, my soul was cured and I was simply exhausted as my cheeks hurt from laughing so much.

Paisan's was closing and I offered to give them a ride home but they said they lived on Doty Street and could walk. I asked them which block and Samantha said the 500. They couldn't believe that I had lived only a few doors from where they had their apartment.

I looked at Amy with my big puppy dog eyes and asked her if I could see her again. She smiled and said. "We really are a couple."

My heart crashed to the floor and it must have been written all over my face as she smiled. I really didn't know what to think. Was she serious or playing with me?

"Well, can we go out, even if it's the three of us? Can we go out again?" I sounded like a begging kid at Christmas. "Can we dad? Huh, can we?"

Amy looked at Samantha and shrugged her shoulders. "It's fine with me. How about you Sam?"

Samantha, the quiet one, said "Sure, why not?"

"When?"

"Sunday night?" Amy responded.

"Great. Should I bring the guy I'm living with too?"

Now Amy was in a box. We were playing a mental game of chess. She had made her move and I made mine. Time to be cool! I didn't know whether to shake hands or hug them. I was afraid that shaking Samantha's hand would do permanent damage to mine. Instead I just imitated Sam and shrugged my shoulders.

"Sunday night. Seven o'clock?"

"Sure."

"Where do I pick you up?"

"Where would you like to meet us?" Amy asked.

"The Capitol Rotunda." I responded.

Amy nodded her head and that infectious smile came into play. She was beginning to realize that the mental chess match would have many moves and many surprises before it was checkmate.

Thursday was supposed to be Great Grandfather's day but the assisted living center called and said that he had some doctor appointments and we would take a week off. I didn't know if it was true, but I thought another week of cooling off was good.

It was Friday night and Big Brother was at the factory. Forty-eight hours and I could hardly wait.

Ann could tell by the spring in my step that something was going on.as she inquired "Who did you meet?"

How do you know I met somebody?"

"Because you've had a silly grin on your face since Wednesday!"

"The UPS driver."

"What? You mean Frank?" Ann countered incredulously.

"No. There was a substitute driver."

"I hope he's younger and better looking than Frank. His legs are too hairy for the shorts he wears."

"She's younger and much better looking than Frank and her shorts looked fine."

"Where are you meeting her?"

"Capitol Rotunda."

"Your idea or hers?"

"Mine."

"Neat choice." Ann said with a smile on her face.

It was Sunday and I was as nervous as a whore in church. What to wear? What fancy smelly stuff to apply? Everything had to be just so. No jeans tonight. No tee-shirt. I got out my best cool clothes and looked in the mirror. Not me! Back to jeans, but I pressed them so that there was a crease. A really white tee-shirt with no stains, loafers and socks! Yes socks! All highlighted by a navy-blue blazer. I posed for Ann and she laughed.

"She must be special."

"Best looking UPS driver I've ever seen."

At its worst, and the Beltline can be bad, it's 30 minutes from Rodney's cottage to the Capitol. I left an hour early and got to downtown at 6:25. I parked in the Edgewater hotel ramp, walked the four blocks and meandered around the Capitol grounds. You don't want to look too anxious. I checked my phone and at exactly 7:00 PM positioned myself in the middle of the rotunda. I looked towards the State Street entrance. Nothing! Towards the West Washington Avenue entrance. Nothing! Towards Hamilton Street and there she was. My God, my heart was melting. She looked fantastic! Gone were the jeans, replaced by a conservative yet, very appealing skirt. Gone was the tee-shirt, replaced by a white silk blouse. Gone was the baseball hat so that gorgeous and I mean incredibly gorgeous, light brown ringlet curls flowed down from the crown of her head to her shoulders.

She had on large gold hoop earrings, a small gold cross and was wearing somewhat high heels. Oh my God!

As she got closer, I noticed the makeup. Not too much, but enough to accentuate her deep brown eyes and succulent lips. I quivered and smiled…she smiled. I smiled again and she laughed.

"Where's Samantha?" I asked.

"Out with her significant other," Amy responded.

"And the partner thing?"

A slight smile crossed Amy's faces as the tip of her tongue slid across her upper lip as if in contemplation as she offered. "Perhaps we were just pulling your chain. But then maybe again not. Would it matter?"

She left me wondering.

"Where's the guy you're living with?"

"Rodney and my other roommate, Ann…who's his fiancée, went up to Black River Falls to see his parents. They're planning their wedding."

With that, all the bullshit was over.

"Why here?" Amy asked.

"Because this was the most beautiful thing I'd ever seen in Madison, until about three minutes ago".

Amy blushed as I continued. "The capitol is 100 years old and filled with both beauty and memories. If they continue to take care of it, like love and friendship, it can last forever."

"I've never been inside before," Amy lamented.

"Most people haven't and they don't know what they're missing." I pointed up to the dome. "Look at the artwork. Look at the statues. Above all else, look at the symmetry…circles upon circle upon circles that all add up to a reflection of time and the seasons. With each passing year, the marble darkens a little bit and yet, the veins within remain the same. With each passing year, the difference between then and now becomes a little more apparent and more defined and yet there is an intrinsic beauty that only comes from appreciation of the talent and commitment that went into its creation. I was pontificating and yet, I seemed to have a receptive audience.

I took her on a tour and showed her all that I knew. "Wisconsin's Capitol is 284 feet or nearly twenty-four stories tall and only three feet shorter than the Nation's Capitol."

"The old Capitol burned down in 1904 and to fund the new one, each citizen was taxed twenty-five cents. It cost over seven million dollars to build this place. The exterior stone is Bethel white granite from Vermont, making the exterior dome the largest granite dome in the world. There are forty-three different types of stone, not only from Wisconsin, but places like Vermont, Italy, Greece, Norway and Algeria. We walked some more and I explained that there were over 700 different rooms in the building and that the crystal chandeliers were made by the same company that created those on the Titanic. Amy was surprised to learn that there were 40,000 light bulbs in the building and they were the same wattage as those installed in 1917."

I added, "It's estimated that to replace the building today would be almost impossible, but, if you could, the cost would be somewhere between three and four billion dollars." When we got to the Wisconsin Avenue exit, I said, "another thing most people don't know is that almost all the streets around the Capitol were named after people who signed the U.S. Constitution. I held out my hand and directed her to "follow me" and held the door as we walked out into the cool May night.

"Where are we going?"

"Do you mind a short walk?" I asked.

"Of course not, I just walked five blocks to the Capitol, Amy replied.

"Are you cold?" I asked. With that I took off my sports coat and placed it over her shoulders. I saw that in a movie once and vowed that if I ever got the chance to do it, I would. So cool! So incredibly cool!

We headed north on Wisconsin Avenue to the Edgewater. I had pulled a favor from the restaurant manager by dropping the Chief's name to make sure that we had table number one where the Chief sat when he wanted to impress the politicians. It overlooked Lake Mendota and the view at sunset was supposed to be spectacular. It was already dark, but the lights shining out upon the Lake Mendota waves made it look spectacular.

Normal chit chat began as if it had never happened before in the getting-to-know-you phase. Where are you from? Outside Milwaukee. Outside Mineral Point. God! She had heard of Mineral Point. I didn't dare throw the Waldwick thing on her. I tried not to be the newsman digging for a story and yet the questions flowed. College? Georgetown. Major? Business, Pre-Law. Why Madison? Friends. Great place to be young. I watched as the light caressed her hair and the candles glistened off her eyes.

How many times today has someone told you your hair is simply gorgeous?

Amy blushed. The girly side was coming out. My God was I smitten as we dug a little deeper.

"I'm mixed race" she announced, awaiting my response as if I was TOO dumb to realize. "My mother is part Spanish and African and my dad is white so I identify with being half black."

"Well I played halfback in high school. Is that close enough?"

Amy looked at me with a quizzical grin as her eyebrows tried to meet above her nose and then caught on to the play-on words….half-black…halfback.

"You're great at being half-black, I was horrible as a halfback!"

Again, a girly giggle! I believe she was being smitten. Anyway, I hoped so, because I surely was as I decided to try my luck with one more… "And, my dad is a dairy farmer and has 250 Holsteins that he milks twice a day and they're black and white, so I guess were pretty close to even, huh?"

Once again, an infectious smile radiated from between her lips as her deep brown eyes darted from object-to-object until they crashed into mine. My God, I wanted to touch her...hold her...smell her, feel her. My body ached, not for sex...anyway I didn't think so ... but simply to reach out and feel this person I had become so enamored with. In seeing each other three times, our skin had never touched. The temptation was so great and yet, I wanted it to be gradual and consensual. There was no rush, but then there was.

"Hold out your hands." I requested.

She obligingly held out her hands as I held out mine with both palms facing down.

Stealing wisdom from Ann I said: "Look. You're not black and I'm not white. You're medium brown and I'm light brown. We're just different shades of brown and, besides that, we are both the same. My great, great aunt was a freed slave. She was the first woman of color to teach in Wisconsin. I wasn't attracted to you because of your race or even how incredible you look. I was attracted to you because you did something to me that had never been done before ... you made me feel alive. From the UPS delivery, to having you test me to see if I would sit all night at the Nitty Gritty ... and I would have, by the way ... to the little 'partner' deal, did nothing more than make me more interested in the incredible person I have met. Please excuse me. I hope I'm not coming on too strong. Don't be afraid, this is not a pressure situation. All I am doing is being profoundly honest and telling you that I wouldn't have cared if your parents came from Mars or Uranus...well maybe if they came from your anus, I would have been a little reluctant".

Another girly giggle as she squiggled up her nose in a funny way.

Amy looked into the candle and then at me. Her eyes, once again, dug deep into mine as she said. "My parents met in St. Martin where my mom is from. My dad was married before, but his first wife died when they were young. He just needed to get away, went to St. Martin and got sunburned and had to go to the clinic where he met my mom. Mom said that he kept coming back to the clinic every day because he thought the burn wasn't healing fast enough. She knew that he was coming to see her."

"The third time he came to the clinic she couldn't handle it anymore and when he asked her out, she said OK. She said that her grandpa was really pissed when he found out her mom went on a date with a white boy and that made her even more determined to see him again. It's a crazy story. Dad flew home and caught the next plane back to St. Martin, where he walked into the clinic with a dozen roses and asked Mom to marry him. The patients in the clinic all applauded. Mom's fellow workers thought she was nuts. Grandpa just about went insane until he met my dad and after only one dinner was calling him son. That was 27 years ago and they're still together. Mom hates the cold weather and dad promised that they would retire to St. Martin."

"Gee, that's too bad…retiring to St. Martin."

"Have you ever been there?" Amy asked, all excited to think that I had been to her favorite place.

"I've never been in a plane." I replied.

"What?"

"Nope, I've driven to Florida for spring break, but my dad is a dairy farmer and we never went many places. When you've got 250 cows to milk twice a day…that's 250 udders and 1,000 teats that need to be pulled and long trips usually aren't part of the deal. Someday, when I grow up, I want to go up in the sky."

My humor made her smile and the glow of the candle on her smile was more intoxicating than the wine that flowed. Her hand came across the table and met mine and the electricity I had hoped for was there. We looked into each other's eyes and knew that the touch was all the dessert I needed. It was 10:00 and she had to get up at five to go deliver packages.

Can I give you a ride home?"

Amy was reluctant.

"Either I give you a ride or I walk you home and then walk back and get my car, which do you prefer? I cannot, will not and do not allow women to walk home alone at night."

She smiled. "Ok, where's your car?"

"In the hotel garage."

"Optimist!" she said as she smiled.

"No realist!" I countered. It's cold and I didn't want to make you walk all the way back home.

The bill came and I almost tried to put the food back. My God, a week's wages! I pulled out the American Excess card and signed. The car came…another two-dollar tip.

"Doty Street here we come." I announced.

"Well, I don't live on Doty Street. Samantha does." Amy said sheepishly.

"What?"

"Sorry. I'm not very proud of where I live."

"Gee, I'm sorry. I know it's expensive to live in Madison. I hope it's safe."

"Oh, it is safe and dull and full of old people. She said with a sad smile on her face. "I live in the condos at 137 West Wilson"

"You mean the Capitol Towers?" Gulp.

"Yes."

"How?"

"My dad bought one of the apartments a few years ago because it was cheaper than renting a hotel every time he came to Madison. It has two bedrooms which he keeps one for himself and I have the rest of the apartment during the summer"

"It's weird, I get up in the morning and put on my UPS uniform and walk out of the building…a mixed-race girl in a brown uniform and a baseball cap and everyone just stares, while I just laugh. Daddy was right. It does them good."

We walked to the garage and I opened the door for Amy. Started Jeepers Creepers #2, pulled out of the parking lot and headed south on Wisconsin Avenue to the outer ring, turned right and headed around the ring until I got to M.L. King Drive, where I turned right and went south one block to Wilson Street. I turned right again and went down to her apartment building which was right next door to Paisan's.

We pulled in the driveway and I wanted so much to invite myself in but knew that with all the concerns she had, it wasn't the right thing to do. This was to be slow, natural and as delicate as lace. I wanted to build a foundation for a long-term relationship and not a one-night stand.

We sat for a very long moment and I kept the engine running. "Can I kiss you, goodnight?" I asked.

"If you don't, you can't ask me out again," she said with a smile.

It was what I call a sister kiss…a way you would kiss your sister and yet it was on her lips, which were soft and tasted of wine.

"Thank you". She said in a soft whisper, almost so low that I couldn't hear her. "Thank you for the tour and dinner and most of all for being you…kind, sweet and a gentleman." With that she opened her door. As she was about to depart, she looked back and said. "Call me."

"But I don't have your number." I responded as she walked away.

I couldn't go after her and didn't understand. I drove home and vowed I would go back every night until I saw her. I got back to the cottage and, as I was hanging up my sports coat, I reached in the right pocket and there it was…a white piece of paper with a lipstick kiss on it with her phone number written inside. It was the best goodnight kiss I ever received. I looked at it and smiled. What a wonderful, wonderful night!

Monday, which was my normal day off, had me back at the factory to fill in for someone on vacation. I didn't mind. My shift was three-to-eleven and my job was to watch the front door. (Like a skinny kid who was still recovering from a bazillion things that happened in the accident could do anything). I felt like Barney Fife. I went to the employee lounge and the lights were off. As I turned them on the word "surprise" echoed throughout the room. I had forgotten: it was my birthday! There were balloons and a cake with 23 candles. Geez. No wonder why mom had tried calling me three times while I was in the shower. It's nice to be recognized on a special day you only spend with about a million other people in the United States.

I thought back on Spring and realized it was the first time in five years there was no trip to Florida for Spring Break. Reality was sinking in.

I called Amy and got her phone message. I thanked her for the evening and said I would call again. I didn't want to seem over-anxious but did want her to know that the interest was still there. Tuesday night, I called again and the sweet voice picked up. "46 hours and 13 minutes." I said after her hello.

"What?"

"It's been 46 hours and now 14 minutes since you said call me."

Amy laughed her girly laugh.

"How's the trucking business?"

"Oh God, some of the packages are SO heavy."

"Too bad I'm not there, I'd rub your shoulders." whoops. I shouldn't have said that! I cringed.

"That's sounds wonderful," was Amy's response.

"I'm at the factory until eleven."

"Darn."

"Yesterday was my birthday and I saved some of my birthday cake for you. This means that we need to get together soon or it will be stale."

"Now that's one of the most unique ways I've ever been asked out in my life. How about Thursday night after you get back from seeing Great Grandfather?"

I agreed, realizing she could have said any time, except during my visit with Great Grandfather.

Amy noted. "It's going to have to be early because I've got to get up at five. After work on Friday, I'm going home to Milwaukee."

Damn!

"I have a tutor who's helping me with the LSAT preparation and we meet every other Saturday morning."

"Understood."

"What clandestine spot do you want to meet this time?"

"Hmmm…early dinner. Favorite food? Myles Teddywedgers." I replied.

"Huh?"

"Corner of State, Mifflin and the Square. A little triangle shaped building that serves authentic Cornish pasty."

"You're serious."

"Yup."

"What's pasty?"

"Oh my God girl, are you in for a treat. You're not a vegan or anything like that?"

"Are you kidding me? I love meat and potatoes."

"Superb! Ok set your watch. It's 8:20 on Tuesday. So, I'll see you in 45 hours and forty minutes. 6:00 PM and then we can decide where to eat our pasty and cake."

"You mean they don't have any place to eat?"

"Nope, take out only."

"You're one crazy dude."

"I'm about as far as you can get from being a dude." I responded.

"I've got to go." she announced.

"Wish I was there to rub your shoulders" I said again.

Her voice got serious … "You know, so do I."

"See yah on Thursday." I said.

"Wilco…over and out," was her reply.

I smiled and thought of Amelia Earhart.

I filled all of Wednesday by reading. I hated doing it at school and yet, I found myself mesmerized by Dr. Ian Barnes "The Historical Atlas of Native Americans". Dr. Barnes is from England and yet, he had more information about Native Americans than I could find anywhere else. I bet, Dr. Barnes would just about shit his English britches if he knew that every Thursday morning, except of course, when some idiot is late, I found myself talking to some of the guys from the past that he was writing about and doing so through Great Grandfather.

Pearl Harbor: It was Thursday and I left at 8:00 AM. I was going to walk into Great Grandfather's room at exactly 10 o'clock, which I did.

Little Spirit, you are here," Great Grandfather said with some levity in his voice.

"Yes, Great Grandfather, I am here and I would like to apologize for being late last time."

"No need to apologize. You have been in the lobby for a while this week waiting until the right moment and that is enough to tell me you are sorry."

How in hell did he know that? He's blind and no one came into his room to tell him. Boy, this guy can give me the heebie, jeebies at times.

"Come, sit with me. We have much to talk about and the spirits are glad that you have come. How are Rodney and Ann doing? I sense joy in their hearts and in yours, too."

"They're fine Great Grandfather and so am I. Rodney is always at the casino and Ann is always either at work or at school and so they are both quite busy."

"Tell me about the woman you met."

"How do you know, Great Grandfather?"

"I can hear it in your voice."

"I met her two weeks ago when she delivered a package to our door."

"She's a mailman?"

"No, she is working this summer for UPS driving a truck and working as a substitute driver."

"Little Spirit, I hear more joy in your heart than ever before."

"Thank you, Great Grandfather. I don't think I have never felt like this before"

"Are you sleeping better?"

How in hell did he know about that?

"Like a baby." I responded.

"You mean you wake up every few hours with wet pants and crying?" Great Grandfather chuckled. It was his favorite joke that he said he heard it when John McCain got beat in the presidential election and thought it was funny. It was good to hear him laugh his soft, gentle laugh.

"Rodney and Ann will be married in four months. September is a good time to be married. I married my wife in September beneath a full moon. Do you know if there will be a full moon when they marry? In the beliefs of the Ho-Chunk, it is a sign of bounty … they will have many children."

I sat and listened to him reflect. Not on the distant past, but on his own life. It was wonderful to hear him talk of his wife and children. It was so sweet to watch the soft smile reflect the joy that had been a part of his life. He had not experienced the material achievements of the recent past and had been poor and yet, even in poverty, there was dignity. Today was unlike the others. Not nearly as intense and there was a smile on his face. Instead of having me pull up the old cedar chest and hold his hands, I simply sat on a chair and we visited.

"Did I tell you that I was in World War II?" he asked.

"No Great Grand Father you didn't."

"I remember Pearl Harbor. It was a Sunday morning and I was 19 years old and working on my first car. While things weren't too good for us back then, I was still an American and like my Indian brothers, my job was to help defeat the Germans and the Japanese. As war was declared by President Roosevelt, we all felt as if he was speaking to each and every citizen, including us. I don't know a single Indian man who didn't volunteer to serve his country. There were only about 5,000 in service before Pearl Harbor but around 40,000 by war's end, which was somewhere near 10% of all Indians in America. And the women! So many Indian women served their country as well. We all tried to be good Americans. One of the things the government created to help finance the war were war bonds. Indian nations purchased $50 million to help save America."

"What did you do in the war, Great Grandfather?"

"I was a Marine, like my son. I made it home and he did not. We fought and he died and he never got to see his only son."

With that he shook his head and his eyes got moist. I knew it was time to change the subject. He was wandering down memory lane and yet, after the last time, I didn't want to make any waves.

"What is your lady friend's name?"

"Amy."

"That's a nice name."

"It's short for Amelia."

"Like Amelia Earhart?" Grandfather said with an excited smile upon his face.

"Yes, Great Grandfather, like Amelia Earhart."

"I was a young boy when she disappeared and all America was saddened. The spirits never speak of her and so I hope her soul was found."

"Tell me what your Amy looks like."

"Well she's about five feet six and has beautiful light brown, very curly hair. Her skin is almond color and she has intensely brown eyes and the most beautiful smile I've ever seen. When she laughs, it lights up the entire room. Her hands are delicate and yet strong, Great Grandfather. She has to be because she delivers packages all day for UPS."

"You're dating a delivery girl?"

"It's only for the summer Great Grandfather. She received her degree in business and pre-law at Georgetown University and wants to go to law school."

"Beautiful and smart?" Watch out young man, you're going to get hooked on this one."

"Not going to, I think I already am."

"Are you being a gentleman?"

"Yes, Great Grandfather, I am being more of a gentleman than I think I ever have been in my life."

"That's good Little Spirit. When you value something, it is necessary to honor and cherish it and let all things come naturally."

"I know Great Grandfather, but it is so hard. She is so beautiful and we have had so much fun in such a short time."

"Be careful Little Spirit, broken hearts are the most difficult to mend."

"I know and I don't want either of us to get hurt."

"Take it slowly and let her come to you. Don't try to go to her."

"I will take your advice Great Grandfather."

"When will you see her again?"

"Tonight."

"Are you taking her to dinner?"

"Yes, Great Grandfather."

"Where?"

"Miles Teddywedgers?" Great Grandfather let out a guffaw.

"Still there? Still great pasty? Still out on east Johnson Street?"

No Great Grandfather, they've moved on State Street right off the Capitol Square."

"That fellow…what was his name?" Grandfather thought for a minute and smiled…"I know Poppi! Does he still own it?"

I responded, "Unfortunately, Poppi passed away Great Grandfather. He had cancer and so many people loved him, when he was sick, they all pitched in to keep the place going. Now, it's owned by a brother and sister and they are keeping it just as Poppi had always wanted it to be."

"That's noble, to think people would help a friend. That's what life is really all about!" Grandfather responded with a shy smile on his weathered face as he inquired, "Do you have a gift for your lady friend?"

"A piece of my birthday cake?"

"No Little Spirit" Great Grandfather exclaimed "You need to give her something that will allow her to learn more about you. A good relationship is like a rose opening its petals slowly to allow the scent escape, slowly let her into your world. Do not force it."

Soon his eyelids were closing and I knew that there would be no "talking" to one of the spirits and yet the Chief was still expecting his 2,000 words.

"One last thing, Little Spirit. Don't wear so much aftershave. You smell like a French prostitute!" With that he let out a cackle and I knew we were back on good terms.

Teddywedgers: On the way home, I thought of what Great Grandfather had said. A photo? Nope way too soon! Then it came to me, a scanned copy of my George the First's book. She could read about the past and hopefully see who I was. I scooted home, got the book, stopped at the Hallmark store and asked the lady if she would wrap it for me. If I did it, it would look terrible. She wrapped it and it looked fancy and nice.

I made it to the square at 5:30 and parked the Jeep in the Mifflin Street dead end. At precisely six, I got out of the Jeep and saw her walking towards the door. I smiled and said, "Hi."

With the weather finally getting winter warm as we called it, Amy was dressed to make certain I noticed. Wearing black tights with white socks over the ends of the legs, a tan cashmere turtleneck sweater covered by a black lightweight vest, her natural skin tone was accentuated only to be superseded by her effervescent smile as she demurely whispered "Hi," in response.

We both smiled and I held the door as she walked in. There was only room for perhaps four people in front of the counter and there were three already inside and so she squeezed in behind me and I could feel her press against my body. I was getting chills up and down my spine. I turned and our faces were but a few inches apart. I wanted to kiss her.

"Can I order for you?" I asked.

"Sure."

We waited our turn and I ordered two of the originals…tenderized round steak and potatoes in a pie crust. The clerk wrapped them in aluminum foil and put them in a bag.

"They smell delicious." Amy noted.

"I think you're going to like them and they go well with birthday cake. Do you want anything to drink?"

"Nope" she replied. "I know a quiet place where they have some great wine and we can eat your birthday Pasty and cake there."

"Can we walk?" I asked.

"If you want, but I think the food will get cold."

OK, the Jeep's just around the corner."

"I know. I saw you sitting there." she giggled.

We climbed into Jeepers Creepers #2 and I asked, "Where are we going?"

"Back to the outer ring and turn left"! We went up past the library and crossed West Washington Avenue and then past the parking garage. "Turn right onto King Drive."

There was a smile upon my face. "Right on Wilson and then into the garage stall number 805."

There was a silver Mercedes convertible in stall 804 and I made sure not to ding it when I opened my door. We took the elevator up to the top floor and she opened the door to the most spectacular view of the Capitol Dome I had ever seen. "Oh my God! You live here?"

Amy smiled in a somewhat embarrassed way and said…"Let me show you around."

She had the entire top floor. Dad had purchased two condos and made them into one. Beyond the obligatory gourmet kitchen, there was a great room that overlooked Lake Monona with twelve -foot ceilings and ceiling-to-floor windows and a master suite with a deck that looked out on the lake as well.

Amy noted. "This is Dad's room when I'm not here. Because I'm living here for the summer, I get the suite and he takes the guest bedroom."

She showed me the master suite and its bathroom. I think six people could fit into the steamer/shower. It was bigger than dad's cow wash in the barn. Then the guest bedroom that also had a walk-in bathroom. Geez!

"We better eat the pasty before they get cold" Amy offered as she got out two plates.

"Do you put anything on them?" Amy asked, nodding at the pasties.

"A little butter."

"Red or white wine?" she asked.

"No just butter. The wine would make the crust soggy"

"To drink ding-dong!" She giggled, and I loved her laugh.

"You choose" I offered, as she opened the wine closet that looked as big as my room at Rodney's house.

"Pinot Noir?"

"Honestly, my favorite."

"Let's see…hmmm…birthday boy, Cornish pasty, birthday cake…a Little Black Dress sounds good."

"On you, I bet it would look good too" I chuckled.

"Someday, dear boy. Some day!"

She set the table and lit a candle and served the pasty.

"Oh my God" was her exclamation as the first morsel hit her mouth.

"Good? Bad? Too Hot? Too cold?" I was perplexed.

"Too good! This is going to mean an extra lap out to Olin Park and back.

Amy made a point of showing me with each bite that she was loving it as she murmured "so good."

"It's the original Mineral Point recipe the Cornish miners brought over, except they took the rutabagas out of it." I added.

"Delicious." she said with a mouthful, as crumbs spewed forth. Her guard was coming down.

I laughed a little laugh and chuckled a little chuckle. Reality was already setting in and I was loving it.

We finished the pasty and she said. "I'll get the cake," as she stood up from the table.

She split the cake and gave me the larger piece.

"It was all for you." I noted.

"I can't eat all that. You'z don wan ta date no fat lady dooz ya? She said in a most slanderous African American imitation. You'z knows what deh say, we all get's big butts ifin we eats too much cake."

I wanted to tell her that I liked the size of her butt just the way it was, but knew better. Instead I just smirked.

Amy walked over to what I thought was a walk-in refrigerator the size of my first dorm room and asked, "Do you want ice cream on your birthday cake?"

Now birthday cake is great, but adding ice cream…wow!

I didn't know whether the cake would be white or chocolate and so I bought chocolate, vanilla, turtle and mint chocolate chip." She said while looking in the freezer.

I noticed the labels…they were from Madison's own Chocolate Shoppe Ice Cream which almost took my breath away. Now there is ice cream and even frozen custard and then there is ice cream from the Chocolate Shoppe. My God! Heaven on earth! Forget counting calories! Forget carbs! Forget anything except some of the best ice cream in the entire world.

"You pick." I said, hoping for the Turtle.

"My mother's favorite was mint chocolate ribbon, but they stopped making it. Mine is Turtle," Amy said.

Ding! Ding! Ding! And we have a winner! We both like the same ice cream!

Slowly, Amy put a huge dollop on my cake and then a smaller scoop for her. It was like heaven on earth…great cake, scrumptious ice cream and a beautiful lady as she sang, "Happy birthday to you. Happy birthday to you. Happy birthday sweet "Q'…Happy birthday to you. I know. I know, don't quit driving for UPS.

She came back to the table with the plates and we both dug in. I watched as each morsel was put into her mouth. I never knew ice cream could be so sensuous.

We ate the cake and ice cream and then I said…"Oh darn. I forgot something in the Jeep," which I'd intentionally left in the car! "You clean the dishes woman while I go to the car."

"Youbetcha!" was her reply. I just shook my head and smiled…a real Sconnie girl.

I headed to the elevator and realized I would need a key to get back. There were keys on the counter and I simply took them. When I got downstairs, I accidentally squeezed the remote on her set and the parking lights went on in the Mercedes. It was hers. No wonder why she walked everywhere.

I pulled the present from behind the Jeep's seat, went back to the elevator, turned the key in the number eight slot and headed back up, vowing to say nothing about the car. I opened the door and walked back in just as Amy was putting the last of the dishes in the dishwasher.

"I'll do them tomorrow. I don't like the noise. How about some music?" she said.

"OK!" Another eloquent response from yours truly.

"I suppose you're into country." She inquired.

"I really don't like country music," I answered.

"Whew." Amy replied. "Me either. What type do you like?"

"Believe it or not" I responded, "I can't stand rap music and actually like female vocals and new age instrumentals. I listen to piano, cello and guitar music without vocals while I'm working, but also love 70's rock, plus U2, not as much for their music, but because they take a stand on a lot of global issues and are trying to use their wealth and notoriety to do something about it."

Amy looked into my eyes, smiled and said "I like old rock music like the Doors, Moody Blues, Queen, Led Zeppelin, Crosby Stills Nash and Young...music my dad listened to when he was my age. Out of all today's really popular singers, the one I really like Lady GaGa. She's got an incredible voice and some of her songs and what she expresses really inspire me. She's all about inclusion and so am I."

The conversation was digging down to a deeper level.

"How about opera?" Amy asked.

"Some" I responded with my jaw clenched. "I don't like fat lady music where they're screaming and all that, but I do like people like Josh Groban and people like Harry Connick Junior even though they're not opera." I was mumbling and spewing forth innocuous mumbo jumbo because I was a nervous wreck.

"Let me put on some music and tell me what you think". With that she opened a small cabinet door in the kitchen, punched a few buttons and a soft opera began as we sat on the couch overlooking Lake Monona.

"Wow"! My ears perked up.

"This is 'The Flower Duet."

"It's beautiful." I responded.

"Do you know what it's from?"

"Nope." Yet another profound answer from me.

"Did you ever read 'Fifty Shades of Grey' or see the movie?"

"No. I heard about it, obviously." I replied, somewhat sheepishly, like I was really up on the times.

Amy' expression changed as what appeared to be a quite cerulean thought crossed her mind. 'Fifty Shades of Grey' is really a sad story about love and what people will do simply to feel wanted. We all have limits and to push another person beyond their bounds is a tragedy and not a love story. In the end, Anastasia wins, but her sacrifice for Christian I believe, was really too much. Perhaps it was liberation, but I don't think so."

Amy was being very serious and I didn't know where she was going with the topic and so I allowed a very pregnant pause to let her get her bearings before responding. "I guess some of the stuff would be Ok, but a lot of it is beyond me. Don't get me wrong, I love passion and feeling passionate but not when there's a huge price tag placed on it."

Having never read the book or seen the movies, I had absolutely no idea what she was talking about other than there were scenes of kinky sex.

Amy continued. "Right now, The Flower Song is associated with the book and movie. In reality, 'Duo des fleurs / Sous le dôme épais'which she said in perfect French. (Any way I think it was French by the way it sounded) "is from the opera Lakme' and is the story of a British solider and Lakme' the daughter of a Brahmin Priest, who fall in love in the late 1800's when the British were occupying India."

"'The Flower Duet' song takes place between Lakmé and her servant Mallika who go to gather flowers by a river. Lakme' meets a British soldier named Gerald. Lakme' and Gerald fall in love, knowing that no one will approve, simply because they are different in race, culture and religion."

"While the flower song is one of the favorites from the opera, I really like L'Air des clochettes or 'The Bell Song' better. In it, Lakme's father forces Lakme' to sing in a public square to entice Gerald to show himself so that Lakme's father can have him killed. The Bell Song tells the legend of a pariah's daughter who saved the son of Brahma the Creator called Vishnu."

"Gerald is stabbed, but he doesn't die and Gerald and Lakme' fall even more in love. Sadly, the social pressure is too great for Lakme' to handle and she eats a poisonous leaf from a Datura tree and commits suicide. It's so beautiful and yet so tragic." Amy said shaking her head to emphasize the sadness.

God! She was into opera! The closest thing I ever did was watch "General Hospital" which was a soap opera on TV, when I was in rehab after my accident.

We sat on the couch as Amy slipped off her shoes, closed her eyes and inhaled deeply. "The opera is beautiful and is about exploration and tenderness and sadly, about judging people for what they are instead of who they are, which is a tragedy!"

Amy opened her eyes and looked deeply into mine. I didn't have a clue what she was talking about. Was she setting boundaries or just talking about the music? I made a silent vow that, until I got to know her better, I wasn't eating any leafy vegetables or staying with her until I knew more about her dad. As Great Grandfather said. "Slowly, open the rose. Never pull the petals off!" Boy, was he right, especially if the petals will kill you.

"I have a gift for you" she said and with that went to the closet. I watched as she walked to the entryway and realized how beautiful she was. I was enamored and the instant she was out of sight it sent a rush of sadness through my brain. I vowed to myself, "don't mess this one up" as my heart was skipping about every third beat and I didn't know why. Quickly, she returned carrying a beautifully wrapped package with a big red bow.

"Read the card." she giggled as she slid down right beside me. Whew! The giggle took some of the intensity out of the room.

I opened the card and there were two men sitting at an old-fashioned townie bar. One had a coonskin cap on. The other wore a skunk skin cap. Next to them sat a bear with a man's bare ass on his head. I opened the card and it said, "Happy Birthday Butt Head."

She giggled again. As I turned to say something, her lips met mine with a deep passionate kiss. "Happy Birthday, butt head" she whispered. I lingered and wanted more, but the kiss was all there was.

"Open your present." she decreed.

With that I slid my finger through the crease and carefully opened the gift. I leaned back and smiled. It was the pictorial history of the Wisconsin State Capitol.

"Open up the cover."

Inside she had inscribed … "the most beautiful thing I'd ever seen in Madison until about three minutes ago" with the time and date of our first Sunday.

I had a shy smile on my face and my eyes glistened with gratitude in the candlelight as I replied, "Thank you. Now I have a gift for you." With that I went to the hall table and picked up the gift that was professionally wrapped at the Hallmark store.

"It's not my birthday," Amy mildly objected as her forehead wrinkled with an inquisitive frown.

"I know, but it's something I think you might enjoy. I know how busy you are with work and preparing for the LSAT, but you might like it."

Amy slid open the paper and looked at the title "Waldwick" with the photo of the painting my great, great aunt had made.

"It's the memories that my ancestor, George the First wrote. I want you to have a copy."

"Oh my God," she said as she took a deep breath. Boy, this girl really breathes deep! She paged through the book and smiled. Then she took yet another deep breath and without opening her eyes whispered. "This really means so much to me, thank you."

The music was finished and the cake was gone, along with the pasty. I looked at my watch. It was nearly eleven. "I should go. You've got to be up in a few hours and drive to Milwaukee."

There was no resistance on her part. We both knew that there was still a line in the sand. I hoped she felt that someday, when it was right, we could smooth away the sand and let the passion flow. She walked me to the door and I turned and we kissed. Not a sister kiss! A deep passionate kiss that lasted a long time. She pulled me close and put her hands on my lower back pulling me into her body so that I could feel her breasts against my chest with our thighs were pressed together.

"I better go." I whispered.

She leaned back and smiled. "You are a gentleman and I do like that."

Great Grandfather was right...oh, so right. Was it a test? I don't know. I do know that the temptation was profound and six months earlier I would have thrown caution to the wind for a one-night stand. This was different. This was the adult world and I was getting used to it.

"Call me next week?" she inquired.

"Can I text you tomorrow?" I asked.

Amy look down at the floor and then up into my eyes as she nodded, smiled her shy smile and quietly said she would like that.

I smiled my goofy grin and nodded yes. With that there was one more, short kiss and then she patted me on the ass.

"That's for next time," she whispered.

I drove home, almost oblivious to streets and signs and speeds and pulled in the driveway. Rodney's truck was parked where it should have been and I knew that in a little while Ann would be home and they would have each other.

"Heh, Little Brother. We haven't seen each other and talked in a long time."

"I know! I know! You're gone or I'm gone, it's like we don't even live in the same house."

"How is the book coming?"

"I'm at 50,000 words and no negatives from the Chief."

"You and Great Grandfather make up?"

"There wasn't really anything to make up. I was late and in being late and not calling failed to show respect. I was wrong and apologized to him. Today, he told me about World War II and your grandfather. He was sad about what happened."

"No voices from the past?"

"Not today."

"Let's hope he's not slipping away."

Man, I hope not. He's looking forward to a big wedding in September." I said.

"When the Great Spirit calls, he doesn't think about weddings, only who he is calling must come home. I hope he can tell you our entire story before he goes. It means so much to him, the Chief and our nation."

"Am I doing enough, fast enough? Some days it's all right there and other days, simply nothing." I asked. "It's tough being creative knowing that when you spill out your heart and soul it's still all subjective, where some people will think it's great while others will think it's a pile of shit. Two-thousand words every week is a lot to ask."

"I think you're doing great, but who knows what the Chief thinks. He's like me or I'm like him, it's all about numbers and not about creative peaks and valleys. How are you coming on the social media?" Rodney replied.

"I've been thinking about it and believe we need to look at some sort of gaming or membership cards where loyal customers are rewarded in some way. Charlie is looking into what is legal. The idea is to get the regulars coming back more often while we try to expand our reach and acquire new customers. Every business has to realize that it will lose 20% of its existing customers every year and they need to be replaced, just to stay even. It's a challenge but I'm putting together a plan to present at our next meeting."

"Ann said you have someone new in your life." Rodney inquired.

"A UPS driver." I replied.

"A guy?" as I saw Rodney shudder.

"No ding dong! She was the substitute driver a few weeks ago when you got that package I signed for. We struck up a conversation and we have been out three times including tonight." I responded.

"Three times and she still wants to see you. Is she like Great Grandfather?"

"What does that mean?"

"Blind." Rodney let out a big guffaw.

"Her name is Amy. She lives downtown, graduated from Georgetown and is taking her LSAT's in a few weeks."

"A LAWYER? Watch those lawyers!"

"Really, a nice girl". I replied.

"What's in your hand?"

"She gave me a book on the history of State Capitol for my birthday."

"Why?"

"Because, our first date was touring the building and dinner at the Edgewater."

"Man, the Chief must be paying you big bucks if you can afford to eat there."

"You only get one chance to make a first impression and dinner only cost me nearly a month's salary."

"How's the love life?"

"I'm following Great Grandfather's advice and playing it cool."

Rodney looked at the ground and then at me and smiled. "Follow his advice. He's really a wise man. You gonna be around this weekend?"

"I have to go home on Sunday as my mom wants to celebrate my birthday."

"When's that?"

"It was last Monday."

"Aw man, sorry."

"No problem. Every day I live here is like a birthday present from you and Ann. You are my family and my dearest friends.

"So, you and your new girlfriend celebrated your birthday tonight?"

"Yup! We had Teddywedgers and then some of the left-over birthday cake from the surprise party at the factory. She even bought four different flavors of ice cream from the Chocolate Shoppe!"

"Four different flavors?" Rodney was incredulous. "That's the best ice cream in the world!"

"I know. She didn't know what kind of birthday cake it was and so she bought chocolate, vanilla, turtle and mint chocolate chip."

"You ate them all?"

"No, just the turtle ice cream…chocolate, vanilla, caramel with a few Rodney's in it"

"Rodney's?"

"Yes…some nuts!" I blurted out and we both laughed.

"Wow! Nice girl and ice cream from the Chocolate Shoppe. I've got the meet this one" Rodney offered.

We went back to discussing the weekend. "I've got to go home for dinner on Sunday as mom wants me home to celebrate my birthday."

"I need to put the pier in. Can you help Saturday morning?" Rodney asked.

Geez! I'm living in house for free. He cooks, Ann cleans and my job is to look out the window. Hmmm! Let me think about it for a millisecond…"Sure!"

The next morning, the texts from Amy began. I imagined her riding all over Dane County in her brown uniform driving a huge UPS truck and so, the subject began there.

What was intended as one text turned into a plethora of one-liners with double-entendre's, whimsical jokes and all kinds of silly stuff intended to not only put smiles on each other's faces, but stoke the fires of what was quickly becoming a level of passion.

I thought I was clever, but she was my match. What started out quite innocent kept getting more risqué. She was the temptress and was doing an incredible job of making me vow over and over and over. "Lead us not into temptation. Great Grandfather…HELP! The rose petals are opening fast…like really, really fast!"

Saturday: It was Saturday at sunrise and when I looked out at the lake, there was Big Brother hauling sections of the pier from behind the garage to the shoreline. It wasn't even seven o'clock and, of course, mister type "A" had to make me feel inadequate. Each eight-foot section had to weigh 100 pounds and he was throwing them over his shoulder like they were forty-pound bags of dog food.

Lake Waubesa water was still really cold. Big Brother got into his waders and took a twenty-pound mallet like it was a finishing hammer and pounded each section of pier in place. My job was to hold the sections perpendicular and then fasten the bolts when he placed each section in line. It was girlie work, but needed to be done. God is that dude strong!

Sunday, I went home. It had been awhile and I called mom from Dodgeville to tell her where I was. Of course, every mention of Dodgeville was responded by "be careful". I got home and dad and Tommie were out planting. May is really serious planting time on the farm. You've got to get the hundred-day corn in on time and then hope and pray that you get rain and good weather. The casinos aren't the only place you gamble. If you want to roll the dice, try farming. Rodney told me to never play roulette because, when you add up all the numbers on the wheel, the sum is 666. So much for mixing analytics and religion.

Jake went ballistic whining and crying that I was home. I was totally helpless in planting and actually had a blister from the pier. My God was I getting soft or what? Mom and I talked and she knew where I needed to go. I put on my work boots and Jake and I headed for the forest. The trees were just budding as it was a late spring and so I stood beneath the naked branches and counted my blessings. The red wing blackbirds were back in full force and their chirps to each other, telling each other where they were, reminded me that spring had come to Waldwick, Wisconsin.

This was my cathedral! I thanked God for my friends and having Amy enter my life. I asked for forgiveness for my tardiness and asked God to keep Great Grandfather around until after the wedding. Jake and I walked to the spring and I saw something I hadn't seen in a long time. Shoeprints in the mud! Someone had been there. Dad and Tommie were too busy and so I knew that whoever it was didn't belong. I walked to where the foundation of the school house had been and found a fresh candy wrapper. The wind never blew hard enough to do that. Someone had been on our land. My attempt at tranquility was usurped and I wondered why I felt violated.

As the afternoon wore on and it was time for dinner, Jake and I made our way back to the house. Mom made a pot roast and more birthday cake. I was a little old for it, but knew that she felt it was her duty. Dad and Tommie came in from milking and chores and got cleaned up.

"Happy birthday." Dad and Tommie announced.

"Thanks." I replied.

I got right to the point. "Someone's been in the forest. I found footprints near the spring and a Snickers wrapper near the school foundation." Now most farmers are good negotiators, but lousy liars. Dad and Tommie fit the bill.

"Don't know a thing about any visitors," dad said.

"Me neither," added Tommie.

I leaned back in my kitchen chair and looked at the two of them. "What's going on?"

"Some guys from the county is all. They surveyed the land."

"For what?"

"We don't know." Dad replied.

My cheery mood of birthday and thoughts of Amy were quickly eroding.

"Dad."

"Son, I don't know."

"Dad, Tommie. Nothing happens to that land. Nothing! I know we are incorporated and all that limited liability corporation stuff and we all have stock but all I care about are those ten acres. Tommie, you can have my share of the rest of the farm, but not my forest."

The birthday party got quiet and mom tried to put on a happy face. No mention of Amy was made. Time was not right. Even Jake knew that there was friction. God, dogs are smart!

After dinner, I excused myself and said I needed to get back to Madison. We all hugged, but the hugs were different…almost like consolations…like those at funerals. Not my land! Not my forest! I headed back to Madison. I needed someone but didn't know where to turn. Amy was in Milwaukee or anyway that's where I think she was. Rodney was at the factory, trying to keep peace and get ahead and Ann was studying as she always was.

I got home and did what I probably shouldn't have done. I called Amy. "Heh, where are you?" I asked.

"I just began heading back to Madison. What's going on? You sound terrible."

I proceeded to tell her about the forest and how special it was and to explain that it meant more than almost anything else in the world to me. I told her about the footprints and the Snickers wrapper, Tommie, mom, dad, the farm and Jake. I shared about Great Grandfather and the deer and how he knew everything. All the pressure! All the fear came tumbling out. There was silence on the other end.

"I know." she said. "I read Waldwick this weekend."

"The whole thing?"

"Yes. The entire book! Your family is so noble and your great-great-great-great-great grandfather was incredible. The sacrifices he made and the decisions of decency so great, I had tears in my eyes. I hope you don't mind, I loaned "Waldwick" to my mom and dad to read. They need to see the dignity of the family of the man who has become my friend."

I had tears in my eyes. "What do I do?" realizing that I cry a lot! "What can you do when you have no idea what's going on and the only person who can tell you is a 94 -year-old blind Indian residing in an assisted living center in Wisconsin Dells who speaks to you in voices?"

"Relax. I'd rub your shoulders if I was there, but I won't be home until late." She said.

My God I wanted her touch, her smell and see her smile. It was all building inside of me. I took a deep breath and replied, "Thank you for listening"

"Thank you for calling me," Amy responded.

Sleep did not come. I lay in bed and twisted and turned. Thursday had almost become a day I dreaded and now I couldn't wait. I needed to see Great Grandfather. The pressure of the LSAT's was building and I knew that Amy and I needed to cool it. Every minute of every day was becoming critical. I texted her Monday night and told her that all was cool, hoping that she would believe me. We agreed to meet Thursday night at Paisan's. After that, it was going to be a long weekend as she prepped for the exam and even the time on Thursday would be short.

Monday and Tuesday at the factory were a blur. My mind was focused on only one thing…Great Grandfather. Wednesday was prep day for social media and I went through the fundamentals. I could have done them in my sleep. I was preparing a power point for our next marketing meeting and researching all kinds of things including market synergies, cookies and using Google to expand our reach. I contacted plastic card companies about manufacturing costs, liabilities, counterfeit, fraud and concepts and added them to the presentation. My goal was not to show up the Ass kissers, but see if we couldn't begin dialogue beyond outdoor advertising and mentions here and there.

White Cloud: Finally, Thursday arrived. It was the first warm day in May. At 8:00 am sharp, I got in the Jeep and drove to the Dells, arriving at 9:20. I went to Mickey D's and had a sausage and egg biscuit and a glass of orange juice and made sure I was in the parking lot of the assisted living center at 9:55 am, walking into Great Grand Father's room at exactly 10:00 am.

As always, Great Grandfather was sitting in his rocking chair with the shawl over his legs. As I entered, his head rose and he smiled. "Little Spirit, you are here and we have much to talk about. The spirits have told me that you are worried". Again, the shit was being scared out of me. "Pull up the cedar chest and hold my hands."

I did as I was told and Great Grandfather's eyes began rolling back into his head as his chant began. Hoiyah. Hoiyah. Hoiyah. Great Grandfather sat with my hands in his. His chant was taking him to another time and another world. After the other sessions, I knew that it was useless to turn on the recorder. I also knew that what was about to be spoken would be burned into my memory forever.

Great Grandfather's voice changed and was unlike anything before. Gone was the soft whisper. Gone was the gentle lilt. In its place was a much harsher tone that I had never heard before.

"I am White Cloud, leader of the Winnebago as the white man calls my people. How can I explain our confusion? All we asked was to live in peace and let the Great Father decide when to call us home. Instead, the white man arrives and brings with him sickness like we have never seen, weapons like we have never experienced and sadness like we have never known. How can man be so brutal to so many others in the name of a few furs? How can a man tell me that my Great Spirit means nothing, simply because he believes in something else and throws that which is sacred to us in the river? How can this be when we have lived without the white man for so many moons?"

"We moved our villages many times simply to remain at peace and yet the white man and those who have aligned with him have not allowed us tranquility. We have done our best to live with those called the French and yet all we do is not enough. In 1718, in the white man's years, the French attacked our homes using their fire sticks and burned our villages. There was no concern for women and children! There was no concern for those too old to fight! Instead many of my people died and yet no one mourns. We cannot bury those who did not live. We cannot honor those who have come before. All we can do is run and hide ... escape from those who have brought so much death to my people."

"A warrior can only allow this to happen for so long until he must fight back. To kill for any reason is not right and yet to kill to defend a life or the lives of many is not wrong. For nearly ten years we fought the French with many warriors until, in the year 1726, we agreed that we would leave and live in peace. What kind of peace is it that only lasts for two summers? What kind of man is it that promises forever and then destroys our villages on our Great Lake and takes away the lives of so many? Is this peace? Is this honor? Is this the way of the white man? Promise everything and give nothing?"

"We could not live as one nation when many of us believed that there would be peace with the white man while others believed that the only peace the Winnebago would ever know was when it was the silence that comes in death. I took those who think like me and we left those who disagreed and moved to Carcajou Point on a lake called Koshkonong. We left family. We left friends, brothers and sisters, but did so in the name of survival."

"While we are Winnebago, we were not willing to live with those unwilling to defend our land. In 1729, a great meeting was held with our brothers from the Fox and it was agreed that we must remove these invaders once and for all from what was ours."

"We, the Winnebago, and our brothers the Fox, attacked the French and those who said our Great Father did not exist. We made certain that they understood that to take our land, our way of life and our freedom would not come without great cost. Our numbers were small and yet the French called this the Fox War. We fought with bows- and-arrows and with axes against those who had firesticks that made holes in our bodies but not in the resolve for what we fought. For five summers we fought the French with many lives lost on both sides. For five summers we defended what was ours and yet, for every battle won, for every warrior killed, there came more and more and more to fight us, arriving from somewhere to overwhelm our lives as if we were but blades of grass upon which they could trample."

"Not all white men came to conquer. Some came to be our allies and to allow us to understand the ways of those who invaded our lands. No one needs death without honor. Captain Pierre Martin came to our village and explained that in order to have peace, we must allow the French to live in our land. Our elders listened to this man and, because so many of us had seen our children die, agreed to allow these people live. In the name of peace, we took our families and all that was ours and moved from Lake Pepin to a river that no one wanted, filled with rocks so large that even the best of those who could manage our canoes could not travel downstream. Our land was the garbage the white man did not want."

"We moved in the name of peace and the name of survival. We could not foresee the future just like we could not tell you about the sun and wind of tomorrow and yet I, White Cloud could see an end to the beginning. Like the snow that falls each winter, more would come and we, the Winnebago, would be forced to move many times in the name of peace. How sad. How true. We must always remember who we are and always pray that the Great Spirit will look over us no matter where it is that we live."

With that, Great Grandfather's eyes pulled back and his hands went limp. All the energy in his body had been used to bring White Cloud to me, to allow his story to be told. My God, the first forced move of the Winnebago. How sad to know that there would be so many more. Great Grandfather sighed a deep breath and I knew it was time for me to leave. I quietly rose and slid the old cedar chest back to the end of the bed. I wanted to peek inside, but thought better than invade his privacy. What could an old man store besides memories?

As I was about to leave, his eyes opened and he spoke..."There is much to be afraid of Little Spirit. What happened to my people can happen again. The spirits are restless and you need to help them. Please help them find peace." I had no idea what Great Grandfather was talking about. The ride home was mundane and introspective. I was hearing the true story of all that happened. There was no whitewash and certainly no bull shit, just sadness…profound, incredible sadness. Great Grandfather's plea on the end did not sink in.

Paisan's: With so much "social" activity entering my life, my mind hadn't wandered to Amy much…well OK…about every ten seconds or so…and I think that was good for both of us. Too fast, would scare her away and that was the very last thing I wanted to do. With the pressure on her, I almost wanted to call off dinner, but I really needed to see her. The session with Great Grandfather had been intense and I thought we both needed a respite.

I arrived at Paisan's at 6:15 and parked in the lower garage. I went in and Emily, the hostess, remembered me. I asked for one of the small booths down the dead end of the first corridor by the front desk. She asked if I wanted the one on the far end and I said that would be perfect. I told her that I needed to wait for Amy and she went and had the table set. I spent twenty cents and bought two breath mints just to make sure.

At precisely 6:30, Amy walked in. Her hair was back under a black baseball cap. She was wearing a black turtle neck and black jeans and had small gold studs in as earrings. I looked at her and she at me and we both smiled. Mine was warm. Hers seemed strained. I could already sense the pressure. I let her sit first and she chose looking out the window at the beige brick wall of her condo next door. I took my place opposite her, facing the wooden partition. I had the better view. I got to see her. Her normally wide-open eyes were half closed in tension.

"You OK?" I asked.

She gave me a weak nod and smile. "I've been studying all day and have a terrible headache.

She didn't need to say anymore.

"Anything I can do?"

"Be patient and tolerant."

I held out my hands and she placed hers in mine. She was trembling. "Listen, you went to Georgetown and got a double major in four years. I'm certain that you did fine in school. You took pre-law and probably aced the courses. She nodded in the affirmative. "You took the ACT and SAT's to get into college and I'm certain they went well." Again, affirmative! "You have been studying that cute little ass of yours off for months" She smiled. "And, you've got me rooting for you. What else could you ask for?"

"I just want it all to be over!"

"Nine days and its done. Nine days and you take the test and the rest is history."

"Í know, but I'm scared."

"Scared of the test? Scared of yourself or scared that you won't live up to what you THINK your father is expecting?"

Her eyebrows raised.

"Ok, Sweetie." I replied.

With that her hands pulled away from mine. "Why did you call me Sweetie?"

I shrugged my shoulders and shook my head. "I don't know. Did I offend you? If so, I'm sorry and I'll never say it again, I promise."

"That's what my dad has called me since I was a little girl. It's his special name for me."

"Then let's save it for him."

"I liked it."

"I still think we should save it for your dad, as you will always be his little girl. There's absolutely nothing wrong with that and I honor it as I honor you and the relationship you have with your family. Family is the most important thing we have. Without family, there is nothing … just a deep abyss of singularity."

She smiled and grasped my wrists.

"You are a very special man, Mr. George Terrill the Fourth."

Now it was my time to blush. Thank God, I was saved by the server.

I ordered an Italian beef sandwich with fries. She ordered a small salad. I asked if she wanted any wine and she shook her head 'no'. She was in training for the LSAT and nothing was going to cloud her mind.

I looked deep into her big brown eyes and watched the light reflect off her pupils. I was entranced.

"What are you looking at?" she inquired.

"I was trying to peek into your heart to see what you are feeling."

"Fear…nothing but apprehension and fear."

"Nothing warm and tingly about the handsome man sitting across from you?" I teased.

A slight smile came across her face and then it broadened into a grin. "You!" as she shook her head.

She changed the subject asking how Great Grandfather was and I told her of White Cloud and the 1700's. By her facial expressions, I know she thought I was full of beans, but my intensity and sincerity quickly convinced her that what I was saying was real.

"How does it feel to be talking to dead people?" Amy asked.

I don't talk, I just listen". I responded. "However, after some of the professors I had, it doesn't seem that much different."

She smiled her girly smile which I adored.

"At first I thought I would just record everything. Three times, when I got home, the recorder had nothing on it and yet I remembered everything."

"Bad recorder?"

"Nope? I actually tested it, you know…'testing 1-2-3". I said as I held my fist like a microphone and went into a horrible rendition of a radio announcer.

"Spooky."

"My voice?" I said with intended levity.

"No, ding-dong. Nothing on the tape."

"At first yes, now, I'm used to it. I am a highly trained professional reporter, you know" I said in jest. "Who doesn't have a clue what's going on. What's really bizarre is that Rodney and

Ann think it's all so normal, while I'm getting the proverbial shit scared out of me." Another girly giggle. Time to switch back to reality … "Where is the LSAT?"

"Bascom Hall."

"What time?"

"9:00 to 3:00."

"How are you getting there?"

"Driving?"

"There's no parking around Bascom, even on a Saturday."

"I'll Uber."

"Nope! I'll be sitting out front at 8:15 as I pointed to the brick wall out the window behind me and drive you. I'll be standing outside in front of Abe Lincoln's statue at 2:30 in case you finish early."

"You don't need to do that."

"There are a lot of things I don't need to do, but there are things I want to do and one of them is to take one less hassle off your plate."

There was a bashful smile on Amy's face as she said "cool."

The food came and I ate while she picked at hers.

"Come on, eat your food," I implored, but Amy kept picking.

I went into my God-awful impersonation of an African American woman with my falsetto voice. "Eat dem greens. You ain't gonna get no fat ass frum dem, so youz better eat dem all."

Amy burst out laughing as I got serious. "Let's look at what happens if, and I certainly don't believe you will **not** pass the LSAT. Gee, the incredibly intelligent, highly educated, beautiful, young lady with the fantastic personality and gift for gab could re -take the test or ONLY have to get a job in business where she would be extremely successful in a very, very short period of time. That isn't a bad consolation prize."

"You don't understand."

I got more serious. "Let's me see if this is right. Beautiful young lady has a very dynamic father whom she loves and adores. Beautiful young lady has always done everything she possibly could to make him happy and has excelled at everything. Beautiful young lady is striving for perfection because she believes that is what her father expects?"

She nodded in the affirmative. "He is so successful and came from nothing. He wants his only daughter to achieve the way he achieved and that means a law degree from Harvard, Yale, Princeton or the University of Chicago."

"Gee. My old man only asks that I don't touch the cows in a naughty way or bring cow shit in the house."

Once again, a girlie giggle as I continued, "Let's take dad out of the equation. Now, let's look at the LSAT. It's a multiple-choice test that focuses on logic and legal doctrine. Other than your current choice in men, you seem both logical and I'm certain well versed in basic law. Half of the folks taking the test will be taking it for the umpteenth time because they haven't been half as serious as you have. Another segment will be totally lost because they aren't as intelligent as you are or as dynamic. That leaves a teeny, weeny" as I put my fingers close together "group who might, and I say **might,** be at your level. Now Miss Amy Goodbody, don't you see that if you play it cool and_forget the stress, you'll be just fine."

Amy leaned back into the bench and smiled her infectious smile. I think I got through to her. Anyway, I hoped so. The check came and as I went to pick it up, she grabbed it.

"My treat Doctor Q". I shook my head but knew that it would be disrespectful.

As we stood, she waited and put her hand in mine. I liked that. We walked into the lobby as if the hand-holding was telling all those who knew her at Paisan's that we were a couple. You couldn't have wiped the shit-eating grin off my face with a spatula.

As we walked out of Paisan's entrance, she pulled me around the corner, near the ramp that went down to the parking garage and gave me deep passionate kiss. I tasted the oil vinaigrette dressing and it tasted good.

We stopped and I added, "I'm going to walk you to your front door and then let you go back to your studies, Miss Amy Goodbody. You have to promise me that tonight, when you're all done studying, you'll get into that great big shower of yours and turn on the water as hot as you can stand it and relax before you go to bed."

"I promise." she replied, paused and then added. "Would you mind if, while I'm in that great big shower, I imagined you were in there with me?"

Wow! Yiikes! Jiminy Crickets! As we walked hand-in-hand all of fifty feet and stopped in front of lahdeedah estates.

Pausing I declared. "Now turn around."

She looked at me with apprehension but did as I requested. I took my fingers and splayed them on her shoulders and used my thumbs to begin massaging the base of her neck. It was the first time I had touched any part of her body except her hands and lips. Her shoulders were square and I could feel the developed muscles from her investment in weight training and a cardio program.

"Oh my God." was her whispered response as she succumbed to the advances of my hands with her head moving from side-to-side. We spent several minutes standing in front of her building with me massaging her back, neck and shoulders.

"Turn around please and hold out your arms." I instructed. Again, she abided and I massaged each forearm and then her hands, taking extra effort to focus on each individual finger. Finally, I massaged her forehead and took my thumbs to her temples and finally gently her ear lobes. I could tell by her expression that she was enjoying it. "Feel better?"

"Oh, my God...More. More. More."

"Another time. You need to go study." I responded.

Amy put her hands around the back of my waist and pulled me in until we were touching from nose-to-knees. Our tongues met and for an instant we were one, parallel in thought, mind and emotion. My heart was racing and I knew we needed to stop or the urgency would overwhelm both of us and I wanted to follow Great Grandfather's advice. "slow and steady".

She kissed me on the lips and leaned back.

"Where did you learn how to do such a great massage?"

"I took a class in massage therapy. I thought it would be a great way to meet girls."

"Did you?"

"Just a bunch of gay guys, but they were cool."

"I certainly hope you got an "A.""

"An 'A' for effort. But, I need to practice."

"You can practice on me anytime." Amy responded.

"Not tonight." I replied. "You need to study."

Again, our lips met and we both knew it was time for her to go back to reality. As our lips parted, her face brushed mine as she leaned into my left shoulder. "Next time…I want a total massage," she whispered as her tongue slid in my ear as she then pulled back and kissed me quickly on the lips.

At first, I was startled and then simply smiled and nodded toward the condo front door. Amy turned and walked into the lobby, realizing I wasn't following. I watched as the elevator came and she stopped. I was then she turned and blew me a kiss, which was incredibly cool because I'd never had anyone do that before. The elevator doors closed and a couple of seconds later my phone dinged, telling me I had a text.

"Thank you…Sweetie." was all it said.

Having only a goodnight air kiss was really special but still tough, especially after the "total massage" teaser. When I got home it must have shown. Big Brother had just returned from the factory and was sitting at the kitchen table eating a snack. "See her again?"

"Yup."

"As exciting as the other times?"

"She's got the LSAT's next Saturday and is totally stressed out."

"Where'd you go?"

"Paisan's"

"Again?"

"She lives next door."

"In the Capitol Towers?"

"Yeah, how did you know?"

"The Dells has a high roller who has a condo there. You gotta have big bucks to live at Capitol Towers!"

"It's her dad's place" I responded.

"What her last name?"

I shrugged my shoulders.

"You've been out with here three or four times and you don't know her last name?"

"It's never come up. But her first name is Amelia like Amelia Earhart."

"Have you been in her condo?"

"Do you remember the number?"

"805."

"I'll Google it."

Rodney went to the computer and Googled the tower and it came back unlisted as he noted. "This might take some doing."

"I want to send her flowers next Friday. Do you think that's cool?" I asked.

"Ask Ann."

Geez, even he didn't know if flowers were cool.

Next morning as Ann was sipping her coffee, I asked her if flowers were cool under the circumstances and she said yes.

Rodney got up and came into the kitchen asking, "Do you have any idea who you are dating?"

"A beautiful woman who has yet to reject me?"

"Any idea who her daddy is?"

"Nope"

"Douglas, The Duke, Williams."

I shook my head with no idea who he was talking about.

"One of, if not the richest man in Wisconsin."

"Huh?"

"Daddy started out as a lawyer, got into real estate and owns half of Milwaukee, along with his law firm and a lot of car dealerships and this huge investment firm, among other things."

"Does it say that last summer his daughter worked as a waitress at Paisan's and is delivering packages for UPS?" I asked.

"Q, this dude is REAL money."

"You know I don't care about that. Money has ruined as many people as it has helped. All I want to be is happy and that means feeling wanted, needed and loved. How do I send her flowers on Friday so that she knows I care about her LSAT's and about her?"

Ann interjected. "I don't know where you two are in the relationship, but there must be something that you can do that will let her know the flowers are for her and you are trying to help her be relaxed about the test."

"I gave her a shoulder massage". Duh! "I could say good luck on the LSAT, but then I'm going to drive her to the exam. I don't want to infer anything physical. I know. I lectured her on not being so tense and said, "STOP AND SMELL THE ROSES.""

Ann smiled and recited my now common expression…"Cool." Even Big Brother thought it was neat.

I called Felly's flowers and ordered a dozen red roses. I gave them the address and they said they knew the building and would call security. They asked who I wanted the card to be signed by and I told them "Q". It took about three minutes to explain the letter "Q". I think the lady was a little miffed when I asked her if she knew how to spell it.

"Nothing more?" the Felly's lady asked.

"Not really". I replied. I thought about putting Sweetie, but not yet.

My days were normal. I could only imagine the growing pressure. Amy's absence was simply killing me.

LSAT: It was Saturday morning and I got to her condo at 8:00. At exactly 8:15 she came out of the elevator. The stress was etched on her forehead. She got in and looked at me.

"The flowers are beautiful."

"Thank you."

"I stopped and smelled them about a dozen times."

She leaned back and took a deep breath as I asked, "Are you ready?"

"As ready as I will ever be."

"Let's go slay the dragon," I reiterated.

"God, I'll be glad when this is over."

"Remember. This is for you!"

"Will you rub my shoulders when this is over?"

I was about to get cute and say I would rub anything she wanted, but stopped myself. "Be cool Q. Be cool."

We got to Bascom Hall in ten minutes. I parked in the handicapped spot using my yet-to-expire, temporary sticker and told her I would explain later. I reiterated the plan and leaned over to kiss her good luck. Instead she just got out of the car and headed in the side door. OUCH.

I had five hours to kill and headed home and wrote more about White Cloud. At two, I got in the Jeep and headed back to Bascom. It was really windy. As I was standing there, it started to rain. Not a soft pleasant rain, but one of those cold, angular, wind-swept mothers, where Wisconsin gets to remind us that Mother Nature is still the boss.

I'd promised myself I would be out in front of Abe at two-thirty in case she got done earlier. I got out and stood under my umbrella and waited and waited and waited. At 3:30, she walked out and saw me standing there. She looked like a total wreck.

"How was it?" I asked.

"Tough. How long have you been standing here?"

"Don't know, about an hour." I said.

"Your feet and pant legs are soaking wet and you've got to be freezing."

"I've been doing a survey."

Amy looked at me, frowned and asked. "What kind of survey?"

I tactfully replied. "Legend has it that the statue of Abe Lincoln will stand up any time a virgin walks by. He's been sitting the entire time. In fact, a couple times I think he even tried to lay down, whatever that means. Come on you've got to walk by."

Amy giggled her girly laugh and that broke the ice as she noted. "We need to get you out of those wet clothes."

My imagination started running rampant as she added. "Come on, let's get you dried off, silly boy."

We went to her place and she gave me her dad's bathrobe.

"Put this on and I'll dry your clothes"

Not what I had in mind, but getting closer. I slid out of my jeans and underwear and Badger sweatshirt and into the plush robe. I walked into the living room and she was staring out the window at the gray Lake Monona. The lake rarely had the white caps it had. Those were saved for Lake Mendota and why Lake Monona was called Fairy Water by Rodney's ancestors.

While still looking out the window Amy noted. "I think I did all right, but there were a couple of questions that were really tough."

"I'll bet you did fine," I said reassuringly.

"I hope so."

I put my hands on her shoulders and massaged her neck and back as Amy whispered, "God, that feels good."

With that, she turned towards me. Our eyes met and she pulled me close to her. Without taking her eyes off my face, she pulled me in and we were nose -to-knee again and she kissed me, slow and deep. Without looking down, she undid the belt of the robe and slid her hands around my bare back. "Did I say thank you for the roses? Did I say thank you for making me realize that this is for me and not my dad? Did I say thank you for driving me and waiting in the rain today? Did I say thank you just for being you?"

With that she opened up the bathrobe and slid herself in. It felt good to have her next to my bare body even though she was still dressed. It felt good to feel her warmth and hear her breathe. It felt good to feel wanted. We kissed as her hands slid around and pulled me in.

"I think I need to unwind, don't you?"

"Uh huh." Yet another profound response from the literary genius.

Amy looked up at me and inquired. "I think a hot shower and a massage would feel good. How about you?"

"Uh huh" Boy was I being the great conversationalist. "Uh huh."

Amy was just reaching for her belt buckle when her cell phone rang and it startled her as she proclaimed, "Shit. It's my mother." I learned later that each person had their own ringtone in her phone.

Amy went to the kitchen and got her phone. I listened, but didn't, as she talked with her mom. I could tell from the conversation that a surprise visit was about to take place. Oops!

"My parents are by East Towne and wanted to surprise me and take me out to dinner."

I reluctantly understood as Amy shut off the dryer and handed me my warm, damp clothes while offering or was that commanding, "Here put these on."

"I better leave" I said.

Amy's frown grew deeper as she asked. "Why? I just don't want them to meet you in my father's bathrobe."

"But I'm not dressed very well and it was supposed to be their surprise celebration".

"Mom knows all about you."

"What?"

I told her about you when I went home. I told her that I had met this really nice guy who's really funny and makes me feel special."

Now it was my turn to have a shit-eating grin.

"Did you tell her I was a white boy?"

"You're not white, you are light brown, remember?"

My shoes were soaked and my hair was still wet. I knew I was going to make a really great first impression.

The bell rang from the elevator and we knew they were on their way up.

Amy's parents were of average height and normal weight and were in their late forties or early fifties. Their clothes looked expensive and Mrs. Williams engagement ring was a real rock. There's something about rich people because they know how to dress. Everything was coordinated and looked expensive, simply because it was.

"Mom, Dad this is my friend, George."

Both parents nodded. I was certain that neither agreed to seeing what looked like a drowned white rat in their daughter's apartment.

Amy got the drift and explained that I stood for an hour in the rain waiting for her after the LSAT and my shoes were soaked.

"The Duke" put the fear of God in me. With a name like THE Duke, I was expecting some really big macho guy. Instead he was about my size and was a little shit. I could only imagine what was going through his head. He had piercing blue eyes that burned right through me and he rarely smiled. But then, I don't know how much I would be smiling if I walked into my daughter's apartment to find some guy in his bare feet, but I guess that would be better than in his bathrobe.

"The flowers are beautiful" Amy's mom said.

Amy responded that I'd sent them and encouraged her mother to read the card. With that there was a broad smile on Amy's mother's face. I learned later that it was one of her favorite slogans for Amy because Mrs. Williams thought Amy was too much like her dad in that way.

We had a brief conversation with each sentence on my part ending in sir or mam. I told them that I had a conflict and was glad Amy wasn't going to be alone on her celebratory night. It was all bullshit, but I felt like the fifth wheel.

Amy looked at me and her big brown eyes narrowed. It was a look I'd never seen before. "Is it REALLY something you need to do? I REALLY would like to have you join us for dinner. Please."

I acquiesced and said I would make a call to see if I could change my plans if Mr. and Mrs. Williams didn't mind. Amy's mom was first to respond. "It would be great to have you join us, if you can, George." Duke didn't say much as he was still sizing me up like some rusty old Chevy he saw at an auction house…bald tires, cracked windshield, rusted fenders…not worth much.

I excused myself and made a fake phone call and came back and said I could join them. I asked if it would be ok if I went home and changed and met them for dinner at the restaurant. It was agreed.

The Duke called someone and reported that we had 6:00 PM reservations at L'EToile across the square. Holy shit! The fanciest restaurant in Madison and the most expensive and virtually impossible to get into and he did it on a quick call. It was then I realized that my Jeep was parked in his stall in the basement. God!

"Sir, I must apologize. When I brought Amy home and didn't want her to get wet, I pulled into your parking space. If you would like, I'll be more then glad to pull my car out and park yours for you."

This seemed to catch Duke off guard. He wasn't expecting a logical explanation that focused on the wellbeing of his daughter, plus an apology and an offer.

"It's still raining hard and there's no sense both of us getting wet." I added.

The Duke smiled and handed me the keys. "Black Mercedes out on the street."

"Yes sir".

I went downstairs and pulled my Jeep out and carefully parked his Mercedes and not just any Mercedes in spot 805. It was a new AMG-S65 Cabriolet coupe. This was the Batmobile's big brother. This car was so expensive that when I got out, I took my shirt sleeve and wiped the water from the door sill.

I looked at the key fob and realized there was no elevator key. I rang the bell and Amy answered. "Heh, you, there's no elevator key on the fob," I announced.

"I'll ring you up. Better yet, I'll come down."

The elevator came down as amy lip smacked me a good one. "Mom's in love with you. The fake conflict was brilliant and dad thinks it's cool that you were willing to get his car and park it in his stall. Now go home and get dressed and meet us at the restaurant. Slacks and sports coat, but no tie would be cool."

Another quick lip-smack. "Oh, and I do want to start in where we left off when they're gone, but they will probably stay the night."

With that she was in the elevator and gone. I just smiled. She was getting back to being her old, funny, self and I was loving it! Love is probably the wrong word, but she really did have a spell on me.

I went home and Big Brother was getting ready to head to the factory for the late, late shift.

"How did the test go?" He asked.

"She probably did fine. I stood out in the rain for an hour and was soaked and was at her apartment drying my clothes when her parents called to say they had come to Madison to take her out. We're going to L'EToile for dinner."

"Holy cow! That place is really expensive."

"I know. I'm glad her dad's paying as there's no way I could afford it. By the way, he's got the big brother to your Batmobile and I got to drive it".

"Really? The AMG63? Black or silver?"

"Black."

"And you got to drive it?"

"Yup, all the way from the street into the parking garage."

"Do you know how much those cost? A quarter of a million dollars." He answered not waiting for my reply. "You can't break up with her until I get to drive it."

"Geez!" I was still trying hard to remove profanity from my vocabulary as I didn't think a gentleman would continue to use it after college. Man was I changing or what?

I took a shower and shaved and brushed my teeth and put on my best khaki pants and a light blue JC Penny Stafford button-down shirt and navy sport coat. I didn't think tennis shoes would look too cool and so I got out my one pair of hard sole shoes and did the old Rodney shoe polish trick on the back of my pant legs.

As I was primping myself, Ann walked in. "Must be a hot date." she said.

"Amy's parents." I replied.

"This must be getting serious."

"No, just inconvenient" I said.

Having said that and leaving imaginations to settle in, I was out the door and timed it so that I found a parking spot and walked into the restaurant at exactly 5:58 and stood and waited as they walked in. I smiled, they smiled and then the hostess took us to our table with yet another incredible view of the Capitol.

The Duke noted that he never got enough of the Capitol. I added a little of the Capitol history, not only to enhance the conversation, but show Amy that I was reading her book.

The wine list was brought and Duke asked what kind of wine I liked and Amy answered Pinot Noir. Mrs. Williams said it was her favorite too. Duke said he would order a bottle for the three of us and that he would have a double scotch of some fancy stuff that was fifty years old.

The menu was in French. Mrs. Williams and Amy were fluent in the language as Mrs. Williams had been raised on the French side of St. Martin and studied In Paris. Thank God, because I didn't have a clue. The food was incredible and was only exceeded by the conversation and beauty of the girl across the table from me. We talked about school, growing up on a farm and my job and how it was expanding. I kept away from the book. How does one explain that every Thursday he meets with a ninety-four-year-old blind man who talks to dead Indians?

I asked Mr. Williams about what he did and pretended not to know. He said that he was an investment counselor. The Duke didn't want to talk about his job. Amy interceded and informed me that her mother was a pediatric oncologist at Milwaukee Children's Hospital. Was I in over my head or what?

We ate dinner and had a light desert. When all was done, the waiter came and placed the bill in front of me. I almost had a heart attack. It was $1200. I looked at it and then closed my eyes and pulled the bill towards me. Nary a word was said and I reached for my wallet and slid the American Excess card in the folio. The waiter took the folio and came back with a total of $1500 including tip.

I took the pen and was about to sign my name when The Duke spoke up. "Son, Amy has said a lot of great things about you and one of them is that you are kind and generous. I have a central bill here and there is no charge to your American Express card."

With that he smiled. It had been his way of testing me to check my level of integrity. I guess both Amy and I had taken tests and I think we both passed. I looked at Amy and she smiled at me and we knew the next round had begun.

Mrs. Williams spoke first. "Well, Don, I need to use the ladies' room and you need to as well." I hoped he wasn't using the ladies' room, but then smart-ass me kept his mouth shut and only chuckled to himself. The move was Mrs. Williams' way of giving us a couple of minutes alone. She was a classy and I might add, gorgeous lady.

Amy sat and smiled, a proud smile as Daddy had put what was now her boyfriend through the paces and he had passed. This was no easy task and yet dating the daughter of someone so dynamic and so proud of his daughter to the point that only he called her Sweetie, meant the test had to be tough and it certainly was.

The Williams returned and The Duke announced that the car was waiting. I walked out with them, holding the door as Amy brushed her hand on mine sending electricity through my entire body. "Goodnight and thank you for the wonderful evening," I responded.

The Duke spoke as he held the car door for Mrs. Williams. "Son, it was nice meeting you. I hope to see you again." His tone was softer and sincere as he firmly grabbed my hand and shook it.

"Thank you, sir," I replied as I closed the door for Amy. "I hope so, too."

I drove home. Ann was cuddled up on the couch watching TV with a fire in the fireplace. It was only ten and yet everyone was beat.

"And?" Ann asked.

I just smiled a big, crazy smile.

"That good?" Ann inquired.

"Better." I filled her in on all the details, the meal, the French. What I think I ate and then the bill.

Ann just shook her head. "What would have happened if you had to pay?"

"I'd be there washing dishes for a few weeks."

As I went to my room, my phone dinged. It was from Amy. Her text said... "Congratulations, you got a perfect score... Goodnight Sweetie."

May: March is the rough month in Wisconsin. You're sick of winter and feel as if it will never end. April is the fickle month when you are tempted yet know there can be days when things will still be bad. May, ah May, that's when it all begins again, four months of the best weather there Is.

After Amy's LSAT and meeting her mom and The Duke, our relationship became more 'stable' if you want to call it that. We talked everyday as she went back to UPS and I kept up my routine...with Monday and Tuesday at the factory and then Wednesday through Friday writing and meeting with Great Grandfather and creating the 2000 words per week. The marketing program was put on hold for a while as everyone was too busy.

The following weekend, Amy had plans. I wanted to know what but knew better. Ask too many questions and people think you're getting possessive. Don't ask any questions and they think you're indifferent. She texted me on Sunday and said that she missed me and she would explain. It was none of my business, but I still wanted to know. All week long the texts flew back and forth and I was loving it. On Tuesday, I asked if she wanted to go out on Saturday and she said yes. Needless to say, there was a big smile on my face. Whoopee!

Saturday night came and time to celebrate the end of the LSAT's. Madison, being a college town, has plenty of bars and restaurants. I had asked her where she wanted to go and she said where we could dance. While Madison has its social scene, there weren't any "clubs" as she called them and we ended up driving to Milwaukee and hitting a spot where there were a few white boys and incredible music.

It took nearly 90 minutes to get to the club and there was a long line to get in and a $20.00 per person cover charge. $40.00! Wow. Amy took me by the hand and walked up to the VIP entrance and a guy that made Rodney look small smiled and the rope came down.

I looked at her and she shook her head. "Long story" was all she said as we walked inside and as I was about to pay the cover charge was politely told that it was "on the house."

I found the entire environment different and exciting as the sounds and people pulsed to the music that pounded in my ears. The level was so intense both acoustically and physically that we couldn't talk. The night was to be action, physical action, engulfed in the primeval arousal of one's senses created and manipulated by intense music rushing through one's ears and into their bones, cascading across every inhibition and negating any sense of decorum.

Amy was loving it! I was loving it! We were releasing the energies that had already been created between us. She had worn what was considered traditional club garb...a very short skirt and tight black tee-shirt that left nothing and I mean nothing to the imagination while I was in traditional jeans and felt completely out of place.

Farm boys from Waldwick, Wisconsin aren't known for their dancing skills, but girls who have soul really know how to dance as they let the rhythm of the music enter their bodies. Mix in the Franco/Spanish/Caribbean influence and oh my God could this woman dance. She put her purse in a locker and gave me the key and we headed for the dance floor. It seemed as if each note penetrated her body and set her nerves in motion. I watched as another side of her came out...rhythmic, like a cat, almost in an erotic manner. Her shoulders kept time to the music while her hands, hips, arms, feet and thighs moved to the rhythm of her soul.

Her body was lithe as she moved in a syncopated rhythm to the beat, making even dorky me seem fluid at times. She had to teach me how to dance. She'd holler right and I'd stick out my left foot. Boy, did she have work to do! Finally, she pulled me close and put her hands on my hips as we danced together to the pulsating sound of who knows what. She was in paradise, moving to the music, keeping a beat, her mind wandering somewhere, anywhere, everywhere!

We worked up a sweat and she wanted more, looking deep into my eyes and lighting me up, she just smiled. She took my hands and placed them on her hips so that I could feel the motion. Left, in, right, out. Left, in, right, out. As the tempo increased, left and right were simply eliminated and her hips began moving in pelvic thrusts. This was the dance style of our generation I was accustomed to and yet, from her, it seemed so much more. As the tempo slowed, she moved her arms above her head and moved to the music, never taking her eyes off me. A slight smile crossed her face. My God, if her goal was to **not** seduce me, she was doing a terrible job as my nerves went on edge in a sense of neural overload.

Her light brown curls became plastered to her forehead, glued with sweat, as our hips gyrated in a manner so close to public concupiscence, I couldn't believe it. Every now and then, a slow song would come on and she would pull me close and let me feel her sweating body emanate its heat as it radiated through my libido. She put her arms around my shoulders and pulled me in.

She was teasing me and I was breathing hard and not only from just the physical strain of the dancing. I was being tortured and she was loving it. I was experiencing her and feeling her in a primal way and wanting her in many, many more. Who was this woman? Why me? I should have wondered. I no longer cared. The sensuous electricity was almost withering as my eyes wandered throughout the masses and I saw that we were not alone. Couples engaged in rituals. Symbiotic rituals of interaction… beyond human, almost spiritual, yet totally, profoundly sexy. This was the way it was and the way she wanted it to be.

She smiled and kissed me. I was nearing purgatory as she slid her tongue in my mouth and pulled my hands down until they were on her butt. She wanted to dance and I wanted to…well, you know. We danced until the wee hours and I was simply exhausted. It was nearly two when we got into the Jeep and began the drive back from Milwaukee. She leaned back in her seat and all the way home I got to glance at two light brown thighs in a skirt that almost reached never, never land.

As we reached parking spot 805 in her condo parking garage the kisses in the Jeep were long and hard and God I wanted to stay. However, logic overcame my hormones as I said goodnight. She was disappointed until I explained I had to go home to Waldwick. I'd promised my family I'd go to church in the morning and help my parents celebrate their 25th wedding anniversary. Damn parents! Why couldn't they have been married some other time of the year except that weekend, twenty-five years ago?

She smiled! I smiled! She said thank you for a wonderful evening. I did too. All I could do was smile and then smile some more, a smile that stayed plastered on my face all the way back to the cottage. My God! This woman was weaving a spell on me that I could hardly stand.

I think I slept, but who knows when your mind is racing. I took my shower, grabbed a blueberry muffin and headed for Mineral Point. The road home was so familiar. I sat looking…seeing everything, feeling nothing but my wishes...hoping and praying that Amy would appear…a waif alongside the road, who would join me on my journey.

How incredibly strange to rearrange the thoughts within one's mind! To bend them, shape them, roll them into emotions that make you sincerely, incredibly, feel that, without another person, you simply can't go on. How could this be happening? Why, in the matter of a few heartbeats, had my heart been taken away? My body ached, not of pain, nor of lust, but simply of wanting that narcotizing feeling that smothered me and made my nerves tingle when we were together.

I couldn't stand it! The abyss was so profound! I craved that feeling of being alive that slid silently away when she was gone.

Was this love? Was this what Rodney and Ann felt? Was this what mom and dad felt so long ago? I drove on and my mind wandered back and forth from before until tomorrow. I could no longer imagine my life without her. I could see her in the windshield smiling at me. I could hear her voice, in the canvas that shivered on top of the jeep. I could smell her perfume and knew that what I saw, what I heard and what I smelled was nothing, absolutely nothing, compared to what I felt. Tears welled in my eyes. Were they tears of joy? Were they tears of remorse because, at that instant, I wanted nothing more than to be with her, to hold her, to feel her body next to mine, to hear her girly giggle and know that it was all just for me.

I drove carefully. One time almost dying is enough to last a long, long time. The familiar road was right before me and yet my thoughts wandered. Is this real? Is this going too fast? Does she feel the same? What if she doesn't? What happens then? What if she does? What happens then? I, the joker, I the clown, had taken off his mask and let his guard down. To stand naked in front of another physically and emotionally exposes one to so much potential pain and yet to not do so would mean regrets today, tomorrow, forever! Life is a gamble! Love is a gamble! What would it take to mend my broken heart, if all this was for naught? I shook my head and prayed for the best.

I headed for Minnie Point and knew there was nothing I could do except travel on, hoping that what lie ahead was a bed of roses and not a bed of thorns. We were so different and yet so much alike. In a few weeks, she had taken my cup-of-life and filled it to the brim.

I reflected! "Am I in love?" "Don't convince yourself "Q" I vowed. Do as Great Grandfather said and let it all flow naturally. I was holding on and yet, what was flowing was a torrent...an incredible rush that was overtaking me. "You're too young!" I countered to myself. However, when what you have, what you feel and what you have always sought, stands before you it's really, really tough. When you realize that it truly is what you will always desired, and could perhaps never be duplicated, never be replicated, and never be approximated again, you reach out and grasp the feeling and only pray that she feels the exactly same way.

I wondered if this was a game of hide-and-seek, where we hide our emotions as we seek an answer. Reality splattered on my windshield as the Mineral Point water tower came into view. My mind shifted to my parents. Would it be so obvious? Would the splendor in my heart radiate out as my eyes focused, not on today and my family obligation, but my yearning to simply go back to where I wanted to be….with her! I whispered to myself… "Slow down! Promise yourself to make sure it's not infatuation and she feels the same way." Slow down I repeated as I parked the jeep on High Street.

Mom and dad were in their favorite pew. Jesus left, about four rows back, but still in line with Reverend Taylor. Close enough to see and hear, but far enough not to be more than just members of the congregation. They were dressed up. I was in jeans! Dad was not happy with that! I slid in as the organ began playing and sat next to mom. Tommie and Heather were on dad's side. It was the first time I ever saw Heather and could see that they were serious.

The respite of church and its solemnity couldn't eradicate the thoughts within me! I ached from exhaustion. Lack of sleep and Amy deprivation! It was a nice day and mom and dad were glad I made a formal, if physically blighted, presence. Boy did I need some sleep! We went out for brunch and mom could tell her son was exhausted and it had been a long night.

We went back to the house and I sat down and zonked out. Mom let me sleep for a few hours and when I awoke, dad was getting into his overalls. The cows were calling! Happy 25th mom and dad! I can only hope that the feelings I have are those within their hearts. I can only hope that the feelings I have are with me when and if I ever reach such a milestone.

I called Amy on my way back from Waldwick hoping that we could begin where we left off. Her week was filled and so we set the following Saturday for our next date. I asked her if she wanted to go to Devils Lake and hike the bluffs. She said yes. I told her I would pick her up at nine. The weekdays dragged by and Thursday, "MY DAY" with great grandfather was cancelled because he had a bad cold and a doctor's appointment. Geez! 94 and he chose a doctor over an idiot! What kind of guy was I talking to dead people through?

Finally, it was Saturday...one of those glorious days in May when the sun is warm and spring has sprung. I arrived at the condo at precisely nine and she was waiting. My God, was she sexy. One time when I'd been at her apartment, some of her bras were drying in the bathroom that she called 'holsters' as she detailed how confining they were and how she preferred going 'sans-a-bra' as she called it whenever she could. To that end, on this warm May day she was 'sans-a-bra' while wearing a sleeveless shirt, one of her infamous baseball caps and cut off denim bootie shorts that had about a half-inch of her butt, I'd been grabbing the week before, showing each time she took a step. This wasn't fair, she was going to seduce me, entice me, arouse me all day long and tease me until I ached and wanted nothing more than to consummate our involvement.

"You look very special," I said.

She pulled me in and we kissed as she cocked her head to one side and whispered. "I want today to be a special day, one we will never, ever forget."

She told me she had a surprise. I had no idea what it was until we walked into the garage and there was a brand-new black Audi R8 ABT in her parking stall.

"Jesus, Mary and Joseph!" I murmured.

"It's daddy's present for taking the LSAT's."

It's incredible." I marveled, referring first to the car, then to myself, about the way she looked.

"It's too much," she responded.

She got behind the wheel and I slid into the passenger's seat.

"Let's go up highway 113 and take the ferry across the Wisconsin River" she outlined.

I didn't mind. I was too busy looking at the long legs and gorgeous thighs pressing on the pedals to care.

We went out East Washington and over to Johnson street and out past Warner Park. She was doing 60 and was still only in fourth gear. We rolled through Waunakee and Lodi, finally to Merrimack and the ferry. We just missed the crossing and so Amy shut off the engine as we sat in line. We got out and stretched and I don't know who got more attention from the other waiting drivers…the incredible car or the incredible girl.

The ferry came back and we rolled onto Colsac III for the seven-minute ride across the river. It seemed weird to be parked on a boat going seven miles per hour in a car that could go at least 160 with the governor on and perhaps hit 200 MPH without.

We got out and looked at the scenery while every guy on the ferry had a different type of scenery to admire at least for the seven minutes it took to get to the other side.

The boat ride was over and we hit the north shore of the Wisconsin River and headed up Highway 113 past Devils Head ski resort and into the south entrance to the park. Even the park rangers noticed the exotic car as we stopped to pay the admission fee and the ranger smiled. God it was cool to feel coveted.

We found a parking spot, locked the car and began our hike. The bluffs around Devils Lake are simply superb. The spring-fed lake is the closest you can get to the Rockies from a thousand miles away.

At first, we walked hand-in-hand. As the path up the bluff became narrow, I put Amy in front just so that I could watch that tight little butt of hers peak out each time she took a step.

Having been there many times before, I knew what the view was going to be. As this was Amy's first time she was treated to breathtaking the panoramic views of Devil's Lake itself, with its a stunning blue, glacier-carved reflection nestled between 500-foot quartzite bluffs accentuated by the lush forests and rock formations such as Balanced Rock and Devil's Doorway with the Baraboo Range in the distance.

As Amy perused the scenery one of her quirks that I'd seen before came to light as she simply took her hands and sort of massaged her breasts without even thinking about it. I don't know why she did it and I really don't think she realized she did but, this was one of those instances when her hands simply did it as we stood there.

I looked around and realized we were all alone. If you want to talk about romantic, God, this was it as I pulled Amy into me and took the liberty of putting my hands around her waist as I noted. "Have I told you that I really care for you, Miss Amelia?"

This was the closest I had ever come to the word love in my life. "Have I told you that the past few weeks have been the very best in my life?"

Her body became somewhat rigid. Was I going too far, too fast? We embraced and she kissed me deeply and yet, I sensed a concern, a trepidation, a reluctance and it worried me.

We sat upon a big rock and looked at the glistening lake below. My God, natural beauty before me in so many ways! I wanted her. I wanted her right then and there. We stood up and my hands slid down upon her butt and I pulled on the bottoms of her shorts making sure that each pull pressed upon her, signaling my desires. Her butt was half way out of the shorts and my hand slid to the front when I heard voices. Fellow climbers... reality...shit!

Amy leaned back and I could sense her mutual frustration. We wanted it, we needed it, we had conspired long enough. The tension was so thick even the sounds of reality seemed distant.

"Let's go back to the condo," she whispered.

"Ok," I replied.

We began our descent and, in our earnest, got careless. In an instant Amy slipped and fell. I reached and grabbed but got nothing but a hand full of air as I watched her tumble down a ten-foot embankment.

"Oh my God. Oh my God No." I screamed as I quickly descended after her. She lay in a pile...blood oozing from her hands and face where the gravel had impregnated itself into her skin. Her top was ripped and dirty and she was numb with fright and was in shock and I could tell by the angle of her foot, her ankle was broken.

I pulled out my cell phone and called 911 announcing the location of the accident and its magnitude and requesting immediate medical assistance. It seemed like forever but was only a few minutes until a small ATV showed up with a ranger in the driver's seat.

The Ranger examined Amy and determined that the cuts and bruises were superficial. However, the left ankle was definitely broken. Amy sat in a heap and looked at me. Our special day was over.

The Ranger slowly took Amy down the hill and asked if she wanted an ambulance. She was getting her senses and said no, I could take her to the hospital, but requested that the ranger call St. Claire Hospital in Baraboo and tell them that we were on our way.

We helped her in the R8 and I took off north on 113, rolling into the emergency entrance just as the pain was setting in. I ran inside and got a nurse's assistant and a wheelchair and we rolled Amy in.

They took Amy in for X-rays and asked me to fill out paperwork. Because of all the laws I did my best. I looked in Amy's purse and got her insurance card and that seemed to appease the finance people.

After what seemed like forever, they came and got me. Amy had cuts and bruises on her face, a bandaged left hand with her left arm in a sling, scrapes on her left leg and a broken left ankle.

They had to cut off her top and so she was wearing a yellow, tie-in-the-back paper-like, hospital gown. What a shitty way to start summer or any season for that matter.

"Sorry." She whispered.

"For what? You slipped" I replied "Baby, it could have been much worse. It could have been me that fell down the hill and then all these people would have heard a grown man cry and cry and cry."

The girlie giggle came out.

The doctor came in and gave her one final exam and handed me a prescription.

"I assume you're her husband" he said. I wanted to say not yet, but kept my mouth shut, letting him assume his conclusions were correct.

"She's one lucky girl. The ankle is set and as long as she doesn't put weight on it she should be fine. All the facial lacerations are superficial and so there won't be any scarring. Her left wrist and shoulder are going to hurt for several days and she's going to need help."

I went to the pharmacy and picked up the prescription. As I was walking back to the emergency room, I was beckoned to accounting and looked at all the forms. Someone needed to sign them and assume financial responsibility. I made the decision and signed.

Amy looked battered and completely befuddled. "I'm sorry, baby," she whispered. "This was supposed to be a special day."

"It is! I get to take care of you for several days. We'll have plenty more." I comforted her.

The nurse assistant and I helped get her into the rocket ship. I reclined the seat and headed east on 33 to the Interstate. God, what a crotch rocket. I thought what in hell do I do now?

I called Ann and explained what happened and where we were. Instead of heading for the condo, we headed for the cottage. I looked over at sleeping beauty and knew that she would be in good hands...hands that loved her, cared for her and would help her recover.

I pulled in the driveway of the cottage and sleeping beauty was zonked. The pain meds were doing their trick. Both Ann and Big Brother's vehicles were there. Rodney had come home from work to help. My friends, my wonderful, caring, friends!

Amy was still asleep when big brother lifted her out of the car and carried her into the house. I'm glad he did. I probably would have either dropped her as I tumbled from exhaustion or had to drag her by the hair. The decision was made to make up the day-bed on the porch while we were driving down and Rodney placed Amy on it.

Amy was still in the hospital gown and shorts which were now both dirty. She had taken quite a tumble. Ann got one of Rodney's shirts which was big enough to be a dress and took off Amy's her clothes.

"Why don't you guys step out?" Ann suggested as she was about to take off Amy's panties. I hoped someday that would be my job.

Ann took a wash cloth and cleaned Amy where the hospital hadn't and slipped the shirt on and covered her up. She looked at the prescription and said Amy would be out for several hours.

Ann looked at me and offered. "I think you should call her parents."

I got Amy's phone out of her purse and scrolled the numbers. When I came to 'mom' I pressed the call button.

On two rings, Amy's mom answered. "Mrs. Williams, this is George Terrill. Amy and I were hiking and she fell." I was shaking. "If it's all right, I'm here with my family and my Big Sister is a nurse and can explain all that's going on."

Ann took the phone and explained in medical terms the simple break and stretched ligaments to the left ankle, multiple contusions of the left arm, leg and hand and superficial cuts to the left palm and face. She explained the medical procedure and outlined the prescriptions and the fact that Amy was resting comfortably and it was her estimate that she would awaken in about four hours.

Ann suggested that Amy spend the next day or two at the cottage as Ann had the days off and we could take care of her. Ann agreed that Dr. Williams should come and visit and recommended coming on Sunday and gave directions to the cottage. Ann then reassured Dr. Williams that any change or aberration would result in a call to Dr. Williams' phone service immediately. We also agreed to have Amy call when she woke up.

Amy moved and I jumped. She was just positioning herself and yet all I could help think was that this was all my fault. I should have gone first. We shouldn't have gone at all.

I bent over and kissed Amy on the forehead. She aroused just enough to look in my eyes and whisper "I love you Sweetie." Then she fell back asleep.

My God, did she mean it? Was it just the drugs or her inner soul? I looked down at the girl sleeping on the day-bed and whispered, "I love you too." Things were changing…fast. Very, very fast!

Early Sunday morning, I heard Rodney's truck leave. It was strange as he normally slept in. As my head cleared, my mind focused on the girl on the porch. I went out to see her and she was still asleep. The bruises on her face had become more prevalent and yet she looked in total peace. I went into the kitchen and Ann appeared while detailing. "I called the hospital and they are loaning us a wheelchair for a few days. Amy is going to need one until her hand and shoulder heal and she's able to put all her weight on the crutches to get around". Rodney went to pick it up."

What wonderful friends I thought.

Amy was stirring and Ann went to her side.

"I need to pee," Amy said, still groggy from the meds.

With a broken ankle, sprained shoulder and lacerated hand, she was going to need help. My God the things you never think of when someone is hurt.

Amy looked around and had no idea where she was. I came into view and a soft smile came across her face.

"Hi baby." I said.

"Where am I?" Amy inquired.

"You're at the cottage. Do you remember what happened?"

"I fell down the hill," she responded.

"Yes, and you broke your ankle and cut your hand." I replied.

Amy held her good hand to her forehead.

"What day is it?"

"Sunday."

"Oh man. I've got to pee and call mom."

"This is Ann," I announced as Ann came into view. "Last night we brought you here and Ann got you ready for bed. We called your mom and she and your dad are coming this morning to see you."

I could see that Amy was a bit confused as she looked at her swollen and bandaged hand and foot in a cast.

"Let me help you to the bathroom," Ann said.

Amy was like dead weight and so Ann and I helped her up and let her lean on us as she made her way by hopping to the bathroom.

"I feel like shit." Amy said.

Needless to say, neither one of us was surprised and when she looked in the mirror she was going to say that she looked like shit, too. Even I could see that one coming.

We got her to the bathroom and Ann got her situated on the pot and then came out and closed the door. Amy had no idea what happened and I knew that when she looked in the mirror and saw the scratches on her face she was going to freak out.

Ann spoke, through the door. "Tell me when you're done and I'll come and help you."

Amy remembered that Ann was a nurse and that seemed to alleviate some of the reservation that might have transpired. After a few minutes Amy called and asked for help. Ann returned with a pair of her sweatpants and a sweatshirt and helped Amy out of Rodney's shirt. Ann called me and we helped Amy back to the day-bed. Her head was clearing and with it came the realization that her ankle was broken, her hand was bandaged and her shoulder was in a sling and in pain.

"What happened?" Amy asked.

"You slipped and fell and broke your ankle, cut your hand and hurt your shoulder."

"I need to call my parents" Amy said again, not remembering she had said that a few minutes before.

"They're on their way." I said. "But if you want to call, I think it would eliminate some of their stress."

I handed her the phone and left her alone. Mom and dad were on their way.

"I feel like shit." she repeated.

"Do you want something to eat?"

"I'm thirsty."

"Water or juice?"

Amy shook her head in indifference. I got her juice and toast in case she was hungry too.

She looked at me and shook her head. "So much for the first time."

"It can wait," I said.

I heard Rodney's truck in the driveway. In a couple-of-minutes he came in with a wheelchair and unfolded it. He extended the left leg and helped Amy into what was quickly called the Iron Maiden. She was in pain and the meds were wearing off and yet she was sitting upright.

"I need to call work and tell them what happened."

I thought, "in other words you were done for the summer."

We heard the sound of a vehicle and looked out to see a Mercedes Sprinter in the driveway followed by the infamous and coveted black Mercedes. Amy's parents brought a Mercedes van to take her home. Damn!

The doorbell rang and the friendly giant went to the front door. It was The Duke and Mrs. Williams with a worried look on their faces.

To see Amy sitting in the chair munching on a piece of toast eliminated a lot of their worries. Mrs. Williams came over and looked at her daughter. At first it was a maternal look and then a professional exam.

Ann introduced herself and provided her credentials. Charge nurse at Meriter Hospital. At first Mrs. Williams seemed suspect of Ann until Ann proceeded to update Mrs. or Doctor Williams in hospital language concerning conditions, treatment and medication including pulse and temperature. Mrs. Williams smiled as she knew that she was in the presence of a fellow medical professional. The Duke was beside himself. He was used to being in control and, at that instant, he was just the helpless father.

I watched as The Duke looked around the house and saw that everything was as it should be, clean, neat and full of love.

"Son, what happened?" The Duke directed at me.

I shook my head. "It's my fault sir. We went hiking at Devil's Lake and as we were coming down the slope I should have been leading. Instead, I was following. Amy slipped and fell and I couldn't catch her. I am so sorry, sir."

The Duke could sense my remorse and indicated that it was an accident and not my fault. Thank God.

Amy was more alert as Mrs. Williams concurred with Ann's diagnosis. While still in pain, she was coming back.

"We brought a van, so that you could come home with us." The Duke announced.

I looked at Amy and she at me. I didn't want her to go to Milwaukee. "Mom, I don't want to come home." Amy replied.

"But you're going to need help."

Ann announced. "I'm between classes and have the next four days off. She can stay here with us."

Amy smiled.

Mrs. Williams looked at The Duke.

"I'll call Frank Goldman at UW Hospitals and you can see him tomorrow morning."

It's funny what power, fame and money wields.

"Would you prefer nine or ten?" Mrs. Williams asked even before calling.

Ann responded nine would be preferable.

Mrs. Williams took out her cell phone and made a call. "Nancy, contact Doctor Goldman at UW hospitals and tell him Amelia will be there tomorrow morning at nine."

"Mrs. Williams turned to us and announced that Dr. Frank Goldman was a family friend and great orthopedic specialist and that she wanted a second or third or fourth or whatever it was, opinion. That was better than Amy being shuffled off to Milwaukee for the next six weeks.

It was nearly ten o'clock and everyone had missed breakfast. As was a tradition at Big Brother's house, Sunday morning meant he was going to cook some of his famous lighter-than-air pancakes. The Williams were invited and everyone gathered on the porch to give Big Brother room to work his magic. At 10:30, we all sat down to heaping stacks of Bisquick pancakes, sausages, fresh squeezed orange juice, wheat toast, fresh roasted coffee and scrambled eggs.

Amy watched the interaction of her parents with Rodney and Ann and smiled. They were meeting real people whose only objective was to provide comfort and care. There were no ulterior motives. Nobody trying to impress someone else. Nobody with their hands out. Just people! Amazing!

The conversation turned to Ann's education and then Rodney's role and how the casinos were doing. I kept my big mouth shut and let the conversation flow until the cadence was one of comfort and laughter. I looked at Amy and she at me and then she winked.

The Duke announced that they were leaving the van for our use until Amy could get into a regular car and would send a driver to pick it up when she recovered. Rodney was shy and so I asked The Duke if it would be all right if Rodney took a look at his car as Rodney had a CLS550. The Duke was happy to show it to him.

The Williams profusely thanked Ann and Rodney for their care and hospitality and as The Duke said, "the best damn breakfast I've had in years". Mrs. Williams gave Ann a hug and thanked her. As they were about to leave, they stopped and both bent down and kissed Amy goodbye.

I thought I was going to be left out until Mrs. Williams came to me and gave me a hug and said "You are special. Thank you very much."

The Duke came and shook my hand and then, as I learned later, did something Amy had never seen before, gave me a hug and whispered "Take care of my baby...but then I know that you will."

Us boys went out and looked at the car. The Duke was proud of his toy and was impressed that Rodney could outline the differences between his car and The Duke's.

"Someday, you'll have to come to the track with me," The Duke said, "and put yours through its paces". The Duke was referring to Joliet where Rodney loved to go.

"I'd love to do that sir," Rodney responded.

Mrs. Williams came out of the house and it was time for them to leave. Again, there were hugs all around.

I was speechless…they didn't blame me for the accident.

We walked back into reality and the four of us discussed the next few days.

First, Ann and I would go to Amy's apartment get some clothes for her. Second, we would take the Audi back and get the Jeep. Third, I would take Amy to see Doctor Goldman in the morning. Fourth, life would go on.

Ann and I drove to the condo and I thought Ann was going to pee her pants. First the R8 was incredible. Second the condo was beyond her expectation.

"Oh, my God" she exclaimed as we walked through the front door. Ann marveled at the view of the Capitol and Lake Monona. I made her promise there would be no mention of the apartment, as Amy was somewhat self-conscious of her digs and reluctant to have anyone know about them.

Ann had a list of things to get and found Amy's suitcase and proceeded to carefully pack all that was requested. I felt uncomfortable going through Amy's clothes so I stood in the living room looking out at Lake Monona.

It only took a few minutes and we walked down to the Jeep and headed home. Amy was asleep on the daybed when we entered and Rodney was out on the pier fishing.

We put the suitcase down and both headed out to the pier.

"How's the fishing Big Brother?"

"Terrible", he responded. "Wrong time of the day and it's too warm for fishing this time of the year."

We talked about our game plan and set our schedule. The goal was to have someone home at all times until Amy was ambulatory. I saw true concern in their eyes and felt true compassion in their hearts.

I went into the house and left the two alone. They needed time together, without me in their way. I sat down at the computer and warmed it up, watching my Sweetie asleep besides me. I looked out the window and saw Big Brother and Ann sitting side-by-side, bare feet dangling over the pier's edge with lines in the water and Rodney's arm around Ann's waist. It was the most beautiful part of some incredible scenery.

I needed to work on my 2000 words and dug deep into different historical websites to see what I could find that would help me better understand the people I was meeting through Great Grandfather. There was so much legal verbiage, I was befuddled. I was a farm boy from Waldwick and not a lawyer. It was then that the idea struck me...a way to keep my Amy occupied, by having her become my researcher. I was so proud of my brilliance...Even a blind squirrel like me could find a nut every now and then, but she knew what to look for and where to go.

I watched as Amy slept and began to memorize the peaks and valleys of her face. I listened to her breathing and watched her facial expressions change whenever she attempted to move. I knew there was pain and only hoped it wouldn't last too long. I was really falling for this girl. However, after Devil's Lake, using the word "falling" was probably the wrong choice.

In my growing passion, there was fear. I was afraid, what if she didn't feel the same way? Could I tolerate it if she went away to school in the fall? If it did work out, how could I afford to sustain the lifestyle that she was used to on a rookie writer's pittance? I thought about what it would be like to lay with her and wake up with her in my arms, feeling her body next to mine, her heart beating in rhythm with mine.

It was four when Amy awoke and Nurse Ann came to her bedside. Ann helped her into the wheelchair and rolled her to the bathroom. Being left handed and having her left arm in a sling made everything difficult. I guess the tooth brushing should have been taped for blackmail as Amy held the tooth brush in her right hand and moved her head back and forth with tooth paste slathering all over the place. Nurse Ann offered to help, but Amy wanted to do it herself. I guess it was hilarious.

By the time Amy was cleaned up and back out to the kitchen, it was dinner time. Big Brother grilled some steaks and we cut the food so we could all eat with some dignity. I looked at Amy and smiled. She caught my glimpse and smiled back. I shook my head and she giggled. Ann got in on the action and within a nanosecond we were all giddy, laughing at nothing, sharing something called friendship.

Ann outlined the next four days and Amy shook her head. "What would I do without you?"

"Well, first you wouldn't have fallen down a cliff," Rodney teased.

"Smart ass!" I thought and just shook my head.

We watched a movie and then it was time for the pain pill and sleepy time for Amy.

Rodney and Ann excused themselves and went to their room.

"Come lay with me." Amy requested.

I lay down beside her and propped my head up so that I could look in her eyes.

"Mr. George Terrill the Fourth, in 24 hours you have shown me dignity, compassion and grace. You have introduced me to two of the most generous people I have ever met. You have made my parents see that money isn't everything and goodness has more value than baubles. What am I going to do with you, except say thank you?"

I leaned over and gave her a kiss.

"I feel really bad that you fell and got hurt." I responded.

Amy closed her eyes and there was a sweet smile upon her face and then sent words that went straight to my heart. "God meant this to be. I can handle a little pain because the reward for me is decency in the people I have the honor of having as friends. You Mr. Terrill are so very, very special."

Her words were getting softer as the medicine was taking over. I watched as her lips moved without sound. I think she, once again, said...'I love you".

I looked at this girl sleeping next to me and mouthed the words..."Me too" as I kissed her on the forehead and arose to curl up in the chair next to her.

Big Brother's days off were Sunday and Monday and so I knew that if he and Ann had plans it would be for the day. I wanted to make certain that they had some time to themselves and tried to make as little noise as possible while I made coffee.

Amy awoke and I put my forefinger to my lips indicating that our host and hostess were still asleep. I helped her into her wheelchair and rolled her to the bathroom. Her bruises were now in their full glory and she looked in the mirror at her swollen face. "Oh my God."

I let her go to the bathroom in privacy and then came in to help her.

"We have a nine o'clock appointment with a Doctor Goldman," I announced.

"A friend of mom and dad's." Amy responded.

"I can't go like this," she announced.

"What?"

"I need to get cleaned up."

"Huh?"

"I need to take a bath."

"You can't get your cast wet and you can't take it off".

"Help me take off these pants and sweatshirt."

"Ok." This wasn't how I had fantasized seeing her naked for the first time...sitting in a wheelchair with her arm in a sling.

I took the wash cloth and got it wet and lathered soap in it and washed her face and then her body. There was absolutely nothing erotic about it. I washed under her arms and everywhere I could while she was sitting and then she stood up and leaned against the vanity as I washed her backside. It was then I noticed the small tattoo on her right shoulder. It spelled out the word 'Survivor ' and had four dots beside it. It wasn't the time to ask what it meant.

Amy leaned over the sink and I poured warm water from a glass into her hair and then rubbed shampoo in. I lathered her and then rinsed it and then wrapped two big towels around her body and her wet head and helped her back into the wheelchair.

"Thank you, sir," Amy noted.

"You're welcome, mam," I replied.

While sitting, I helped slide a pair of running pants with side zippers up over the cast as she slid into them. She had asked Ann to bring a loose top and carefully took her arm out of the sling. I thought she wouldn't make it through the pain of getting into the sleeves, but she gritted it out and we put the sling back on.

A little deodorant, some lipstick and perfume and she looked somewhat like her old self.

I leaned down and kissed her and I think she appreciated that.

Big Brother was in the kitchen when we came out of the bathroom.

"Someone's looking a lot better" he said with a smile.

"Thank you," Amy replied.

"I wasn't talking about you Amy, I was talking about that guy behind you." He snickered.

It was my time in the shower and I did so quickly. I came out and it was almost eight and announced that we needed to head for Doctor Goldman's office. I got the keys to the Mercedes van and was expecting that we would need to lift the wheelchair into the vehicle. When I opened the door, there was an aluminum ramp. The Duke and Mrs. Williams thought of everything.

Rodney brought Amy out and pushed her up the ramp. We set the brakes on the wheelchair and found two tie downs used to affix the chair to the van floor.

"Take me to the city George." Amy said in a phony English accent like I was her chauffer.

"Yes Miss Amy." I replied.

Mrs. Williams left an address and suite number for Doctor Goldman and I punched it into the van's GPS system. Little was said on the way to the doctor's office. I was nervous driving the big van in morning Beltline traffic. I got off at the John Nolen exit, turned left on Olin Avenue to Park Street and then to the medical complex at Park and Regent. It seemed like a long way from UW hospitals until I learned later that Doctor Goldman was one of the top orthopedic surgeons in the world and had privileges at all three hospitals in Madison.

I wanted to pull into the parking garage, but the van was too tall. I circled around to the front with the idea that I would drop Amy off and go find parking. As we pulled up, the security guard came out and asked if I was Mr. Terrill. I said yes and he said that I should just leave the van and he would take care of it and would wait for us.

We got Amy out and into the building lobby. Doctor Goldman's office was on the fourth floor. We rolled into the elevator and I punched four and rode up. When the doors opened there were two people waiting for us who took Amy right into the examining room and helped her up onto the table. Dr. Goldman was already waiting for us. Geez! Mid-fifties, salt and pepper hair, glasses and you could tell one of those really, really smart guys.

"Hi Amy."

"Hi, Doctor Goldman," Amy responded. "This is my boyfriend, George."

I liked the sound of that.

"Well, your mom said that George pushed you off a cliff up at Devils Lake"!

I was appalled.

"Yes. He's such a klutz. I was walking along minding my own business when he just pushed me."

Humor in the examining room...ha, ha.

"I had the attending physician e-mail the X-rays and looked them over. The ankle break was clean and so it should only take four-to-six weeks to heal. The cut on your hand could have used a couple of stitches but the scar won't be too bad. I'm most concerned about the shoulder as the MRI's show some minor tearing of the labrum that might take some time and will need some physical therapy. Under normal conditions, the contusions should be gone by this weekend unless of course, George hits you again. However, with your meds, it might take a couple of weeks."

"The cast they put on in Baraboo was a basic unit. I've got one of the new air casts ready for you and want you to go down to third floor and my physical therapists will fit you with it. It's going to feel tight when they inflate it, but with the clean break and the immobility, you can probably begin walking on the ankle in a few days, just no dancing or waterskiing for six weeks and stay away from cliffs please. As the swelling goes down, take the little pump and keep the boot tight and take it easy for the rest of the week, but start walking by this weekend. The cast is designed to be worn all the time, even in the shower. Your mom said that you are staying with friends and one is a nurse."

"Yes, she works at Meriter" Amy replied.

"Who's that?" Doctor Goldman asked.

"Ann Wolf"

"Annie?"

"Yes, sir."

"How do you know Annie?"

"She's engaged to George's best friend."

"The really big guy who she met in the hospital?"

"Yes."

"Great love story. Some guy is in a car accident and when he comes too, he meets this wonderful girl and introduces her to his friend."

"That was me" I included.

Doctor Goldman turned to me and smiled. "The nurses still talk about you and how it was such a love story. Good job, we need happy endings every now and then."

"Well Amy, go downstairs, they're waiting for you and say hi to your dad and thank him for the great deal on the car."

"Q. Do me a favor, don't push my little Amy down any more hills please" he said as he shook my hand and headed out the door.

"How did he know my nickname?" I asked Amy as we were in the elevator.

"Everybody at Meriter knows you."

Amy responded. "What?"

"They know about Ann and Rodney and that you came back and defended her honor and not only to defended Ann but saved Rodney from doing something he would have regretted."

I had chills as we made our way down to the third floor. Once again, there was no waiting. They were waiting for us. In fifteen minutes, Amy was fitted with an inflated walking boot, given instructions on inflation and we were out of the medical center.

The van was where we left it and we headed home. Amy called her mom to fill her in and found out that Doctor Goldman had already called and briefed her. Mom was happy and that was good.

As we drove out Park Street I turned to Amy and asked what was going on. I wanted the truth and nothing but the truth. She looked me in the eyes and with earnest began ... "Five years ago I was diagnosed with chronic lymphocytic leukemia. I was a junior at Georgetown and thought the world was at my doorstep. The prognosis was not positive. Mom, being a specialist in the field, knew that my chances weren't very good. I went to John Hopkins and they did what they could for me and it was pretty rough with chemo and I was miserable. I lost all of my hair and 30 pounds and was sick all the time. They did their best and I went home to die."

"Mom learned about an experimental drug called Venclexta that was having some success here in Madison and was able to get me in the clinical trial. At first, the treatments consisted of medication and weekly checkups but the trips here and back from Milwaukee were more than I could handle, so dad bought the condo. Within a few weeks I began to see some improvement and got some hope."

Amy was being very matter of fact. "Just like people, cells in our bodies aren't in any hurry to die. Research in the early 1960's by Leonard Hayflick determined that normal human cells, beyond stem cells, will only divide, on average, 50 times before they stop. This has become known as the Hayflick Limit that can be affected by disease, stress and genetics. I wanted to know what was going on and learned that the basic composition of our chromosomes has what are called, telomeres at both ends. The telomeres protect chromosomes from damage and from fusing with each other. If I've got it right, every time a normal non-stem cell divides, somewhere between 50 and 100 of the telomeres cease to exist and the telomeres get shorter and shorter and shorter until they reach a minimum length at which time cell division stops altogether and a process called apoptosis happens, which eliminates old cells to make room for new ones."

"The problem is that, sometimes cells cheat death by living off certain proteins in the body that allow the rogue cells to not only live but spawn. Better known as metastasis, this eventually can kill us. It is called cancer. Venclexta restores the normal cellular life cycle to those of us who have a specific gene mutation, by blocking the protein lifeline to the cancer cells. In so doing, the malignant cells end up committing suicide."

"Besides the drug, one critical factor seems to be that stress can shorten telomeres at a much faster rate than that of people who lead a less stress-filled life. This seems to be attributed to elevated levels of the hormone cortisol and might be one reason why stress can cause cancer. While it is impossible to eliminate all stress, identifying and reducing it can slow the aging process and improve the overall quality of life and perhaps even prevent cancer. With my genetic disposition, I need to take it easy. Taking the LSAT was stress-filled and so, I don't know what just it might have done to me."

"Are you clear?"

"Right now, yes. They think that as long as I keep taking the pills, I'll probably be fine. I always keep some in my purse and Ann got more for me this morning. I'm still in the trial and have been cancer clear for four years. I need to take my meds every day and then once a month, I need to go for blood work where all my blood is cleaned and tested and stem cells are harvested and stored in case I have a relapse. With any type of cancer, it takes five consecutive years before you are considered clear. After ten years you are considered cured and then considered a cancer survivor."

"Thus, the word survivor on your shoulder and the four dots?"

"Yup. Four down and six to go. I need one more dot to make it to the clearing."

Amy continued. "There's a routine to the treatment and at first I felt sorry for myself…you know…the 'why me' syndrome, until I started seeing all those other people who came to the clinic who were in much worse shape than I was. I started helping them in any way I could to give them positive reinforcement and we have our own little group who gets together with some of the staff. When you've been doing something for over four years, you get to know the routine and the people, especially the nurses."

"Like Ann?" I added.

"Like Ann! We bonded because we are both of color in an otherwise white world. One day she told me about this really funny guy who had been in a terrible car accident and while he was in the hospital introduced her to the man she loved...a Native American like her. She said he was not only kind and generous, but noble. She explained how she had been groped and that, to save the man she loved from probably going to jail, this funny guy came back to the hospital and proceeded to teach the jerk a lesson by cranking his bed up and down."

"Everyone on the hospital staff knew who the guy was from the time he was there and then to have him come back and do what he did, made him their secret hero. He did what they couldn't do. This guy went by the name of "Q". Incredibly, hospital security did their 'thorough' search and couldn't find a single person named 'Q' who had ever been a patient and the day of the purported event the security tapes accidentally had been erased."

"Word spread about this guy named 'Q' and even the doctors and administrators cheered for him. Ann and I talked about this guy and I needed a hero in my life. I told her that I wished that I could meet him. I wanted it to be natural. I didn't want pity and, after all the jerks I've met who only looked at my parent's money, I wanted to be accepted for me and not my dad."

"I did try and work for UPS because I wanted to be accepted for being me. Incredibly, one day, on my day off, it was arranged for me to deliver a package to Rodney. Ann had me make a delivery to your house and we met. Frank, the regular driver, was hiding in the back of the truck. I hoped and prayed you would talk to me. I did everything I could to make you want to see me again."

"What would have happened if nothing had clicked that day?" I asked.

"I would have been back with a delivery the next day and the next and the next until it did."

I smiled and inquired. "And the Nitty Gritty?"

"I wanted to make sure you were interested."

"From then on?"

"The humor, the nobility, all that everyone said would be there has been there. I believe you have accepted me as me. I almost cringed when dad brought the new car. That's not me. That's dad. I've met too many people corrupted by money and power and it's not for me. Don't get me wrong, I like nice things, but I like quiet, nice things and not the bullshit that comes with wealth."

"How are you now?" I asked.

"Health-wise, I'm clear, but I need to have my treatments every month that clean and check my blood and harvest "T" cells.

"That's where you were two weekends ago?" I asked. The riddle solved. Here I'm thinking another guy and she's lying in bed recovering from having all of her blood taking out of her. I felt like a jerk!

Amy nodded 'yes' and continued on. "This is insurance in case the drug stops working. It knocks me out for two days…one for cleaning and one for recovery. Emotionally, I have this guy on a pedestal who treats me like a princess not for what I am, but who I am. There are no guarantees regarding my health as the program is still experimental. I could be a walking time bomb and even if I can have kids, they could have the same challenge because the issue is genetic. I wanted Saturday to be special and then, I was going to fill you in. I wanted to show you how much you mean to me and let you see that I really care for you, my noble prince. Then, I was going to let you decide if you wanted to continue knowing that things might not be good. That time might be short. That all that I have might only be for a short while."

"Mom knew medically, what was going on. She's an expert in the field. I wanted dad to meet you and see that you are different than any other man I have ever met."

"Yeah, I'll bet I'm the only one who talks to dead Indians every Thursday morning."

She chuckled. "Dad tested you in the restaurant and then saw your profound regret about the accident. He saw you, Rodney and Ann go out of your way to take care of me, not in an artificial, sterile way, but with love, kindness and compassion."

"Dad giving you a hug was his sign of acceptance. He's never done that before to any other man that I know of in his life. He sees the nobility, senses the commitment and respects that you are for real. To call you son is spooky. He's never called anyone I've dated that before and I hope it doesn't scare you. Mom told him about the hospital and how we met and he smiled. Dad likes good people. I'm not saying Dad isn't tough. He is! He fought his way up and doesn't back down, but the people he likes can always count on him."

"Well, the cat's out of the bag. The good doctor took care of that by calling you "Q", but I'm glad. Two people who have feelings for each other should not hold secrets, especially one like this. You've got a woman sitting next to you who might be dead in a few years. You've got a woman who also might live to be a hundred. There is a high probability that I can't ever have children and that is one of the saddest parts."

We were on Olin Avenue and when we went over the railroad bridge I pulled into Franklin Field and stopped the car next to the Goodman pools. What I wanted to say came from the heart. "I have never had a woman want me before. I've always had to be the initiator. I am not noble, nor do I want to be placed upon a pedestal. I am just a guy who knows right from wrong and good from bad, whose only goal is to be happy and make those people around him happy as well. The past few weeks have been the happiest of my life. I met a beautiful woman who is kind, compassionate and caring, a woman who has filled me with more joy than I ever imagined and I don't want it to end."

"I'm going through a major change in my life from being a boy to hopefully, becoming a man. For the first time, I am accepting responsibility, not only for myself, but for those around me. I am a witness to love and devotion, kindness and generosity, compassion and, above all else, the purity that comes from goodness from those with whom I have the honor of living."

"Whether we last a few weeks, a few months or forever, neither of us knows. What I do know right now, is I don't want it to end. There will be days and times and instances when I will be wrong. There will be times when you will question your judgment and wonder what you are doing with me. However, there will never, ever be a time, instance or circumstance when you will need to question my dedication and commitment to you and your happiness."

We both had tears in our eyes. We hugged and kissed...not a romantic kiss, but one of acceptance, as I wiped the tears, first from her eyes and then from mine. We drove back to the cottage and I got ready for work. Ann and Rodney were on 'duty' for the night while I went to take care of drunks, punks and jerks. It was my humility detail. God, people can be stupid!

I kissed Amy goodbye and looked at Ann. "You and I need to have a conversation" I said, looking Ann in the eyes. She knew that I knew and she had the grin of a kid who just got caught with their hand in a cookie jar.

At the factory, I went through the paces and counted the moments until my shift was over. It was the week before Memorial Day and that meant business would be slow. The casino business is just about opposite everything else. When things are busy, casinos are slow.

I got home to a quiet house and slipped into the chair next to Amy's bed. Sleep came quickly and I was awakened by the morning light.

"Morning Sweetie" I said as Amy awakened, stretched and smiled.

"Wheelchair?" I asked.

"Let me try walking. Can you help me up?"

Das boot" as we began to call it, was cumbersome, but one hell of a lot better than the wheelchair. We took it slow and she made it.

I closed the door and went back to the kitchen. A few minutes later, the door opened and she made her way back towards me with a great big grin on her face. She had a towel wrapped around her head like a turban and was in new clothes. It was like she was walking for the first time ever.

"Freedom! But next time, I think I'll need someone to wash my back" She murmured.

We sat at the kitchen table. "I have an idea," I said. "What's that?"

"I need to know more about these dead guys I'm talking to and also about the legal aspects of what happened back then in terms of the treaties. They are all written in mumbo jumbo and I don't understand them. Do you want to be my legal researcher?"

Her eyes lit up...a project in law that we could do together. I added, "Step one is to read what I have written so far and correct it for grammatical, thought process or logical errors. Step two will be staying one step ahead of what or who I think I'm going to be talking to."

"Neat"

"I can set up the computer and you can work at my desk."

"I can't afford to pay you much beyond love and kisses."

"Can you print it so that I can lay down to read it and also have it redacted?"

"You think it's too long?"

"No, not really, it's just that one handed typing doesn't work so well and I can hold a pencil and mark it up and then we can go over any questions I might have."

"Will you need a box of crayons?" I asked.

That got the girly giggle out of her.

I printed off 20,000 of the words I had written and had it ready before I went to work.

When I got home, Amy was sitting at the desk and still penciling in changes. They looked like chicken scratches until I remembered she was using the wrong hand. Duh!

"This is really good." Amy surmised.

"Really?"

"Seriously. You are telling it like it was and yet it's not a bleeding-heart story. It's very balanced."

"Unlike the author," I added.

I glanced at the pages and there were margin notes and changes everywhere. She was doing an incredible amount of work. I put my hands upon her right shoulder and her head leaned into my hand. With that, I began massaging her neck.

"Oh my God, that feels good," she whispered. "I can't wait until I can reciprocate."

It was time for bed. Big Brother and Ann were long gone and I was exhausted. "Come lay with me." Amy beckoned.

I got her settled and then lay beside her. We lay, staring in each other's eyes. Our lips met and there was passion or as much passion as you can with a one-legged woman whose arm is in a sling. We kissed and kissed and kissed some more until we both fell sleep in each other's arms, or arm as it was in her case.

I awoke first to realty…her beneath the covers and me above. Big Brother was in the kitchen.

"Heh, little brother, how you doing?"

I just smiled.

"Do you have anything going on this morning?"

"I need to finish my 2000 words."

"How many do you have written?"

"I don't know, my editor in chief has been didactic."

Big Brother just grinned.

"Want to go with me to get my boat? I need someone to drive the Batmobile home while I bring the boat home.

"Sure, where is it?"

"Out at the Marina on Northport drive."

"They called and the boat is ready."

"Sure, when do you want to go?"

"'After the girls get up."

Amy awoke and I helped her out of bed. She wanted to ditch the sling and see if she could handle it. I thought she was pushing it. She was. Ann came out of the bedroom and smiled. It was her last day off before six straight working days. Rodney and I thought they needed some quiet time together and announced we were going to get the boat. The girls acted indifferent, but I knew it meant girlie talk.

We took off in the Batmobile and made it to the marina a little after nine. The fishermen were long gone and the day trippers had yet to arrive. Being with the friendly giant who was dressed in a black tee shirt, cut offs and flip flops made me feel macho. This dude could have played in the NFL.

Small talk transpired and then Rodney flipped me the keys to the car. "I'll see you at home little brother."

I went out and got into the Batmobile and headed home. Once again…seat forward, mirrors down, seat belt shortened. I felt like the tallest midget in the circus! The girls were all dressed and Amy was at the computer. She was going to keep the pressure on me in terms of the book.

Two hours later, I looked out and saw Rodney coming. This wasn't just any boat. This was a 1957 Chris Craft Capri, the ultimate in wooden boats with a modified straight six, Chris Craft engine in it. This was a classic and one of only a few brands of boats ever built that's worth more each year from when they were built.

My God it was spectacular! The hand rubbed Mahogany finish, inlaid mother-of-pearl highlights, real leather seats and chrome hardware that glistened in the sunlight, made the boat look simply fabulous. The boat was built for four…perhaps five people and the majestic dub-dub-dub of the exhaust was simply incredible. This was from a different time. A different era! Rodney called Ann and invited us to come outside. None of us had seen his pride-and-joy or even knew it was in the works and we all went out to the pier to welcome him home.

He smiled. You could see the pride from across the lake in what was his.

"Nice boat." I said. Little did I know!

"It was my dad's and he gave it to me to give to my son, someday. They just finished restoring it. It took two years, but they got it right. They disassembled all the exposed wood and checked the frame and then reinstalled the chines and keel with marine adhesive and stainless-steel bolts."

"Once that was done, they installed the inner layer of premium Okoume Marine plywood that was registered and manufactured to British Standard #1088. Some of the wood needed to be replaced and new mahogany outer planking lumber stock was selected and cut in book-matched pairs, then milled to final thicknesses so that both sides of the boat are exactly the same."

"They soaked some of the lumber used in the bow to allow it to bend to the curve more easily. They were able to reuse the outer, mahogany-stained deck, but the inner deck had to be remade. The entire deck got new screws and 3M-5200 so that it's much stronger and any expansion/contraction splits in the varnish at the deck seams won't happen. They put wooden bung caps over the screws that were cut to fit the slope of the sides and then sanded until they were flush so you can't see where the bung holes are. I added a custom dashboard with solid bird's eye maple and mahogany and had the original Chris Craft gauges restored with custom colors to compliment the wood and leather interior."

I had absolutely no idea what Rodney just said...chines? Okoume Marine Plywood? British Standard #1088? Book-matched pairs? 3M-5200? Bung caps? That's Big Brother. All I know is that it sure looked and sounded expensive to me.

Rodney climbed out and we tied his prize to the pier making sure all of the foam bumpers were in place so as not to rub the finish. My God, with all that he had done, the last thing I wanted to do was nick it, scratch it, bump it or even have it fade in the sunshine when I was around.

"Take a look at the stern," he said with a smile.

We all went back and saw what he was most proud of...the new name "Queen Ann"

"This weekend, we can go for a ride".

Rodney and I put the canvas cover on and slid the boat into the hoist and lifted it out of the water. Rodney ran a chain through the lift wheel and locked it. This was simply too valuable to let stand alone. He pointed up to the tree and we saw the video camera. He had 24-hour surveillance from a security company and there was a motion detector on the hoist and one hidden in the boat with a GPS finder as well. If someone did get it down, the boat could be located in a matter of minutes.

Rodney needed to go to work as did Ann. I had Rodney help Amy back into the house while Ann and I stood outside.

"Well Nurse Wolf. I don't think I can ever forgive you for what you've done". Ann looked at me with saddened eyes. "I expected a few years of wild and crazy life filled with all sorts of debauchery. Instead, because of you, I have met the most wonderful person in my life. Instead of five years of fun and games, I find myself living for each and every moment and cherishing the fact that right now, I am the luckiest man on earth. I have wonderful friends and an incredible woman in my life."

I smiled and hugged her. "How can I ever thank you?"

"By treating Amy, the way, you have. She is a special person and in the past few weeks, she has been the happiest I've ever seen her and so have you. That's more than enough gratitude."

Ann and Rodney left and reality was all about us. Amy and I sat home and worked on the 2000 words. God, she was smart! We made the changes and I decided that instead of emailing just 2000 words to the Chief, we would send the entire revised edition. We printed off the pages, found a binder, went to the Stoughton post office and mailed it, Priority Mail, to Black River Falls.

We had lunch at Culver's and headed back to the cottage, devouring our chocolate custard with marshmallow topping sundaes on our way home.! It was fun watching Amy eat with the wrong hand and get custard all over her face and not be able to wipe it off.

Tomorrow would be a Great Grandfather day and so I elected to prepare by discussing the next chapter with Amy. It was a glorious May-day so I pulled two chaise lounges out and we sat out in the sun enjoying the tranquility. I got out my I-Phone and Bluetooth speaker and put on some music from Pandora called 'Healing Massage' and we both dozed in the warmth of sunlight and each other.

"If we were at our house in St. Martin now we could be getting tan all over." Amy said, first without opening her eyes, then looking deeply into mine.

My expression must have got to her and so she continued on. "Imagine walking naked down Orient Beach with hundreds of other naked people. Doesn't that sound romantic?"

I thought it sounded intimidating but wasn't going to spoil her fun and so I replied…"Not really because right now you can't get naked and walk on the beach because you've got your walking boot on. Can you imagine the scene of a gorgeous naked girl dragging her left foot through the sand? My God what would the perverts, voyeurs and exhibitionists think watching you take a step, drag your foot, take a step, drag your foot, and the impressions in the sand. Right foot. Club foot. Right foot. Club foot. Right foot. Club foot."

That got a girly giggle out of her.

"You mean if I wasn't wearing das boot you'd go naked with me on Orient Beach?'

"Lady, I'd go naked with you right here in Lake Waubesa "

Now she had the weird look on her face...tee, hee.

"Well, then I think I'll take off my boot". Volley back to me.

"Well then I'll take off my pants."

"Well then, I'll take off my, my, my sunglasses." as one of her now famous girly giggles erupted.

"Well then, I'll take off my shirt and expose all my scars."

"Well then, I'd ask you to kiss me."

"Well then, I'd ask you where you wanted me to kiss you."

She looked right in my eyes and said..."All over and I mean ALL over."

"Pretty hard to do with das boot on your left foot."

"You could kiss my toes and then go from there."

With that I reached over and kissed on her lips. "Tomorrow, we will add another spot until we've got you completely covered in kisses."

"That could take weeks"

"I figure about five more, if my math is correct."

Amy smiled a bashful smile. Our verbal intercourse would need to suffice.

After a few moments I turned to her and said. "Would you really walk naked down Orient Beach?"

She turned to me with a quizzical smile and said. "Again?"

 Oh my God!

With me on 'Amy duty' for Thursday and her deeply involved in the book, I asked Rodney if Amy could go with me to the Dells. He called the Chief who thought someone new would be good for Great Grandfather and also give her insight into what was going on.

The drive to the Dells was smooth and we waited in the lobby until exactly ten.

There was soft smile on Great Grandfather's face.

"Little Spirit, you are here and on time."

God was he ever going to let me get over it?

"Yes, Great Grandfather."

"Come sit with me. Who is that with you? Her spirit is strong."

"It is my dear friend, Great Grandfather.

Your hearts beat as one and they are strong.

"What is your name?" Great Grandfather inquired, knowing all along what it was.

"I'm Amy."

"Amelia, correct?"

"Yes." Amy gave me a strange look.

"You are named after your great grandmother from France.

"Yes." Amy replied.

"Your family is very proud of you Amelia. You are a great warrior and have battled a mighty foe. For now, you are the victor, but you must never let your guard down. Your grandmother is sorry for all that you have endured and is blaming herself. She is happy that your heart is light." Now Amy was getting the heebie jeebies as Great Grandfather continued, "She has said that you need to fight hard and you will live a long life and have many children."

"Come Amelia, hold my hands. Little spirit, pull up the old chest so that Amelia and I can visit."

It was difficult for her to do but we persevered and I did as I was directed.

Great Grandfather closed his eyes and spoke. "When you fell, the poison in your body was replaced by love. Your family can feel your joy and for the first time ever, your father asks no more of you than what you have done. He has joy in his heart, as does your mother. It is wise that a broken bone can release pain and invite happiness." There were tears in Amy's eyes.

Great Grandfather motioned towards where I was standing. "Little Spirit, please come sit on the chest and let us all hold hands. I want to feel what flows between you."

I quickly joined Amy on the chest. There was a broad smile upon Great Grandfather's face.

"The spirits are happy and the energy between you is great. There will be much joy in your lives, but be careful, there are clouds upon the horizon that will bring storms and yet your energy is such that they cannot harm you."

His face turned somber. "Little Spirit, you must persevere. Do not let the dark clouds take away your sunshine."

"What Great Grandfather?"

"I do not know, except that you will be challenged and it will take all of your strength to win, but you are a brave warrior and the Gods are with you."

"Amelia, your beauty falls beneath your skin. Make sure you let it flow, as it will win the hearts of those who think less of you. You have my blessing."

I looked at Amy and she at me. I knew that Great Grandfather was about to go to sleep as Great Grandfather added, "Please tell Rodney that his boat is in peril. He must not trust so many people and be so kind. There are those out there who are not as good as he is."

Amy and I stood and looked at the old man sitting in the rocking chair. We held hands and walked outside.

Amy's eyes opened wide. "Oh my, God" as she put her hand to her mouth.

"At least the dead Indians didn't talk to you. They only will speak when I'm alone with him."

"I would never have believed it." Amy said. "I thought you were making it all up. You're sure he's blind?"

"Completely."

"How did he know so much about me?"

I just shook my head.

"I'll never forget that. Let's hope what he said comes true."

Amy said it. I wished it as we headed home and I checked the boat. It was there. That night when Big Brother got home, I told him of Great Grandfathers warning and could see that Rodney took it to heart.

The Invitation: It was Memorial Day weekend, the official beginning of summer in Wisconsin. When you're in the entertainment business or the medical profession, it's just another weekend. Someone's got to run the store. Friday, Amy needed to go in for her monthly blood cleaning, Saturday had Big Brother working, as would Ann. Sunday we all had off and then Monday I was working my normal shift. It didn't seem possible that I had already been out of college for over a year.

Ann took Amy to the hospital and it seemed strange to be home alone. As I was sitting pondering my next 2000 words, the phone rang. It was Mrs. Williams. "I'm sorry, Amy isn't here right now" I said.

Mrs. or Doctor Williams said she knew and that was why she called when she did. She wanted to speak to me. She indicated that I had learned of Amy's condition and wanted to make sure I understood what was going on as she was certain that Amy had minimized everything.

I agreed that Miss Amelia had a way of not wanting other people to worry about her. Mrs. Williams said that she could see that we were getting close. I concurred. She then outlined what was going on in regards to Amy's condition. It was doctor talk, but she dumbed it down for me.

"The activity of human cells is controlled, or programmed, by our DNA, much the way software controls what a computer will do. If the DNA programming runs amok, the genes lose control. It is as if the computer operator were hitting the command key over and over again without hitting the program key to give it direction. Cancer cells are normal cells which have developed the ability to multiply at an abnormal rate and are out of control. They do not attach to normal cells, but they do form abnormal groups and patterns. Cancer cells proliferate on their own and become autonomous. This is how they become "differentiated," meaning capable of forming unique groups and patterns of their own." Dr. Williams said.

"Most DNA damage…i.e. cancer growth…is caused by mistakes that happen while a normal cell is reproducing or by something in the environment such as cigarettes that trigger the cell to mutate. Some people are prone to mutation simply because of a genetic hereditary weakness such as with Amy". She noted, "It's rare to know exactly what causes any one person's cancer and this is what makes the illness so foreboding and unpredictable. We got lucky with Amy. Without persistence six years ago, she wouldn't be with us today.

Dr. Williams continued, "One thing that is known is that the body has a naturally occurring protein called epidermal growth factor or EGF that signals cells to grow and divide, regardless of whether they are normal or cancerous. By creating a vaccine that temporarily impedes the body's creation of EGF, it is believed, it may also limit or stop some types of tumor's growth that are more sensitive to EGF's existence."

"Leukemia is different. Instead of a tumor it is the creation of abnormal blood cells that are produced in the bone marrow. Usually, leukemia involves the production of abnormal white blood cells, which are the cells responsible for fighting infection. Abnormal white blood cells do not function in the same way as normal white blood cells. The leukemia cells continue to grow and divide, eventually crowding out the normal blood cells. The end result is that it becomes difficult for the body to fight infections, control bleeding, and transport oxygen. Tiredness and easy bleeding were Amy's first symptoms."

Mrs. Williams added. "Few people die from Leukemia. They die from its complications such as the inability to fight infections or if the cancer spreads to other organs like the lungs, liver, bladder, bones, brain, pancreas or kidneys, either through the bloodstream or lymphatic system. Metastasis tumor cells are not overnight developments. They involve a series of sequential and interrelated steps called neoplastic progressions that can include genetic, molecular, cellular and even small organisms themselves. When this happens, the metastasis detaches from the primary tumor, moves into the circulatory or lymphatic systems, evades immune attack, invades distant blood and begins to grow."

"The outcome of cancer depends on multiple interactions between metastatic cells and stable cells that belong in the environment. For this reason, treatment of metastasis is not only aimed at the specific cancer cells but also against host factors that contribute to and support progressive growth and survival of metastatic cancer cells. This is why Amy and so many people get so sick when they go through chemotherapy. While Amy's current medication is working, there are no guarantees that it will keep going long term. To this end, we continue to research immunotherapy options of which the most promising is called T-cell therapy. Here, T-cells are removed and genetically modified to enhance their cancer -fighting abilities and reintroduced back into the patient's body. In early tests more than 90% of those who were terminally ill went into remission. So, we have a back-up plan if we need it, but hopefully, it can remain a back-up plan for a long, long time."

"Right now, our…your Amy is in pretty good shape. She took time to rest after all the treatments and recently I've seen energy return that wasn't there. The job at UPS was her first real challenge. At Paisan's last summer, she was only able to work a couple hours per day as she got so tired so quickly."

There was a change in Mrs. William's tone of voice from medical to maternal…softer and rich in emotion. "I've seen the smile return that had been missing for a long, long time. I can feel her happiness and called first to thank you and second to make certain that you were aware of all that is going on. Happiness is not a cure all, but it is a big step in the right direction. Having your blood cleaned once a month is not fun and tomorrow, she's going to be listless, cranky and not so much fun to be around. I hope that by explaining what's going on, you have a better understanding because, I really don't know what she or we would do without you."

Once again…damn tears were in my eyes as I responded. "I met a wonderful person a few months ago that means everything to me. She has shown me so many virtues, so many attributes and so many emotions that I really didn't know existed. Understanding who she is and the battle she is facing makes me even that much more attracted and supportive of her. Not out of pity, but of being in complete awe of her. There are no complaints from her. There are no excuses from her. There has never been a time, an instant, even a thought that she was anything less than someone I completely respect and honor."

"Doctor Williams, please tell your husband what I am telling you, I am here for the long run if Amy will have me. However, I want to take it slow-but-sure, not because the passion isn't there and certainly not because of the risk involved regarding Amy's health. I want to make sure that those days, moments, and situations when we will both question our allegiance, will not be for an extended period of time, but only for an instant to be replaced by our true love for each other. By adding time and layers of experiences, I believe we can build a foundation where we realize that those few days, moments and situations were nothing more than this thing called life…little valleys from which all mountains of happiness gain perspective."

There was a long pause on the other end and I could almost hear the tears rolling down Amy's mother's cheeks. She had gone from doctor to mother and the emotions were there, exposed, raw, in complete view and I knew that she was relieved…relieved that her daughter was in the arms of someone who truly cared.

"Thank you." she whispered. "Can we keep this conversation between us?"

"Of course! Thank you for giving me a better understanding of the battles within. She is a warrior and will fight. I can only hope that I am allowed to be by her side. The objective is to act as if nothing is wrong, yet accept the fact that there will always be a risk that we must be aware of."

With that, the call ended. I knew I could not pity the crazy girl who entered my life as that would be terrible and yet I also knew that hidden deep within her heart was fear…fear that it all would come back and that she would not see her dreams come true. My vow to myself was to treat her openly, honestly and with respect, while still being aware that there was still a long, long time before it would all be normal.

Amy came home and she seemed fine. She was walking slowly, but then I thought that was from the boot. Her arm was out of the sling and the gauze on her hand had been replaced by a large bandage. She came in the house and gave me a weak smile and then a soft kiss. Ann nodded towards the day bed and I shook my head 'no'.

"Baby, why don't you go sleep in my bed? It will be quieter and you can get some rest."

There was no fight, just one very tired girl walking to my room. She had worn sweat pants and a sweat shirt, even though it was a warm day. As I walked into the room, she was pulling off her clothes and crawling into bed. She looked exhausted.

"Always a rough day," she murmured.

"Tomorrow will be better" I assured her.

She slightly shook her head 'no'. This was number forty-seven and she knew that tomorrow was going to be awful. She would be tired, have an incredible headache and only want to sleep. She slid under the covers and pulled them up to her chin. I kissed her softly on the lips and began pulling down the shades. Why hadn't I put her in my bed in the first place? God only knows. By the time the curtains were drawn, she was asleep. I quietly closed the door.

Ann was in the kitchen as I approached.

"How did it go?" I asked.

Ann continued to make a salad and without looking up noted. "Normal procedure, but she'll be wasted for the next 24 hours. If you hear her moaning, it's probably that she's got leg cramps. They're quite common and she seems to be more prone than most people. With the cast on, she can't get up and stretch and so, she might need you to massage her legs." Looking up from the sink, Ann suggested. "You might want to sleep with her tonight and the combination of the cramps and cast might mean she'll need help."

For the first time Amy and I slept together. She didn't wake up and never knew I was there. Saturday was just as Ann and Amy said it would be. Rough! Three times I went in and massaged her legs and helped her to the bathroom. She looked like a disaster hit her but didn't care. There's something romantic however, about seeing someone you care for at their worst. It gives you a perspective, especially when they need your help. Let's just say the day wasn't wasted as I was able to get 2000 words done for the next week.

Sunday morning arrived and the old Amy was back, full of smiles and girlie giggles. "47 down and 13 to go." was her mantra. "Next month, I get to add another dot." The team cheerleader had spoken. Rodney made breakfast and then he and I went out and got the Queen Ann ready for the day. For a Memorial Day Sunday, it was warm and that meant the lakes would be busy.

Amy hadn't anticipated the weather being so warm when Ann and I went to the condo and so she had her choice…the bootie shorts and sleeveless shirt that had been cleaned or clothes that would be too warm. Even with Ann being a nurse and Rodney seeing all that he did at the factory, they were still quite conservative and traditional.

I knew that Amy was prepared for the possible conflict of propriety and so I offered to drive to the condo and pick up some different clothes for her. Ann immediately said "no" that there was nothing wrong with the clothes Amy had been wearing when we went hiking and that, if fact, she just wished she could wear clothes like that. I don't know if Ann meant it, but it certainly took the edge off the situation.

We all went out to the boat and Rodney simply carried Amy and put her in the back seat. Ann followed and sat up front. Big Brother put on his captain's cap and got behind the wheel as I pushed off and climbed in back with Amy. Needless to say, the boat was gorgeous as we spent the day traveling up the Yahara River from Lake Waubesa to Lake Monona, passing by the condo before heading further north, through the Tenney Park locks and into Lake Mendota. Everywhere we went, people waved at our boat as it was really something special.

We made it to Picnic Point and Rodney opened the bow and took out a cooler. He had made lunch for us and we had a picnic. For the first time in my life, I was actually having a picnic on Picnic Point. The afternoon was filled with laughter and the joy of all of us being together. Amy was still tired, but the laughter was great medicine. The warm sunshine felt great and we were all glad summer was upon us. The girls had girly talk about the wedding while Big Brother and I talked sports and fishing. Boy, did he know Lake Mendota. He outlined that the deepest spot was right off the point and where the bass were biting at different times of the year and why ice fishing for perch was always better on Lake Monona.

As we were about to leave, Amy asked Ann and Rodney where they were going on their honeymoon. Ann said they really hadn't thought much about it. Amy indicated that she had spoken to her mom and dad and they offered the use of the family house on St. Martin. Both Big Brother and Ann were taken aback.

"Are you sure?" Ann asked. "We don't want to impose."

Rodney had a big grin on his face. "Wow, that would be neat."

"Where would we fly out of?" Ann inquired.

"Why, here in Madison." Amy responded, almost incredulously.

"They have flights from Madison to St. Martin?" Big Brother inquired.

"No, you can use the family plane." Amy responded.

"You have a plane?" Rodney incredulously asked.

"I don't. Dad does." Amy replied.

And he'll fly us there?"

"Dad has a pilot."

"It can go that far?"

"Sure, it's an eight passenger Gulfstream 650 that is equipped for over-water and international flight."

"Oh my, God." both of them were incredibly excited.

Amy continued. "My uncle Frank works for dad and takes care of the property Dad has down on St. Martin. We have several houses and condos that we rent out, but our house is only used by family and special friends." Amy replied. "Uncle Frank will take care of everything when you get there, sailing, snorkeling, diving and even the restaurants. If you want, he can arrange a personal chef to come to the house, but the restaurants on the French side in Grand Case are really good."

"I think it would be cool to go sailing and scuba diving," Rodney noted.

"Amy added. "No problem. We have a catamaran and all the equipment and you can use it whenever you want to. Uncle Frank can arrange for the crew and diving partners so that you're with professional divers who know the area. For that, he will probably need a day's notice"

"How about renting a car?" Rodney asked.

"There's a car at the house for your use. All dad asks is that the tank is full when you leave. The whole deal is pretty cool, as Uncle Frank loves company. He makes a big deal out of making people feel special."

I watched the two of them squirm with excitement. It was the most fun with them since the day they met.

"Your dad doesn't really need to do this." Ann said.

"My dad doesn't do anything he doesn't want to. The house sits empty most of the time and this is his and mom's way of saying thank you for all you've done for me".

We headed home knowing that the couple in the front of the boat had great big grins on their faces while the two of us soaked up the good feelings that wafted from them.

Memorial Day and Tuesday were just like normal days at the factory. Wednesday, Amy started filling me in on what she thought would come next in my conversations with Great Grandfather. She was beginning to believe that if she went along, the dead Indians wouldn't come out and speak to me and so I was going solo.

Greendeer: I awoke early Thursday and made my way to the Dells. You could tell schools were out because the town was packed. I made my way to the assisted living center and arrived in Great Grandfather's room precisely at ten.

As was always the case, Great Grandfather was sitting in his rocker and a smile came across his face. "Little Spirit. You are here, but you are alone, where is the one who puts so much joy in your heart?"

"She had a conflict," I lied to Great Grandfather.

"Don't let her slip away Little Spirit. She fills your heart with too much joy."

"I know Great Grandfather"

"Come, pull up the chest and let's talk. I believe that the spirits have much to say today."

I pulled up the old chest as I had done before and put my hands in Great Grandfather's. Once again, the chant began. Once again, a different voice emanated from the old man. It was deeper, sharper and more intense than ever before, filled with anger and frustration.

"My name is Greendeer. I am the leader of the Winnebago or what is left of our nation. With each summer, we find more white men on our land. Not their land...our land...taken from us...not purchased from us. There is a great war in a place called Europe between the British and the French. Our only wish is that they destroy each other and leave us alone. Yet, we can already see that their war is becoming our war, their hatred our hatred, their demise, our demise."

"The British claimed the Ohio in 1744 with the Treaty of Lancaster with the Iroquois and the Shawnee with the Treaty of Logtown in 1748. The Iroquois and Shawnee were fools to sell their land. Where will they go? A beaver who builds a damn does not give it to the otter and move away. He fights to keep what is his. While many days away by horseback, the war clouds of the east blew back towards our peace when the Ottawa and Ojibwa warriors supported the French and attacked the British in 1752 at a place called Pickawillany and killed Demoiselle, the great Chief of the Miami."

"We were but observers as the French took Fort Necessity from General George Washington. When one must take sides in time of war, it is better to deal with those who are the strongest than the weakest and it is still even better to deal with those with whom you have had dealings than complete strangers, which the British were…cold, aloof, indifferent, towards all nations, believing they have all the answers and we have none. Our Gods! Our way of life! To them we are nothing but animals to be harvested like the deer and bear. We along with the Ottawa, Algonkin, Wyandot, Nipissing, Ojibwa, Potawatomi, Sauk, Shawnee and Seneca reinforced our alliance with the French in a war called 'The Seven Years War'. We do not trust the French any more than the British, but at least they do not treat us as fools."

"In 1755, Major General Braddock of the British army attacked the French with four columns of infantry and naval vessels. We were asked to show our support of the French in our alliance and 100 Winnebago warriors along with 500 warriors from the allied nations fought side-by-side in the forests beside Fort Duquesne in the Monongahela Valley."

"General Braddock was assassinated along with 800 of his men. They lost because we knew how to fight and they did not. We fought with passion. They fought because they were ordered to. Our warriors claimed the forest and attacked the regiment. 800 British died not knowing who or where the enemy lay, while just 39 warriors died of which only one was from our nation. While the Winnebago and all Indian nations who sided with the French were victorious in battle that day, we all lost the Seven Year War and it would take many moons until we realized that the consequences upon our nation would never end."

"In 1763 the Seven Years War was over and all land formerly called New France came under British rule. All Indian nations went from trading partners with the French to subjects of the British. The end of the French fur trade met with dire circumstances for our people. The British did not forget that we had been their enemies and so cheating and high prices for goods became the norm and we were forced to sell our furs at British forts where our men were treated like little boys, made drunk with fire water, made fools of and let go in disgrace."

I could actually feel the anger in Greendeer's voice. I could sense his frustration, humiliation and degradation. A proud man, a proud people, a proud nation brought to its knees by the British.

"A great leader by the name of Pontiac could not tolerate the abuse of the British and so he sent messengers to all nations asking them to join him in his battles at Fort Pitt and Fort Detroit while others attacked other forts within the region. On June 1, 1763 an allied group attacked Fort Quiatenon and it fell into our hands. By September all forts west of Fort Detroit had been overrun and over 2,000 encroaching settlers had been killed. They did not belong on Indian land.

By fall when Fort Detroit had not come under his command, Pontiac realized that there was a stalemate and Fort Detroit could not be taken. With winter nearly upon the north, Pontiac realized he needed to negotiate a peace settlement with the British. As part of the settlement, the British provided blankets for warmth. Within the blankets was a disease called smallpox, intentionally put there to decimate and destroy all those who came in contact with them. Some Shawnee and Delaware received the sick blankets and their nation's women, children and elderly who had not been in battle became victims of the British war covered in British blisters as they writhed in a painful British death.

The British realized the bravery of our Indian warriors and wanted security for their settlers. In 1763, the British issued a proclamation that created a boundary between the settlers in the east and the Indian nations in the west. This line was to stop the settlers from taking land that was not theirs. This line was to bring peace to all. In the end, all that it did was hold back what was to come. Defer it until, like the beaver's dam, until the pressure for more broke open the line and the settlers flooded in. We fought as warriors. We thought we fought against honorable men in their red and white suits who drank tea from fancy cups. I ask you, what kind of people make women and children suffer and die by giving them sick blankets? What kind of people agree and then break promises? What kind of people fight for land and not dignity, only to spread their way of life amongst those who wanted nothing more than to live in peace?

Great Grandfather was wheezing with the energy of contempt that spewed forth. I knew his body could not take much more and then he slumped forward and there was silence. Greendeer was gone. Greendeer had spoken his piece. Greendeer had shared his frustration and his anger and left me sitting, wondering about all those who came before me.

As had been the case previously, I expected Great Grandfather's hands to go limp, but they did not. Instead his eyes opened wide and he warned me. "Little Spirit, beware of the forest. Many men have been there and they are not your allies. Stop them before it is too late."

I had no idea what Great Grandfather was talking about as his hands went limp and he dove into a deep sleep…a little old man in a rocking chair with a quilt on his lap. My God. What was happening?

Lockheed: I hadn't been home in nearly two months. No one in Waldwick knew about Amy. I met her parents twice and the time had come to have her meet my family. I called home and talked to mom and told her that I had met someone special and wondered if I could bring her home. Mom, of course, said "yes" but then what was she to say…"no?" Moms don't do that.

I asked Amy if she would like to meet my family and she said yes. I called mom back and it was set for the following Sunday. I chose that day as I thought Ann and Big Brother needed a day in the house without the two of us, even though Amy was getting to the point she could be on her own. As the day neared, I was nervous. What would happen if they didn't like her? What would they think when I came home with a mixed-race woman? While it was the twenty-first century, there are still those folks out there who simply don't get it and I didn't know where mom and dad stood on the issue as it never came up in lily-white Waldwick.

Sunday came and we headed out. We took Highway 39 and missed the Madison Madness called the Beltline. Amy loved the scenery. To me, it was just more farms. I headed for Waldwick. We took the Jeep as Amy wanted my family to learn who she was and not what she was and the Audi actually embarrassed her. Tommie would have fallen in love with her, had he seen the car.

We made our way up the driveway and our official greeter was at my door when we stopped, tail wagging, barking, whining, happy to see me. Amy got out and Jake went to her and she bent down to pet him and it looked like he had a smile on his face. We made our way up to the house and opened the door. Jake, of course was the first one in. He didn't want to be left out of a family get together.

Mom came out of the kitchen and had a big smile on her face. I introduced the two of them and mom did something I'd never seen her do before…she gave Amy a hug. Mom is/was a conservative farm girl and she never did things like this before.

Mom noticed the walking boot and asked Amy what happened. Amy, of course, told her I pushed her down a cliff at Devil's Lake and did one of her girly giggles before telling the truth. Mom asked if it hurt and Amy said in the beginning yes, but now, it was just the inconvenience of the boot and it would be gone in three or four weeks. She spoke of her shoulder and hand and showed they had healed nicely.

We went out and sat on the screen porch and mom asked a million questions about school, where we met, when we met, all the girlie stuff. Jake sat with his head in my lap. He wasn't going to be cut out of the attention. Dad and Tommie were next door, which was over a mile away, helping fix a tractor and would be home in time for chores. They left Jake home just to see me. When it seemed like all the possible questions could be answered, mom asked Amy if she would like to go to my favorite spot in the entire world. I was shocked.

With the boot and all, I didn't know if Amy could handle the walk, even if we took the ATV to the edge of the forest. Amy was up for it. I went and got the ATV and pulled up to the house. Jake wanted to go, but mom held him back. This was to be our trip to my favorite place on earth. We both put on helmets and slowly headed out. It's only a mile and I took it real slow. As we came to the edge of the forest, Amy tugged on my shoulder and told me to shut off the engine. I did.

"My God, it's beautiful." she said as she looked into the valley. "It's just like George the First said it was." Amy closed her eyes for a moment and smiled. "Is this where the apple trees and the school were?" She remembered what had happened from George the First's book.

"Yes," I replied as I looked around for signs of intrusion but found none.

"It's so peaceful here. It's no wonder why you love it. I don't know why, it almost feels religious."

The soft breeze was willowing across the tall hay and you could see the wind as it moved each blade of grass and Amy's hair. Quite honestly, I don't know which looked more beautiful. However, I did realize what was going to happen to the hay and what it would become, namely cow shit and voted for Amy's hair.

We slowly made our way down to where Skunk Hollow School once stood and Amy and I got off the ATV. The only sound was the soft June breeze in the trees. I pointed out where Running Deer had been. I outlined where my ancestors had walked and then took her to the spot where George the First had saved Rodney's ancestor. Amy was struggling a bit with the boot but pushed on. We made it to the little brook where the water came from beneath the rocks. I bent down and cupped my hands and gave Amy a drink. Her head tilted back and she looked deeply into my eyes. "There is something I've been wanting to do for a long, long time. Something that I have been saving for a special time and place."

With that, we found a small patch of long grass and I matted it down and we made love. This wasn't about sex. This was about two people sharing themselves with each other. It was quiet. It was peaceful. It was splendid and everything I had dreamt it would be. This was our first time and it would always be remembered. This was my special place with my special girl and the love and joy within my heart had taken what we shared and moved it beyond anything physical, beyond anything emotional and into a realm unlike anything I had ever felt in my life. My God, it was special.

We lay in the grass, holding each other listening to our hearts beat. We got up and dressed and walked back to the ATV, kissed and climbed on board. Amy gave me a hug and I could feel her joy as we headed home.

I think mom knew what happened as what little edge that had been there before we left was replaced by smiles all around. It wasn't long until dad and Tommie came home and were introduced to Miss Amelia Williams, better known as Amy. There was no resistance. There was no second guessing. There was no delineation. Within a few minutes, all parties were laughing at my trials and tribulations and smiling and enjoying each other's company. Poor Amy had to answer all the same questions again as mom was in the kitchen making dinner.

Mom wanted to eat in the dining room. Dad wanted to eat in the kitchen. Mom's was a sign of respect. Dad's was a sign of acceptance. We ate in the kitchen. I smiled. After dinner, Tommie excused himself and indicated that he would go start milking…a reminder that 250 Holsteins needed tending to. I could tell that Dad didn't want to join him, but duty called.

Amy asked if she could watch and Dad politely told her that cows get skittish when there are strangers around and so, if she wouldn't be offended, she could watch through the window.

We all walked out to the barn and looked into the milking parlor. I explained to Amy that each Holstein cow costs about $22,000 to raise from birth through full maturity. I explained that each cow had a microchip implanted in its leg that was tied into the computer. As the cows came into the barn, they were weighed and their temperature taken. If there was any problem, the cow would automatically be sent to the infirmary area to be examined. The cows all went through what I called the "cow wash", where they were cleaned by soft brushes. Some cows loved it and others really didn't like it at all.

I added. "At each milking, the cows got in line and it never varies, unless one was missing for whatever the reason. As they enter the milking parlor they always go to the same stanchion where they receive a prescribed amount of feed and, if needed, vitamins and medication. The bar across their back is to keep the cow from "humping" to relieve itself as it would get a shock if it touches the bar. Tommie or Dad adds the milking machine and the milk goes through the pipes where it is weighed and the butter fat measured."

"An average cow produces 70 pounds or about 8 gallons of milk per day. Milk production is always measured in hundred-weight, or 100 pounds of milk. Our herd of 250 cows produces one large tanker of milk every -other-day that is picked up and taken to the dairy where most of it is made into cheese. Over a year, our 250 cows total milk production averages about six million pounds. At about seventeen dollars per hundred-weight the gross revenue is about a million dollars a year, which, if all went well, is the break-even point for the business."

Amy seemed shocked as I continued. "Dairy farming isn't as simple as you might think. It's agribusiness that works on high costs, varying levels of income depending somewhat on a free market plus the government, including tremendous risks. You have to go through the routine twice each day, and then make sure each cow is healthy and calves each year. Without calves, there would be no milk. To be a dairy farmer, you have to do it because you love it. Tommie does. I don't."

The show was nearly over. It was getting dark and Amy put her good arm through mine as we walked back to the house. Jake was at our side. He knew he was getting the night off as his job was to make sure any strays were rounded up and sent through the process. We went back in the house and Amy outlined everything I had told her to mom, who was incredulous to think that she had such recall.

We were about to leave when I asked Amy if she could make it up the stairs so that I could show her my room. There was something special, I wanted her to see. She carefully climbed and I took her into my bedroom. I knew that mom would be counting the minutes and there were no ulterior motives. I showed her my high school letters and pictures of me at the fair. She laughed and giggled and squeezed my hand. The thing I wanted to show her was up on a shelf….it was the model of Amelia Emhart's Model Lockheed 10E that I had made. I carefully took it off the shelf, wiped the dust off and handed it to her. "To the new Amelia in my life. I want you to have this in memory of today."

Amy had tears in her eyes and then a frown and then more tears before she kissed me. "I will always cherish this and today."

Now I was getting a lump in my throat which was certainly a lot better than the lump I had in my pants for the past few weeks.

We went downstairs and mom saw the model plane in Amy's hands and knew this was more than just some girl from Madison. I hugged mom goodbye and so did Amy.

"It was so nice meeting you Amy. Please come again." Mom said with a smile on her face as she nodded her approval.

As we were walking out the door, I looked at mom and her at me and she winked. It was her way of saying that everything was OK.

Amy wanted to say goodbye to dad and Tommie, but they were still working. Instead, she took a piece of paper from her purse and wrote a note thanking both of them for their hospitality and she hoped to see them again and slipped it under the wiper on dad's truck.

Jake was still following us and I told him to go into the barn. He understood that we were leaving and it was all right for him to go and be with Tommie and dad and so he left as we got into the Jeep. Mom was still at the front door and waved as we pulled out and headed for home just as the outside lights came on. Amy slid her hand in mine and held the plane in her other only letting go to slowly twirl the propellers on Amelia's plane as I drove. I looked at her and had a smile on my face as we drove in silence. I think she did too.

As we neared the cottage I got a text from mom. It said, "WONDERFUL." All in caps. Next a text from Tommie giving his approval. Dad never text anybody and I don't even think he knew how, but I could tell by the way he took time to outline what was going on in the milking parlor that he liked Amy.

We entered the cottage and Big Brother and Ann were watching TV. They had been out in the boat for the afternoon and the sun had set upon their faces. For the first time, I felt like I was intruding and I think Amy felt the same way. That night Amy and I went to my bedroom and she popped the question…did I want to move in with her? I had been with Rodney and Ann for six months and it was time. They needed their privacy and space.

"Do you really want me to?"

"Yes, dummy."

"What about your parents, what will they say?"

"I already talked to mom and she thinks it's great."

"What about the Duke?" It seemed weird calling Amy's dad, The Duke, but I really didn't know what else to call him.

"He's not going to be as excited, but if you say yes, mom can begin the process of softening him up."

"Well…OK." I said with a smile. "But you're sure your dad won't mind me using his bedroom?"

For that I got punched in the stomach. At least it was with her right hand and not a left hook.

The next morning, we called a breakfast meeting of the fearsome foursome. Amy took the lead…"I cannot express my gratitude enough for your generosity and kindness the past four weeks. You have opened your home and your heart to me and I will always be grateful. However, I think it's time for me to move back to the condo."

Rodney and Ann shook their heads in agreement. "There are still a few things I can't do and so I've asked 'Q' to join me."

Again, nods of affirmation. I think they knew it was coming. It was my turn to speak. "How can I ever say thank you for all that you have done, all that you have tolerated and all that you have given me? We are only a boat ride away and we will still see each other at work."

"When are you thinking about doing this?" Rodney asked.

I replied. "If I take all my worldly possessions and add them to Amy's, it should take about fifteen minutes."

There were guffaws all around the table. We finished breakfast and loaded the Jeep. It actually took twenty minutes, so I must have had more than I thought I had.

We all hugged and once again said thanks, got in the Jeep and headed towards the condo, riding up Stoughton Road, west on the beltline, across John Nolen drive and up west Wilson Street. I parked in spot 805, next to the Audi and went upstairs where I carried Miss Amy across the threshold. Needless to say, it was a while before I started moving in as we had something we needed to do to consummate the agreement.

I told Amy to get settled and I would bring everything in from the Jeep. As I was riding down on the elevator, some old lady got in and looked at me. "You live here?" She asked.

"Yes, Mam."

"You living with that black girl?"

"She's not black Mam she is just a richer shade of brown than you and me. And yes Mam, I am living with her! She is the woman that I love…kind, gracious, funny, intelligent and dignified enough that she wouldn't have taken your comments as an insult, but only as an observation. Have a nice day."

I got off the elevator and went to the Jeep. Comments made were to be kept within the elevator and Amy was not to know. I came upstairs and handed her the suitcase and her clothes on their hangars. As she was unpacking, I got mine from the truck and walked into her dad's bedroom.

"Where should I put your dad's clothes?" I questioned.

"Ha, ha, ha, silly man. I made room for you in the closet and you get three drawers in the big dresser."

I only had clothes to fill two drawers and my jeans and sports coat took up less than six inches in her closet.

"Four basic apartment rules… Amy said "First, no dirty clothes on the floor, only in the basket! Second, no going to bed angry at each other. Third, all opened food put away. Fourth, no more loud snoring."

My eyes must have opened wide on number four as she gave me one of her girlie giggles and then hung her arms around my neck and kissed me.

"Welcome home." she said.

I kissed her back. "Tomorrow, my dear, das boot goes away and you get kissed all over."

"I can't wait for that." she said.

"Do I really snore?"

Amy just giggled.

I sent a text to Rodney and Ann and told them that we were all moved in and all was well and asked them to dinner the following Sunday night. Big Brother had never been to the condo and it was our way of saying thanks.

Two minutes later, the response was 'yes' and 6:00 PM was set.

Something to look forward to!

Our first guests as a couple.

Das Boot: Monday morning we went to see Dr. Goldman and the boot was taken off. The break was repaired and no more thump, thump, thump. The good doctor encouraged Amy to see one of his physical therapists regarding the shoulder. Amy asked the doctor if he knew any therapists that could help me. The doctor replied, he knew therapists…not miracle workers. Tee hee!

Amy wanted to go shopping, so we went home and she dropped me off and took the Jeep as it was automatic and didn't require shifting like the Audi did. I got to work on the 2,000 words and called mom and informed her that I had moved into Amy's apartment. She wasn't surprised and asked where Amy put Amelia. I noted that it was on a shelf above her computer. Mom said she knew this one was serious and I said "yes". She said she could see it in my eyes when we first arrived and that even dairy farmer dad caught the gist.

I asked if there was any problem with the different shades of brown and mom said she hadn't noticed. I thanked her for that and hoped that dad felt the same way. I told her that I needed to come home to get some stuff and would fill her and dad in on all that was going on. She asked when and I told her I didn't know. I was about to go to work at the factory and would check my and Amy's schedule. She understood, but then moms usually do.

When Amy got home, I told her I called mom and that they really liked her. Amy asked if there was any problem with the different shades of brown and I told her absolutely not and she smiled. With everything going on and Amy able to drive again, she needed to go to Milwaukee and we both thought that if she went home, I'd go to Waldwick on the same day. She thought she would go to Milwaukee Friday afternoon and come back Saturday afternoon. I told her, I'd do the same. Our first night apart in nearly five weeks. Yikes.

I called mom to check and see if Friday night was going to work and she said yes. I thought we could go into town for a fish fry. I hadn't been to one in months. Mom thought that would be cool. The week flew by and it was time to go see Great Grandfather again.

Chaurachon: Ten O'clock sharp. As usual, Great Grandfather was in his rocking chair with the quilt over his legs. Walking in, I was met with his gracious smile and told to bring the old chest over and take his hands. I did as I was told. The chanting began and the voice changed to a deep, almost sinister, tone as Great Grandfather's head tilted back.

"I am Chaurachon, the leader of the great Winnebago Nation. I am a warrior who has fought the white man my entire life, taking many scalps from my enemies including the Illinois. We have not had peace during my lifetime. Only war. Why can't the white man just leave us alone? The red coats treat us like dogs and yet, we need them for our weapons. They have come to our village and told us how we must live and how we must die. I will only die with honor and for my people."

"The white settlers had not forgotten the Pontiac War and they wanted revenge against Indians and the British. We were told there will be a great war and once again, we will be called upon to fight with our oppressors. At first, we said 'no', we only wanted to live in peace. Then we heard from many different people that a group called the Paxon Boys led by a Presbyterian church Elder butchered six Christian Indians at Conestoga, Pennsylvania. When the remaining members of the Susquehannock tribe...old women and children mind you, searched for safety and found it in a safe blockhouse, the mob broke down the doors and killed them all. A Mr. John Penn wrote...'they were divided into their families, the children clinging to their parents; they fell on their knees, protested their innocence, declared their love of the English, and that, in their whole lives, they had never done them injury; and in this posture they all received the hatchet. Men, women and little children! Everyone was inhumanely murdered! These Indian people were doing what the white man wanted and yet it was not good enough. If that was not enough, these butchers marched into Philadelphia and murdered 140 more Christian Indians living there. What kind of God did these people worship? What kind of man kills women and children? They are not warriors but cowards and if they come to me, I will kill them all and hang their scalps around my waist to remind me that they are animals and not people."

"All Indians who had been in touch with the settlers felt threatened. The settlers came and took land that was not theirs. General Stuart, a British solider, asked many of my brother nations to fight with him against the settlers. At first, it was intended that the Indians and British would fight together as our numbers were great. However, the way of war of the British was organized and structured. The war of my people was one of silent attack, using the land as its ally. The nations took it upon themselves to attack settlers along the edges that led to harsh retaliation by the Americans. Villages were burned and food stores destroyed with many, particularly the Cherokee, abandoning all that was theirs…homes, fields and livestock. The efforts of the Cherokee and of the Americans was settled when the Cherokee gave up all land east of the mountains where my ancestors came from."

"Cherokee Chief, Corn Tassel spoke of the many battles and the difference between the white settlers and his people. He said. 'I am sure that if we give up these lands the British will give us more than 100 pounds. They will spoil our hunting grounds; but the land will always remain good to raise families and stocks on. However, when the goods we receive are rotten and your stocks are tame and marked and we don't know ours, because they are wild what will we do? Hunting is our principal way of living."

"Our council sat and voted to assist the British in what was called the Revolutionary War. We did so, not because we liked or trusted the British, but because they were the ones who put guns and bullets in our hands and allowed us to fight our wars and the British could control their soldiers while the Americans could not. When we learned that the American soldiers had murdered the neutral Delaware Chief White Eyes and the neutral Shawnee Chief Cornstalk, we realized that our future safety required our alliance with the British, even though neither side could stop the tide of settlers who broke every promise ever made by their great leaders."

"As the war continued and we saw the British begin to lose ground, our council voted to make peace with the Americans as a way to prevent further bloodshed within our nation. When, in 1777, we learned of the Battle of Saratoga that saw British General Burgoyne lay down his arms as 5,000 British soldiers surrendered, we knew that we were on the wrong side of the war. In 1778, we met with General George Rogers Clark who represented the United States and entered into a treaty that we believed would provide peace to our nation and safety to our families."

"We fought and we signed a treaty that, in the end, was not worth the paper it was written on. The Treaty of Paris of 1783 ended the hostilities between the British and the Americans. The British, with no right to the land, ceded it from the great water where the sun rises to the west and the great river, now called the Mississippi. This was not their right. Much of this land was Indian land, not British land. The Proclamation of 1763 limiting land of the settlers to that east of the great mountains meant nothing. Once again, the white man showed he did not respect the rights of the Indian nations and its people."

"The Revolutionary War was over, but the war we were willing to fight to save our land, our people and our way of life had just begun. I am an old man and yet, I would raise a musket against those who take away what is mine. I would rather die with honor than live as a coward humiliated by broken promises and the greed of others."

Great Grandfather was completely exhausted. He released my hands and I saw tears in his eyes. So much pain and suffering had been channeled through him. So much sorrow! I didn't know how many more times he could endure. I only hoped and prayed that all those in line waiting to tell their stories would get their chance before this last bridge to the past was permanently broken.

I went back to the condo and Amy was hard at work. I outlined the session and she said that she had been studying the effects of the Revolutionary War on the indigenous people from a legal perspective. She noted that she was researching the Northwest Ordinances of 1784, 1785 and 1787 that established the basic structure for territories and statehood.

Amy noted that the ordinance of 1784 established the national American domain while that of 1785 decreed all land would be surveyed and divided into six-hundred-forty-acre parcels that would be sold by the government to fund the infrastructure and educational systems. Amy found it interesting that when a defined area's population reached 20,000, that area could hold a constitutional convention and become a Territory with its own government and representation in Congress. When the population reached that of the smallest state, or 60,000, it became a State of the Union. Finally, and critically, the 1787 Ordinance stated that good faith was required toward the Indians and their land and that it would never be taken from them. Suuure!

Fish Fry: Friday morning Amy left early for Milwaukee and I worked on my 2,000 words until around three when I headed for home. I got to Waldwick around 4:30 just as Tommie and dad were finishing milking. Damn Beltline! I waited in the house as the cows didn't like me either. They…Tommie and Dad…not the cows…came in to get cleaned up and I could tell by the look on dad's face that something was up. At first, I thought it might be Amy, but the furrows in his brow were too deep.

Mom got home and had a weird look on her face, too. Tommie said hello/goodbye and never looked me in the eyes. I was getting worried. We went out to dinner in Mineral Point and I detailed Amy, how I met her, the challenges she was facing and how we had decided to give cohabitation a try. Mom was worried that I was rushing into things. I told her that I had never felt the way I did about any other person and I couldn't risk losing her.

Dad asked about Amy's parents. I told him that Amy's dad was in finance in Milwaukee and that her mom was from St. Martin. I told them how they met and how Amy's dad came home and caught the next plane back to St. Martin to propose. I didn't tell them that Amy's parents were some of the richest people in Wisconsin.

Now it was my turn to ask the questions…What's going on?" I asked.

"What do you mean, son?" Dad responded.

"Is it Amy?"

"Heavens, no." Mom replied, shaking her head to make certain I completely understood.

"Since I've been home you two and Tommie have been tiptoeing like you're walking on broken glass. Tommie wouldn't even look me in the eye."

"It's the county, son." Dad answered.

"What about the county?"

"They want the forest."

"What do you mean, they want the forest?"

"They want to put a park in the forest."

"They can't just do that. It's our land." I retorted.

"They can if they want to and there's not much we can do about it."

"They can't just take my forest." I was getting agitated.

"They've offered to buy it."

"It's not for sale."

"Son, you don't understand. If the government wants the land, they can take it."

"Why, you've paid taxes on it all these years? It's been in our family for nearly 200 years." The volume of my voice was increasing with each word.

"Son, please calm down."

"Dad, that small amount of land is the only thing I ever wanted. You know that."

"I know, son. But they are having planning meetings and if they want it, they can take it"

Now my anger level was really bubbling up as I threatened, "I'll fight them."

How? With what? You know that milk prices are low and we're hardly making a profit. I'll need to hire a lawyer and son, I simply can't afford the fight." Dad responded in a raised voice.

"Sell me the land, dad."

"What?" dad said incredulously.

"Sell the land to me and let me fight them."

"How in hell do you think you can afford to fight them? You just graduated from college and don't have any money." Now he was getting irritated.

"Tell you what. Give me the ten acres and I'll sign an agreement that Tommie gets everything else."

"What?" Now dad was shaking his head in disbelief.

"Dad, I have no interest in the farm or being a farmer. Tommie loves it. Give me the land and let it be my battle"

Dad shook his head 'no'.

"Dad I haven't asked for much and I don't expect much, but I am willing to fight for the land and for our ancestors."

"Please, dad! Mom, please let it be this way! You know Tommie deserves the farm, not me. All I want is my forest, please?" I was begging her.

I went back to the farm and that night and I couldn't sleep. I got up around two and walked to the forest and cried. This was our family. This was Rodney's family. This was all that we had that linked us to the past. I sat and felt the dew around me. I watched as the sun rose in the east and then slowly made my way back to the house.

Mom was in the kitchen making breakfast. "I'm going home to Madison. Please tell dad that my proposal stands."

The drive home was long…much longer than ever before. I pulled into slot 805 and made my way up the elevator. I opened the door to the solitude and looked out at the lake. The sailboats were already skimming across the water and the joy that should have been in my heart was gone. I sat staring when the door opened. It was Amy. She took one look at me and knew that something was wrong. I told her all that was going on and began to cry. I held her and we trembled together. After a few minutes, she let go and said, "Let me call dad."

She got The Duke on the phone and explained what was going on. He must have told her to get a piece of paper and she began writing things down. "Uh huh. Uh huh. Uh huh." was all I got out of her.

"Dad said that if the land has not been improved, the county can come after it under eminent domain, taking private land for public good. He noted that the value established by the county would be based on tax assessments and not on sale prices because the land had been in the family for so long. He indicated that one option was transfer the land into your name and that the purchase price should be half the value of the farm. This would make the county think twice about taking it as the cost should be prohibitive. He noted that the county would fight the valuation and it would only be a delaying tactic until something else could be done. He said that he would have one of the partners get hold of us and work through the details."

I asked how much all this would cost and Amy looked at me incredulously. "After all you've done for me?"

Fifteen minutes later the phone rang and it was Mr. Raskin, one of Amy's dad's law partners. He indicated that he felt we could stymie the process for a year and The Duke would make a few well-placed calls on Monday to see what was going on.

I told him I had a different idea. "What would happen if I went into partnership with the Ho-Chunk nation and they purchased half the land with me with the understanding that it would always remain unfettered as a place of spiritual significance?"

Mr. Raskin said it would need to be justified and I outlined what had happened to Rodney's great, great, great grandmother and all about running deer. He noted we needed proof. I told him about the journal George Terrill the First had written that outlined everything. He said he would need a few days to have an aid look into the laws but having a recognized independent nation as part owners would certainly slow things down, if not completely stop the process altogether. He told me to chill out, that these things could drag out for months or years. However, he did feel that something needed to be done or the land would be foreclosed without a fight.

I was tense, to say the least. I needed to get dad to sell me the land. I needed to get Rodney to believe in the property. I needed to get the Chief and the Ho-Chunk board to agree. I needed to develop a strategy and needed to do it all fast. I called mom and told her of the plan and asked her to see if dad would go along with the restructuring. The only thing that would change is primary ownership, as the land would stay exactly as it had been for all of time. She promised that she would talk to dad. Then I had another idea, why not take Rodney and Ann down to

Waldwick and let them see the land. We were having dinner with them the next night. If they could come early, we could easily go down there.

I called Rodney and explained what was going on and asked if we could leave a little earlier. He said yes. I called mom and asked her if we could all come for dinner. She said yes. We would have to go in the Jeep as four people would never fit in the Audi or the Batmobile and Ann's Hyundai was the small one.

Ann and Rodney showed up precisely at 2:00. Amy showed Rodney the apartment and then we all climbed in Jeepers creepers and headed for Waldwick. We went down 18&151 past Verona, Mount Horeb, Ridgeway, Barneveld, Blue Mounds and then Dodgeville, where I pointed out where Jeepers creepers number one went into the ditch with me in it. I told them to start looking for the Mineral Point water tower and how Tommie and I used to see who could see it first when we were little. We took the road into town and went down Shake Rag Street past the brewery one of my ancestors built and then Pendarvis and the limestone cottage my mother's great, great grandmother built herself when she met a farmer and they married. We turned towards Darlington and got off at the Waldwick exit. It was just past four when we pulled in the driveway. Of course, Jake was there to greet us, getting up from his favorite outdoor spot beneath the old oak tree.

Tommie and dad were just finishing chores. Mom came out onto the front porch and invited everyone in. We went out on the screen porch where mom already had extra rocking chairs. Pleasantries were exchanged as Rodney and Ann got to bring mom up-to-date on the wedding plans. Amy got to show off her left foot with no boot. Soon dad and Tommie joined us with dad all smiles. We discussed the county and what was going on. Dad had calmed down and that helped me calm down too. Big Brother was his normal analytical self. Tommie excused himself as he was having dinner at Heather's house. Dad had a hay wagon attached to the John Deere and we all went for a hay ride to the forest.

Dad helped Ann, Amy and mom down from the wagon and the six of us walked into the forest. Rodney stopped and I saw tears in his eyes. Ann stopped as shivers went up and down her spine. The intensity of the spirit was so great that I think any Native American would have felt them. We truly were at a spiritual place that was affecting them to a much greater degree than it ever affected me. Rodney's head tilted back and his eyes closed. Ann looked at him for a moment and then slid her hand in his. The energy was between them. It was spiritual energy and they were convoluted in love.

"Oh, my God!" Rodney said. "Oh, my God. I have never felt like this before. The feelings! The emotions! Everything you said is truly here. I don't need to go any further. We cannot allow this sacred place to ever change." He said as he looked at Ann.

Rodney stood for a moment as we watched in total silence and then began the tour…where the school had stood…where his great, great grandmother had survived, to which he knelt down and grasped some of the cool earth and rubbed it between his hands. Finally, we walked to the spring where Rodney cupped his hands and drank in its purity. I watched as a shiver went through his body. Not a cold shiver, but one of total encumbrance to the magnitude of what transpired. The tall grass that had been Amy and my bed was still flattened and it brought back pleasant memories for the two of us as Amy squeezed my hand.

"Can I bring the Chief here?" Rodney asked.

"Who's the Chief?" dad asked.

"I'm sorry, Mr. Terrill, my father."

"Certainly!"

We all walked back to the wagon and dad drove us back to the house. Steaks were put on the grill with assurances to Amy that dinner hadn't been one of the 'cute' cows she had seen the week before. We ate dinner together in a quiet manner as if we had all just come from church. When dinner was over, it was time to head back to Madison. The mood was quiet and respectful as the reverse trip unwound.

As we were just passing Verona, Rodney noted that whatever it would take, we could count on him and he was certain that when his dad visited, the entire nation would be behind the plan. I hoped so as I couldn't afford to go it alone and knew for certain that mom and dad wouldn't even be able to start.

Monday meant back to the factory and no call from Mr. Raskin. Tuesday was the same. I was getting anxious. The Duke had done some digging and found out whose idea it was to create a county park and it happened to be someone who had never been in the favor of the Terrill family. He had gone to the planning commission with photographs of the land and taken the time to outline the plan for the park. It would consist of one parking area and an outhouse. This was going to be their park. They wanted to put the outhouse right on top of the old school foundation and create a walking path to the springs. They wanted to violate the sanctity of the land "for public good."

Dad was coming around to the idea of selling the land to the Ho-Chunk and me. We broached the subject with Mr. Raskin and he indicated that he could draw up a Quitclaim Deed to speed up the process. I asked what it was and Mr. Raskin replied. "In general, quitclaim deeds are useful when it comes to transferring property between family members who trust one another. They also come in handy when deeding a property as a gift to a person or estate. They can even be used to transfer property owned by a business entity to another business or a person. In some cases, quitclaim deeds are also used to actually eliminate any clouds or encumbrances that can end up on a title."

He said the best thing to do was to have dad initiate a Quitclaim Deed to me and then have me sell half of the property rights to the Ho-Chunk. In so doing, the property would be expedited and the county would face further delays. I called dad and asked him and he agreed to go forward with the plan.

I called Mr. Raskin back and told him we had a go. He noted that the property would need to be surveyed. He didn't want Iowa County to know about it and so they would send a surveyor from Milwaukee that The Duke used. Mr. Raskin called back an hour later and said the surveyor would be at the house on Friday if that was convenient. I called dad and he said it was fine.

Spoon Decorah: I made another journey to the Dells to meet with Great Grandfather. His spirits were low and the soft smile had faded as he spoke. "The clouds are darker than ever Little Spirit. The holy land is at risk. The spirits wander and have asked the Great Spirit to use his power to save this sacred spot. I am disheartened that the white man must take everything from us and won't even leave us a few memories."

I needed to cheer up the old man and so I outlined who Amy's father was and all that was happening. I explained the quitclaim deed action. The plan was to "sell" half interest in the land to the Ho-Chunk nation so that the battle was not Iowa County against one dairy farmer, but against a nation of people who had the resources necessary to finally draw a line in the sand and say "Enough is enough. You have taken everything before, but not this time."

We would use the public relations arm of the Casinos to get the message out. We were willing to mobilize protestors to stop any incursion and had other political allies of The Duke who were willing to bring pressure on whomever it took to have the matter dropped. My outline brought the spirits of this dear old man back from darkness as he smiled and said that I was truly a warrior but instead of a bow and knife, I was using the weapons of today in battle…public opinion.

Once again, Great Grandfather's head tilted back. Once again, the soft chant began. How many more times could he do this? I did not know. All I knew was that deep within his soul there was a need for the anger, frustration and humiliation that these people had experienced to escape and I had been chosen to be its recipient, allowing me to reach back into time and tell their story. Was it because of George the First? Was it because of the land and how important it is to me? Were they joined in one long emotional chain where each link, each voice, each experience represents yet another part of the story? I was about to tell that would determine my place in history and eventually my happiness.

Once again, a strange voice emanated from the little old man in the rocking chair. "I am Spoon Decorah, I speak for the Northern Tribes as I am the one who would not back down to the great white fathers in Philadelphia. I, along with my brothers from many nations, including the Winnebago, met in 1784 at Fort Stanwix to discuss the new America. While the British had agreed to the Treaty of Paris, we were not consulted and believed that our land belonged to us. The great white fathers in Philadelphia said that our land belonged to them and **they** would decide who would have rights to it. Our many peoples worked to create our own unified nation so that we could establish a boundary between America and our nations. Even together, we could not hold back the force of the settlers."

"Construction of forts on our land, such as Fort Washington on the north bank of the Ohio River, was a violation of all that we had been promised. How can you trust a man who gives you his word one day, makes an agreement the next and then violates your trust and dignity by doing the opposite of what was agreed…to which we made concessions in good faith?"

"The only way to fight dishonor is with force. Little Turtle and Blue Jacket of the Shawnee and Miami fought back, taking back the land that was stolen from their people. Many people died. At the same time, other nations were also realizing that peace was not at hand and were beginning to stand up for their land and ways of life. We met with a General St. Clair and told him that the land the settlers wanted was our land and that the treaties signed agreed that the land would be ours forever. For what? So that the white man could lie to us yet again?"

Once again, battle raged. Once again, a treaty was signed called the Treaty of Greenville where our nations ceded 25,000 square miles to the American's with a promise from a General Anthony Wayne that the United States would renounce all claims to all other Indian lands north of the river Ohio, east of the Mississippi and west of the Great Lakes and the waters uniting them.

I was given a copy of the agreement. In it was written…'The Indian tribes have a right to these lands and are to enjoy them so long as they please, without any molestation from the United States; but when those tribes…shall be disposed to sell their lands, or any part of them, they are to be sold only to the United States; and until such sale, the United States will protect all the said Indian tribes…against all citizens of the United States and against all other white persons who intrude upon the same. And the said Indian tribes acknowledge themselves to be under the protection of the said United States, and no other power whatsoever.'

"Those who signed the treaty only wanted to go home and tell their nations and their families that they could live in peace without fear of someone taking what was theirs. Once again, the word of the white man was not worth the paper it was written upon and yet, 25,000 square miles of Indian land was taken away."

Great Grandfather's head dipped in exhaustion. "Do not allow it to happen again, Little Spirit. You are our last hope." Great Grandfather whispered as his hands went limp and I knew it was time to leave.

As I was walking out his door, I looked back at the tired, old man and wondered if I would ever see him again. He was failing and his energy was being sapped as he shared so many tragedies with me, time after time after time.

As I was driving home, my mind reflected on yet another broken promise. My God, where would it all end? My resolve was to fight the county and win. Ten acres is a long way from 25,000 square miles and yet, it had to be done for Great Grandfather, for the Chief, Rodney, Ann and all those who had spoken to me.

Round One: Friday came and Mr. Raskin called to tell me that the property had been surveyed and papers would be delivered to me on Saturday morning. Mom and Dad agreed to come to Madison. I told them the address, forgetting they had no idea about Amy's parents. They had to come mid-day as dad needed to get home for chores. The neighbor who usually substituted for him was on vacation. I told them we could go to Paisan's for lunch and they thought that would be cool.

At 11:30 the bell rang and I coded the elevator. Amy was waiting for them when they got off. "Oh my God." mom said. "Your apartment is beautiful. And the view. Holy cow."

Dad and I sat at the kitchen table as Amy showed mom the condo. We signed where all the little stickers were. "How can you guys afford a place like this?" dad whispered.

"I can't." I replied. "It's Amy's parent's place. They bought it when she was going through her treatments four years ago."

"They gotta have some bucks."

"They do. Amy just doesn't want people to know. She wants to be accepted for who she is and not who her parents are."

"Son, hang on to this one." dad said with a smile on his face in another whisper.

"I'm not planning on going anywhere dad as long as she will have me. I don't care about the money. All I care about is having someone make me feel important in their life and special and she certainly does that."

"This place had to cost at least a quarter-million, dollars."

Dad was so far off, I didn't even respond. Madison is an expensive city.

We went to Paisan's and sat in the Lake View room and celebrated. Dad reached for his wallet and I told him that the bill had already been paid as my way of saying thank you. He just shook his head. "We have to do what is right son and fight for what's ours. Nobody else is going to do that." I was glad he was on our side.

We walked back to our building and mom and dad got in the truck and headed home. We went upstairs and scanned the signed documents and sent a PDF to Mr. Raskin who noted that a courier was on his way to the condo to pick up the originals and take them to Milwaukee for legal documentation. First thing Monday morning, a representative would be in the Iowa County Courthouse in Dodgeville, filing the papers.

The Chief: Rodney called and explained everything to the Chief who wanted to go visit the land. I asked when and Rodney said on Monday. I told him I was scheduled to work the night shift. Big Brother said "not anymore." The Chief was driving to Madison on Sunday afternoon to have dinner with Rodney and Ann and wanted to know what time we could leave on Monday morning. I said anytime and he said 6:00 AM. I told him to tell the Chief I would be outside the Edgewater to pick him up. Amy told me to take the Audi. I thought it would send the wrong message and took Jeepers creepers.

We made our way south and into Waldwick arriving at 7:45. Damn Beltline! Along the way, the Chief and I talked about the casinos, marketing, Amy, Rodney and Ann when he wasn't on the phone, which wasn't very much. Mom was waiting with coffee and fresh donuts. The Chief was very gracious and was interested in the milking parlor. Dad and Tommie were just finishing the morning chores when everyone was introduced. I think dad was impressed when the Chief turned down the offer of a ride to the forest and asked if we could walk. He also put his phone in the Jeep. This trip was to be without interruption. As we walked, the Chief and dad talked farming and the history of the farm. The Chief knew that George the First traded for the land with Blackhawk and that in Blackhawk's memoir's there was mention of how the Chief's great-great grandmother had been saved, as she was Blackhawk's daughter.

Dad, the Chief and I walked to the edge of the forest and watched as the Chief's demeanor completely changed. Gone was the confident attitude, replaced by humility. Gone was the urgency, replaced by respect. Gone was a feeling of superiority, replaced by a total sense of reverence. The leader had become the follower…not of people, but of honor, dignity and trust. The Chief opened his arms and began a quiet chant. He looked into the sky and his face turned ashen and then back to a golden hue. His head bowed and his knees bent as if he was about to tumble.

Dad and I stood back and watched. The Chief took a deep breath and realized that he was not alone. There were many spirits whose energy he was feeling. His head tilted back again and he took another deep breath.

Without word, he began walking into the woods. First, he stopped at the school foundation. "Many children, including Indian children, learned here. I can feel their laughter and their joy." He walked further to the spot where his great-great grandmother had been saved. "This is where my life began because hers did not end." Like Rodney, he reached down and lifted soil and rubbed it between his hands. Now there were tears in his eyes. "My soul has reached its sacred spot. My heart is filled with joy." We walked further to the springs and, like his son, he cupped his hands and drank the pure, clean Wisconsin water. "This is to wash my body of all that has been bad. The spirits are here! I can feel them! I can feel them!" as a huge smile crossed his face and tears rolled down his cheeks.

He was as excited as a little boy on Christmas day as he exclaimed, "Thank you. Thank you. Thank you. We must save these sacred grounds. Whatever it takes, the spirits are here and they are calling to me." With that he was spent like Great Grandfather the day before. Dad asked him if he wanted us to go get the truck for him and he said no. We began the walk back to the house with the warm June sun on our shoulders and the Chief's hand upon mine. It was a sign of gratitude and one of acceptance. All that Great Grandfather had spoken of me now made sense to Rodney's dad.

When we got back to the driveway, I opened the door to Jeepers Creepers and took out a Manila folder. "I have taken the liberty of drawing up a purchase agreement between George Terrill the Fourth…namely me and the Ho-Chunk Nation for half-ownership of the land outlined in the attached plot description. In the agreement it states that the land shall be held in trust in perpetuity and with no rights by either party to modify or develop the land in any way until either party wishes to rescind the agreement, at which time, it would revert to the other party for half the initial purchase price.

The Chief put on his glasses looked at the document and read it carefully. Everything had been written by Amy's dad's firm and outlined the rights of each party in terms of co-ownership. Before the Chief could get to the last page he looked up and smiled. "You are very thorough young man."

The last page dealt with the selling price and terms and conditions of the agreement regarding payment. The Chief looked at the figure and then at me and shook his head. "I don't know if this is a fair price or not."

"It's what I believe the price should be, take it or leave it." I responded.

Another smile on the Chief's face. "You drive a hard bargain."

"Thank you."

"I accept the terms and conditions" With that he opened his wallet and handed me a twenty-dollar bill with Andrew Jackson's photo on it.

I took out the matches brought for the occasion and we lit the twenty-dollar bill on fire and watched the image of Jackson burn before we both signed on the dotted line marking payment in full.

"For our ancestors! For the other nations! For the reservations! For success! For our children's, children, children!" I reiterated the mantra from the counting room as the twenty-dollar bill slowly burned.

Dad watched and smiled and was totally moved when the Chief hugged me with tears in his eyes. "You are as noble as they say you are Little Spirit and we will always be grateful."

Mom came out of the house and saw three men crying in the driveway and knew that the deal was done, even though the war had just begun.

The Chief and I climbed back into the Jeep and waved goodbye. Mom and dad stood in the driveway and watched us leave. I don't think there was ever a moment when my dad was more-proud of me.

"Thank you, son." The Chief said as he turned on his cell phone and saw all the calls, texts and emails that had come in. "I've got to call my son" he whispered as he dialed up Rodney. "Little Spirit drove a hard bargain, but the deal is done. Yes. That's right we did burn it. You knew. Rodney, you son-of-a-gun."

It was back to reality as we rode back to Madison. I was the quiet chauffer, which almost killed me…the quiet that is, as he was enveloped in the daily ritual called business, supporting 7500 people and making sure that those who helped make it all happen, the guests, were treated properly.

Treaties Made, Treaties Broken: Amy was looking deeper into the treaties, particularly the Treaty of Vincennes, which had delivered a large part of the Illinois Territory while the Sauk and Fox had relinquished fifteen million acres in Southern Wisconsin in 1803 and 1804, including the land where Waldwick stood. It wasn't long until Fort Crawford was built in Prairie Du Chien, Fort Armstrong on the Mississippi, near where the Quad Cities lie, Fort Dearborn in what is now Chicago and Fort Edwards in what is now St. Louis. In all of them, land was deeded to the United States in return for promises of safety, security and stability, none of which meant anything to the ever-growing number of settlers or it seems the long-term intentions of the US Government.

In 1808, the Treaty of Fort Wayne was signed that sold three million acres of Indiana by the Delaware and Potawatomi. The western movement of the settlers was gaining momentum. Amy reported that in 1811, William Henry Harrison, who had signed the Treaty of Fort Wayne, felt threatened by the growing number of Tecumseh followers, including hundreds of Winnebago, who built a village called Prophetstown in Northwest Indiana. With 1,000 men, Harrison attacked and the battle of Tippecanoe took place in which warriors on both sides met with death as Harrison drove the Indians from the village and burned it to the ground. When Decora returned to the Winnebago villages he was reported to have said "We have been killed; your comrade Harrison has killed us. Look at us who have escaped; look at the way our blankets are pierced with bullets."

This was the last time the Winnebago would ever be involved in a war against the United States. The government's power, size and resources were too much and all the Winnebago could do, was accept their demise. Their pride, their dignity and their hope were like a withering tree whose roots are slowly hacked away, with each day, the nation was becoming smaller and weaker, more susceptible to the demands of the ever-encroaching settlers, including my family.

While the British were out of the United States, they still controlled Canada and the U.S. government believed that the British were providing the Indians with weapons they believed were then used to attack settlers. Amy learned that Tecumseh, who was highly educated, saw the War of 1812 as a way in which he could unite the different nations and establish an Indian state. Tecumseh supported the British and was killed in the Battle of the Thames in 1813. With his death, any opportunity to unify the different northern tribes into one State aligned with the United States died as well. As Amy noted, they met all population requirements needed to become both a territory and a state except one…their skin wasn't white.

Amy found yet another treaty…The Treaty of Ghent signed on December 28, 1814 that secured the rights of occupancy, fishing and planting for Indians. Rights, according to Amy's research, they already had. One critical omission dealt with hunting rights. In return, the fate of all Indians was now in the hands of the US Government. In other words, all freedoms and liberties as independent nations outlined in the Constitution were null and void.

Sunny Saturday: It didn't seem possible that a month had gone by and Amy needed to go in for her "deep cleaning" as she called it. The time was set for Friday morning and I took her. The procedure took about four hours plus recovery and so I dropped her off, went up to the sixth floor of the hospital and said "hello" to everyone and then headed home. She called me when she was done and I was at "parcel pick-up" as I called it, before they even rolled her down. Madison is a big, small city and the condo was only about two miles from the hospital. She came out and looked like she had been through the wringer. After June, I was prepared but still depressed to see her that way. We went back to the condo and I put her in bed and got to work on the 2,000 words. Amy's mom called to see how she was doing and I told her that when Amy woke up, I would have Amy call her. I knew Saturday would be shot, but it also gave me another day and more words.

Saturday was one of those spectacular summer days and my little one was out of it. She awoke just after noon. Instead of lying in bed, she wanted to go out on our deck and get some fresh air. Being on the top floor with the road probably 150 feet below and 400 yards away with a solid wall to the east and the living room to the west, we had plenty of privacy, but I don't think it mattered to Amy anyway.

She came out in her dad's robe. She looked better but was still a long way from 100%. "Here, sit down." I requested pointing to the empty chaise. As she was about to sit, another wave of cramps hit her. Her calves and quadriceps were attacked. She had all she could do to not scream. "Lay down," I commanded and she abided. Pain was racking her body.

"Where first?"

"Calves" as she rolled onto her stomach and I began the vigorous kneading of her calf muscles.

"Ohhhh" she moaned. I could feel the tension in her muscles and worked feverishly. As quickly as they had come, they were gone.

She flipped over and slipped open the robe. "The quads." As she was writhing in pain, the insides of her thighs tightened. Once again, I began the process of kneading the muscles, attempting to bring circulation back where it belonged. She untied the robe and, yet another time, having her naked before me didn't arouse me. I was helping her come out the other end of her two-day tunnel and knew that this was the admission price to normalcy. I did wonder why she was so uninhibited. Girls in Mineral Point or even in mega-liberal Madison, or anyway the ones I knew, were never that way. Finally, the cramps were gone and she smiled a weak smile.

"Rub my back?" she whispered, almost pleading with me as she flipped over on her stomach.

"Sure, sweetie if that's what you want."

"I want you." she whispered.

"I want you too." I thought to myself, not only in a physical sense but an emotional sense that I could feel growing inside of me.

As she lay on her tummy, I spread lotion on her back and butt and then did her legs. She was out of it and yet, I think that the massage did her good. I know it was her way of showing me that she was still sexy, even when she was totaled. A month of living together and we were still very much exploring each other physically, emotionally and intellectually. In a month, she had shown me that she was the most uninhibited person I ever met. It was quite a difference from what I was used to, even in Madison. I never brought the subject up and didn't know if it was because of the French, St. Martin heritage or because so many doctors had poked and prodded and examined her over the past few years. I just knew that she was comfortable with her body and I was getting comfortable with her body too.

With her out like a light, I covered her with the robe and decided to make dinner. It was my first time doing so in the condo and it was my way of saying. "I'm here for you." Nothing fancy, a salad and one of my not -so-famous Ham and Provolone Cheese toastwiches, that restaurants call Panini's. Two slices of wheat bread, ham, cheese and mayo with butter on the outside then fried. Amy had never had one and I could make them and so they were the main entrée'. She took one bite and almost fell back asleep but smiled a weary smile knowing that I had cooked for her. She dabbled in her salad and then it was time for her to go back to bed.

"I'll be fine tomorrow," she promised.

Raskin: Amy was sleeping as the phone rang. It was dad. The eminent domain papers were served and the hearing was set for Wednesday, August sixteenth at 7:00 PM. No surprise. I told him to scan the papers and send me a copy. I would forward them to Mr. Raskin and also Charlie Birdsong, as he would be representing the Ho-Chunk nation. Dad did as requested and I tried reading the verbiage only to get tied up in all the mumbo jumbo about this and that and everything else. Copies were forwarded and I didn't expect any response until Monday. Instead, within thirty minutes both parties had responded via email. God, don't these guys ever shut it off?

It was suggested that we either have a meeting or conference call to discuss roles and responsibilities. Charlie noted that he needed to go to Milwaukee on other business. Mr. Raskin indicated that he could clear an hour from his schedule the following Tuesday. I said I would need to get permission to take the day off from work.

Charlie chuckled. "I guess they haven't told you."

"What?"

"You don't work at the Casino anymore."

"I've been fired?"

"No promoted."

"What?"

"You're now head of marketing."

"What about the team in Black River Falls?"

"It was their idea. The Chief will fill you in, Mr. Executive."

Oh, my God. I needed to call Rodney but then he probably already knew.

Sunday we just hung out at the condo. I called Rodney and, of course, he knew. He said it was the Chief's idea and there would be a raise.

Amy was feeling better and I asked her if she wanted to go with me to Milwaukee on Tuesday and see her mom. She said her mom was probably at work, but she would like to ride along.

Monday, I started looking at all the marketing projects that needed addressing at the casinos and felt that since we were going to be in Milwaukee anyway, I could go see KissAss advertising. I called them and announced the change in status. I didn't think they were too happy. Tough!

The meeting with Mr. Raskin and Charlie was set for 2:00. We left at 8:00 and made it to Milwaukee by 9:30. We went to KissAss and I introduced Amy as my Administrative Assistant. They took us on a complete five -minute tour of the offices and were introduced to everyone. It was a typical agency, like the ones I had applied to when I graduated. We went into the conference room and I inquired about their public relations efforts and asked if the PR team could come in. The "team" was one girl about my age. She was scared. Amy's eyes got big I an incredulous way. We were introduced and I learned that her name was Karen that she pronounced Kah-rin. Welcome to the world of advertising.

"Tell me what your resources are." I inquired.

"You mean like the computer and stuff?" she responded.

"No, I mean like social media, newspaper and broadcast contacts, things like that."

"I just started a month ago. I just graduated." There was a very apparent squirm by those in the room.

"OK. Everyone has to have a beginning, Karen. Let's detail what needs to be done and then build a Gannt Chart concerning projects and time lines."

"What's a Gannt Chart?"

At least she was being honest when I outlined that a Gannt Chart was a visual representation of projects that broke down the different components of an entire project and established deadlines. Amy had never seen me "at work" and there was a smile on her face as we spent the next hour going through different projects...Facebook, Twitter, Snap Chat, broadcast and newspapers and what needed to be done.

I asked Tom, our account executive what was happening between the agency and the Ho-Chunk lobbyist in Madison. Tom had a blank look on his face. I shook my head.

"Ok Team. Let's consider today as day number one. I need Gannt Charts developed on the different projects and ready for me by next Monday when I'll be back. Tom, please call Black River Falls and get the name and phone number of our lobbyist. I would like a report regarding his activities and what he is working on. Effective today, you are responsible for him as well. Finally, because I've done all the work today, none of this was billable."

An appointment was set for 10:00 AM and I allocated two hours the following Monday. We walked out of KissAss and Amy grabbed my arm. "I didn't know you had it in you, Mr. Terrill."

"Just getting started, my dear. Just getting started," I replied.

It was 11:30 and time for lunch. Amy asked if I had ever eaten at Kopp's and I said no. We went and had one of the biggest hamburgers, best fries and incredible chocolate custard shake for lunch. "God that was good. If we lived in Milwaukee, I'd weigh 200 pounds." I announced.

We still had an hour to kill and so Amy asked if I wanted to go see her parent's house as it was close to the law offices. I was all for that until we pulled up this long winding driveway and realized her "house" was a mansion on Lake Michigan. Shit. I had forgotten her parents were rich. She punched in some numbers to shut down the alarm system and we walked in the front door. On each side of the foyer were curved stairs that allowed you to look through and see the lake. To say the house was gorgeous would have been an understatement.

Come on, let me show you my room. With that we climbed the stairs and went into her room. Typical girlie stuff everywhere which was to be expected. On the tall dresser were photos of Amy as a little girl with her parents. In one photo she was standing with a tall, handsome guy and they were smiling.

"An old boyfriend?" I inquired.

"My brother." Amy answered.

"I didn't know you have a brother."

"I don't. He died."

"I'm sorry."

"He went away to school and started doing drugs and OD'd on Phentenol and heroin. It almost killed my mom and dad. That's why when Dad called you son I was so shocked."

"God, what a waste." I replied.

Amy looked at me with sorrowful eyes and noted. "He had everything and he threw it all away…looks, intelligence, personality … He had it all. It almost killed my parents. Promise me you'll never do drugs."

"I promise, I saw too much of that at school. I don't need drugs to be happy, I've got you."

"Derrick and I were a lot alike. She confessed. "Both wild and crazy! Everyone thinks it's easy when you're wealthy and yet a lot of it is simply bullshit. Don't get me wrong, I love my mom and dad and respect all that they have accomplished and all that Derrick and I were given and yet, at times, the pressure was incredible. Everyone knew who we were and wherever we went, we were scrutinized."

"Both Derrick and I rebelled. He went into drugs and I went into my crazy world and had to get out of Milwaukee. When you live as a mixed-race person, you are judged no matter what you do and you really don't know where you fit it. Am I white or am I black? Do I hang with rich white kids or go down and hang with the sisters? I tried both and never felt like I fit in at either juncture. I just wanted to be me. I wanted to be accepted for who I am…a person…a person who needs other people who will not judge her for the color of her skin or kinky hair…a person who will be allowed to herself and certainly not the daughter of Douglas, The Duke and Dr. Marie Williams."

Amy continued, "I struggled to understand my own identity. Being a light-skinned African American, with a white father and a mother who is black, I often felt like a minority within a minority. Not black enough! Not white enough! Like a stranger in two lands. I'm still struggling with that feeling and yet I have endured and have no regrets. My physicality is such that I have lost all sense of inhibition towards so many things, indifferent and oblivious to what people think, say or do. All I want, above all else, is to sincerely feel wanted, needed and loved…not judged, but accepted. Does that make sense?"

"Very much so." I replied.

Amy added, "When I went away to school, I wanted a clean break and so I changed my name from Amelia to Amy. Daddy wanted to take me in one of the corporate jets and I went on Frontier Airlines. Daddy wanted to inspect my dorm room and I told him no. I just wanted to be Amy Williams from Milwaukee, Wisconsin, just another kid going to college. Dorm life was fun and no one knew anything about me and accepted me for simply being some girl from Wisconsin. I made a lot of friends and my roommate Cheryl from Atlanta and I are still great friends today."

"My sophomore year, Cheryl and I wanted to get an apartment. I found an old house and amazingly it was purchased by Wilco and the rent was cheap for four girls who shared it. Junior year it was the same and then I started getting sick and dad kept the place and the rent remained for my roommates even though I wasn't there. I was able to arrange all my classes and still graduate, but I was in no shape to live there."

I held her and felt the trembles within her body. She had shared with me her fears and aspirations and stood before me stripped naked…not physically, but emotionally and our lives took one step closer towards together and I began to understand. We kissed and realized we needed to go to the office. Reality was upon us. The actress needed to put on her happy face and walk out upon the stage once more.

As we headed towards her dad's law offices, Amy pointed out a big white building with the name Wilco on the manicured front lawn. I surmised that the named stood for Williams Company and was corrected. Amy pointed out that the word "Wilco" is short for "Will Comply" in military jargon and that was what it really stood for. "Dad had a set of goals and ideals and all people who will comply would be rewarded, therefore Wilco."

Amy went on to explain the structure. There were ten independent divisions and each had a director. Each division had an inter-related specialty that was 49% owned by primary investors who were considered experts in their industry and 51% owned by Wilco, who put up the money and operational expertise to start the business. Each division did work for the corporation, but they also had outside customers. The two most noted divisions were the auto group and the law group but the most lucrative was the financial arm.

"Wilco itself has two sets of owners. The first is the Williams family. We sit on the board and own 51% of the stock with the other 49% owned by the employees. In other words, Wilco earns profits from the divisions and then nearly half are returned back to the employees in the form of stock dividends. Each employee begins earning stock after five years with the company when they are awarded five shares. Every year of service means another share. Sissy, dad's Administrative Assistant has been with him for 30 years and has 30 shares. Sissy and her husband can retire whenever they want to because the dividends have been that great."

Every year we have a stockholder's meeting on a Sunday in February. That's when bonuses and dividends are announced and dad gives his state of the business address. What's really cool is that one employee from each of the ten divisions is selected, based on merit and earns an all-expense-paid vacation to one of the properties in the islands. We've had janitors and guys who change oil win because they busted their butts and did their job. No one knows who's going to be selected. Each group head submits five names and why they are a candidate and then dad makes the decision. It's really cool, to watch the excitement as dad names the finalists and why they were nominated. Their families are invited and are given special attention. For the four runners-up, there are cash awards ranging from $ 1,000 to $5000 and so everyone wins. Once an employee has won, they cannot be nominated again for five years to keep everyone striving to make the team."

"The Marketing Group handles all the advertising, promotion, public relations and lobbying along with all visual creative and social media for all of the divisions. With each group standing on its own, each has a different set of needs and a different set of external customers and so Wilco Marketing functions as an advertising agency and lobbyist" Amy added with a sly smile, knowing that KissAss had some new competition on the block.

"The Legal Group is in a separate building because the Wilco building is full and also because legal deals primarily with corporate law not only for Wilco but a whole plethora of other companies ranging from manufacturing to car dealers and it's where dad started."

"Dad got screwed once by a banker. When he got enough money together, he started his own finance company that turned to investing and stock brokerage. The client list is small and quite exclusive and it handles all the finances for all the divisions."

"The final group is the Williams Foundation. This was established to not only give back to the community, but keep all those who are asking for donations channeled into one place. The foundation has built schools on St. Martin and St. Lucia, donated computers to classrooms, set up scholarship annuities at both the University of Wisconsin Madison and Georgetown and donates money for cancer research and drug prevention programs."

"Every month, each division leader must make a presentation lasting no longer than 10 minutes on what they achieved in the previous month and what their goals are in the upcoming month.

Dad attends these meetings and at times, the meetings can get a little testy. Dad doesn't lose his cool too often but he hates excuses. His favorite line is 'excuses are like assholes. Everyone has one and no one wants to hear about them. The meetings start at three and are over at five. He will look at his watch and at five, he's gone and you had better have spoken your piece."

I laughed as Amy continued, "Dad has a program developed that, should something happen to him and mom and then me, if there were no heirs, the 51% of Wilco would revert back to the employees and they would own Wilco completely.

"Wow, your dad really has this thought out." I added as Amy pulled into the law offices parking lot.

"My dad doesn't have any real hobbies except business, his family, flying and Badger sports. He's a good man who is trying to take care of those who have made him very wealthy including not only the employees, but the people who have been his clients and customers. There's going to be a big to do about me being here so please be prepared. Miss Amelia doesn't come often and every Ass Kisser will be fighting for my attention. It just goes with the territory."

"Will your dad be here?"

"He keeps a token place here but is hardly ever in the building. Sissy works here and does my dad's scheduling while looking over all the administrative staff. Dad works out of the house a lot or if he is traveling, works out of a cargo van like the one we used for the wheelchair that has a mobile office for him, that Dennis drives."

"Long ago, dad decreed authority to so many others who have worked for him, reported to him and honored his presence at the law firm. These people bust their butts. However, there is one rule … the offices are closed on Sunday and no one is allowed in. Sunday is family day! Dad loves cars, planes and fancy clothes and Dennis makes sure that everything is the way dad likes it and yet, they are just good friends as well."

When we walked in, you would have thought it was royalty, but then The Duke's daughter was almost considered royalty in the law firm as daddy was making everyone there at least comfortable, if not rich. People were congregated near the receptionist and Amy shook hands with them all. Charlie was there and we headed to the conference room where I almost got lost in the thick carpeting as I looked out on Lake Michigan. There were fresh flowers on the table and a bowl of fruit. Coffee, soft drinks and ice water were on a server and there were small cookies on a plate.

Charlie looked around and just smiled. I could tell he was impressed. At precisely 2:00 PM, Mr. Raskin walked in with Denise, his administrative assistant. Discussions took place concerning the Iowa County letter and options regarding the next step. Amy seemed to know what everyone was talking about. I attempted to keep up. It was decided that using Amy's dad's law firm would put a degree of imbalance in the entire matter as they were one of the top firms in the state and it would look like overkill. It was agreed that Charlie would serve as lead council. It was also agreed that Miss Amelia Williams would serve as his law clerk. She smiled. She already knew it was coming. Surprise.

When everything of a legal nature had been discussed, I spoke of our meeting with KissAss advertising that morning and how I had directed them to develop project sheets for a program called Project Frisco that included public relations, social media and integrating the Ho-Chunk lobbyist into the realm of things. I also noted that KissAss had no idea what the project was and that they would be informed if and when the time was right. I then noted that the right time would be decided by the legal team. There were smiles and nods all around the table and I felt Mr. Raskin was beginning to see that I was more than his bosses' daughter's boyfriend.

The meeting adjourned at 3:00 as scheduled. Punctuality!

We climbed back into the Jeep and headed for home. "Do you think the agency is strong enough?" I asked Amy.

"Give them a try and see what happens. If not, put the account out for bid. It keeps subjective people on their toes." The business side of Amy was coming out.

"I think we need to stop at Brookfield Square." Amy noted.

"For what?" I asked.

"If you're going to be a junior executive you need to look like one. Don't take this the wrong way, but I believe part of the problem today was that you looked like a college student."

I got her point. With three pair of jeans, one dress shirt and one sports coat to my name, along with two pair of tennis shoes and one pair of slightly scuffed loafers, I really didn't look much like an executive. We went into the mall and I headed for J.C. Penny.

"Nope, come with me." as we headed to Brooks Brothers.

"Jesus!"

We walked in and the clerk looked at me like I was from outer space.

"My friend just got a major promotion." Amy noted to the somewhat indifferent clerk. With that, we walked by him and went to the pants department. Size 32"x30". Skinny Minnie me. I liked the flat front and so I tried a pair on. While I was doing that, Amy picked our five pair...black, navy blue, tan and grey. They were $200 per pair. Yiikes! She knew I hated neck ties and so we went to the button-down shirt department. Three for $200.00. Size 16"x32" She picked out six. My God. Next two belts...one brown, one black. Then to the shoe department where I picked out two pair of Alan Edmonds loafers...one pair brown and one black. The pile was growing. Sports coats? Armani...Navy blue, of course! My infamous over-the-Amy shoulder wool-polyester blend that was in the closet at home was from the famous French designer Jacque Penne. Amy giggled as she understood...JC Penny!

Next was a black double-breasted doozie and finally a light tan coat as she added two pocket squares and four pair of black socks. The sales guy was in pig heaven. He had a smile on his face like he'd just won the lottery. My pants were about to be filled and it wasn't with money when he rang up the total of $3230.49.

Amy pulled out an ID and handed it to the clerk. Discount $807.53. Net bill $2422.96. Then she pulled out a second card and an additional 10% discount. $2180.66. I had no idea what was going on as I reached for my wallet. Amy looked at me and told me to stop. It seemed that The Duke had a deal for all employees of his companies as he wanted them to look professional. Then on top of the company discount, The Duke had a personal discount as Brooks Brothers knew that the company would spend over $100,000 per year in this store. When her dad came in, they would have a tailor from Chicago present as he only wore custom made suits, dress pants and shirts. I said I wanted to pay and laid the American Excess card on the table. Amy pushed it back saying, "You can't get the discount because you're not an employee. I need to buy them for you"

"I can't let you do that."

"Yes, you can. You just did" Amy said as the clerk began bagging everything up.

I just shook my head. We just spent more for clothes than I had in my life. We headed out Blue Mound Road, past another Kopp's and hit the Interstate by Waukesha. On the way home, we talked about Ann, Rodney and the wedding. It was only six weeks away. "What should we give them as a present?" Amy asked.

"I thought the trip was their present."

"That was from mom and dad."

"I don't know, what do you think?"

"Will your book be done by then?"

"Close."

"A leather-bound copy that was signed by the author would be cool".

I placed my knee against the steering wheel and cupped my hands together and made a roaring sound.

"What's that?" Amy asked.

"The blow torch was being lit and applied to my ass."

A girlie giggle erupted as Amy said, "We've got a lot of work to do in six weeks, Sweetie."

I looked at her and thought, "We? What, you got a mouse in your pocket?

Wednesday morning the phone rang. It was Carol from Black River Falls. KissAss had called and complained that I came into the office all high and mighty and ordered them to do all kinds of things they had never done before and that my Administrative Assistant was some bimbo I brought along.

Wrong thing to say! I let my blood pressure come down and told Amy.

"Give them enough rope and they will either swing or hang themselves. Let it ride until Monday and then be critical. In the meantime, let's put together a list of agencies to invite to the bid." Amy's fangs were out for blood.

I plunked out 4,000 words that day. We were at 80,000 words with a minimum of 90,000 for printing. We were up to the 1920's and the Great Depression. Between the blow torch and the adrenaline, I was very productive. Amy was working on all the legal aspects with Charlie and still helping me with research. We had two computers and they didn't seem to be enough. The condo looked like a war room with paper everywhere. I saw a new side to my lady...intelligent, capable and now driven.

The blow torch was lit and the mantra was...Produce. Produce. Produce and I wasn't at the grocery store picking our asparagus! A marketing strategy was developed for the casinos and also for the land. The boys down in Dodgeville were in for a surprise consisting of not only the legal aspect, but the court of public opinion...the fifth estate...especially in an election year.

Red Bird: Thursday morning I was up at 5:00. I had much to do before visiting Great Grandfather. I hustled and bustled, but never took my eye off the clock. I was out the door at 8:30 and in Great Grandfathers parking lot at 9:58. Whew. Even the Interstate can get crazy in the morning!

I walked to his room and, as always, he was sitting in his rocker with the quilt on his lap. Without looking up he called. "Little Spirit, you are here"

Yes, Great Grandfather, I'm here."

"Is your Amelia with you?"

"No Great Grandfather, she isn't. We are afraid that the spirits would not come if she is with me."

"That is a good rationale, Little Spirit. They sense that you are the chosen one and they are reluctant to come forth to anyone else. Come, pull up the cedar chest and sit with me. We have much to learn."

I pulled up the old chest and held Great Grandfather's hands. His chanting began and his eyes rolled back. The voice that came forth was different, filled with sadness and remorse as if it were exhausted and confused. "My name is Koo-zee-ray -Kaw but am known by the white man as Red Bird. I am a warrior willing to defend my people and what is mine with my life. I am a man of peace. When I am ready for battle, people always know as one side of my face is painted red; the other green and white. This is to warn the spirits that I am at war. I am proud to be a Winnebago leader and wear the clothes of such with a collar of blue and white wampum, claws of the panther and a Yankton dress made of elk skin that is almost pure white. Across my chest is a war pipe of horsehair, feathers and bills of birds to give me strength and power. I have seen many white men come into my village. Most mean no harm and yet they take what is not theirs and give nothing in return. I have learned that it is best to live in peace and have always felt welcomed in Prairie du Chien, where I have often eaten and drank with the settlers in their homes."

"While I am a leader of a village, I cannot control the actions of others. But, to take a man's food is wrong. While we lived on the morning side of the great river, many of the trees that produced maple sap were located on the evening side. Our men would go each spring and use their tools to make marks in the trees where the sap would flow and then use reeds to have the sap run into our birch bark buckets. We would collect our buckets and heat the sap until the water was gone, leaving behind the maple syrup that we used to cook our meat and provide our nourishment. To go find the trees, do all the cutting and collecting and do so on one's land and then have someone steal the food from their mouths can make anyone … white person or Indian angry. In the maple sugar season of 1826, our braves came across just such thieves … stealing our food. A battle broke out and two of our warriors killed two Frenchmen, which they believed was just the thing to do."

"Word spread and our warriors were found and brought to Fort Crawford in Prairie Du Chien. There was a flood on the Mississippi that left the fort under water and so, the army moved the two warriors to Fort Snelling in what became Minnesota."

"We believed that the white man would treat our braves with honor. However, in the spring of 1827, a Sioux warrior came to our village and reported that the soldiers had killed our warriors and chopped them into little pieces so that their souls could not go to meet the great father. I had no reason to doubt this brave and his story, nor did my people."

"After hearing from the Sioux, my people wanted justice and demanded that the ancient Winnebago law be upheld which meant killing two-for-one of their own killed and that we should attack Prairie Du Chien. I did not want to do this as I had many settler friends who I did not want to hurt. I was called old and weak and a coward by the young, until I reluctantly agreed to lead a small war party. We went to the village and I returned saying we couldn't find anyone to kill. Again, I was mocked as being too old, too weak and too much of a friend of the white man."

"In June, the tribe voted and it was determined that there must be justice as we set out to fulfill the tribal command. After stopping in Prairie du Chien, we went to the farm home of Mr. Registre Gagnier where we attacked Gagnier and his hired man, Solomon Lipcap, who were killed immediately. In our anger, one of my warriors scalped Gagnier's infant daughter and flung her to the floor. This was wrong and I admit that the child should not have been hurt. We stopped and Gagnier's wife and her son went to Prairie du Chien, where she spread the alarm."

"A few days later, two keel boats, moving up the Mississippi and carrying supplies to the garrison at Fort Snelling put to shore with firewater and got all of us drunk before leaving with seven squaws that they used for their own purposes of pleasure. These women were our wives and daughters. They were not someone's property or for their pleasure."

"Two days later, the boatmen believed they could simply drop off our abused squaws and go on their way back from Fort Snelling as they all had their ways with them. As they reached the mouth of the Bad Axe River and were about thirty feet from shore my braves were in waiting and let out war hoops as they experienced one round of bullets. We asked if they were English…those who treated us like children and when they said yes, we invited them ashore to which, the crew answered back that they needed more squaws for their pleasure. Thus, commenced a second round of fire and one of the sailors was killed."

"There was a gun battle that lasted nearly all day. Of thirty-seven Indians from my village, seven died and fourteen were wounded. We put 693 bullet holes in and through that boat and then fired on a second boat later that night. The keelboats got away and when they reached Prairie du Chien they reported what happened. After the Gagnier mishap, the settlers crowded in Fort Crawford for protection."

"I am of man of religion and peace and see nothing wrong with what we did to the keel boats. To take seven women and use them for pleasure is wrong. To bring them back abused and disgraced and say that you want to do the same to more of our women is wrong. Do we not have rights? Do we not have dignity? Do we not have any value as people of this earth?"

"Sadly, the events of those two days turned into what the white man called the Winnebago War. This was not a war. All we wanted was to be left alone, in peace, to live our lives, but this was not good enough for the white man. The soldiers at Fort Crawford captured a dying Winnebago chief named Old Dekauray, who was simply trying to live out his remaining days. The commander at Fort Crawford demanded that if I was not turned over, the chief would die instead."

"To save my village and DeKauray, I left my family, while those who were with me in Prairie Du Chien traveled towards where the sun rises. But it was not enough for the white man. Soldiers and the volunteer militia moved north from St. Louis while more soldiers and even more militia came down the Fox River from Green Bay to an area called Portage. At this point, a meeting between the Winnebago elders and the soldiers was held and my people were warned that the existence of our entire nation depended on my surrender along with the killers of the one sailor and two settlers."

"I think our leaders realized that this was the end of life as we knew it. Our land was gone. Our livelihood was gone. Our dignity was gone. Our women were not for their pleasure. All that was left was our existence and to some of us that wasn't worth the price we had to pay."

"On September 2, 1827, I sent a single Indian to the soldier's camp carrying a white flag. He promised that before the sun set the following day, I would surrender. I kept my word. As I stood on the opposite shore of the Fox River; I sang my death song, for my life was over and then surrendered to the white soldiers."

"I reported that I had accompanied two of the three other braves, but that the other had escaped. I simply asked for kind treatment with no irons for the prisoners and food and tobacco for my starving people. I stood up when the white men finished talking and faced a Major Whistler and said…'I am ready. I do not wish to be put in irons. Let me be free. I have given my life away. It is gone.' I stooped down and took up some dust between my thumb and finger and blew it away.' I would not take my life back. It is gone."

"I was taken to Fort Crawford and put in a cell where I wrote the following… 'I do not know that I have done wrong. I come now to sacrifice myself to the white man because it is my duty to save my people from the scourge of war. If I have done wrong, I will pay for it either with horses or my life. I do not understand the white man's law, which has one set of words for the white man and another for the red. The white men promised the lead mines would be ours, but they did nothing to the men who took our possession away from the lands. If an Indian took possession of something belonging to the white man, the soldiers would come quickly enough. We have been patient. We have seen all this. We have seen our ancient burial grounds plowed over. We have seen our braves shot down like dogs for harvesting corn….We have seen the white men steal our lands, our quarries, our waterways by lying to us, cheating us and making us drunk enough to put marks on papers without knowing what we were doing. When first the Long Knives came, the prophets told us they would never be honest with us. We did not believe them. We do now. When word came that our brother was slain, I went forth and took meat. I did not know the report was false, so I did no wrong. I fulfilled the law of the Winnebago. I am not ashamed… I come because the white men are too strong, and I do not wish my people to suffer. Now I am ready, take me."

"I wanted to die because imprisonment of me was worse than death. The Winnebago concluded their captors were too cowardly to kill me. Many in the US government felt that if I was tried and put to death, war would break out. Based on my actions and that of five men, my entire Winnebago nation was forced 1828 to relocate across the Mississippi river. Both the Sauk and Fox nations were also to be removed from Wisconsin as well, and settle on the west side of the Mississippi River. I am a Winnebago not a Sauk or Fox. I am but one man and yet, because of me and that of a few others, my people suffered. I exist forever with that on my soul and am restless as my spirit wanders looking for the only thing I ever wanted…peace."

Great Grandfather's eyes began their roll forward. He was exhausted. I don't know if he knew what was being said. I only know that when these sessions were over, there wasn't a single ounce of energy left in his body. As I stood, he faced me and smiled…"Little Spirit, what is being said will never be forgotten. You are the chosen one. You will do battle for justice so that all the spirits can rest in peace. All we want is justice. All we have ever wanted is peace.

I walked out of his room and down the hall. There was a family in the lobby and two of the people were crying. I knew that the great spirits had come for someone. I only hoped that their spirits would not wander. That they would live with the eternal peace Great Grandfather asked me to find. I came home and filled Amy in. Some of it could be added to the book. A lot of it went straight to the heart. My God, these people got screwed. We all think of Hitler and all that he did. From what I was learning, it didn't seem that much better for the Indians.

AssKissers: Friday, Saturday and Sunday were like finals week. We both were cramming. We had so much to do and so little time. The only good thing was that we were doing it together. We took a little time out as Amy asked if she could cut my hair. It was shaggy…no, it was a mess. I had worn it long since I was a freshman. I was reluctant until she told me that she cut her dad's hair and I went "Holy shit!"

She tied a towel around my neck and washed my hair. God it felt good. Then I sat in the kitchen and she clipped and snipped and fluffed and puffed. Finally, she had me lean back and she put a hot towel on my face and then a shave. The 'mountain man' look was laying on the floor. She dried my hair and put some really good smelling … and I'm certain … quite expensive … aftershave on me.

"Go look in the mirror." Amy urged.

I got up and went into the bathroom. My God, what a difference. I actually looked like a young man instead of an old college student. I just shook my head. Boy had I been wrong.

"Well?" Amy said as I came out of the bathroom as she was sweeping the floor. "I don't like it" I said with as much earnest as possible. "I love it. Time to grow up."

Monday rolled around and Amy told me to take the crotch rocket. At first, I was reluctant and then thought "what the hell". She was staying home researching international law of the 1700 and 1800's looking for any morsel that would help win the case.

I rolled into Milwaukee and went to the agency. I walked in dressed in khakis, light blue shirt, navy blazer and shiny black loafers. The look back was one of total shock. Gone was the smart-ass punk, replaced by a young businessman. With all that had transpired, you could cut the ice with a butter knife. I asked for the Gannt Charts and was told that they had been too busy. I asked what they had done and Karen walked in and said she spent the week researching social media and saw no value to it. I was royally pissed.

"Where's Tom?" I asked and was told he had an emergency meeting with a client.

"Who runs this place?"

I was told that the owner was in an important meeting.

"Tell him to see me now or the contract was being pulled."

The little girl who thought the world of advertising was all so cute and nice and all about comp'd tickets to everything quickly realized there was a business side to the world as well. This old dude came out and asked what the problem was. I elicited that I had driven from Madison to review projects and that not only wasn't anything done, but the account executive responsible for the Ho-Chunk account had an "emergency meeting" and couldn't be there and didn't think enough to call me. Now my undies were really twisted.

"Let's talk respect…you and I," I said staring straight into the eyes of the old guy with the dyed comb-over hair and tight jeans, trying to be young.

"I should just fire your asses and find someone else. Your contract states 30 days written notice and I'm giving you that right now. While I'm at it, tell Tom that if he's got a gripe with me, call me and not Black River Falls. Also tell him that the woman with me was not a bimbo but my fiancé who graduated with honors from Georgetown University with a double major in Business and Pre-Law. While you're at it, tell Tom that as far as I'm concerned, this case is closed and that he, personally, just caused you to lose a client…probably not your biggest, but the ramifications go way beyond what his feeble mind can comprehend."

"As for today, we are deducting $500 from your monthly retainer. Don't like it? Tough shit. Take it out of Tom's salary. If I wanted to deal with arrogant, incompetent clowns, I could hire some idiots in high school to do a better job than your firm is doing!" God I was pissed. I headed for the door and then spun on my heels. "One last thing, to be in advertising and not know anything about social media is a joke and to have a public relations department of one, with some girl named Kah-rin, who doesn't know her ass from a hole-in-the-ground is simply not good enough for me."

The guy just stood there. He really didn't know what to say before he spoke. "Well I'll call the Chief and get this straightened out."

"Go ahead. In fact, let's do it right now. Oh, by the way, do you have his private line? Otherwise you won't get through."

Now this guy's undies were in a bundle.

"Here, use my phone."

The guy took my phone as I punched in the number. Ann, the receptionist is Black River Falls answered. "Good morning, Mr. Terrill."

"No, this is John Schnelnicht at Advanced Advertising Associates"

Mr. Schnelnicht, what are you doing on Mr. Terrill's phone?"

"He's in my office and we've had a discussion about the services provided and I need to speak to the Chief".

"I'm sorry Mr. Schnelnicht, but Mr. Terrill is the head of all marketing for the Nation and the Chief is directing all marketing and advertising calls to him."

The sorry son-of-a-bitch almost wet his pants.

"Jesus, I'm sorry" was all Schnelnicht could say.

My foot was on his throat and I didn't want to let up. I needed to put fear in him. From that I hoped there would be respect and more important, productivity.

"I know we're only a small, multi-million-dollar billing for you and that you probably have accounts more important, but I am paid by the Ho-Chunk Nation to create and implement a comprehensive marketing plan. The choice you have right now is whether you want or have the resources necessary to provide the services you are being paid to do. If not, I'm walking out of here and finding someone else. If you do, you've got one more week to produce what was asked or you're wasting my time. And tell Tom that if he ever disrespects my fiancé again it **will** be personal.

The old man with the tight pants and dyed comb-over got the message.

I pointed my finger at comb-over and said, "Next Monday, 10:00 AM in Madison at the casino. A full marketing presentation that will determine whether you keep the account or not. Understand?"

He nodded his head in the affirmative as I turned and walked out of his office.

I was completely flooded with testosterone and swagger and jumped into the crotch rocket. Mr. Combover was looking out the window and I can only imagine that he almost shit his pants when he saw a $160,000 Audi roar out of his parking lot.

As my "energy" levels started slowing down, I reviewed the meeting and wondered if I had done the right thing. They had dissed me and insulted both Amy and me and I wasn't going to tolerate that. In my fervor I had called her my fiancé, not once but twice. Was there a subconscious message there? It had only been four months and yet, I already knew what the end result was going to be. I drove west on I-90 and headed back to the condo. Along the way the phone rang and it was Rodney.

"Heh, little Brother, I heard you gave it to the Asskissers really good"

"Yup."

"How did you know?"

"You forgot to hang up the phone" with another belly laugh from Rodney.

I explained all that had transpired and told them about the bimbo comment. Rodney responded. "What? There wasn't a hospital bed to raise up and down?" as he laughed.

I asked if the Chief was pissed for me doing it and Rodney said, just the contrary. He liked someone with some balls kicking the shit out of people, especially if the guy doing the kicking was a white guy. I smiled and felt better. When I got home I told Amy all the details, except of course the fiancé part. I needed the right time and place for that.

Wingra: Madison is called the Four Lake City, referring to Mendota, Monona, Waubesa and Kegonsa with the last two not even in Madison. In reality, there are actually five lakes with the fifth being called Wingra, which Rodney told me meant duck in Ho-Chunk.

There seems to be some disagreement as to how Madison got the name Four Lake City, but then, Madison is the center for politics and politicians never seem to be able to agree on anything. One story has it that a team of surveyors named the lakes First through Fourth as they traveled north, showing what is now Lake Wingra as simply a pond they left unnamed.

In 1849 the names Monona and Mendota were applied to the northernmost Third and Fourth lakes respectively. Mendota, is a Dakota name that means "confluence of rivers" and also "great water" in HoChunk. Monona, is a Sauk-Fox name that was translated as "fairy water" because it is so much calmer than Mendota. Kegonsa is Ojibwa for "little fish" and Waubesa means "swan".

Another story about my favorite lake is that the reason Wingra was never considered a lake was because it was so shallow and was only marshland until the small dam was built that raised the water level. At one time there was a seventy-foot tall hill between Lakes Monona and Wingra that was an Indian burial ground. The citizens of Madison, used the hill to fill in around the Capitol while folks would have picnics on what was left and dig up Indian artifacts. In other words, digging up Indian graves. I don't know what I would do if I found someone digging in the Mineral Point cemeteries, but it certainly wouldn't be pretty. The last vestige was an area called Keyes hill, which was located where Fish Hatchery Road and Park Street meet that was levels ion the 1920's also used as fill.

A third story is that, while the first four lakes are water-shed lakes and connected by the Yahara River, Wingra sits alone, and is spring-fed, keeping it colder than the other four. Most people don't realize that Lake Wingra actually is connected to Lake Monona because there needs to be some way for the spring water to go somewhere and so Wingra or Murphy's Creek, as the old-timer's called it, was simply created by not filling in all the marshland as the creek meanders south, parallel to Wingra Drive, turns east under Fish Hatchery Road, Park Street, through Franklin Field and under John Nolen drive to where it enters Lake Monona next to Olin Park.

In 1934, most of the shoreline of Lake Wingra was deeded to the University of Wisconsin as an arboretum consisting of woods and nature that includes tallgrass prairies, savannas, several forest types and wetlands. It is one of the oldest and most varied collection of restored ecological communities in the world. I have always loved the arboretum because their woods are the closest I can get to my forest without driving home. Whew! That's a lot of information about a little lake, but it deserves it as it will always be a very special place for me and there is one reason why.

Saturday still meant our sixth day of work and Amy and I promised each other that Sunday was our day off. No work and just each other! After breakfast, we went to the Henry Vilas Zoo and looked at all the animals. After the zoo we drove into the arboretum and parked in an area called "Lost City". At one time they were going to build houses there until someone realized that the water table was so high the houses would sink, along with the roads, sidewalks and dreams. There are a few houses up on a hill in the woods, but none by the lake and the normal picnic area is positioned to the west where the road ends and away from where we decided to go hiking.

We made our way through the woods to the shore and my favorite spot where we could see the world but few If anyone could see us. I was certain there were no cliffs for Amy to fall down. It was like we were the only living beings in the world...other than the mosquitoes, of course. We spread our blanket and watched a few sailboats on the other side of the lake.

"Let's go swimming." Amy said.

"We don't have our suits." I replied.

Amy answered by simply taking off her top and shorts and getting naked. I reluctantly followed suit. In a matter of seconds, we were up to our necks in the cold water and giggling like little kids.

"Have I told you, Mr. Terrill, how much you mean to me?" with that she wrapped her arms around my neck and legs around my waist.

"Have I told you, Miss Williams, that I love you?" Ooops! True feelings exposed, but then that wasn't all that was exposed.

Amy pulled back and I smiled.

"Yes, I have fallen in love with you." I said.

She had a great big shit-eating grin on her face.

"You know what, Mr. Terrill, the feelings are quite mutual."

We splished and splashed and giggled and hugged until our skin was pruned and discreetly made our way back to shore, drying off by wrapping the blanket around us. It was time to go and I had an idea as we got into the Jeep and headed up West Washington towards the Capitol square. Amy thought we were going back to the condo but I went through the outer ring and onto the square itself. It was Sunday and parking on the square was plentiful. I abruptly pulled into some politicians reserved parking space right next to the Capitol building. We still had Amy's temporary handicap sticker that I hung on the mirror. What I wanted to do wouldn't take long.

"Let's go inside. There's something I want to show you". Amy had a frown on her face.

We walked to the middle of the rotunda where our first date officially started. I told her to close her eyes. She obliged. I got down on one knee.

"Open your eyes."

Amy pulled back and giggled her girly giggle. I thought the smile on her face was going to stretch her ears.

Are you proposing?" she asked.

"I most certainly am. Will you marry me?" I responded.

She nodded her head. "I accept."

"I'm in the most beautiful building, with the most beautiful woman I have ever known. I am committing myself to you Miss Amelia Marie Williams for the rest of our lives."

Amy began to cry. Two people, hugging and kissing in the State Capitol in Madison, Wisconsin might have been a sight, but we didn't care. The few people that were there, all began to clap. I knew that I was in love and she did too and that's all that mattered. Her fight would be our fight. My burdens would be her burdens. We were to be a team and together, we would conquer the world.

We walked back hand-in-hand to the car. A Capitol policeman was just about to write a ticket. I explained that we had only been there long enough for me to propose. He thought it was cool and let us go with a big smile on his face.

"I'll need your father's approval, of course."

"He'll say yes."

"I want to do it the traditional way."

"I was going to wait until after Rodney and Ann's wedding. I don't want to steal their thunder."

"Let's ask dad now and let my parents in on the secret. It will make mom very happy."

Permission: We headed to the condo and Amy called her mom and asked what she and dad were doing. Amy told her mother that with all the work, we needed a break and wondered if we could come to Milwaukee and have dinner. I think Mrs. Williams knew what was going on. Amy asked if it would be all right if we ate at home instead of going to a restaurant. Mrs. Williams agreed, but noted that it wouldn't be very fancy. I offered to bring Cornish pasty. Amy thought that would be great. Mom was reluctant and then concurred. I quickly got cleaned up, dressing in some of the new clothes and went to Miles Teddywedgers just before they closed and bought four, half-cooked, traditional pasties and put them in a small cooler to stay warm. We took a second cooler and got some of Amy's mother's favorite mint-chocolate ice cream from the Chocolate Shoppe, along with a quart of Turtle for Amy and me and, later I found out, her dad. I noted that I always wondered how those coolers knew when to keep things warm instead of cold and it was one of my worn-out jokes, as we headed for Milwaukee.

We arrived at Amy's parent's house a little before six. As always, the house looked spectacular. Amy opened the front door and called to her mom. Amy's dad was out on the patio watching the sailboats on Lake Michigan with a drink in his hand. I handed the pasties to Mrs. Williams with the heating instructions. She looked at me and smiled. I think she approved of my new look. Amy took me out to her dad and then went back into the kitchen. The view from the patio was spectacular.

"How are you, son?" Mr. Williams inquired.

"Very good, sir." I replied.

"Very busy, you mean."

"Yes, sir."

"How's the case going?"

"Still in the formative stages, sir."

"And the casino? I heard you're head of marketing."

"Yes sir. They asked me and I said yes."

"And the book?"

"About 80% complete, sir."

"Raskin said you've got a good head on your shoulders."

"Thank you, sir."

"Very organized and punctual."

"I try sir."

"Surprise visit? What's up?"

"We needed to get out of the city and away from the temptation of going back to work on our dedicated day off."

"How's my daughter?"

"Special. Very special." I replied.

I was as nervous as a whore in church. I breathed deeply. "There's something I would like to ask you sir."

"What's that?"

"While it has only been six months, four days and fifteen hours since I met Amy, I have fallen deeply in love with her, sir and I would like your permission to marry her."

Whew it was out.

"What if I say no?" Mr. Williams inquired, still looking out at the sailboats.

"I, at first, would be profoundly disappointed and then would ask what steps I needed to take to have you change your mind."

"Good answer. Six months is not a long time."

"I know sir, but longer than four days and two airplane rides."

That brought a big smile to his face.

"When you know, you know." Mr. Williams said. "That you do and you really love her?"

"Yes, sir, I do. I know that there will be others who think that this is about money…a struggling writer and a rich girl. To show my sincere love for your daughter, I would like to develop an agreement that indicates that nothing that belongs to Amy today or in the future, other than what we acquire together, is mine without your written consent. I'm not interested in material things as the ultimate goal in life. My goal with Amy is to sincerely feel wanted, needed and loved and no one I will ever meet will ever fill those needs like your daughter has."

He had a look of surprise on his face. "You're a better man than I thought son and I pride myself on being a good judge of character. Amy is all we have. Derrick is gone and with him part of our legacy. My only goal is that she is happy and healthy and for the past six months she has been happier and healthier than she has been in a long, long time. There will be days when you will question your decision. There will be times and instances when people will judge you simply because of the color of Amy's skin or by the fact that you married my daughter. Money does funny things to people. There will be instances when you will want to reconsider your logic. Are you ready to face all those challenges?"

"Yes, sir."

"You know, when Derrick died, I lost my son...my only son. When Amy got sick, I was afraid I was losing my only daughter and all I had hoped and dreamed about would be gone forever. Instead, a young man has walked into our lives that can give Marie and I joy and happiness that will hopefully fill some of the holes in our hearts that desperately need filling, simply by making our daughter happy. Of course, you can marry Amy, but there is one caveat." He said as he turned and looked deeply into my eyes.

"What's that?"

With tears in his eyes he said "You call me, dad."

"Yes, dad"

We hugged and both of us wiped the tears from our eyes.

"Come on, let's go in and tell the girls."

We walked into the kitchen and Mr. Williams...err Dad Williams, put his hand on my shoulder. "We have an announcement to make" Dad blurted out. "Tell them, son"

"Yes, dad."

It was all that needed to be said. The girls hugged and we hugged and Amy kissed me and there was joy in the Williams kitchen unlike any that there had been in a long, long time. We ate our pasty and outlined the plan of waiting to make any public announcement until after Rodney and Ann's wedding. With so much happening so soon, no date was even discussed, but we both knew that it would be the following year, after Amy made it to the clearing and got her fifth dot.

Mrs. Williams and Amy would have much to do and plans would need to be made. I knew that it could be the social event of the year in Milwaukee if that's what Amy wanted. We would cross that bridge when we got to it. In my heart, I wanted it to be a simple ceremony, in the forest. Amy would have final say.

The ride back to Madison was one happy ride. Amy was all giggly and I was in love. You couldn't wipe the shit-eating grin off my face. I asked Amy if I could tell my parents. She thought that it was only fair. We called from the car and mom let out a shriek. She and dad promised to keep it between them until after Rodney and Ann's wedding and then we would come home and let everyone know at the same time.

I told mom. "Life is good."

Mom concurred. "Life is good."

That night Miss Amelia Marie Williams and Mr. George Terrill IV consummated the agreement between both parties and lay in splendor thinking only of their future together and it was bliss.

Vampire Day: Friday was "V" for vampire day as we began to call it when Amy had to have her blood cleaned. I dropped her off at the clinic at 9:00 and told her I would come inside and get her at 3:00. She kissed me goodbye and walked through the double sliding doors. She turned and smiled. It was a sad smile, as once again she had to endure. At 2:30, I returned and she was just finishing up. She had tubes in her arms and was already getting weak. God, what a process. I don't know how those on dialysis can take it, but then realized that it was what kept them alive.

We got home and there were a dozen roses on the table. I had stopped at Felly's on my way home and thought they might cheer her up. She was wasted and gave me a brief smile. She went in and went to bed. I knew that our Friday night would consist of her sleeping and me working. You would think we had been married for ten years.

About seven, the cramps began. She started moaning and I knew they were bad. I massaged her legs and it didn't seem to do much good. Her head was tilting back as she was in so much pain.

"Medicine cabinet" she directed. "Brown bottle! Nimbex"

I looked and found a bottle with the name cisatracurium and brought it to her. She weakly shook her head saying, "Sorry, the insurance company went generic on me and I forgot."

I got her a glass of water and she took two pills.

"I'll be out for about 12 hours. Sorry. I love you."

As she lay back down, I began massaging her calves and could feel the chemicals rush through her body. Within three minutes, she was like a dish rag.

Fourteen hours later she awoke…still groggy. "I try not to take the pills, but sometimes I just have to. Sorry."

"Sorry for what, that you were in pain? Sorry that you slept for fourteen hours? There's nothing to be sorry about. You and I are in this together. I just wish there was more that I could do for you."

She wrapped her arms around my neck and kissed me. "I love you."

With that she went back to sleep. She was my Sleeping Beauty and all I ever wanted to be was her Prince Charming.

Around noon, Mrs. Williams called and inquired. I told her about the Nimbex and she understood. She thanked me for taking care of her daughter and told me that this happened every now and then. I told her what I told Amy, that we were in this together. Mrs. Williams seemed touched by what I said.

More Treaties: By Sunday, my fiancée' was back to normal and trying to catch up by doing her homework and researching all the treaties. As she worked, she was simply shaking her head. She wasn't one for profanity but every now and then she would look up and said, "These people really got screwed!"

She began with the Louisiana Purchase in 1803 from France that took the Winnebago homeland from the edge of the frontier to the center of the new American territory. Before it was signed, America was a distant enemy. Now it was within a day's ride by horse. The next year, William Henry Harrison had entertained a visiting Sauk and Fox delegation in St. Louis where he got them drunk and convinced them to sign away all rights to any land east of the Mississippi for a few small gifts. Those in attendance weren't even leaders of the Sauk and Fox nations, just a group who didn't understand what they were doing. The anger of both nations was so great that in 1810, they burned the city of Dubuque, Iowa to the ground. The threat of American takeover was so great, that the once indifferent Winnebago became concerned that their land would be next. Little did they know.

In 1816, the first treaty between the Winnebago and the American government was signed by, amongst others, a William Clark and, amongst others Choukeka or Dekare the Spoon. In this treaty, both sides agreed to forgive the others for all transgressions. In so doing, the Winnebago agreed that all land cessations made to the British, French or Spanish became in effect with the United States of America and that all members of the signed group were now exclusively under the rules and regulations of the United States and no one else. This treaty was in effect for nine years.

In 1825 another treaty was made encompassing all the warring Indian nations within the region. In this treaty, the US government, designated specific geographic areas and established boundaries between the different nations with the Winnebago area reduced from its traditional boundaries in the name of peace. Gone was any claim for the area around Green Bay or that which lie within Illinois. Once again, all tribes agreed that they were to be governed by the laws of the United States to such point that whenever the President may think it necessary and proper to convene such of the tribes, either separately or together, as are interested in the lines left unsettled herein, and to recommend to them an amicable and final judgment of their respective claims, so that the work, now happily begun, may be consummated. This too was signed by William Clark and De-ca-ri of the Winnebago, along with nine other nations. Amy pointed out that this meant that in 1825, the US government took control of determining the boundaries and territorial rights of the ten nations and there was absolutely nothing the Indians could say or do about it.

In 1827 and 1828, yet another treaty was created that extinguished any and all claim to land by the tribes who signed the 1825 treaty, including the Winnebago, to lands in Illinois or Michigan, including the Upper Peninsula. In signing the treaty, the Winnebago agreed not only the cessation of more land, but to allow miners into the remainder of their territory for purposes of mining. For relinquishing all the land, the joint tribes were promised $ 20,000 in goods to be divided amongst the tribes and that the government would determine any damages caused by the miners to the land. Needless to say, this is when George the First came to Mineral Point and how he was allowed to mine, but wasn't supposed to farm. This agreement was signed by Lewis Cass for the US and Koan-Kaw for the Winnebago.

In 1829, or only one year later, Major General Winfield Scott and John Reynolds, Governor of Illinois, amended the treaty stating. "The Winnebago nation hereby cede to the United States, forever, all the lands, to which said nation have title or claim, lying to the south and east of the Wisconsin River and the Fox River of Green Bay" in response to Red Bird. In exchange, the Winnebago were granted land in what was called 'the neutral zone' in Iowa on the western side of the Mississippi River. Whereas the US government agreed that the Wisconsin land was worth more than that in Iowa, the government agreed to remit $10,000 per year for 27 consecutive years to the Winnebago nation beginning in September of 1830. The government also agreed to erect suitable buildings, including a boarding school, near Prairie Du Chien for the Winnebago children, along with providing people to teach the Winnebago how to farm. As part of the treaty, the Winnebago were given 10 months to relocate at which time it is expressly understood that no band or party of Winnebago shall reside, plant, fish or hunt on any portion of the country herein ceded to the United Sates' signed by the above Americans and signed by Tshee-o-nuzh-ee-kaw, war chief and Khay-rah-tshaon-saip-kaw of the Winnebago tribe.

Three years later, in 1832, yet another treaty was signed where the Winnebago ceded to the United States forever, all the lands, to which said nation have title or claim, lying to the south and east of the Wisconsin River, and the Fox River. In exchange, the remaining Winnebago living in Wisconsin were "allowed" to have ownership in the land already owned by the Winnebago people who were forced out in 1829. In other words, they gave up Wisconsin and got nothing except the same stipend of $10,000 per year for 27 years now based on the people living in the designated area at time of payment. Thus, began the initiation of a welfare program for the native Americans. This too was signed by Scott and Reynolds and Khay-rah-tshaon-saip-ka.

This twenty -seven-year agreement lasted five years, or until 1837 when all the remaining land east of the Mississippi was ceded to the United States, along with the land west of the Mississippi, except for land designated as theirs for hunting, that they agreed to in 1832. For relocating again, a sum of $200,000 was designated as payment to specific individuals, with the balance to be applied to certain debts the Winnebago had with traders and other individuals along with a total of $50,000 to the chiefs who came to St. Louis "representing" the Winnebago nation. The treaty also promised "to invest the balance of the proceeds of the land ceded in the first article of the treaty amounting to $1.1 million dollars such that interest on the money would be spent for education, interpreters to teach the Winnebago English, a miller to grind their corn, agricultural implements and medical services" for the remaining 22 years and done so at the discretion of the President of the United States as signed by C.A. Harris for the US Government and Watch-hat-tyke or Big Boat for the Winnebago. With this agreement, the US government was now beginning to determine not only where the Winnebago were to live, but how they were to live…as farmers.

Nine years later, in 1846, the US government's treaty begins…It is solemnly agreed that the peace and friendship which exists between the people of the United States and the Winnebago Indians shall be perpetual; the said tribe of Indians giving assurance, hereby of fidelity and friendship to the government and people of the United States, and the United States giving to them, at the same time all proper care and protection." With this wording, Amy pointed out that the US government was now considering this independent nation, as protected by the US Constitution, a ward of the government. In signing, the Winnebago relinquished any and all claim to land within the United States, anywhere and thereby negated the twenty-two-year agreement signed in 1832. In so doing, the Winnebago nation was forced to relocate again and were to be compensated a grand total of $150,000 less $50,000 in concessions that the tribal elders made. Once again, the US government retained control of how the funds were to be allocated and that the funds were to be determined by the government. This was signed by a group of really brave Americans and Hoong-ho-no-kaw of the Winnebago tribe.

This twenty-two-year agreement was changed in 1853, after just 11 years, when the Winnebago ceded all lands where they had resided and were forced to move yet again giving up 897,000 acres for the sum of $70,000 along with a "permanent" home consisting of eighteen square miles in Minnesota. The US government realized the Winnebago nation had been splintered with segments living in the Kansas territory and some remaining in Wisconsin and therefore allowed additional time to create farms before they would be forcibly moved. For the first time, the agreement indicated that the government would assign to each head of family, or single persons over twenty -one years of age, a reasonable quantity of land, in one body, not to exceed eighty acres in one case, for their separate use.' To agree to this, the treaty of 1853 also indicated that monies owed by the US government from former treaties would be used to develop the land for the Winnebago in terms of schools, etc. and no funds were to go to individuals.

Even though the Constitution indicated otherwise, this agreement also stated that Congress had the power to create and enact laws concerning trade and intercourse with the Indian tribes including a complete prohibition of the creation or consumption of alcohol, even though it was readily available and legal to all other parties, as signed by George W. Moneypenny for the US and Waw-kon-chaw-koo-haw or The Coming Thunder for the Winnebago.

This treaty lasted all the way until 1859, when the government determined that the Winnebago had too much land that was "productive" and reduced the size of their holdings, classifying the remaining part as the "Winnebago Reservation". In the treaty, it was clearly stipulated in Article 1 that no white person was allowed on Winnebago land without written permission. For this protection, the land taken away was divided into one-hundred-sixty-acre parcels and sold at auction with all funds to be applied to the Winnebago as the Secretary of the Interior determined was best for the nation. In other words, the US government decided that land, agreed to six years previously, would be sold, even though it was owned by the Winnebago. Then the US government would decide what to do with the money for the land. If the money earned wasn't adequate, the Secretary of the Interior would determine a method of welfare for those in need as signed by Charles E. Mix and Baptiste Lassalleur.

Amy had another sad story to share. In 1865, or only six years later, the Winnebago ceded the remaining part of their reservation in the Dakota Territory to the US government and once, again, were forced to move to the Nebraska territory, with no compensation, as signed by William P. Dole and Little Hill for the Winnebago.

All-in-all, there were eleven agreements signed that saw the Winnebago Nation forcibly moved, eight times. With the move in 1865, they relinquished any and all claim to land and became undefined within the US system of Indian reservations. With so many moves and so much disruption, many wanted to return "home" to Wisconsin where their forefathers had lived and where their spiritual roots existed. As individuals, they took the risk of moving back, suffering the indignations of being outcasts in land that was once theirs. Their freedom was gone, their dignity was gone, their way of live demolished by a series of agreements that had but one goal, to totally dismantle their way of life and their rights as stated in the Constitution of the United Sates.

Amy had done her homework. It was a tale of two worlds colliding and only one victor... the white man. We couldn't let government win again. It was only ten acres and yet, just once, the Winnebago needed a victory on land that had once been theirs.

Combover: Monday morning meant back to work. I had an early conference call with the team in the Dells and listened to their gripes about signage and hotel promotions. I briefly worked on the book and put on some of my new clothes and still made it to the casino for the one-hour meeting with the agency. Mr. Combover was present, but Tom was not. Mr. Combover was surprised by the new duds.

"Tom has been reassigned" was enough for me.

"Let's see what you've got" as I listened to reach and frequency analysis and positioning in the high roller room.

"What about social media?" With that Mr. Combover turned on the projector and went through the thematic and structural aspects along with the required budget. I liked what I saw until he got to that part.

"Why, is it so expensive?" I asked.

Combover shook his head and said that all media buys cost money. I looked him square in the eye and told him that the position was good, the thematic were fine and reach and frequency analysis made sense, but I thought he was way off base with the social media.

"Tell you what." I said. "You keep the traditional advertising for now and I'll find someone more contemporary for social media"

"Why you can't have mixed messages in the marketplace," he blustered.

"We won't" I replied as I looked at my watch and the hour was up. Combover wasn't quite done, but I'd heard enough and learned a lesson from the Chief and Mr. Raskin. Authority means control and the best way to show your authority is to sustain a timetable. The Chief and Amy's dad taught me well as I stood and smiled and thanked him for coming and walked out thinking to myself. "Go tell Tom to shove it up his ass."

I walked out of the high roller room and some of the casino employees came up to me and said "hi". I think they were shocked by the new look and demeanor. Everyone was happy for me and the promotion and realized that in the scheme of things, I was now a step higher than last week and I hoped that my new look, attitude and role would result in a better life for everyone.

I had a plan. It was crazy, but I thought it might work. I called the Journalism Department and got hold of Doc. Snyder who had been my advisor. After a brief, but pleasant conversation where I filled him in on what I was doing, I asked if he had a couple of sharp social media students who would like to earn scholarships for the second semester. He said "of course". I gave him my phone number and told him to have his top four candidates call me. They would put on competitive marketing presentations and the two selected would be given the job. For simply competing, all four would be paid $250. If they were one of the two selected, the award went to $1000. If we chose their plan we would give them half the tuition for the first semester. If they implemented the program, the second half would be awarded as the Derrick Williams scholarship in honor of Amy's brother. I told Doc Snyder I would have the agreement drawn up and on his desk in 48 hours. My total cost for a completely integrated program would be less than $20,000 or $280,000 less than Mr. Combover wanted.

There was a pause and then Doc Snyder said something I will never forget. "You have become a man. The talent and creativity were always there, but it was trapped inside a little boy. Congratulations!"

Within 20 minutes, the phone was ringing. Two people I knew from Journalism classes called first. They thought it would be a slam dunk until I outlined what was expected. I think they were shocked that smart ass "Q" was grown up. The other two were more cautious. We set a deadline for the first Wednesday in September because I knew they would be back in school and I told them to email me and I would send them the details. Then I called Black River Falls and told the girls to plan on a day in Madison to see the presentations.

Amy came up with the name Project Frisco. The name meant nothing but it was to be the PR campaign about the forest and eminent domain designed to put public pressure on the government. We developed plans regarding the core message…"The government, once again, trampling on the rights of citizens" and the secondary theme…"Native Americans having more sacred land taken from them". We polished off the timetable based on hearing number one, the possible court case and the probable appeal. I learned that over 90% of all eminent domain cases are won by the government mainly because people can't afford to fight. I also learned that those which were lost by the government usually happened because of public awareness and resistance. Amy learned that, beyond the initial hearing, there could be a court trial and then, if the government won, the defendants could sue and become the plaintiffs.

Concurrently, Amy was developing the social media plan and how to put pressure on traditional print and broadcasting to cover the story locally. Ten acres in Iowa County, Wisconsin wouldn't get national coverage unless something dramatic happened. Amy asked her dad if he would talk to the politicians he knew and he agreed. He said that, with the money Wilco spent in both Madison and Milwaukee for advertising in both the newspapers and broadcast, he would ask for coverage from both, but couldn't predict anything. We knew we needed some surprise element and so no one was allowed to know what Project Frisco was all about.

We took Amy's Dad's condo bedroom and turned it into our war room where we had charts and graphs and stacks and stacks of paper all coded and in folders pertaining to different aspects of the case. Amy was writing a brief for Charlie regarding Winnebago treaties while studying Constitutional law and the right of government to take property with religious meaning.

For me, it was time to meet with the Ho-Chunk lobbyist. An appointment was set and I went to his office. He had the old time used car salesman look to him. I spent about an hour there and thought it was a waste of time. He didn't have a clue what was going on and was all BS about the people he knew. I went home and told Amy he was simply taking the Nation's money and they were getting nothing for it. I looked at the Gannt chart and added another line to the project list, replace lobbyist.

Our work hours kept increasing as the Ho-Chunk marketing team took on thematic issues within each of the casinos and began calling them "gaming centers" as casinos sounded negative and where you went to lose your money. Research indicated that the word "gaming" sounded more exciting and more participatory and people felt that that they were actually competing, which in the case of the Class II properties, they were.

The idea of making Madison non-smoking was implemented and required new signs, new ad campaign from KissAss and total cleaning of the property to get the cigarette smell out. In addition, an outdoor smoking area was added. We knew there would be some push-back, but the overall response from the target demographics outweighed the negatives from the smokers.

I had a video conference call with the demographics team and interior design specialist to make certain that the message within the casinos matched the target customer demographics. Rodney and I developed target analysis dependent on the market served. With Rodney's analysis, our performance expectations met the socio-economic profile of the target market and we quickly learned that our two worst performing clubs were the most discordant from the customer profiles we were developing.

All this was happening while writing the book, visiting Great Grandfather and waiting for the Waldwick shoe to drop. There were nights when Amy and I would look at each other through blurry eyes and say, "enough is enough." then we would crawl in bed and snuggle until we fell asleep in each other's arms. Sunday remained our day and as summer reached August, Ann and Rodney's wedding loomed on the horizon. God we were busy and yet Sunday remained our day.

Sunday, Funday: Rodney and Ann invited us out for a Sunday boat ride and dinner. We countered that they pick us up in the boat and then come to our "house" for dinner. Rodney was worried about where to leave the boat and not have it vandalized or stolen. We agreed and went to their house. We were four weeks, minus one day, from their big day and all that we knew was that the wedding would be in the Dells and the reception at Grand Geneva Resort in Lake Geneva. I questioned the difference in geography and Rodney indicated that the owners of the resort were personal friends of his dad and had several pending business opportunities they were looking at. While the distance was over 100 miles, the only ones who would traverse were those in the wedding party and everyone else would only be at the reception. He noted that arrangements had been made for everyone and it was what the Chief wanted. I had learned early on, the Chief got what he wanted and this was his plan.

Ann told us that it would be a small traditional wedding and then a big party at the Grand Geneva. The Chief made all the arrangements and because it was his only son, you knew it was going to be a big deal. All the Madison big-wig politicians had been invited along with virtually every major officer of all the region's Indian nations. I imagined guys in tuxedos and headdresses.

Ann said over 500 people would be there including both Amy's and my parents along with Tommie and his girlfriend Heather. I asked about accommodations and Rodney said that his dad had talked to the owners and 60 rooms had been blocked at the resort. This would be the first time my parents and Amy's would have met and so we were both a bit nervous.

Ann and Amy went to look at Ann's wedding dress. Amy told me later that it was traditional Native American made of beige Chamois buckskin with a beaded front that the old ladies had sewn for her. Amy said it was drop dead gorgeous. Rodney had not seen it. I guess the tradition of seeing your bride in her wedding dress before the wedding was bad luck with them as much as it was with us.

Rodney and I talked business for a while and then about the wedding. He said he would be in traditional Ho-Chunk garb consisting of buckskin breeches and a buckskin shirt. I asked if I was supposed to wear the same thing and he laughed. "You're my little brother and always will be, but this is traditional Indian dress and it's reserved for those still in the tribe. A dark suit would be fine." Holy shit! I didn't have a suit, but never let on.

We had a wonderful dinner and then headed home. I told Amy about the suit and she said not to worry. I said, "not worry, the wedding was in four weeks." When we got back to the condo, Amy called her dad and explained. The next morning, I got a call from Brooks Brothers and they told me to go out to West Towne Mall and meet with their tailor. Instead, Amy called the tailor and gave him her corporate number. Instead of me driving out to the store, Brooks Brothers had the tailor come to our condo with about twenty different fabrics for me to choose from. Amy narrowed it down to four…black, navy blue, silver gray, like the one the Chief wore the first time I met him, and a dark, charcoal gray pin stripe. I was going to pick the charcoal gray and she told the tailor "one of each". I almost messed my pants! I thought she was done and then told him to also make navy blue, double-breasted and black single-breasted blazers as well. The smiling tailor also brought material for neckties and Amy picked out two that went with each suit. Eight silk, custom-made neck ties and then she ordered four custom-made white shirts with spread collars and French cuffs.

I just shook my head. Here I was, a farm boy from Waldwick, Wisconsin whose last suit came off the mix-and-match rack at Burlington Coat Factory Outlet for $99.00 and Amy selected four custom made suits, eight neckties and four more shirts. Geez!

I needed dress shoes. Amy told me there wasn't enough time to have them custom made like her dad did. Instead, we went to the Allen Edmunds store and picked out a pair of Park Avenues…all black, plain, wing tip, lace-up, dress shoes. I just looked at her and shook my head. "This has got to stop." She just did her girly giggle. "I want you to be the best dressed man at the wedding and you can save the navy-blue suit for our wedding next year." That put a smile on my face. I tried to figure out what the total cost was and it had to come to over $10,000 in clothes. I just shook my head. "I can't afford these."

"I know" Amy said. "But I can and these are my way of saying 'thank you' for all that you have done and all that you are to me. I know you don't want to be a hero. I know that I am not supposed to put you up on a pedestal and so, let me do the next best thing and give you something that reminds me every single day of my gratitude for being the best thing that has ever happened in my life."

"These would have easily paid for five really good heifers." I replied.

Amy smiled and went "moo, moo, moo!" I asked her if it would be chocolate milk. She had a devilish grin on her face and said "we'll just have to keep trying to see if any babies come along, and then we'll find out."

"OH MY GOD!"

Happy Anniversary: We got back to work. The days were long and the nights short. I was back not sleeping again…shit. I'd wake up about three and Amy would be sound asleep. I'd lay there for a while and then think of all the things that needed to be done. I'd quietly get out of bed and go in the guest bedroom and shut the door. Was it Great Grandfather? Was it the book? Was it the marketing? Was it the wedding? Was it Amy? I didn't know. All I knew is that sleep was not part of my repertoire. Amy would wake up in the morning and stretch and reach for me and I wouldn't be there. She'd come in and see that there were dozens if not hundreds of words on the screen and know that I had been up for a long time. I hoped…no prayed, that the pressures would subside. I vowed once the book was done, I would slow down… but slow down to what?

She needed her rest. I needed to produce. I wanted the book done. I wanted the marketing plan complete. I wanted Iowa County to go away and let me live in peace. It was Tuesday and she awoke and saw me blurry-eyed looking at the screen. She enticed me into the shower with her and rubbed my back. I knew what I needed and so did she. We got into the car and went to Waldwick. Mom was at work. Tommie and dad were farming. Jake was in the house. We parked the car and walked to the forest. This is where I should have proposed, I thought. We sat beneath the mighty oaks and felt the damp ground around the school foundation. We walked upstream to where the water came from beneath the rocks and the grass had been matted. I looked at her and held her tight.

"Amy, will you marry me?"

She had a surprised look on her face.

"Of course."

I smiled and kissed her on the forehead.

"I love you."

She was getting a little concerned.

"This is where I should have asked you in the first place"

"It didn't matter where you asked me. I would have said yes, anywhere."

"I know, but this is where I should have asked. I want to pay for all the clothes you bought me."

Now, she had a very concerned look on her face.

"Why?"

"It's wasn't right for you to spend all that money on me."

"Honey!" She called me honey for the first time. "I bought the clothes because I love you. I bought the clothes because I am proud of you. I bought the clothes because I wanted to, not because I had to. I have the money and wanted to. Please don't ever let money come between us. Please!"

I had tears in my eyes again…I know, cry baby! As I shook my head. "It's too much. I'm trying to do too much."

Amy held me close and then kissed me.

I looked at her as she implored. "Sweetie. Let's look at everything…The book. Almost done. The marketing…Your changes will be implemented. Ann and Rodney…Three weeks away. The land…We WILL win. You and I…We're forever."

I held her close and realized she was right. I hadn't mentioned that it was the first anniversary of the Dodgeville debacle…my car accident.

"Where were you a year ago today?" she asked.

I breathed deep and shook my head. She knew.

"Without a year ago today, nothing and I mean nothing you mentioned would exist. Take the good with the bad. God was looking out for you and changed you in so many ways."

I smiled a weak smile and she kissed me and hugged me and held me close. It was what I needed.

"Have I told you that I love you?" I asked.

"Have I told you how sexy you are in all those new clothes?" she replied.

"Have I told you how sexy you look in no clothes?" Touché!

That was all it took and I was fine. "Let's go home," which for the first time meant 137 West Wilson Street, Madison, Wisconsin.

Blackhawk: It was Thursday. The weeks were flying by. I felt as if I was getting close to finishing the book promised to the Chief. I also felt as if I was being pulled in a dozen different directions not knowing where to turn or were to go. I made what was becoming my obligatory weekly trek to the Dells and arrived with ten minutes to spare. Each week, my 2,000 words were added with no response from Black River Falls. When you are creating anything, something is better than silence. It can be deafening.

I walked into Great Grandfather's room and he was sitting as he normally was, in his rocker. "Little Spirit, come in," Great Grandfather said without his normal soft smile. "I sense that you are troubled. What is it that makes you sad?"

"I'm simply overwhelmed, Great Grandfather. I am trying to do so much and there isn't enough time. I want to be a good employee. I want to be a good son. I want to be a good person and above all else I want to be a good friend to all who care for me."

"Come sit with me and let me tell you what an old man learned long ago."

I pulled up the cedar chest and Great Grandfather began sharing how important it is to simply write down everything that needs to be done and putting a number by them. "There should never be more than seven items on your list as there are only seven days in the week" He said. "Don't start one project until you have finished the one before and never let it move up your list until the one above it is done unless it is an emergency."

"Life is not about what you do. It is about who you are. You, Little Spirit are a warrior. Had you been born and were part of the Winnebago tribe, you would have, someday, been its chief. You have the patience of the turtle, the intelligence of the owl and the determination of the wolf. That is why you are the chosen one. We do not get to select who we are, we do get to select what we are and what we will become. Be strong Little Spirit and you will become a great leader who will help many people. Fight for what is right and always remember that you are the chosen one."

With that, I put my hands in his and his chant began. As his eyes rolled back into his head, there was a different expression on his face. Instead of tranquility that I had seen so many times before, there was one of pain as tears welled in his eyes. Once again, a different voice emanated and I sat in fear…

"I am Blackhawk, leader of the Sauk and yet my soul runs deep through the land of the Winnebago. My wife was Winnebago. My daughter was then half Winnebago. We lived in peace with each other and honored our similarities and respected our differences. We are honorable people. Our word is our bond. We have taught this to our children as we learned from our fathers and those who came before them. What good is a man whose word is not kept? What good is a written word that is broken? What good can I find in a man willing to take what is mine and give nothing in return?"

"We, the Sauk, built our villages in an area called Saukenuk where there was plenty of water, good land for growing everything from corn to pumpkins and many animals for food and clothing. This was our land and yet, because of a few Winnebago, we were forced to move to Iowa where there was no food, only more broken promises by the white man."

"We moved because we knew that if we did not, we would be killed. My people were starving and, like any leader, I was angered by the loss of my birthplace. There was no food and in 1830 and 1831 we came across the river called the Mississippi into our land now called Illinois several times simply in search of food from the crops that we had planted. The white settlers were afraid of women, old people and children when all we wanted was something to eat."

"In June of 1831, because of the Winnebago incident, the government forced me to sign a treaty stating that my people would never return to our homeland on the east side of the

Mississippi River without government permission. In return, Keokuk and I, the other Sauk elder, were promised enough corn and food to feed our people throughout the winter. They had taken our land and now they were taking our pride. We did not want what was handed to us, we wanted what was ours. No man should suffer and it is understood why I was angry. The government never provided the promised food and so, with little food and my tribal members starving, I elected to return to my homeland once again. Did I break my word? Yes. But only because the white fathers broke theirs and my people were starving."

"I was not alone in my anger and my frustration. I did not sit by myself peering into a looking glass to see anger. Instead, I spoke to the leaders of the Fox and Kickapoo and in April 1832, encouraged by promises of alliance with these nations and Britain, I moved what the white man called the "British Band" of more than 1200 of my people, back across the Mississippi River. We only went where our former cornfields had been simply to harvest what crops had grown. Who would have thought that something as basic as wanting to feed your family could lead to war, if you want to call it that?"

"I heard that the settlers who had moved into Saukenuk lived in fear that we would return. They had fenced in what had been the Sauk fields and their animals had eaten or trampled the vegetables that we came for. Our leaders heard about the situation and went to the settlers carrying a white flag, meaning they meant no harm, simply to tell them that we had only come back to harvest food for our families. The settlers didn't seem to care about the white flag or the fact that my people only wanted to eat. Instead, their excuse was that they didn't speak the Sauk language and killed two of my people, white flag and all. I was enraged. We came in peace only to live and so we began killing white settlers."

"The Sauk nation's "incursion" into land that was once ours, simply to find food, was considered an invasion by the United States Government and volunteers were sent to fight us. In May 1832, the volunteer militia was supported by regular U.S. Army troops who drove my people to a point of exhaustion and starvation. With our supplies running low, I sent out a truce party bearing another white flag of surrender. The white militia volunteers saw the three representatives I sent and rushed out and killed one, while capturing the other two. These "soldiers" then pursued five warriors who had followed the truce party, killing two of them and attacking our encampment. Needless to say, I was enraged that the dignity of surrender could be sullied and integrity did not exist. I took my men to battle and dispersed the militia, many of whom simply went back to their homes, without ever firing a shot. These were not warriors. They were drunken cowards who cared, not for honor and dignity, but for the bravado that comes from killing another man and thinking nothing of it."

"Enraged, I made plans for war. Using small groups of warriors to randomly attack while the women and children remained safe in the marshes of Koshkonong, no one knew where we would next attack. The white man's armed forces attempted to stop us and for four months the "war" went on as we eluded capture by leading these forces around southern Wisconsin. The toll on my people, who had no food or water, was tremendous and yet death was a much better choice than living the life we were."

"In late July, what was left of our people were traveling through the four lakes area called Tychobera. We were traveling between two of the lakes with the soldiers in pursuit. As our malnourished and exhausted stragglers fell behind, they were simply shot by militia throughout the day. One-by-one, my starving people were destroyed as if it were a sport…a game…a happenstance, not out of anger but out of sport, simply to see who could kill the most of my people. I heard that they laughed as my people died. I heard that they brutalized them and raped the women and young girls. I heard that they humiliated them before they shot them dead, leaving their bodies to rot in the summer sun. It wasn't difficult to track my people as flocks of buzzards and carrion crows swooped above the bodies as they fell in exhaustion or, if lucky, in death."

"We repeatedly attempted to surrender, only to be met with volley after volley of weaponry. As darkness was setting, what was left of my Sauk nation reached the Wisconsin River at a point called Wisconsin Heights with troops and militia in pursuit. I had a choice…continue to watch my people die one-by-one as they fell behind or try to get back to safety in Iowa. It was my belief that the existence of my entire nation was at stake and so I took 50 warriors and moved about two miles from the river, leaving the balance to help the old people, women and children cross the river. Another 70 warriors volunteered to fight to save our families and our ways of life but I told them to stay behind in case we failed."

"We defended the pass against nearly three thousand soldiers and militia and made our way northwest to a point above Prairie Du Chien at the Bad Axe River. Here some families fashioned rafts and floated downriver toward the Mississippi as they believed their only hope to save themselves was to get back to Iowa. Few escaped. They either drowned or found themselves facing soldiers who stood on the steamer "Warrior" and simply killed the women, children, old people and braves as they floated by. To the soldiers, it was great sport. They didn't seem to care these people begged for mercy and again, waved white flags, desperately trying to surrender. The soldiers simply shot them."

"One story told was of a little boy…starving, his arm half blown away, begging for a piece of bread. Instead the little boy was shot along with those of his nation. As they fell into the river, their bodies floated away, and the river, as Captain John

Throckmorton so vividly boasted, "blushed to a scarlet red" with Indian blood, washing away our hopes, our dreams, our love for life and the land that had once been ours."

"Those who hid in the reeds along the shore were hunted down and bayoneted to death as they tried to surrender. About 70 of my nation escaped across the Mississippi River only to be hunted like animals by bands of Sioux at the direction of General Atkinson. Of the 1,200 followers who came 'home', less than 150 lived to tell of the horrors they experienced."

"I surrendered at Fort Crawford to an Indian agent named Joseph Street. I was a tired, broken man, no longer able to fight for my freedom, no longer willing to fight for my people who were, for the most part, decimated by disease, hunger and the never-ending, ever-eroding tide of settlers. They took me east and made me a spectacle. I learned the power and might of the government and realized that the way of life of the Indian was gone forever. Gone was the peace. Gone was the tranquility. Gone was the harmony with God and nature, replaced by the ever-growing insidious presence of a mankind hell-bent on controlling everything and making it work for them."

"They took me to New York City and let me see all of the people and them see me. It convinced me that my fight was futile. My people were dead and each day there were more white men than the day before."

"They say I died of a broken heart somewhere out in Iowa. Iowa, land that was supposed to be the Sauk's forever. Death was a welcome event. I only wanted to rest in peace until some grave robbers dug up my body and my soul and paraded it around for more people to see. I went from being a great leader to a great sadness all because of someone else's dreams. Now my soul wanders looking only for a place to rest. I will go on forever, looking, looking, looking. There will be no peace for the white flag of surrender was stained red with the blood of my people and I see them all looking at me with tear-stained eyes simply asking, Why?"

Tears running down Great Grandfather's cheeks. This had been the most difficult. This had been the most traumatic. This intercession took every ounce of his body and every gram of his soul and spread it thin, exposing it to the raw consequence of reality.

As his lids closed and I was about to leave, Great Grandfather spoke again. "Please don't leave me. I cannot bear to be alone. Please stay awhile and let me feel the warmth of your goodness".

We sat in total silence for almost an hour with him holding my hands until the pain that he had endured had subsided. His head tilted down and then there was a nod. The spell had been broken. More of the sadness within him had come to the surface cleansing his body once again of the pain and agony that had been building for so many, many years. When would it all end? I did not know. All I knew was that I was the chosen one into whom all the pain and suffering of a people so long, long ago was being channeled so that those who came before could finally rest in peace.

I walked slowly out of the assisted living center and reached the Jeep. I stood for a moment and caught my breath as I leaned against the Jeeps door. As I headed out of the parking lot, I did not turn onto the Interstate. Instead I traveled south on Highway 12 through Sauk City and turned right on the south side of the bridge, stopping in a small spot along the Wisconsin River where the Sauk had tried to flee, where I broke down and cried and cried and cried.

I made it home and Amy could tell I was despondent. I shared with her the words of Blackhawk. She added that Ann knew that Blackhawk was a friend of George the First and our family had purchased land from him before having to purchase it two more times from the government. She found it appalling to think that someone would dig up a dead man and parade him around the country and no one would stop them. Amy looked at me and shook her head and then she cried.

Round One – Iowa County vs. George Terrill IV: Charlie met us at the condo at 3:00 and we headed to Dodgeville, eating dinner at the Culver's near the cut-off. We walked into the old courthouse and up the stairs and into the council chambers. Mom and dad were there and it was a lot more casual than I expected. I don't think those on the Iowa County board were expecting the turnout they got. Normally, a rubber stamp and "bang". What was once private land becomes that of the government. The argument is normally about the value of the land and not whether the government had the right to take it in the first place. As the meeting came to order, Mom, dad and I sat in the "audience" seats. Amy and Charlie sat at the table.

The meeting began and Charlie raised his hand and introduced Amy as his legal assistant and then himself, representing both the Terrill family and the Ho-Chunk nation. The board was perplexed in wondering what Charlie was doing at the meeting. Charlie outlined how the land in question had been owned for nearly 200 years by the Terrill family and that ownership had been transferred to me per the Quitclaim deed that he offered as evidence. The board examined the deed and accepted it as evidence.

Charlie pointed out that "Subsequent to acceptance of the transfer of said property, Mr. George Terrill IV, who had assumed ownership, sold 50% stake in the property to the Ho-Chunk nation for which full payment was made". Amy provided copies of the receipt and the second Quitclaim deed and receipt of submission of both sets of title transfer papers.

The board members were surprised. They knew what was supposed to be a normal transfer of ownership just got a whole lot more complicated and they weren't ready for what was presented. Because the County wasn't expecting the challenge, they didn't have the County Attorney on hand and had a clerk run down the hall and get him. Charlie asked for permission to outline all that was in the process and was given permission to speak…

"Ladies and Gentlemen, eminent domain compulsory purchase resumption, resumption compulsory acquisition, or expropriation is the power of a local, county, state or national government to take private property for public use. However, it can be legislatively delegated by the state to municipalities, government subdivisions, or even to private persons or corporations, which they are authorized by the legislature to exercise the functions of public character. Based on this ability, it is our belief your board has acted and we accept the ability to act therein." To which the board nodded in the affirmative.

"We accept the fact the property may be taken either for government use or by delegation to third parties, who will devote it to public or civic use or, in some cases, economic development. The most common uses of property taken by eminent domain are for government buildings and other facilities, public utilities, highways and railroads, or for public safety. In this case, it appears the intent is to develop a small public park. Some jurisdictions require the acquirer make an offer to purchase the subject property, before resorting to the use of eminent domain, which was not done." Again, the board agreed, but you could see that they were beginning to wonder where the line of reasoning was going."

Charlie continued. "However, once the property is taken and the judgment is final, you, the condemner may put it to uses other than those specified in the eminent domain action. This means that, should you so elect, you could put a gas station or Gentleman's Club on some of the County's only remaining virgin property, unspoiled by farming or development, with no rights allowed to those who currently hold ownership to the land. We understand that property of an owner may be taken either in its entirety (total take) or in part (part take), either quantitatively or qualitatively…either partially in fee simple or, commonly, an easement, or any other interest less than the full fee simple title…and that, should this board so deem it, you could take the entire Terrill farm. However, at this point in time, we do not believe that to be the case." Again, heads nodded in the affirmative.

"People do have a right to their property and that is what we are here to discuss today. In some cases, it is all they have to show, not only for their, but their ancestors, work. In other cases, the land is the only thing they know. I am of the Ho-Chunk nation and it would be safe to say that many people look back on what was done to the Native Americans and say, 'That was wrong.' Their land was encroached upon. In the past, the US Government made treaties and made many of my ancestors feel safe … much like granting someone ownership of property in today's standards … then the US Government forced my ancestors to continue to move as it fit the government's needs. While this happened in our ancestor's times, it is our belief that the ten acres of land under consideration is similar to what is happening today: land is being seized against people's wills, without just compensation, and without proper reasoning. It was irresponsible then; and it irresponsible now." At this point, the committee sat in earnest. "This is why we are here today."

Amy had done her homework and Charlie continued: "Most states use the term eminent domain, but some U.S. states such as New York use the term appropriation or Louisiana uses the word expropriation as synonyms for the exercise of eminent domain powers. It is our belief that any and all three terms need to be placed in public record to ensure no misunderstanding as to the intent of the board. Based on our position, we formally request the cessation of all processes towards the application of eminent domain, appropriation or expropriation towards land held by the Terrill family and the Ho-Chunk nation as sacred land to both parties, upon which the proposed changes and modifications would result in a defamation of the moral, religious and sanctimonious integrity of the property and unjust emotional duress to the parties herein."

The board sat flabbergasted. This was 10 acres of unused farmland that had been fallow since the beginning of time. The Terrill family had been residents of Waldwick and Mineral Point since the village began. The Terrill children had gone to school and had been part of the community forever. A fifteen-minute recess was requested while the board got their bearings.

When the process began again, the County lawyer was present where he stated the county's case…"Our attempt is to take undeveloped land and put it to use for the good of all residents. We have attempted to work with the Terrill family and they have not been cooperative, taking devious steps to transfer ownership from the rightful owner to first one son…George Terrill the Fourth and subsequently partial ownership to the Ho-Chunk Nation. We, as representatives of Iowa County, have worked in good faith to determine a fair value for the ten acres in question and have outlined our intent for the property. Unfortunately, the Terrill family, George Terrill the Fourth and now the Ho-Chunk nation have not been cooperative in allowing our due process to transpire."

"Based on our actions, it is our belief that an act of condemnation be implanted, thereby allowing the County, within its rights, to exercise the formal act of this power to transfer title or some lesser interest in the subject property. Where this happens, such as when an easement or a leasehold is taken, we agree that we the condemner must pay just compensation, the same as in total takings, while outlined within the Constitution of the United States."

"Pursuant with this document, upon which our society is based, we have acted, in good faith, to provide the constitutionally required "just compensation" measured by fair market value of the part taken, plus severance damages subjected to the diminution in value of the property remaining to the owner, whomever that may be at this time, when only a part of the subject property is taken. Where a partial taking provides economic benefits specific to the remainder, those must be deducted, typically from severance damages."

"Should the Terrill family, Mr. George Terrill the Fourth or the Ho-Chunk Nation or whomever it is that owns the property at this moment, disagree with our intent we are prepared to allow the courts of Wisconsin and those of the United States to determine our rights." This was the attorney's way of telling us that he expected to wring us dry financially by using County tax dollars to win his case.

Charlie rose and looked squarely at the County's Attorney. "Counselor, it is our intent to show that, without a doubt, the land in question was legally transferred to the parties herein under the laws and protocols established by Iowa County and the State of Wisconsin and this is now a federal case where the County of Iowa superseded the independent rights of the Ho-Chunk nation as also outlined in the Constitution of the United States."

"In so doing, it is then also our position that, subject to federal law, the United States Congress may take private property directly without recourse to the courts by passing an Act transferring title of the subject property directly to the government. However, because the United States is dealing with a nation protected by the Constitution of the United States, certain precedents have been established by the United States Supreme Court defining the rights of such nations as it applies to the taking of sacred land. In such cases, we, the property owner, will seek cessation of all claims of eminent domain. And, in the instance that it is decided by the United States Supreme Court we are not due such protection, fair and just compensation from the United States government in the U.S. Court of Federal Claims, shall be requested."

In other words, we're about to move to the big leagues and we're taking off the gloves.

The County board sat there and realized that the pissing match was about to begin. "Gentlemen, unzip your flies!"

We all walked out of the Courthouse and Charlie had a smile on his face.

"They got the shit scared out of them." Charlie whispered. "They thought this would be a slam dunk and all of a sudden they don't know who they're fighting or why. It certainly doesn't mean that they're going to back down. This is an election year and that means anything can happen."

Amy told me that there were two critical issues that consisted of who owned the land and if the land was truly sacred. The first challenge would be who owned the land. This would probably not require a court appearance but just letters back and forth showing that all papers were signed and registered, which Charlie had proof they were.

Seven days later, Charlie called and said that he had received a letter from Iowa County. It was their position that the sale was invalid and done "in anticipation" and that they were proceeding. Charlie was not surprised or dismayed. It just meant that we would have to show why I sold the land before anything could happen in regards to Ho-Chunk involvement. Charlie had expected it and knew it was their way of trying to get us to give up believing we didn't have the resources to fight the next round. Boy were they wrong.

The Wedding: It didn't seem possible that Rodney and Ann's wedding was in a few days. All arrangements had been made. Amy and I had been informed that we would be picked up at the condo on Friday afternoon at three and a schedule had been set for the rehearsal and dinner in the Dells. We were told that we would be transported after the wedding to Lake Geneva and then back home on Sunday. It was going to be a full weekend. I had been told by my new boss (named Amy) to bring two of my new suits and she picked out the silver gray for the wedding that somewhat matched the really nice, conservative dress she was wearing. We had no idea what to expect.

At precisely three, the bell rang and we loaded Amy's two suitcases and my overnight bag into the limo. Geez, women need a lot of stuff. The limo was huge and fancy and I expected more people to join us, but we were alone in the back and stretched out with my feet trying to touch the wall in front of us. For me, it was a hoot, because I had never been in a limo before. For Amy, I don't think it was the first time and she did her girlie giggle at my excitement.

Having driven to the Dells many times to see Great Grandfather, the trip was routine and I got to enjoy the company of the limo driver asking a dozen questions about everything and anything about the behemoth and having the gorgeous woman sitting next to me. After the hour drive, we checked into the hotel and went to a really nice room with fresh flowers on the table and no water slide. There was a note saying rehearsal was casual and asking us to be downstairs at 6:00. Knowing Rodney, I knew that it meant precisely at that time.

Just before what I called the witching hour (which Amy, my new boss, told me was the first hour after midnight and so I was off by only six hours), we went to the lobby and a shuttle bus arrived to pick up the rest of the wedding party, none of whom we knew. There were Ann's parents and Rodney's college roommate and his wife. Within five minutes everyone met everyone else and the delineations evaporated. I guess I was the star of the show because they all knew how Ann and Rodney met.

The Dells is a really beautiful place. I learned back in Geology 101 that the Dells' rocks were formed about 500 million years ago or so when I think my dad was born and Wisconsin was at the bottom of a shallow sea. Now these half-million -year-old rocks had it pretty good until approximately 19,000 years ago, when the Dells sat at the edge of the continental glacier. The melting glacier formed what was called, Glacial Lake Wisconsin, which I learned was about the size of the Great Salt Lake. The lake was held back by an ice dam created by the remaining glacier. As everything was warming, the ice dam finally burst and kaboom there was a huge flood that cut deep, narrow gorges in the sandstone creating these really neat pillars with deep valleys between. Because the stands are so different, the Ho-Chunk considered them to be a very special and sacred place while the developers turned them into Wisconsin Dells "Water Capital of the World".

Enough on history! We went out to a park and made our way out into the woods and down a long tree-lined path until we came to a narrow bridge that led over to one of the escarpments called Stand Rock. A long time ago, some guy took pictures of his kid jumping from the main land to Stand Rock and it became famous. For years, they had shows there with a German Shepard jumping over and back to the ooohs and aaahs of the paying public. The problem was that all the tourists were destroying sacred grounds and so the area was closed for ecological reasons. However, because it is a sacred place for the Ho-Chunk, their use is allowed a special permit basis. I guess the wedding of the head of the nation's only son and the counties' largest employer was considered one of those events.

While many people would wonder why Indians got married on a rock instead of in a church or religious building, I learned from

Rodney and Great Grandfather that, while the Indians ancient civilization world-view was quite different from the one of their modern people, each Indian child is still taught to perceive the world as one whole and not of separate parts and to respect every life, regardless of its form. They are taught to live and act on the Earth impeccably, disturbing neither the harmony, balance, nor beauty of the environment and to listen and understand the world around them such as the sun, stars, wind, forest, rivers, lakes, animals…and to follow the laws of nature in their life. Indian children are taught that, violating these laws causes unnecessary pain to the living. Rodney told me that for him little things like crossing a river, walking forest trails or swimming in a lake always made him feel as if he was one with the wind, water, mountains and birds. Since a young age, Rodney said he knew and accepted that his own body was but a small fragment in the world of matter, no more important than pines swaying in the wind, clouds floating in the sky, squirrels frolicking in the trees or fish swimming in waters and this is from one very large man. I think this is why we get along so well.

At the wedding rehearsal, there were several other people and everyone was in jeans and very casual as we waited for the soon-to-be bride and groom to show up. As they arrived, they came with an elderly gentleman, the Chief, Rodney, his mom and Ann's parents. I learned that the elderly gentleman was the shaman or minister. Compared to traditional Christian weddings, the wedding was going to be a lot more complicated. Everyone would be seated around the bridal center which was circular. Before the services began, both fathers would give a speech and thank everyone for coming, and acknowledge the aid given by the drum spirit.

Next, there would be music. However, not organ music, but drum music with lutes. After Ann and Rodney's fathers spoke there would be dancers who would perform the dream dance and then Ann and Rodney would be formally presented. The ceremony would revolve around a number of sacred drums made from wooden washtubs, each supported off the ground by means of four stakes that were stored in a vault in Black River Falls. They were covered with calf hide and elaborately decorated with paint, beadwork, and other symbolic decorations. Each drum had an organization of tribal dancers attached to it that were spoken of as "belonging" to a certain drum. Each member had a particular place in the dance ring and there were specific duties for each: speaker, singer, drum beater, pipe tender, and heater of the drumhead. The calumet, or peace pipe, would also be an intrinsic part of the ceremony and it too was an antique and only used for very special occasions with the dream dance, such as marriage, divorce, and removal of mourning and done to ensure social cohesion within the family and the nation.

As the bride and groom arrived, they would take their place and the following words were spoken:

> Now you will feel no rain.
> For each of you will be shelter to the other.
> Now you will feel no cold
> For each of you will be warmth to the other.
> Now there is no more loneliness,
> For each of you will be companion to the other.
> Now you are two bodies
> But there is only one life before you.
> Go now to your dwelling place
> To enter into the days of your togetherness
> And may your days be good and long upon the earth.

Next, an antique, sacred, two-stem, wedding decanter would be handed to the bride and then the groom from which they drank a honey-mead drink, first from one side and then the other, in reverence to nature, earth and life. The bride and groom would then present the decanter to their parents and grandparents as each was to taste the sweet nectar of their marriage.

The bride and groom would kiss and prayers and invocations of prosperity, good health and brotherhood would accompany the ceremony and anyone could participate. At this point in time, the ceremony would be over and all parties were to join hands and sing the words of praise, Hoiyah! Hoiyah! Hoiyah! Those which Great Grandfather had said so many times. The drums would play softly with a reed lute accompaniment and then Rodney and Ann would walk across the bridge to their new lives together.

In all, it was pretty cool. There were only about 20 people in the party and I learned that on Saturday, there would only be a few more. The wedding ceremony was VERY religious and was intended only for those closest to the bride and groom. Amy and I felt honored.

When rehearsal was over, we walked back to where the van had dropped us off and caterers had set up a dinner tent and we had roast duck with wild rice and all the trimmings. The Chief was in his best of moods with a smile from ear-to-ear. I had never seen him happier. Ann's parents were common folks from Milwaukee, where her dad worked for the city. I think they were a bit overwhelmed by everything. We sat with Rodney's college roommate and his wife and enjoyed ourselves watching the families blend together in love and laughter.

Saturday morning arrived and we were ready to go when the van came at 9:30 to pick us up. We were told to have our luggage packed and downstairs and it would be taken to the Grand Geneva Resort in Lake Geneva. As always, everything was clockwork. We arrived at the wedding site and walked back down the path, now strewn with small pine cones and rose petals. As we crossed the bridge, the railings were covered in floral garlands and each of the chairs from the night before was covered in a white slipcover with flowers everywhere. It was beautiful.

We took our places and at precisely 10:00 AM the ceremony began. Great Grandfather was there in a wheelchair. He could walk, but it was thought that, because he couldn't see, it would be safer for him. He looked small without the rocker and the shawl and yet he sat in a position of authority with a smile upon his face. The Chief and Great Grandfather and the elders of both the Ho-Chunk and the Potawatomi were all in suits, but they wore their hair in two braids with one white eagle feather, which they saved for very special occasions such as this. The wives and ladies were in their finest dresses, some of Native American design and some in a more western style, but all had their hair braided in a single braid with one white feather. I learned that it was improper for white people to touch the feathers. I wondered about Amy. Perhaps she would only be half wrong if she touched one.

As the drummers completed their songs and dances, everyone stood and Ann was escorted across the bridge by her father. She looked absolutely incredible in her tan buckskin dress with the hand-inlaid beads on the front. Her hair was also braided in a single braid, also with her new white feather. Next it was Rodney who was also dressed in a buckskin shirt and breeches who walked alone, proud and brave. Being a big guy, his outfit made him appear even larger and yet, it was totally foreshadowed by the huge smile on his face.

Ann's father took his seat and the priest began his services with the words from the night before. As the new husband and bride held hands they looked in each other's eyes and repeated what had been said during rehearsal, taking the two-spout decanter and drinking from it. With that, they went to Ann's parents and the Chief and Rodney's mom before handing the vial to Great Grandfather who took one huge swig that made everyone smile. The drums began again and the lute played as the new husband and wife made their way across the bridge and into the rest of their lives as we all applauded.

As we were leaving, the Chief came to me and said that Great Grandfather wanted to speak to me. He would not be making the trip to Lake Geneva as it was just too much for him in one day. I walked up to the little old man in the wheel chair and knelt down beside him. Amy stood beside me.

He spoke in the same soft, eloquent voice. "You, Little Spirit are a good friend, not only of my Great Grandson, but the entire Ho-Chunk nation. The words you are writing are honest and noble. The battle you are fighting is for the good of all. I bless you and Amelia and wish you many years of happiness together."

"Thank you, Great Grandfather. I am honored to have Rodney and Ann as my friends and to enjoy the dignity of those I have come to know."

Great Grandfather held out his hands and I put mine in his. "You are a great warrior, Little Spirit. May the peace of God be with you always."

I bent over and did something I don't think he was expecting…I gave him a kiss on the cheek. He smiled a deep and reverent smile and whispered…"Thank you my son. Thank you. Where is the one you love?"

"I'm right here Great Grandfather." Amy replied.

"Don't you have a kiss for a little old man?" he said with a smile on his face.

With that, Amy leaned over and kissed him on the cheek.

"Don't ever let him go" he whispered.

"I won't Great Grandfather. I won't.

I hadn't noticed, but the Chief had been watching as had Rodney. As I walked towards the van, the Chief came and gave me one of those father-to-son hugs and smiled. Rodney, the big lug, had tears in his eyes and gave me a bear hug as well. The wedding spectators got in the van and headed for Lake Geneva. Rodney and Ann and the families stayed for photographs. The two-hour ride to Lake Geneva was filled with laughter and bonding as strangers became friends.

The Reception: How can one describe a wedding reception? The official definition: A confluence of tradition, mandated social propriety, anticipation and potential tedium. My definition…A cacophony of pledges and speeches usually fermented by alcohol, before taking place in an arena overflowing with talk of forever that happens less than half the time.

Those in attendance represented the traditional amalgam of strings tied to the bride and groom through blood line or social interaction who became the automatics. The rest of us were simply additions to the story of this thing called life, ever extending, forever rendering primary, secondary and tertiary alliances to a position predicated on inclusion, based simply on fate. Was a wedding reception to be the celebration of the uniting of two individuals bound in holy matrimony, one decreed by the father or simply a raucous party that was determined by the bride as she manifested her first decree in the rest of their wedded life?

Whatever the intent was, for Ann and all, the range of socio-economic paradigms from Rodney's parents to Ann's was simply so profound that her concepts, dreams and aspirations were overwhelmed by the wishes, not of Rodney, but of the Chief himself. This was his only son. This was the one time In the Chief's life that he could show how far he had come, leaving the realm of social gravity and attaining a point on the edge of the social stratosphere. We were along for the ride, all of us. Participants, observers, spectators in his dream. Knowing and loving Big Brother and Ann, I knew that they had been convinced, cajoled and certainly pressured into the entire reception.

Our goal…mine, Amy's and I believe the new bride and groom, was to take the pomp out of the night and fill the circumstance with fun, so that formal boredom could be replaced with smiles and memories that would curtail some of the aspirations of the Chief. Now, don't get me wrong, the Chief was a great guy, but a magnanimous spectacle was set in place whose objective was to create an event so spectacular that all that came would walk away impressed not only by the event, but the feeling of joy for the newlyweds and, for the Chief's accomplishments. Having said this, let me take a few minutes to outline a celebration unlike any I had ever attended. Was it spectacular? Incredibly. Was it extreme? Most certainly. Was it able to render a night that no one would forget? I completely believe so. Did the Chief achieve his dream without offending those who came? I certainly hope so as the costs were extreme and absolutely nothing, was left to chance or without his personal consideration.

The Grand Geneva Resort in Lake Geneva, Wisconsin began as a Playboy Club and through the years, it has mellowed like a fine wine. Beautiful grounds that are kept impeccable and "oh my God, scenery". It has great facilities and a staff that makes you feel special, based on their down-home goodness that few states and fewer locations could ever offer, thereby making it the ideal location for an upscale wedding reception.

Our van arrived from the Dells and we disembarked. By the time we arrived, the laughter had died down and we were all ready to prep for the main event. As we exited, we were given our room keys and directions to suites where our bags had already been placed. Our room had fresh flowers and chocolates along with full bottles of Amy and my favorite wines, and a hand-written note from Rodney and Ann thanking us for taking part in their special day. On the dresser sat a framed photo of the two of us from the wedding along with a photo of the bride and groom. The miracles of electronics never cease to amaze me. Two hours and the photos had been printed, placed in frames and delivered to our rooms.

Our suite was on the top floor and overlooked one of the two golf courses and the small lake within which floated a pontoon with a floral arrangement of two white horses raised up on their hind legs, with red plumes and the initials "A" and "R" where the quarter-sheets would have been. These weren't tiny little horses, but full-size replicas. My God, there must have been a thousand flowers in each one. The view was spectacular and the September sun glistened on the lake, trees and fairways.

It was only four o'clock and nothing started until 6:00. Amy and I each had a small glass of wine and cuddled as we watched the Badgers on the Big Ten (even though there are fourteen teams) Network. It was an away game and they were winning. The game was what was happening in the lives of so many others. Badger football is Wisconsin!

At five, it was time to get ready. Amy went first as she took the longest. A quick shower and she came out wrapped in a towel on her head and one around her torso. I wanted to pull one of the towels off, but knew better. She saw my glimpse and did her girlie giggle. There's something about making a woman feel sexy that is so wonderful. I went in next and took my shower and then put on the charcoal pinstripe suit with a silver and black tie that my valet (Amy) selected for me. While I was in the shower, Amy slipped into a little black dress...not modest, but certainly not extreme. There were new flowers for us to wear...I got a boutonnière and her a wrist corsage both in red roses with white baby's breath which she helped me with. We made a dashing couple, or anyway I thought so.

We went downstairs and were directed outside to where we were given silver bracelets with Ann and Rodney's initials on them. Cocktails were being served poolside with a small jazz combo playing in the background. Amy and I had another small glass of wine and watched as mom and dad came in. Dad did not look comfortable in his new black suit that mom made him buy. I'm certain they had gone to Madison to the Burlington outlet, but it made no difference. We smiled and they joined us. We learned that Tommie and Heather had broken up and so Tommie sent his regrets to that he wasn't coming.

A few minutes later, Amy's parents arrived. Both sets of parents were meeting for the first time. Yiikes! I took the lead,

"Mr. and Mrs. Williams, I would like to have you meet my parents, George and Mary Terrill". The men shook hands and the women nodded. There were polite smiles all around.

After a somewhat pregnant pause, Amy's dad was first to speak. "Q, says that you are a dairy farmer."

"That's correct. We milk around 250 head that we then process through our cooperative into cheese."

"Wow, that's a big responsibility."

"Twice a day. Every day." Dad replied with his head switching from side-to-side.

"Who's watching the farm today?"

Mom replied..."Our other son, Tommie and we have a friend who helps when we're gone."

"What do you do Mr. Williams?" my dad asked. It seems I forgot to tell them much about Amy's parents and dad assumed that everyone worked.

"I'm an investment counselor, but please call me Doug."

"Well thank you, Doug."

"And my wife Marie is a doctor."

My dad politely nodded and mom smiled.

"I can only imagine the tasks on the farm, but do you work outside the farm as well, Mrs. Terrill?" The Duke inquired.

"Please call me Mary. Yes, I'm in the personnel department at Land's End."

The conversation turned to us and smiles and whispers began as everyone was sworn to secrecy on Big Brother's and Ann's day. The ladies paired off and so did the dads. Amy joined the moms and The Duke, dad and I discussed farming and Badger football. The Duke offered to take dad and me to a Badger game and dad thought that would be cool. The three Badgeritos! Perhaps we could get grumpy Tommie to join us.

There were about 500 people poolside when the lights flashed and we were directed to the edge of the area where you could see the golf course and the cart path below just as the sun was setting. It was quite the mixture of young and old, rich and poor, Native American and Caucasian along with one lady from St. Martin and her daughter Amy, who was truly lovely, I might say.

"Ladies and gentleman." The loudspeaker blared. "May I have your attention. Please look to your right!" With that spotlights came on as Rodney and Ann appeared in a white carriage all trimmed in red being driven by a man in a tuxedo and pulled by four white horses with quarter-sheets and red plumes, just like the floral statues on the island. "I present Mr. and Mrs. Rodney Whitehorse."

Everyone applauded as the bride and groom slowly made their way past our somewhat formal reviewing stand. As they passed, dusk had fallen and fireworks began. Fifteen minutes of ooohs and aaahs with music behind. Totally cool!

With the fireworks over, we all headed inside to find Rodney and Ann already seated at the head table. Amy and I took our place to their left with Chuck, Rodney's college roommate and his wife to his right and Ann's sister and her husband beside them. The Chief was in his glory.

Everyone was seated and in Grand Geneva fashion we were all served great food with much merriment. It was time for speeches and the Chief went first, talking about Rodney and Ann and how proud he was of them and what a wonderful couple they made, and how he and his wife were looking forward to numerous grandchildren, which got a snicker.

Ding. Ding. Ding. Went the glasses. Time for the bridal kisses! It seems that the same traditions were everywhere. Amy squeezed my hand. Next it was Chuck's turn who told of Rodney's college days and how they had grown together as roommates and friends, filling in with just enough humor to make his speech interesting and palatable.

The Chief introduced Ann's sister and her parents who politely stood and waved, all too nervous to say much. The Chief looked at me and shook his head and handed the microphone to Rodney.

Big Brother spoke: "George Terrill the Fourth" better known as "Q" without you, none of this would be happening. You walked into my life as a smart-ass college kid, who was such a bad driver that it took almost getting killed for me to meet the love of my life. In the past 18 months you have become the little brother I never had. You have shown me generosity, kindness, friendship and above all else commitment to what you believe in. I am humbled to call you Little Brother. I am honored to love you and to respect you for the man you have become...a noble and brave warrior who I will always defend. Ann and I welcome you into our lives until the day we die."

There were tears everywhere including in my eyes. I took the microphone and tried to speak but nothing came out. The audience fell silent. I looked at Rodney and then at Ann and clenched my eyes and let the tears fall as I walked towards them. I wanted to include Amy in all the toasts but she said it would ruin our surprise.

"Big Brother. Big sister. My spirit will be with you always to share your happiness, to comfort your sorrows, to witness the joy that is in your heart. I would like to propose a toast"...to which I and the entire assembly raised their glasses…

"To your health, without which all else will have little meaning. Not only your physical heath, but the health of your love for each other and those who mean so much to you."

"To your wealth...not from a monetary sense, but from a wealth of love and laughter and merriment and joyful experiences, for they are the tapestry, upon which your life together will be woven from the people whose lives you touch and those who have the honor of entering yours."

"And to your happiness that comes from keeping the love in your hearts glowing long after the shine of your youth has gone away."

Big Brother in such a short time, you have become my best friend. Today I willingly and joyously relinquish that title to the woman sitting next to you as she is and shall always be the best friend you can ever have."

"Like the mountains to the valleys, there will be days and events when things are not as wonderful as tonight and yet, please never forget that whether you are on the top of the highest mountain or deep within the darkest valley, I will be there for both of you in sickness and in health until death do you part."

I raised my glass a little higher and nodded to everyone and concluded, "As you walk the path of life together, may you remember those who were here tonight and continue to feel the joy and happiness that they share with you now and forever."

Everyone cheered and sipped from their glasses. I went to sit down and almost sat on Amy's lap, I was so nervous.

There was a round of applause as Big Brother came and gave me one of his famous hugs.

"You will always be my little brother" he whispered as he kissed me in the right cheek.

I sat down and Amy squeezed my hand in approval.

The Chief took over and asked everyone to retire to the adjacent ballroom with lines formed so that everyone could not only meet the bridal party but each other. The room was decorated with red and white balloons and the two white floral horses that had been out in the lake were on display. God, they were much bigger than I thought! The procession began as a full orchestra started playing softly and everyone shook hands. In attendance was the governor, a US senator, with the other sending his apologies and two US Congressmen. The Chief had power.

As they walked down the receiving line, mom and dad were adjacent to Amy's parents. It didn't take long for everyone with political clout to realize and recognize that The Duke was in the receiving line. As everyone quickly shook hands, people of power would stop and want to continue talking to "The Man". He was gracious and kept the line moving until he finally got to the wedding party and the Chief held The Duke's hand in an extended handshake.

"Thank you for coming" the Chief said.

"We thank you for the invitation and for being so kind to our daughter Amelia." It was then that the proverbial cat was out of the bag and I knew that things would never be the same at Ho-Chunk for me again.

My Amy Goodbody was actually Amelia Williams, daughter of one of the wealthiest and most powerful men in Wisconsin.

Dad still didn't understand and all Amy's dad wanted was to be a guest at his daughter's secret fiancée's friend's wedding.

We completed the receiving process and the bar opened and the music began in earnest. The tables were set around the edge and in the middle were the two horses with lights shining down on them. I was told that there were placards for assigned seating and after much "discussion" Ann got her way and all the mucky mucks were mixed in with the common folks, except for one table that was for Amy and me with my mom and dad and Amy's parents and Chuck and his wife Sue. Amy and I sat initially between the two moms until the glad-handers started coming over to The Duke. He was there to enjoy the night and having the governor, then the senator and then the representative come over to say "hello" got a bit tedious. Amy's dad was more than gracious in introducing everyone at the table and I think dad was impressed but somewhat bewildered. Dairy farmers don't meet governors and senators and politicians who were "excited" to meet them very often.

While we were sitting, the Chief came to our table and pulled up a chair and expounded on my speech and how much he appreciated everyone attending. It got a bit thick, but then, I guess everyone in life looks up to someone, even the Chief. The Duke was one that the Chief looked up to.

Ann and her dad and Rodney and his mom had the first dance, then we all joined in. I watched as mom did everything she could to get dad on the dance floor. Rodney saw it too and after dancing with his mom and Ann's, asked my mom to dance.

Amy and I danced and danced and then we started pulling people out on the dance floor. I danced with anybody and everybody who wanted to dance with a skinny kid from Waldwick Wisconsin. I made a point of keeping eye contact with Amy and we both knew that our role was to get folks off their butts and out on the dance floor. Every few songs Amy and I would nod and the next song would be ours. I would hold her tight and feel her next to me. My God, what a wonderful feeling! We were in our own little world trying desperately not to be too obvious, but it was tough.

I glanced over at our table and it looked like dad and The Duke were actually smiling and laughing, which was good for both of them. Mom and Dr. Williams were deep in conversation and I knew what that was all about...our little secret. I thought I would split a gut when Amy asked my dad to dance and he finally said yes and I asked Dr. Williams to dance. That left mom and The Duke and they followed suit. When the song ended, mom took over and she and dad actually showed me they knew how to dance. At the same time the ice was broken for Amy's parents as well.

I looked around the room and everyone appeared to be enjoying themselves. I glanced at Ann's parents and they were sitting alone and I nodded to Amy, indicating that we should double team them. They were reluctant but we got them out on the dance floor.

While we were dancing, Ann's mom looked at me and smiled "Thank you, for just being you. You have brought so much joy to our family." I was honored.There was an elderly couple sitting alone. You could tell that there wasn't much material wealth and yet you could see their love for each other. Mom nodded towards them and I caught her message. Amy and I walked over and wouldn't take no for an answer. It had probably been years since they had danced and had never been to such a fancy shindig. But then who had?

I danced slowly with the lady and she said that she had known Ann since she was a little girl and had babysat for her. They had come from Milwaukee and she was concerned about her husband driving home so late, as his night vision wasn't very good. Halfway through the dance, Amy and I switched partners and the old couple found themselves dancing with each other. It put a big smile on mom's face.

I took Amy by the side and told her that I had an idea. With that, we left the ballroom and went to the lobby and asked if there were any rooms left. There was, namely Tommie's. I pulled out my American Excess and paid for the room and got the key. Amy and I went back and the old couple was still dancing. We cut in and I told the lady that my brother didn't make it to the wedding and that we had the key to his room and that she and her husband were welcome to use it, as I slid the key into her hand.

She looked at me and smiled and I could feel her relief. She let me know that she and her husband had never stayed in a hotel in their lives. She kissed me on the cheek. It was a warm kiss of gratitude and something I will never forget. No one knew, nor would ever know about that night when an old man and an old lady stayed in a hotel for the first time in their lives simply because someone cared.

Near the end, I got Dr. Williams to dance with me again. She kept the Duke on the dance floor and away from the predators and it was my turn, as Amy danced with her dad.

"Thank you, Mr. Terrill, for coming into my daughter's life."

"Thank you, Doctor Williams, for allowing me to do so. I have never been happier."

"Nor have we," and with that she gave me a kiss on the cheek.

It was nearing eleven and the old folks were beginning to fade. Ann and Rodney took their place by the exit door so that they could talk to those who were leaving and say "thank you". Everyone had been told that there were to be no gifts and many abided. Those who brought money were later informed that their money had been donated, in their name, to the Make-A-Wish foundation.

Mom and dad went early, followed shortly thereafter by Amy's parents. Boy, parents do go to bed early, but then perhaps, they were reliving their wedding night. Amy and I took over the dance floor as it was time to pick up the tempo before heading to bed. For those who hung on, we shut everything down at midnight. With hugs and kisses from the bride and groom, the Chief and Rodney's mom made their grand exit and the night was officially over.

When we got back to the room and crawled into bed, Amy asked me what I thought. I said I thought it was a great evening. She asked what I thought of all the ass kissers who bugged her dad. I had never been around it before and didn't know what to think.

"That's why dad loves St. Martin. When he goes down there he's just Doug and no one is kissing his ass."

It was a point well taken. I hadn't realized the downside of wealth and power. You need to watch your back and always remember who your friends really are as well as your enemies. My concern was my dad. He had never seen anything like that before.

Sunday: Sunday morning brunch was at the lobby buffet. We wandered down and mom and dad met us. Amy's parents had departed early. Dad was still bewildered about Amy's dad. He asked where Ann and Rodney were going on their honeymoon and I told them St. Martin. Amy gently kicked me under the table. I was saying too much. The house and the plane were not for public knowledge.

We went back and packed and called the front desk. Amy reminded me that we needed to check out of Ann's babysitter's room. I went to the front desk and got the folio. Besides the room charge, there was a charge for $ 56.50 for the in-room bar. It seems that the old folks had cleaned out the candy, nuts and chips, not realizing that there was a cost for them. We laughed and chalked it up to experience, realizing that we had added a memory to the lives of two people who would always be grateful, if not a little fatter from all the snacks.

Mom and dad volunteered to drive us home, but The Chief already had a limo waiting for us and we felt obligated. We rode home in the limo watching the Packers and so our weekend was complete.

Just before dinner I got a text from Big Brother. "INCREDIBLE. Plane ride and house are simply superb. THANK YOU. R&A." They were already at the house in St. Martin and had flown there on the family jet.

It didn't seem real that the two of them were married and on their honeymoon and what I figured was a $200,000 wedding reception was all over as nickels and dimes saved became dollars spent. That was reality.

I called home when I knew that Tommie and dad would be doing chores. I wanted to talk with mom alone. From her visit to the condo she had some inclination that the Williams were well off. She just didn't realize to what extent.

After the normal glad you made it home stuff, mom got to the point of asking why all those politicians came to our table. I laid it all out for her ...The Duke and all that he did and what I heard he owned, the money, the jet, the big house in Milwaukee and St. Martin. I also told her that I was drawing up an agreement so that nothing came my way that wasn't Amy's and mine, which we earned together, to which mom said "good."

"I don't want a single person to ever think I was marrying Amy for her money."

She said that dad thought The Duke was a politician. I told her no, but that politicians seem to have a keen sense for money and power and that's why they all crowded around Mr. Williams.

Morning Star: It was another Thursday and that meant another trip to the Dells to see Great Grandfather. With such a routine, one would expect boredom. However, each week was filled with yet another emotional juggernaut that tilted my brain and made me wonder.

Once again, I arrived on time. Once again, Great Grandfather was sitting in his rocking chair. Once, again, I pulled the old chest forward as he took my hands in his. Once again there was chanting and eyes rolling. As Great Grandfather went into his trance, I expected to hear the sounds of a man…an angry man who would share with me his frustration. I was shocked when the voice of the old man softened and I heard an effeminate voice emanate.

"My name is Morning Star. I am the daughter of Sunshine Also Follows of the Winnebago and Blackhawk, great leader of the Sauk. Because so many are enemies of my father, my mother and I live in peace amongst the Winnebago. My father comes to visit and does so only at night when no one knows he is there. He does this, not because he is ashamed, but because he has so many enemies."

"When I was fourteen, I went with some of the men of our nation as they hunted and I looked for berries. I wandered up a small stream and came across a spot where the pure water came from beneath a rock. The Great Spirit told me that this was where my life would begin. As I knelt to take a drink of the pure water, two white men came across me and forced themselves upon me. They dragged me into the forest and ripped off my clothes. While women of the Winnebago and Sauk had been raped and others sold their bodies to many white men for nothing more than food, I was clean and pure and fought with all my might to save my innocence. While my spirit was strong, I did not have the strength to stop the two men. As one held me, the other was about to violate me. I wanted to scream, but the other held me in such a way that I could not. When I thought my purity was lost, a man appeared in the forest. I heard a soft whistle and watched as he motioned to others as he saw what was happening. Slowly, he began walking towards me and these two men. His gun was in front of him, cocked and ready."

"What do you think you're doing?" the man asked.

"What is it to you?" one replied.

"You're on my land." he answered.

"Won't be long and we'll be gone," the same one replied.

"Leave the girl and go now," he said.

"No." the other replied. "Not until I'm done with her."

"What you're doing is wrong."

"Just a God Damn Indian!"

"What you're doing is wrong and you are to stop right now."

With that, the first man picked up his gun.

"You think you can use that?" one of the men asked, pointing at the hunter's gun.

"It's not just me." he replied.

"That so?"

"Yes. Now put down your gun and let the girl go." the hunter demanded.

There was a pause as if to solidify the reflection and then Morning Star's story continued. "I remember the man released me and moved toward his gun."

"As I said, I'm not alone" the hunter said.

I remember the filthy man's grin as he thought the hunter was pretending. As the would-be rapist reached for his rifle a shot from nowhere splintered his gun's stock, kicking the gun about 10 feet from where it had been.

"As I said, I am not alone." the hunter replied.

"Now, the other rapist began to circle and I guess whoever else was in the woods thought he was a threat and so they let go with a shot that hit the man in the leg, right above the knee, knocking him to the ground. The first man went for his pistol and the hunter took a shot hitting him in the shoulder, ripping his shirt as the blood splattered out the back and all over me. I remember how I was shocked at the noise and then the warmth. He had been such a cold-hearted man that I thought his blood would be cold too. I stood, naked, frozen in fear with two men lying near me. Quickly, the three rescuers moved in just as the one who had been shot in the leg pulled his knife. With that one of the boys took aim and hit the man in the temple. I remember watching the man's eyes roll back and then come forward. First there was disbelief and then a total loss of any emotion as his head jerked back as he saw what had been part of his skull lying on the rocks beside him."

"With all the noise from the gunshots, no one had noticed that hunting party had returned. At first, they sensed that the hunter had been the cause of the problem and appeared ready to attack. The man and boys who saved me raised their arms and dropped their weapons so that all could see that they were not a threat to them. With that, I quickly put on my clothes and crumbled to the ground crying. The braves were angry …at all white men … at everyone who had promised peace and brought lies, disease and corruption."

"One from my tribe came forth and bent down next to me. I looked up and explained what had happened as he looked at the hunter and his boys and then at the dead man and then the living one. Quickly he stood and went to the one who was still alive. Without hesitation, he took out his knife and slit his throat. I remember hearing the gurgling sound as the man gasped for air before falling into a puddle of his own blood. While he was still alive, the young brave took his hand and pulled the man's head back and scalped him, pulling the hair and flesh from his head before pushing his now expressionless face into the dirt upon which he knelt."

"The two boys stood watching, their mouths open. They had never seen a man die before and to watch them go the way they did had left them without words. I know that the hunter was concerned for his son as he had killed a man and for his other son because he was so young. I sat crying asking the Great Spirit why he had allowed this to happen to me. I had been taken to the edge and threatened to the point that I would never forget what had happened."

"It seemed like forever! Then, without a word, we melted back into the forest. The bodies were left for the wolves or whomever it was that would stoop so low as to eat vermin. Without the hunter and his sons, I would not be alive. Without their honor and bravery, I would not have grown to be an adult and married and had three children. The world is full of cruel people willing to do harm to others. Fortunately, the world also has those who see what is wrong and do what they can to make it right. My people have suffered at the hands of the white man. They have taken our land, our lives and our dignity. They have cast us aside as victims of their ways of life. Because of one man and his sons, I continued on. Because of them, my life was not over and their honor, their dignity and their purity allowed me to live a full life. My spirit lives where my life was almost lost. Like the pure water that trickles from beneath the rock, I am the life, I am the love, I am tomorrow and those who drink from me, shall receive the abundance of purity, decency and cleanliness that can only come when one cares enough to risk everything for the good of others."

Great Grandfather's eyes rolled back. However, the exhaustion that I had seen so many times before was not there. There was a smile upon Great Grandfather's face. I knew that the pain and suffering of all the spirits had been released. I knew now why we had to battle for the land. I finally understood why I was the chosen one and why this small parcel of land meant so much to so many. Without my ancestors, the little girl would have died. Without the purity of their actions, the purity of the water would not exist. This was not just a spring coming forth, this was a baptism and all those who drank from the spring of life would be forever changed. My God! It was all finally making sense.

Great Grandfather and I sat for another hour. Few words were spoken and yet emotions were sent like bolts of lightning between us. I could feel what he was feeling. I could sense what he was thinking. All that had been constricted within his body was transmitted to me…innocence, purity, decency. I was Little Spirit whose responsibility it was to carry forth, to protect the point in time and space when the goodness of George the First had transcended all forms of prejudice as he had done what was right, simply because it was the right thing to do. This is why I could not sleep. The spirits wrestled within my soul with all the thoughts and emotions that were not pure. This is why I was tormented because I did not know. Now, I understood. Now, I was no longer a boy, I was a man. A man whose role in life was to honor and defend what was good. A man challenged with the bounty given and using it to make sure that others could flourish.

Rodney had become my best friend for a reason. The accident had been for a reason. Great Grandfather had been for a reason. Without the forest they would not have been and without them, the person who was fulfilling me had come into my life, giving me the direction I needed to make my world, their world and hopefully, the entire world better for us all.

My God! I walked out of the assisted living center finally understanding what this had all been about and thanked God for giving me the opportunity to learn what I had learned and pledging to him and to everyone else that I wasn't going to piss it all away.

I went home and Amy saw that I was perturbed. Boy, I like that word perturbed! No one ever uses it anymore…now people are pissed off, upset or angry, but never perturbed. Amy put her arms around my neck and gave me a sloppy kiss. "You look like you have had a rough day!" she whispered. I knew what she had in mind and, like any normal man the thought crossed my mind. Instead I detailed how confused I was talking to so many dead Indians. I had their side of the story but how did I know if it was all true. With so many dead Indians hollering at me, I didn't know heads from tales. The stories about Red Bird and what I remembered about Blackhawk from what George the First had written all made sense. But now I was getting hammered about this treaty and that treaty and who was right and who was wrong.

Amy looked at me with her big brown eyes and said. "Why don't I spend some time researching all the treaties and then you will know?" My, it's nice to have a resident Google at home who could take everything I had been hearing and cross-checking it. Instead of raucous or even steamy or for that matter any sex, Amy dove into her laptop and began writing. When it was nearly midnight, I went to bed…alone, leaving her still gathering her information.

I awoke at 7:00 and Amy was still typing. She had done her homework. First, Amy recognized that the United States had violated international law when it came to recognizing the rights of all the indigenous people and had done so, simply to take the land away. Unlike the British and the French, who compensated the Indians for their land, the US government did so through force or by treaty, many of which were either signed by individuals without legal authority or in such a manner that the Indians had no idea what they were agreeing to.

Amy broke the six treaties that the Ho-Chunk had signed down into two classes…the first three to create peace with either the United States or other nations. The second three were land cessation treaties in the hopes of creating some sort of permanence for what remained of their land and their way of life. This was about the Ho-Chunk and not the other nations and so Amy had focused only on them knowing the stories of others were as sad.

Amy noted. "Until 1963 the folks in Nebraska and those who came home to Wisconsin were all called Winnebago Indians. I asked Amy what Ho-Chunk meant and she said that Ho Chunk means 'People of the Big Voice' or 'People of the Sacred

Language'." Miss Smarty pants had looked it up too. Amy added that in 1963 the Ho-Chunk gained federal recognition and the scattered land in Wisconsin that the nation owns became federal trust lands. I had no idea what federal trust lands were and so Amy explained that land held in trust by the government is protected and is under jurisdiction of the federal government and not state, county or local government. That land can only be only change hands and still maintain its sovereignty with approval of the Secretary of the Interior.

All that I had been hearing in my visits with Great Grandfather was true and they had spoken in a sacred language that I had the honor of hearing. All the sadness! All the frustration! All the anger! I sat and thought what I would feel like if someone did to me what happened to them...to simply have your land taken away because big government wanted to and realized it was happening to me!

Happy Valley: Casual conversation usually leads to nothing and that's what was expected from the talk about the Badgers and going to a football game. Amy got a call from her mom and The Duke wanted to know if dad and I would like to go to the Penn State game in two weeks. I thought that it would be cool and asked Amy if she would mind. She said no and so I called mom and asked her to see if dad wanted to go. You can't leave 250 lactating cows without some plans.

Dad called Harvey who said that he could help Tommie with the milking. 250 cows is never a one-man job. When everything was set, I realized the game was in Happy Valley and would be my first airplane ride. Plans were made and dad and I were to be at Truax Field at 8:00 AM. The jet would pick us up and then stop in Milwaukee and pick up The Duke and head for Happy Valley.

I don't think I slept 20 minutes Friday night I was so excited. Dad was at the condo at 6:30. He had a small cooler with him and I knew what was in it…the five kinds of cheese that were made at the co-op along with two boxes of Ritz crackers. We were at Truax at 7:15 and stood in the executive terminal until the plane landed at 7:45 when we were escorted across the tarmac and onto The Duke's…Miss Amelia I…as if we were some sort of royalty. Miss Amelia One was a Gulfstream Maverick, five passenger jet with a range of 1200 nautical or 1380 statute miles, enough to get us to Happy Valley and back again twice. Dad had a shit-eating grin like I had never seen before.

We were introduced to Dennis, the pilot who I had heard so much about and he took us on a quick tour. The flight plan called for an 8:00 AM departure and so we buckled ourselves into the deep, red leather seats with a scripted letter "A" in the headrests.

In 15 minutes, my first ever airplane ride was over, as we landed at Mitchell Field in Milwaukee and taxied to the private area where The Duke got onboard. "It's only about 70 minutes to Happy Valley," Mr. Williams said. "What do you think of my Amelia?" I didn't know which one he was talking about, but knew

I was in love with both of them. Dad was like a little kid on Christmas day.

As we got airborne, the conversation turned to the Badgers and the season so far. I could tell that one of The Duke's passions was Badger football. He went through the lineup, what he thought of the coaching decisions and then the entire athletic department. He knew everybody. I looked out the window and realized we were nearly five miles up in the air. It was cool.

After the Badgers, quiet dad and The Duke started talking about cheese as dad opened his cooler and offered The Duke some of the cheese from the co-op. At first, I think The Duke was being polite until he took a couple of bites and realized that it was really good shit. Swiss and Brick and Cheddar too. Gouda. Gouda. I couldn't get the silly song out of my head that Tommie and I had come up with one night at the Iowa County Fair. Dad and The Duke pigged out as I watched two guys bond.

Dad explained that George the First realized there was more money in processed rather than fresh milk and started a cheese factory. Dad added that in order to be profitable, it took a lot of volume and that meant a cooperative owned by about 20 farmers. He then explained how you made cheese which I would have thought The Duke would have rolled his eyes. Instead, The Duke had a big grin on his face as, for the first time, dad broke out of his farmer mode and was really enthusiastic about what he was talking about.

As the Mustang's wheels touched down in Happy Valley, dad added that cheese is easier to store than milk and thanks to the acid and salt, keeps much longer and is why people have been making it for centuries. The Duke had seen a side of my dad that few of us had ever experienced…a passionate soul who lived and loved what he did for a living. I looked out the plane window to see an SUV drive right out onto the tarmac.

Dennis opened the door and we walked down the stairs and got into a Tahoe. There was no delay. We went to the stadium where the driver had some kind of pass that got us within 50 feet of the main gate only to be met by a host in a navy-blue sport coat with the Penn State logo on it who escorted us to a skybox with some other Badger fans. Dad just shook his head and smiled.

At halftime, The Duke asked dad if it was all right that I went with him to meet some people. Dad said "sure" as he was talking farming with some other guy and snarfing down the chicken, ribs, cookies, cake and Spotted Cow and Moon Man Pale Ale beer that someone brought from New Glarus that was being served.

We walked about 75 feet and The Duke told the attendant who he was and we walked into the Penn State Athletic Director's private enclave, where I was introduced by The Duke as his future son-in-law. The AD shook my hand and congratulated me and said that if I was half as good as The Duke said I was, I was one heck of a kid. The AD then asked about Amy's health and The Duke said "healthier and happier than she has been in years." My first formal introduction was over with the Penn State man of power. Next, the Duke sought out the Assistant AD and introduced me to him. There were pleasantries all around. Trust me…it's a long way from the student section in Camp Randall to the AD's private box!

As we we're walking back to our suite, The Duke put his hand on my shoulder and outlined the AD and his respect for him and then the Assistant AD and how he was on the short list for when the day came that the Badger AD retired. He said it was good for me to begin to get to know some of the people who "made the wheels turn". I was humbled.

All-in-all, the entire day was an incredible experience, except for the fact that the Badgers lost. The Duke seemed to know everyone and introduced dad and I to all these high rollers in the skybox. It was a very unique experience for a couple of farm boys from Waldwick, Wisconsin, to say the least.

After the game we headed back to the plane and once on board, there were numerous expressions of gratitude on our side as there should have been…especially when there were so many firsts….first airplane ride, first VIP treatment…first skybox…first time dad and Amy's dad got to do things together, to which I sincerely hoped, would not be the last.

Dad Williams smiled. "I think we should have a toast" and with that, he punched in a code on a keypad and opened a secure liquor cabinet hidden within Amelia I. To the left was a black bottle of fifty-year-old Chivas Royal Salute scotch which was his drink of choice on very special occasions. Next to it was a bottle of Marquis de Montesquiou 1904 Vintage Armagnac brandy and next to that a bottle of Glenfiddich fifty-year-old whiskey, then Magnum Grey Goose vodka and finally, Nolet's reserve gin. This was the booze that dad William's kept on board "just to close the deal" as he would like to say.

My dad just shook his head. He wasn't much of a drinker and when he did, it was mainly Korbel, the brandy of Wisconsin. He nodded towards the Marquis de Montesquiou and dad Williams poured him a three-finger glass as he poured himself some of the Chivas. He knew that I was a red wine guy and so he smiled and pulled out a bottle of Edelton Shiraz from Australia. "I know you like pinot noir but give this a try" as he poured a glass for me.

"To Amelia and George!" dad Williams said looking at my dad. We all clinked! Then, looking at my dad he said…"and to many happy, healthy grandchildren!" They both smiled and nodded.

We were somewhere over Indiana and could have been on cloud nine. I don't think dad had ever tasted anything like what The Duke had poured or even knew existed…or for that matter, cared. What a different world! The Duke offered a second and dad held up his hand and said "No thank you". He had to drive home to reality and enough was enough.

"You can't let a great bottle of wine go to waste" and so The Duke put the cork back in the Edelton and told me to bring it home to Amy as it was her favorite. It wasn't long until we were wheels down. (Boy it was neat learning all the cool terms of flying)!

The Duke couldn't have been a more gracious host. We thanked him for the generosity and the hospitality and he said he was glad we could come. As we walked across the tarmac, I turned to wave, but The Duke was already on his phone. I'm certain he was catching up on all the things he missed during the day when he was providing undivided attention to his guests.

As we were driving back to the condo, dad had a look of total satisfaction on his face. As we got close dad turned to me and told me he would never forget the day. That was all I needed to know as it was exactly what I felt. "Man, that was neat" dad said.

We had spaghetti dinner that Amy made and dad headed for home filled with memories of a day he would never forget, that was just another Saturday in the life of Douglas, The Duke, Williams.

Before The Duke was home, I had already written a thank you text and sent it to his phone.

He responded..."You're welcome son. I hope it's just the first of many more."

Round Trip: After dad left, Amy came and put her arms around me in one of those suggestive ways and I wondered "What now?"

"I have an idea, Mr. Terrill."

"What's that Ms. Williams?"

"We promised to pick up Ann and Rodney at the airport tomorrow."

"Yes."

"Why don't we surprise them and go pick them up?"

"You mean fly to St. Martin?"

"Sure, the plane will be empty going down and there's plenty of room."

I wondered, how would we all would fit in that small plane and questioned it.

"You were in Miss Amelia I. Daddy also has Miss Amelia II. It's the Gulfstream X+ that is set for over-water and international flying which Ann and Rodney took to St. Martin. It's normally a ten-passenger plane but dad had it customized when I got sick so that it seats eight but has a bed in the back. You deserve a break and we will be back tomorrow night."

Geez. Never having flown and then two flights in one weekend. Wow.

"We'll need to get up early, but we can sleep on the plane on the way down. That way you can meet Uncle Frank and Aunt Julia, my mom's sister. We can surprise Rodney and Ann and let them in on our little secret."

The more she talked, the more I liked the idea. Amy did one of her girlie giggles that I love and said she would call Dennis and have him pick us up. She went to the phone and called and made the arrangements. We needed to be at Truax Executive at 5:30 AM.

We spent the rest of the night watching Shawshank Redemption, which is one of my favorite movies. Amy cringed at the escape scene. I guess crawling through sewage to freedom was more than she could handle. At 10:00, we slid under the covers and, in what had become our custom, reiterated the day. Among other things, I filled her in on everything, making sure that she understood that it was a very special day for my dad and I and how grateful I was for her and her parents. She knew.

We got up at 4:00 and headed to Truax. I was really blurry-eyed. When we arrived, Dennis was already waiting with Miss Amelia II. He introduced me to Beth, the co-pilot, who was also his wife and we got onboard. While Miss Amelia One was cool, Miss Amelia Two was drop-dead gorgeous. There were four red leather swivel chairs in the center cabin with a closet and lavatory separating the back section. I peeked in the back and there was a bed….not some tiny, scrunched-up bed, but a real bed. Amy said that it was actually two units that slid together. Totally cool!

We had put our cell phones on call forwarding to Miss Amelia II and the plane phone rang around 8:30 and it was mom. "Where are you?"

"We're going to pick up Ann and Rodney."

"You're flying all the way down there?"

"Sure, there's enough room and Amy wanted me to meet her Aunt and Uncle."

Mom called to say that the normally stoic dad just kept blabbering on and on and on about the plane, the sky box and feeling important. Dad wanted the William's address to send a thank you note and gift. I already knew what it would be. Five one-pound packages of cheese made from milk on our farm. What I didn't know was that dad was having them carved in outlines of the State of Wisconsin, the Motion W, Bucky Badger, a Badger football helmet, and an outline of The Duke's Gulfstream with the script "Miss Amelia I" on the side. The Duke would get a chuckle out of that.

After mom's call I was already beginning to get drowsy. Amy said, "let's go take a nap". We went back and I pulled back the blanket to see pillows that each had the letter "A" embroidered into their cases. I went to lay down and Amy said. "You're not going to sleep in your clothes, are you?"

I hadn't thought about it.

"What about Dennis and Beth?"

"I'll press the privacy button and they know that they're to stay in the front cabin."

"What happens if they have to use the bathroom?"

"They have their own just behind the cockpit."

My worries removed as we crawled under the covers. It was really bright from the sunshine and I didn't think I could sleep. Amy reached for the console and pressed a button and soft, blue LED lights illuminated the floor. She pressed another button and I heard soft music begin to play. It was Lakme', Act I: The Flower Duet the same song from the first time we had dinner at the condo. Next, all the windows went instantly black. They had photo-voltaic membranes in them. Incredible! I put one and one together and realized what was on her mind and smiled. As we lay there, I began feeling her big toe slide up the inside of my leg. It wasn't long until we joined a very special little club providing yet another experience in the lives of George and the future Mrs. Amelia Terrill. Wow!

After consummating the flight, I was out like a light until Dennis came on the intercom and said "Miss Amelia, we're forty minutes to touchdown". I slept for nearly three hours. I had packed shorts and a tee shirt and sandals and got dressed and went into the center cabin. It was 9:45 AM Madison time, we were landing at Princess Juliana airport in Phillipsburg, St. Martin and it was 82 degrees. My God! I looked out the window and saw people on the beach waving at us as we landed. What a hoot. Amy was just smiling at my smile.

After we landed, Dennis pulled off to the side of the tarmac where a black Range Rover LR-V6 was waiting. It was Uncle Frank. The stairs lowered and the warm, Caribbean air hit me and I was already in love with the place. The Rover pulled up and a man in a uniform got out and asked for my passport which I provided and thanked God that I had applied for one when I thought my roommates and I were going to spend spring break in the Bahamas one year. He nodded acceptance. The officer looked at Amy and said "Good morning Miss Amelia. Welcome back."

I shook hands with Uncle Frank and saw the infectious smile that Amy had told me about. We got into the Rover and Amy had me sit in front so that I could get to know Uncle Frank a little better.

"Nice wheels." I said.

"Thank you, George. We own the Hyundai and Range Rover dealerships on St. Marten. Needless to say, we sell a lot more Hyundai's than Rovers. We don't sell many of these and it's only the V6 diesel because you can't go fast anywhere on the island but this one is my favorite.

"Mine, too." I responded.

We drove the winding road into Phillipsburg. Because it was early Sunday, traffic wasn't bad. Amy said most of the time the traffic was like the Beltline in Madison and I just cringed. We went downtown and pulled in behind a store where the sign said "Reserved parking. All others will be violated". I didn't get the humor, but as the day wore on, I found out that Uncle Frank loved to laugh.

We rang the back buzzer and a voice came out of the speaker. "Who is it?" even though there was a security camera aimed right at us.

"It is a tall, dark, handsome man who has come to sweep you off your feet and make mad passionate love with you." Uncle Frank replied.

"I'm sorry, I'm already married to this old, decrepit, sorry lot who likes to make eyes at the pretty girls" the speaker said as the door unlocked.

We walked into the back of this very high-end, jewelry store and I was introduced to Aunt Julia.

She reminded me of Amy's mom…same infectious smile and soft lilt to her voice.

Aunt Julia looked at Amy and gave her a great big hug. "You look fantastic Amelia. The best I've ever seen."

The employees all gathered around and everyone had to give Miss Amelia a hug with big smiles everywhere.

"So, this is your fiancée?" Aunt Julia inquired.

"Yes, Mam." I replied.

Julia looked at Amy and then at her hands.

"No ring?"

"Not yet."

"Amelia, give him the finger."

With that Amy lifted her left hand and extended the ring finger instead of the Pointer salute.

Aunt Julia shook her head and noted. "We need to take care of that."

The fear was setting in. No more charity from the Williams would be allowed. How much was this going to cost?

Aunt Julia turned to the head jeweler and said, "Cecil, what do we have that would be very special for my God Daughter?"

Cecil nodded and smiled and went into the vault and came back with a velvet tray full of gorgeous rings.

Holy Shit!

We went over and sat down at the table and Amy started looking through the different rings.

She wanted something nice, but not too pretentious. I wanted something I could afford.

She shifted from solitaries to complete settings and then back to solitaries. She pointed at a design she liked but the center diamond looked too small. "Cecil, don't we have some loose stones that will fit in here?"

Cecil went in the vault and came back with a tray full of loose diamonds. My eyes almost bugged out.

Taking a tweezers, Cecil picked out a two-carat diamond and placed it next to the setting. 'This will be more balanced" Cecil said. "Miss Amelia, what do you think?" Amy just nodded her approval.

"If you don't mind, I'll need about an hour and I can have it ready for you." Cecil promised and with that, he went to his workshop.

"Aunt Julia, I must pay you for this, how much will it be?" I asked Aunt Julia took her calculator and began adding and subtracting. "Retail minus family discount, plus tax, minus God Daughter plus new soon-to-be nephew in law who looks like he will take care of the only girl in my life discount equals $2,500."

I leaned back. It was a lot for me, but I knew that there was no way I could ever match the price or the sentiment at Goodman Jewelers in Madison. I pulled out the American Excess and smiled.

Amy did one of her girlie giggles and gave me a hug. It was decided that instead of waiting, Uncle Frank would take us to meet with Rodney and Ann and come back for the ring as we had lunch. I thought it was a lot of extra driving but Aunt Julia insisted.

"Should we tell Rodney and Ann?" I asked.

"How about on the plane on the way home?" Amy responded.

It was already 12:30 St. Martin time and we needed to go.

Amy said to save time, we needed to get into our bathing suits, as she was certain Ann and Rodney would be at Orient Beach for lunch and she wanted to walk up the beach and surprise them. We dressed in the shop bathroom and then there were hugs and kisses all around as we got into the Rover.

Uncle Frank told us that he had asked Rodney to take the island cell phone with him. He gave Rodney a call under the auspices of letting him know the plane was scheduled to leave at 4:00 for Madison. Uncle Frank asked Rodney where they were and Big Brother said that they were sitting on the beach in front of Le'String restaurant.

It was a twenty-minute drive from Phillipsburg to Orient Beach and Amy asked Uncle Frank to drop us off by Pedro's, adjacent to Club Orient, which was the nude beach area. As Uncle Frank pulled into Pedro's parking area and we got out, Amy slid out of her shorts to show her cream colored, low rise, half-assed, string bikini bottom that matched her very tiny, bikini top. Crafted from soft sheer stripe mesh with enticing peek-a-boo stripes, the 3D raised texture literally consisted of four tiny triangles with some string in between! I don't know if I was aroused or concerned with what every other guy on the beach was thinking.

Because of her genetic heritage, Amy already looked like she had been on St. Martin for a week. Me, of course, looked like the skinny white kid from Wisconsin who now knew the meaning of the term 'pale face', plus pale arms and pale legs and pale chest. Casper the ghost had more color than me.

I asked Amy how dark she would get if we stayed a while. She said she really didn't have any point of reference because she never had any tan lines. Gulp!

This got a little laughter out of her. I didn't know if she was serious or teasing me. She noted that when she did spend a lot of time in the sun, she would have a skin color closer to her Aunt Julia's, which was a chestnut brown, showing the combination of so many different races all blended together…African, Mediterranean, Middle Eastern and European … in other word's the world in 100 years.

I was envious. The closest I ever got to being tan was the infamous farmer tan on my forearms and back of my neck. At least I didn't do like my dad and wear a Badger baseball cap all the time so that my cheeks were brown and the top of my head pale. Now that's a real farmer tan!

We left our shoes and clothes and what I later learned, any inhibitions in the Range Rover with Uncle Frank, who didn't seem to mind that his niece was 90%, no make that 95% naked. Uncle Frank needed to head back to pick up Amy's ring and said he would meet us for lunch at Le'String.

"If you want to go in the nude area, we need to get naked." Amy said with a giggle.

"Uh, that's ok" I said as I looked at a lot of people who probably shouldn't have been there and started walking the other way.

Amy noted that Club Orient was the most popular naturist resort in the world and drew thousands of cruisers every year. While topless sunbathing was allowed everywhere, the nude section was welcomed because it did a great deal to help the economy by bringing the cruisers from the Dutch side of the island where the cruise ships came into port, over to the French side. Amy noted that when 90% of your country's economy is based on tourism, they needed any way possible to entice visitors to spend time and open their wallets, even if it meant having them take off their pants.

Next to Pedro's were eight adjoining, pastel colored buildings. Amy said at one time, there had been some old decrepit buildings that were smashed by a hurricane in the late 1990's and her dad bought the property at her mom's request. It seems that Amy's grandma spent her life peddling straw hats and clothes on the beach and Mrs. Williams wanted to have an area where the locals could set up stands and sell locally-made goods that probably came from China.

The Williams set up a subsidized, non-profit corporation and charged rents that were low to the locals and gave them pride. The building literally had two fronts. Most of the shore-side stores were small like Juicy Fruits with some really ugly, pale mannikins out front and a couple of small bars and beach activity outlets for parasailing and jet skis. The parking lot side of the building had clothing stores filled with bathing suits, wraps and hats, just like what the ladies were selling, who were walking on the beach.

As we reached the back side of the first cubicle, word quickly spread that 'Miss Amelia' was there and all the ladies came out to give her hugs and kisses. She was like royalty because of the generosity of her parents. The shop owners knew Miss Amelia and Dr. Williams, but had no idea who The Duke was and he wanted to keep it that way. He loved his anonymity and when he came to St. Martin, he was just Doug.

I was introduced and offered virtually anything I wanted for free. In one stall, Amy pointed to a woven, wicker basket of men's thong swimwear and giggled as an embarrassed me vigorously shook his head 'no'. "Maybe next time" she whispered. Definitely never, I vowed to myself.

I thought Amy's bathing suit was a bit extreme until I saw what they were selling in the stores, glanced at the beach and realized Amy's was the norm if not conservative. Just because it would be considered extreme in Wisconsin didn't make it out-of-the -ordinary somewhere else. Once again, I had made a judgment call without understanding the situation.

I was surprised by the acceptance everyone had for the way others dressed. No one gawked and there was nothing lewd. It was simply people being people. I actually began to feel sorry for the cruisers Amy talked about. They came with cameras around their necks to see a different way of life and be titillated and/or offended by those who chose the lifestyle the cruisers did not have. I shook my head as Amy added, "many came in a voyeuristic mode, first to satisfy their curiosity about the world-famous Orient Beach and have their picture taken next to the sign that read "Nude Beach" or "Plage Naturist" which said the same thing in French. Either way, the voyeurs were too timid to join in."

We made our way from stand-to-stand along the parking lot side until we came to the end and went around the corner to the shore side to a small, non-descript, restaurant with a sign that said Le'String. I gazed past the bar and those eating lunch and then out at the beach where I saw this very large Native American with his beautiful wife, sitting on chaise lounges, under red umbrellas, watching the crowd walk by.

A waiter, who I learned later was named Maxx, walked up with a huge St. Martin smile and gave Amy a big hug as he kissed her on both cheeks. I could tell by the joy in his smile that Amy and he were good friends. "My Amelia, our wishes have been answered. You have returned! My wife and I have said a prayer for you each day since you left. What a wonderful, wonderful gift…simply to see you again," he said.

Once again, I felt the warmth of spirit that only comes from acceptance and friendship. Amy nodded towards Rodney and Ann and asked if they had eaten. Maxx shook his head 'no' and indicated they had just ordered ice tea.

"Can we serve it?" Amy asked.

"Most certainly" Maxx replied.

We got the drinks and walked up behind Rodney and Ann as I announced, "Why look who you run into in St. Martin" to two very surprised friends, who almost jumped out of their suits, but then they couldn't do that, because they weren't on the naked side of the beach.

"What are you two doing here?" Rodney asked with a huge smile on his face.

"We told you we'd pick you up." Amy replied. "We just didn't say where".

There were smiles and hugs all around.

"Great time?" I asked.

"Incredible!" Rodney replied as he detailed all that they had done. Sailing, power boating, para-sailing, jet skiing, snorkeling, scuba diving, golfing on Anguilla and shopping on St. Barths, where we went twice.

"The sunset cruises were fantastic and we took like 500 pictures," he added shaking his head.

"So, you enjoyed the boats?" I asked.

"Incredible!" Rodney replied. "And sailing was fantastic!"

"Now you can tell your dad he had a red son in the sail set." I joked.

It took a minute for it to sink in and then the big guffaw I hoped for came blaring out of my best friend. "Red sun in the sail set!" Rodney giggled.

It was Ann's turn. "The food! Oh my God! We had a chef come to the house our first night and again last night. Uncle Frank made all the arrangements. He had menus at the house and we could just pick where we wanted to eat. He would call and we would go and it would be all set for us and they wouldn't let us pay. Everywhere we went the food was simply superb."

"Uncle Frank really knew where to eat! Down near the bikini beach end" Ann pointed, "there is an entire courtyard filled with great restaurants. Our favorite was Le Piment. It was packed every night. Once you ate there you knew why. In Grand Case, our favorite was Le Auberge Gourmand where Rodney ate three lobsters." "In one sitting?" I asked, Ann just shook her head up-and-down in disbelief as Rodney shrugged his shoulders with a big shit-eating grin on his face.

Ann continued. "Our all-time favorite though was a tiny outdoor café under what looks like tarps that is called LeTaitu, over on Mont Vernon. The food was superb and a man and his brother are owners who have been here for over 25 years. It's a local place and one night, we were all alone with just the one brother and it was really neat having him talk about his love of cooking and how they made a go of it doing what they love."

"And that plane!" Rodney added with a big smile. "That plane is so cool!"

Words cannot express how excited they were and what a wonderful time they had. They were simply bubbling over with happiness. For Amy and I it was the best gift they could have given us...pure and simple joy!

In two weeks, both were dark and glistened in the sun. I guess they had become adjusted to the "lifestyle" where everyone just kicks back and enjoys the water and the weather. I was surprised by Ann and Rodney's social ambivalence as I always considered them to be conservative like me. I realized that within a few minutes, what I thought all these years about propriety was simply wrong. The majority rules and the rules were of tolerance, acceptance and laughter. What a dichotomy from uptight Wisconsin, even liberal Madison.

Sydney, the restaurant manager, had been called and came quickly down the beach. It wasn't often that Miss Amelia came to town and she wanted to personally say hello. Sydney looked like she was probably in her early 30's with short blond hair and a tight, muscular body. She was a beach person and, like every other Orient Beach regular, completely feckless of her body wrapped in nearly nothing, that made Amy's suit seem conservative. Amy caught my glance and her composure completely disintegrated.

"Miss Amelia, it is so wonderful to see you again", Sydney said, in her French accent, as she kissed Amy on both cheeks. I could immediately sense that there was more to this than met the eye!

Sydney asked "How's your mother?"

Amy politely replied that she was fine.

"You look wonderful. Turn around! Turn around!" Sydney directed as she twirled her finger in a circular motion. Amy obliged as Sydney inspected her barely covered bottom.

"My goodness. The best, I think, you've ever looked. You've filled out, but not too much. Magnifique!" Sydney exclaimed as she took her fingers to her lips and then kissed the air in an expression of perfection, before patting Amy on the behind. "Had I known you were coming…"

Amy uncomfortably shook her head in tiny, rapid motions. The last thing she wanted was to be put on a pedestal or display or, for that matter, receive any recognition.

Amy introduced Rodney and Ann and told how they were celebrating their honeymoon.

"You have been here before. You should have told me you are friends of my Amelia and the food would have always been on the house." Sydney offered.

Rodney and Ann just shook their heads in gratitude, as everyone had already been so kind and generous.

Amy introduced me as her very special boyfriend, not wanting to let the cat out of the bag.

Sydney politely smiled and nodded towards me, shaking my hand with the type of handshake of one meeting an ex-girlfriend or boyfriend would do when meeting a former lover of someone they were involved with.

Turning back to Amy, Sydney quietly said "I've missed you so much," and then spoke in French. *"Nos caresses me manquent. Notre amour l'un pour l'autre me manque. Tu me manques, et toi, je te manque. Tes baisers et tes étreintes me manquent."*

I had no idea what she said. I do know it's amazing how a few words spoken, can ricochet at the speed of life and only after they reach someone else, are they regretted. I saw Amy cringe as she was uncomfortable with the comment that I let slide.

Sydney pointed to the tables and indicated we needed to eat. We reluctantly agreed.

"You stay here and visit. When the food is prepared, I will come for you" Sydney directed.

"This is why I like to stay at the other end." Amy whispered. "No one knows me there."

Sydney ordered something in French and soon the food came and we were called to our table. There were enough shish kabobs of beef, chicken, lamb and shrimp to feed an army. Sydney asked what we would like to drink and we both said in unison, "water". "Sparkling or flat?" Sydney asked. I had no idea! Amy ordered flat….in other words, Wisconsin water.

Maxx served the food. As we ate, I made small talk with Rodney and Ann with laughter all around. However, I noticed a degree of reticence from Amy as she warily glanced at Sydney. Uncle Frank appeared and helped us finish lunch as he flirted with all the girls. I guess Rodney and Ann had become accustomed to the European ways. For me it was still an adjustment as my eyes followed the people walking the beach in all kinds of attire.

Rodney asked what I thought of the house and I told him that we hadn't been there yet. He just smiled and said, "Incredible!"

The Truth Be Told: We finished our lunch as Rodney and Ann excused themselves and offered to ride with Uncle Frank back to the house to pack. We switched cars as they left the keys to their Hyundai with me. Amy wanted to play in the ocean and so we left the keys and towels at the service counter in Le'String, along, I might add, with Amy's top. As we waded in the warm water, Amy tried to pull my shorts down and we ended up having a water fight. It was a hoot!

After about a half-hour of Amy making absolutely sure that I realized I was the only one for her, we called it a day, picked up the towels and keys, got in the Hyundai and headed for the house. Amy, at least, put her top back on. However, with the clothes in the Rover, Amy was still just wearing her bikini as I was beginning to understand the source of her lack of modesty back home.

We headed west past the backs of all kinds of beach restaurants with Kon-Tiki and KaKao being the big ones. I just kept driving with Amy staring out the window as her reflection ricocheted her countenance. When we got to the end by Bikini Beach restaurant, Amy quietly directed me to turn left. I did.

Without emotion, Amy pointed out a small restaurant named 'Good Morning' and noted that it was where her mom and dad got croissants every morning as they were coming out of the oven, the croissants that is, not her mom and dad. We drove a couple of blocks up the "retail strip" filled with all kinds of tourist stores and Amy, emotionlessly told me turn right in the round-about.

I slowed down as we traversed a few hundred yards of scarred speed bumps where those in a hurry had bottomed-out. The last thing I wanted to do was tear the drive shaft out of the car. Slowly we went through a housing area called Parc De La Baie Orientale and out to the highway marked N7, which I learned was the only road that went around the entire island.

At the intersection, I looked to the left at all the traffic coming down the hill, then across at Les Jardins D' Orient Bay and then to the right at more traffic coming down the other hill and waited for directions.

Instead, Amy said. "It was a long time ago" as she stared out the front window at nothing.

"What?" I asked.

"Sydney."

I thought I knew what she was referring to, but was willing to let it slide.

There was a car behind me and so I needed directions. "Left? Right? Straight?"

Amy pointed to the right and I put my blinker on. When she spoke again, I could tell by the tone of her voice that she was troubled. "I was recovering and needed someone. She taught me a lot."

"I came here and lived in the house. Friends would come and friends would go, but I was all alone. I was here nearly a year. Aunt Julia and Uncle Frank were wonderful, but I needed someone, anyone, who would make me feel completely alive and not half dead."

"I'm ashamed." she said in a very unconvincing way. I sensed that they were just words to justify what she thought I learned and her weak apology was simply a futile attempt at appeasement. I don't think she had ever lied to me before, but this time, I sensed it was one of those occasions. I wanted to let it slide until I saw the furtive tears welling in her eyes.

We sat there for a long, quiet, tension-filled moment as the pieces fell into place. Amy and Sydney had been lovers and Amy wanted to keep it a secret. As we sat in silence, I could sense she felt fallible as her normal self-confidence evolved into tears as she convulsed in sadness.

While Amy's words rattled around in my soul, my mind wandered and I asked myself whether it had been simply a dalliance or debauchery. I concluded it really didn't matter. What had happened or to what degree wasn't going to have any effect on my love for her and I needed to make absolutely certain she was aware of that. I took a deep breath and considered what to say so that she understood there was absolutely no way I would judge, minimize or deprecate what she had experienced.

After what seemed like twenty cars and a half-dozen crazy people on motor scooters, I turned to the right and slowly headed up the hill. When I saw Amy's, hands go to her mouth in regret, I pulled the Hyundai into a parking area next to a French BBQ restaurant called Rancho Del Sol. I didn't have any idea what French BBQ tasted like and was too full to find out, but knew that we needed to have a very serious conversation.

With the lunch crowd gone, I parked the car so that we could peak through the palms and see the ocean below and shut off the engine. I knew I needed to stop the drama and did so the only way I knew how and asked, "Ashamed or embarrassed?"

"What's the difference" Amy asked.

I looked her in the eye and said, "The main difference is that "embarrassed" is about what other people think of you, while "ashamed" is more about what you think of yourself. That's why you can never feel embarrassed when you're alone. Being ashamed, however, is something personal. It's often related to feeling guilty. If you are ashamed … ashamed of what?

My goal was to efface her admission and yet it was a meek attempt on my part that met with little or no reaction, which really raised my ire. For only the second time in our relationship, I sensed her distance. As had been the case when I dropped her off to take the LSAT test, she was emotionless and I was hurt.

Amy sat staring out the front window and shaking her head as if to say 'no' as I continued. "Are you ashamed that you had a relationship or embarrassed that I found out? There is a big difference," to which there was no response.

I tried a softer approach. "Don't be ashamed by what you did. Don't ever feel ashamed about what you feel. You did absolutely nothing wrong! A person should only be ashamed if they intentionally hurt someone or something."

The tears continued to flow as I continued on. "Remember what Amelia Erhardt vowed when she agreed to get married? If we are to have an existential relationship, we both must accept the foundation of a free will and the ability to think, act and be what we were or are! This is critical, Amy! Finding out the way I did might be a little embarrassing … not for you, but for me. There were inferences that went over my head and I need to be more attuned to what you say, what you do and above all else, who you are. As we go through life together, little things will come out about both of us that we might be embarrassed about, but never, ever, will there be anything to be ashamed of … especially when it comes to emotions."

Amy was afraid to look at me and continued to stare out the front window as she wiped the tears from her cheeks. I added, "There are things in your past that are yours and things in my past that are mine. They will always be there and cannot be erased. What you did. What I did and with whom we did It, doesn't matter. It's really none of the other's business, unless we want it to be. How do we learn? By doing, from which we grow! We are together. You and I! We are a couple. We are in love, now and forever. The past changes absolutely nothing."

"I wanted today to be perfect." she whispered, still peering straight ahead.

I just shook my head and raised my hands in exclamation… "It is! It's absolutely **incredible.**"

Tears continued to roll down her checks and I could feel her profound sadness…not at what happened, but that I had found out. I needed to show Amy that what she had done wasn't wrong, but the feelings she had were making indelible streaks upon my heart.

"Why are you crying?" I asked.

"Because."

"Because you were attracted to another person and enjoyed their company? Because that person was a woman? What difference does that make? Two people who had feelings for each other and shared each other. What can be more beautiful than that?"

I think Amy was a bit startled by my response...the conservative, farm boy from suburban Mineral Point...make that Waldwick, Wisconsin, who was more accepting and tolerant than she thought he would be.

I continued to elucidate. "It makes no difference! If the two of you cared for each other, that's all that mattered. I cared about Theresa, who I dated before you, and she moved back to Cleveland. If we went there and ran into her, I wouldn't be embarrassed. It was another person and another time, that's all."

"But!" Amy responded.

I looked at her and noted. "It's not wrong for a woman to be sexually attracted to another woman. Sexual attraction is a natural and deeply personal aspect of human experience, and there's nothing inherently wrong with being attracted to someone of the same gender. A lot of people experience same-sex attraction, whether as a core part of their identity or as a fluid aspect of their sexuality. What matters most is that relationships and attractions are based on mutual respect, consent, and emotional well-being."

"But!"

I was getting a little perturbed. "There's no difference, Amy!" I interrupted. "You took your own boundaries and expanded them. I would be a hypocrite if I judged you on that." Once again, I softened my voice and added, "In fact, Sweetie, I think more of you now than before. When you and Sydney were together, you experienced ephemeral things that I can never duplicate. In the end, you have chosen **ME** and I will always be profoundly grateful for that. Of all the men and **women** in the world, YOU CHOSE ME! Instead of half the world, it's **all the world** and I'm the one."

I could tell she wasn't 100% convinced and so I continued on.

"With Great Grandfather, I have had the honor of being in the presence of a wonderful man who shared the turmoil and profound sadness that comes when people are judged simply for what they are and what they believe in. This great man has shown me dignity and honor and yet I was allowed to see how insipient, judgment of others can be. I was chosen because an Indian girl was saved by my ancestors from being raped and probably murdered, simply because that girl was different. I have heard story after story of the pain and suffering incurred simply because these people weren't like you and me."

"I have lived with a man and woman who have treated me with honor, dignity and generosity beyond anything anyone could ever expect. In so doing, I have learned to respect others who are different. I have learned that there is no such thing as right and wrong, only good and bad and that boils down to one critical thing…it is good if it makes you happy without making anyone else unhappy. It is bad if it makes you or anyone else sad. This is what I have learned. This is what I truly and profoundly believe and if there is one thing I hope I can show you, it is the tolerance I have for those who are different from me."

I attempted to share my logic … What had Amy done, after all? Sydney gave her pleasure and joy that only comes from a sense of freedom, liberation and acceptance beyond the confines of values she had sheltered. Sydney had been there in a time when Amy profoundly needed to feel wanted. Amy needed to be liberated from the confines of fear and remorse, giving her a sense of being and passion and above all else, the drive she needed to regain her health and Sydney sincerely helped her heal.

I wondered, if only for an instant, what her response would have been had I told her that I had been with a man who was my lover. Would she still want me? Would things be different? Would she have asked about what we did and with whom? My God! Where did that come from?

What Amy and Sydney did really wasn't any of my business and I wondered if I should continue and elected to move forward adding, "Sex is really only touch…the closest of all touch, and it's the touch we are all afraid of. Yet to touch another person can be the most rewarding of all emotions when there is commitment and passion involved. It doesn't matter who the person is, as long as both people sincerely care for each other."

In an effort of equanimity, I reached for her chin and turned her head towards me and looked deeply into her beautiful brown eyes so that I could feel her soul close to mine. "There will always be some negativity in our world and there is always going to be pushback, just as there are always going to be people out there who will chastise our relationship and won't like you or me … people who will be reticent to us speaking our mind or being true to who we are. Those people really don't matter. It's about whether you like yourself and I like myself and we love each other. If we like ourselves, nobody else matters. If you love yourself as much as I love you, you going to live a wonderful life."

My head cocked to one side as I continued. "My dear Amy, the world will go on. The weak will fall and yet we … you and I … will still be standing. The world is more or less a fixed thing and, externally, we must adapt ourselves to the world, not the world to us! We can please ourselves or we can please others. Emotions will constantly change ... but our life together will always stand as one!"

I released her chin and looked out the windshield at the ocean below. "Of all people, you Sweetie, must stick by living life to the fullest as far as life sticks by you. Please! Please! Always remember ... We must please ourselves because no one else ever will."

I hoped and prayed that Amy had learned enough about herself and about me as I added that my only goal for the two of us was to be happy... satisfied with who we were and not what we were, content that each day be filled with one and only one thing ... sincerely feeling wanted, needed and loved so that when our last breath was taken, those who remained would look back on how we touched **their lives** and we were fondly remembered and truly missed."

She shook her head in agreement.

"Do you still want to be with her? I asked.

Amy gently shook her head no, but was not convincing.

"I love you so much. If you need to, you can."

More tears....

I added, "All I want is for you to be happy and if that means sharing you, I will, or, if you would be happier, give you up." I said, hoping and praying that would not be the case. Many more tears and convulsions of sadness....

I looked out at Orient Bay and spoke again. "I once wrote that rarely can one's soul rise up, gasping through the fathomless fathoms under which we live. I believe we are all nothing more than fish swimming in the sea, endlessly swimming, as we seek our own true joy in the mucky murk called loneliness. To find someone ... if only for an instant ... can provide hope that there are others who will also allow us to breathe the sweet nectar of acceptance." She slightly nodded in the affirmative.

As we sat there, I did my best to make her understand it's not where the love comes from, only that it comes and that it is completely natural. I added, "Nothing is normal that is forced. If it's natural, then there's absolutely nothing wrong with anything for anyone with anyone else. Forget culture! Forget taboo! Forget what people and society might think! What matters is that the relationship provided the respite you needed in a time and place you needed, to give you hope and let you heal."

I was doing my best to overcome her reluctance. I prayed she was calming down as I continued on. There were small signs that she was relinquishing her trepidation as she slid down in her seat relieving the tension that had forced her into an upright stance as if in battle.

I continued. "I sincerely feel that when we live alone, we are all only half-conscious and only half alive. To live, we must all come alive and be whole. Look at Rodney and Ann! Look at how happy they are! This is what we all search for and this is what you have done to me. You, Miss Amelia Marie Williams have made me feel alive and aware, conscious of who I am and what I want to be…the greatest husband and best partner I possibly can. I don't care about jet planes and fancy cars. I don't care about expensive clothes and people kissing my ass. I don't care about where you were or who you were with before we met … except perhaps, Frank the UPS driver," which got a slight smile on her face. "What I care about, and the only thing I care about, is that the two of us sincerely feel wanted, needed and loved by each other. I only hope and pray that what I do and what I have done makes you as happy as I am today."

Amy shook her head and smiled, a sad smile just the same. This had been her deep secret, the one I knew she wanted to keep that way. I asked who else knew and Amy said she thought her mom did because the housekeeper walked in on her and Sydney in bed one morning.

I added, "Well, let's just believe that there might now be three people, besides you, in the entire world, who know your secret. Three people, all of whom profoundly love you. You can decide if you want anyone else to know. You can be certain that it will be **you** telling them and not me and if you do tell someone, please add that when I learned, I really didn't care and thought it was great, because it made you happy."

There was relief on her part that I could see reflected in her eyes. I watched as Amy focused on the horizon, staring at nothing, yet seeing everything. I knew that what she was about to say was going to be difficult. There is always security when there isn't another set of eyes to catch each word and reflect them back at you. Amy took a deep breath as if it would help her clear her soul. She wanted to let It all out. I wanted her to.

Amy began. "The hospital in Madison wanted me to have the treatments there. However, because it was mainly administration and blood work, mom thought it could be done here where there would be less pressure and a lot less stress. Mom has known Doctor Archibald, who is a great doctor and wonderful friend, from when she was in residency. Doctor Archibald who promised to come and visit me every day, administer the meds, take the blood samples and check my vitals."

"When I first got here, mom and dad came for the first two weeks and then had full-time nurses stay with me. I weighed eighty -four pounds! After mom and dad left and I began to improve, Mom had the nurse still came every day to check on me and Doctor Archibald came every other day as well."

"At first, I was so weak I only got up to go to the bathroom, but the medication began working. I started eating and feeling a little stronger. By the third week, my progress went from just getting out of bed, to making it all the way down the seventeen steps to the end of the walkway by our parking area. My goal became to add ten steps each way, every day. By the end of six weeks, I was down to the end of our driveway. Now it seems so trivial, but then it was a milestone. After nearly two months, I was walking half way down the hill towards the subdivision entrance."

"One day I felt I needed a break and took the car and went to the beach. It was good to get back to reality. All of mom's tenants were surprised to see this emaciated girl with peach fuzz for hair under her baseball cap as I slowly made it all the way to Le'String at the other end of the building. I sat there for a half-an-hour the first day, exhausted by my diligence, but vowing to come back."

"The waiter's name is Maxime but everyone calls him Maxx. That first day, Maxx looked deep into my heart and felt my pain and made me feel welcome without pity. I will always be grateful to him. I added 10 minutes each day until I could handle two hours. In the beginning, they put one of those orange parking cones in a spot behind the restaurant for me. If they hadn't I probably wouldn't have come back. I just didn't have the strength."

"Because I was coming every day and became a regular, Maxx reserved a table for me. At first, I was in back near the kitchen where I wasn't noticed. As my strength returned, I got healthy enough to move up front so that I could people watch without making those eating lunch feel uncomfortable. No one wants to sit next to a skeleton at lunch!"

Amy continued, "Sydney and I started talking and she asked me if I wanted to start walking the beach with her in the morning and that gave me the incentive to begin. At first, I came dressed in long pants and long sleeve tee-shirt but could only go a little way and then needed to turn back."

"We kept walking and talking until I made it all the way from Pedro's to the condos at Mont Vernon on the other end. That's nearly two miles! Two miles! I would never have made if it weren't for Sydney! She would run back and bring the car. As I got stronger, I started walking down the beach and part of the way back with my goal being Bikini Beach or nearly three miles. Finally, my daily regimen became a round trip. I hit a milestone! Then Sydney and I started slowly running until I was able to run the entire length. First all the way down and then down and back."

"Each day, we added a little more. We would run together and then talk. I was getting stronger as my weight increased. Besides running, Sydney and I began lifting weights and doing yoga. I wanted to not only gain weight, but add muscle, and so my regimen of cardio and weight training became pretty intense. I was feeling better each day."

"One day we kicked it in at the end, like they did in the Rocky movie and I beat her. When we got to the end, she hugged me. It just felt good to have someone touch me. As we walked back to the car, she held my hand to help me up, over the rocks by Pedro's and kissed and congratulated me. It was the first time in over two years that I had been kissed by anyone. There were so many days when I thought it would never happen again."

"Being with her so much, I felt comfortable and we talked about everything…and I mean everything. We had been walking the beach for nearly six months and I wanted to repay her and invited her to the house one night for dinner. She brought a couple bottles of wine and one thing led to another and then it just happened. I was so alone and needed someone so bad. She started sleeping over."

I guess I wasn't surprised, but more resolved. One of my questions regarding her total lack of modesty was being answered.

Amy added, "Fighting cancer takes all of your energy. Think of fighting to the death…both physical and mental. In order to do that, I began looking at the holistic programs to supplement the medical treatments I was receiving. Some people rely on one or the other. My thought was to incorporate both to see if I couldn't enhance the curing process and, if it worked, make myself be a better person."

"Sydney and I discussed being healthy and she mentioned, and I began reading about a pattern of physical and mental health called Wim Hof. The entire Wim Hof concept is based on human evolution where, over time, humans have developed a different attitude towards the nature around us and we actually forgot one thing, 'inner power' which is the relationship between our physiological mechanisms to adapt and survive and our natural environment, which is direct and effective."

I nodded in agreement, having absolutely no idea what she was talking about. However, I thought of my conversations with Rodney and realized that, although he never called it Wim Hof or any other German name and I'm certain the creator of Wim Hof never mentions the Indians, their philosophies sounded very much alike…adapting one's body, mind and spirit to meld with the environment, instead of changing the environment to meet our needs.

Amy continued, but threw me a curve. "Because we wear clothes and control temperatures at home and work, we have changed the stimulation on our body, thus the old mechanisms related to survival and function are not in order. As these deeper, physiological layers are not stimulated anymore, we have become alienated from them, thus our bodies are weakened and we are no longer in touch with our inner power. The inner power is a force accumulated by fully awakened physiological processes. It also influences the very core of our self. In other words, be naked and be healthy," she said in all earnestness.

I inquired. "So, you ran around naked all the time?" as my mind went from caring to some sort of erogenous manifestations. I know! I know! Shame on me!

Amy shook her head 'no' and responded, "While Wim Hof provided the internal justification for my acquired lack of modesty, I also began participating in the Japanese activity called Shinrin-yoku or "forest bathing" which consists of purposeful walks for meditation and that's why Orient Beach in the morning became so precious. Here, I could walk and periodically sit down to do deep breathing and use all my senses…sight, touch, smell, taste and hearing. When I did this, I could see things I normally would not see, hear things I would not normally hear, smell things I normally did not normally smell and sense things I normally did not feel. The best example I can give is taking a beam of light and running it through a prism so that all the different colors are shown. The beams are always there, but we never take the time to look at them individually."

I was beginning to believe it was the 60's and I was getting involved in some sort of hippie cult. I think my eyebrows must have raised as Amy continued on in earnest. "It's amazing how attitudes change based totally on perspective. On the west side of the rocks, right below Pedro's, wearing a tiny bikini or going topless is 'unique' and for some offensive. Some people stare ... particularly the cruisers, who come to be titillated and are then upset because people from a different culture or different concept of modesty are enjoying their way of life."

"What's crazy is that just five feet away…on the club side of the same rocks … going topless or wearing the same tiny bikini is also 'unique' and again, somewhat offensive, because everyone else is nude. It can be the same person, in the same attire, who has done nothing more than walk from one side of the rocks to the other. Yet, what people think, completely changes, simply because of which side of the rocks they are on."

Amy continued. "Five feet makes all the difference in the world! But then, isn't life like that? People judge others based on their own perspective and not on reality. At first, I was nervous on both sides of the rocks and then, like everything else, I became comfortable and indifferent to what people thought."

"So, you would go nude?" I asked.

"Certainly!" Amy responded in an assenting, yet unemotional, way. "I began to wear what the locals wore and eat lunch at Le'String and go topless for a swim if I felt like it. Some days, I would go down to the club section of the beach and sit naked on the soft sand and focus on my sense of touch, not only on my hands, but any part of my body that was in contact with the sand, air or even the sun. I practiced until I could focus on a specific body part and appreciate how it was being caressed."

She was getting serious and looked deeply into my eyes and continued. "In doing this, I began to have a much deeper sense of 'me'. Along with the medications, I was able to focus on my fight back to good health. The human brain can do a lot to help a person heal, if it knows where to focus. Cancer cells have a way of tricking the brain into thinking they're non-existent. By the combination of the medications and my focus, I believe I was able to assist in taking the right steps to recovery. In the end, I was able to ameliorate my own self-concept and live a more-healthy life."

Amy continued, "Sitting naked on a beach alone isn't for everyone and did come with some risks. There would be those who would look at me and covet me physically and I really got tired of that. In the beginning, after all that I had been through, I must admit, I was honored. To come back from the depths of oblivion to the point that you are looked at from an erogenous perspective was quite gratifying and yet the short blips of physicality were replaced by my inner spirit that had, as its goal, emotional tranquility … I wanted people to accept me as me, not as a figment of someone's erogenous imagination."

"Ok! Big, or in my case, little guy, chill out!" I thought to myself.

Amy or Amelia or whatever she was today, continued on… "I love the smell of the ocean as it is clean and crisp and yet, when I would focus I could also smell the hibiscus and sea grapes and even the decaying sea weed that floated up on the shore down near Mont Vernon. Even today when we were at the beach, I tasted the salt in the air and my own perspiration on my upper lip and that brought back pleasant memories."

"Like everyone else, I not only hear the ocean, but the breeze in the trees, the call of a bird and even the crunch of the sand as my body shifts its weight. What is different is that I have learned how to focus on them one at a time, like listening to an orchestra and being able to listen to just one instrument. In so doing, I became in touch with nature throughout my entire body to a point of relaxation and peace and did so to such a degree that the rest of my body could help fight my battle."

"Just like Rodney and Great Grandfather," I added, nodding my head in the affirmative, realizing that the depth of conversation was much, much more than where it had begun.

Amy smiled as I, her now-official fiancée, was catching on. "When I combined Shinrin-yoku with Wim Hof, I became more relaxed and drawn to my own, "inner power" which I find to be, in my case anyway, direct and effective. Add to this my health experiences and I have become completely indifferent towards so many things that used to bother me … only wanting to take each day, each experience and each relationship and maximize it to the point that it helps me enjoy life to the fullest. In the time that we have known each other, there is only one instance when I let go … the LSAT's. What you saw then was pretty close to the way I used to be all the time."

Amy's stare at the ocean subsided and she looked into my eyes to the point that her sincerity penetrated my heart. "I love you and I love it here. I love you because you are kind, generous, funny and sincere…and most of all, because I know that you love me. I love it here because of the sense of freedom I can have."

Amy looked back out at the ocean and continued. "Before sunrise, people allow you to be yourself and people running the beach wearing little-or-nothing raise no eyebrows, no judgment and no altercations. You are free to be whatever you want and that's when I lost my remaining inhibitions. I realized who I was and my body didn't play a single part in any of it. A few months earlier, I had been this scrawny waif who was enduring and simply surviving. I started as a walking skeleton and was about as physically unappealing as one could be. People would glance at me and look the other way. They didn't want to be reminded of death. Yet, for the very first time in my life, I was free…free of the constraints that had controlled my life for so many years and no longer the object as I had always been…the half-black, half-white, rich girl who never fit in."

Amy's head turned back to my gaze. "While what I went through was demoralizing, it was also liberating, as people I got to know, accepted me for me, the mental being and not the physical being. I never asked for pity, only acceptance! I went from what I was to who I am and I cherish that!"

As she continued, Amy looked at the floor of the Hyundai. "Looking back, I think the metamorphous began before I even got here with the doctors and nurses who didn't consider me to be a person…simply a patient. When they would talk about me, even when I was in the room, it was never Amelia. I was 'the patient' that they could inspect from head-to-toe, like a head of cabbage, at the grocery store."

Amy looked back into my eyes and shaking her head in disbelief added. "Poke here, prod there, with no thought regarding my feelings or inclinations. To have total strangers looking at every part of your body and probing you, takes away any inhibitions you have in a heartbeat. You were there last year when you were in the hospital. Remember the sign at the nurse's station 'Check your modesty at the front desk?'"

Amy looked out at the ocean and continued, "I'm certain that before today you have been surprised and probably somewhat shocked by my lack of modesty, yet I hope not dismayed by my indifference. When you feel people consider you to be ugly and repulsive, you lose any sense of inhibition because you feel that no one wants you. However, once you are there, there is a sense of freedom … your own bond with the earth, the sky, air and water, just like Rodney has told you about. When that happens, your body becomes insignificant and you are spiritually one and that's when the entire concept of "who" comes into play. When people look at you and judge you by the way you look, you can be distraught or finally get to the point that you simply do not care!"

Amy reiterated. "As I continued to gain weight and look somewhat normal, opinions about me and responses to my presence began to change and once again I was "what" and not "who" and yet the profound feelings of freedom remained. There were those who looked at me and found me attractive. There were those who began to judge me physically and yet I never forgot where I had been. To lose that sense of freedom, to have it encased in what others consider righteous and holy is something I simply cannot do, as it will limit me, encumber me and take away my total sense of being. I have been to the edge of darkness and seen the sun rise. Today, I am liberated because I have set my own bounds. It's not for everyone, in fact it's probably not for most people, but for me, it's who I am and what I hope you can accept."

Amy let out a long, slow breath. "My days with Sydney are part of my past that will always remain there for which I am not ashamed. If you've never run naked on a beach or swum nude in the waters of the ocean, you cannot comprehend the sense of freedom that comes from feeling the ocean, the breeze or the water caress your entire body, giving you a sense of exhilaration and total immersion with nature and with each other."

A slight smile came across Amy's face as if in revelation of a thought or memory that had once existed came to light. "During the day, I would read or listen to music and go out on the veranda and rest on the ottoman and dream about tomorrow instead of feeling sorry for myself."

Amy looked at me with a smile on her face. "One day, I was feeling guilty about my relationship and needed some assurance. When I was digging through all the books in the house, I found a book buried on the shelf and pulled it down. It was the Bible and I read it...the whole thing. It was about humility, generosity, compassion and forgiveness and I knew that there was something I would never forget and that was what I found in the book of Ruth."

"Like you, I had been taught to be with a like-person was wrong and yet the Scriptures say – 'without apology, embarrassment, or qualification -- Ruth felt the same way toward Naomi as spouses are supposed to feel toward each other.'

"Far from being condemned, Ruth's feelings were celebrated as I had felt that my relationship with Sydney was wrong. Yet, at that time, it felt so right. I kept reading and, to remove any doubt about how Ruth felt toward Naomi, the Scriptures go on to talk of the details of the vow that Ruth made to Naomi. Here are her words, which I memorized. 'Do not press me to leave you or to turn back from following you! Where you go, I will go; where you lodge I will lodge; your people shall be my people, and your God my God. Where you die, I will die — there will I be buried. May the Lord do thus and so to me, and more as well, if even death parts me from you!' This is my wedding vow to you Mr. George Terrill. If you will still have me, on the day we officially become man and wife, this is what I want to say."

I looked at her and smiled. "I am in love with you now more than ever my Amelia! Now more than ever!"

Amy was returning to her old self as her confidence was coming back she continued, "Perhaps I read too much into it. Perhaps, I was looking for an excuse. In the end, you are right! I rationalized that what was happening wasn't wrong. Sydney was a chapter in my life that ended. I did what I did, when I did what I did, simply because, at that time, my actions filled a deep, dark hole in my heart with joy."

The truth be told and I understood and accepted it. There was no more fear of a secret escaping! There were no more concerns about what would be thought or said at a later date! There were no more worries about my reactions. Amy's secret was my secret and there was relief that I could see in her eyes, her face and in her heart. How great to have a burden lifted! How wonderful to have a fear removed and replaced by what she had only hoped could possibly be ... acceptance ... not only of what had transpired, but of her, all of her, the way she was and the way she is, without any more worries or concerns.

Amy continued, "As time went on, Sydney introduced me to her friends and I Europeanized myself in many ways … socially, mentally and physically. Because of the St. Martin culture of acceptance and so many mixed marriages, I was just Amelia! For the first time ever, I wasn't considered an odd -ball…a half-black, rich girl, who didn't fit in and wasn't classified or adjectivized, as Ann calls it. I was just another person who came to live in a dream world, away from those running the human race instead of taking time to slow down and enjoy it."

As she looked out the window, Amy's left hand went to her right shoulder as if to read her tattoo as she spoke. "It was then that I got the idea for the tattoo and had myself inked with the word "Survivor". Mom wasn't too happy and I don't think dad was pleased, but they understood it was a message to myself and a symbol of the journey I traveled. Each year, I add a dot to reflect another year of existence."

Amy stopped for a moment and became quite pensive. "What I've done isn't for everyone. Yet, for me, it made all the sense in the world. I get up every morning, look at survivor and the dots after it and thank God I'm alive, vowing to be a better person than the day before"

Amy had run around naked on the beach, had a physical relationship with a woman, has ink on her shoulder that reflects her survival and wanted me! I just got engaged to someone a lot more dynamic than most people and still **really** had a lot to learn.

Amy looked at me and smiled softly. "With you, my dear, sweet man, I have added a wonderful piece of my life puzzle. I now have the type of love I was missing that is different from what I've always received from my parents and family. Because of you, I have the joy I never had and finally have the complete and total concept of inner peace I aspired to that allows me to live in peace and tranquility that has come because I absolutely know you love me and accept me for who I am! And, I sincerely believe that what we have is a bond so strong it will never, ever be broken. We both know that our time together might be measured in days or weeks or months and yet, I know that those moments however short or long, are going to be filled with love and laughter, joy and happiness and I can only and will always simply say 'I love you'."

Whew! She wanted me! Now there were tears in my eyes as she leaned across the console in the car and kissed me. I took a deep breath and smiled. She had turned the tables and I was hoping that she still wanted me. After yet another deep breath, I looked at my watch and realized that it was nearly three o'clock and time was of the nigh.

"We'd better get to the house" I whispered and with that, turned the key in the ignition and began the drive west on N7 as Amy continued. "One day, mom called and said I needed to return to Madison for "T" cell treatments and dad was sending the plane the next day. That night, when Sydney got home, I had candles lit and her favorite wine chilled and told her I was going home. I told her the reason wasn't her and explained why I needed to leave. I thanked her for all that she had done. I think we both knew it was over. Whenever someone who has been an important part of your life is gone, there are always regrets and I will always be grateful for her patience, tolerance and acceptance and hope that our time together will always be remembered as such."

"When Beth and Dennis arrived with the plane the next day, they were shocked by the improvement in me. I had gone from this bald, emaciated, pile of bones to having some hair and a smile on my face with my weight coming back to almost where I began. We flew home and I sat up the entire flight. The custom bed dad installed in the plane had been used only once to fly me down here … until this morning," Amy whispered with a quiet little smile.

Amy continued, "I was still sick, but the medication was working and the second part of the trial was designed to finish off the cancer, hopefully once and for all. With that first treatment, I really had no idea what I was in for. When I got to the clinic, I was told that there would be procedures for five years consisting of monthly blood filtering and testing and harvesting 'T' cells. The doctors told me what it would be like. I thought they were exaggerating! After the first treatment, I just wanted to die. The nausea and cramps were incredible! They gave me prescriptions, but I said 'no, I could endure'. After a few sessions, I acclimated and the pattern set in and I met new people and new friends like Ann."

"Everyone in Madison knows me as Amy, not Amelia. Until Ann and Rodney's wedding, no one, besides you, Ann and Rodney knew who my dad is and that's the way I want to keep it for as long as I can. I want to be happy. I want to be me, unidentified by my heritage. I want to be with you for the rest of my life! You, Mr. George Terrill the Fourth have accepted me for **who** I am and I will always, always, be grateful. I haven't been back here in nearly two years. I missed it so much. I love it here and never, ever want to be gone this long again. Promise me! Please, please promise me that we can come back again!" She let out a sigh of relief and slumped back into her seat with her thumbs nestled between the strings of her bikini bottom and the front of her thighs. Her deepest secrets were told.

"One question though" I asked, which made her sit erect and in a defensive posture once again. "What about Samantha?"

Amy slid back down in her seat, took a deep breath and exhaled, while finally shaking her head "no". She put her fingers to her lips and waited a few seconds before she began to answer. "I think Sam and I might have been getting close to something physical. Then this crazy farm kid swept me off my feet and changed everything."

"Was Samantha disappointed?" I asked.

"I think so, but Sam had another relationship going and so what might have been, never happened."

"Were you disappointed?"

"Not really. If it happened, it happened, but Sam lived in a different world that I really don't think I wanted to visit then. However, it was all that I had at the time. I was really concerned about some of the things she was excited about. Sam was trying to convince me they were all right, but I didn't see them that way."

I responded. "She scared the shit out of me. I thought she was going to beat me up."

This got the ice-breaking, girlie giggle we both needed as Amy noted, "she wouldn't have done that. Anyway, I don't think so."

"But she could have." I retorted as I hunched my shoulders and flexed my muscles and growled, which resulted in yet another girly giggle.

"Remember the first time we had dinner and the music we listened to?" Amy asked.

"How could I forget it? The Flower Duet?" I said with the smile of a cat who had just eaten the canary.

"As I told you, the music score is from *"Fifty Shades of Gray"*. Read the books and you will have a better understanding of Sam. She wanted to do all the things in the books and some of them made me uncomfortable and I was reluctant."

"In other words, you established your own boundaries?" I offered.

"Yes." Amy responded adamantly.

I continued. "You, my dear, are one of the lucky ones. You found **your** own limits. You expanded **your** bounds beyond where society mandates they should be. Then, when you thought of going further, you and your values, not society, held you back. You set your own limits. You drew lines in the sand regarding what you were, or are, willing to do. My God, you are the lucky one. So many of us don't have a clue where our limits are and so we sit and let society or religion tell us what is right and wrong and then we judge others based simply on that."

"Do you think bounds are forever?" she asked.

In the few seconds it took to exit the parking lot, my mind wandered. Like almost everyone else, I knew what *"Fifty Shade of Gray"* was all about. Having lived in an apartment also meant I would go grocery shopping, which always concluded with a wait in line and a look at the magazines. Blaring out at me was always *Cosmopolitan* and headlines barking about this sexual act or that, which women could do or have done to them that was supposed to push the envelope and provide greater pleasure. Was this something Amy was referring to?

I waited for traffic as my mind went back to the word 'some' and her reference to *"Fifty Shades of Gray"*. My journalistic mind reminded me that while there are words like 'always' and 'never' which are absolutes, the word 'some' is not one of them. 'Some' meant partial and I was curious whether Amy was telling me she wanted to try something more and if so, what? How do you ask someone, especially a person who was crying a few minutes before because you found out she had a relationship with another woman, what she meant?

I didn't know what to say and took the safe route, as I replied. "I think the bounds a person creates for themselves are dynamic and change depending on where they are in life. Imagine what it was like back before the sexual revolution, women's liberation and the civil rights movement. We can't even pretend to think what is acceptable today was approved back then. Society moved those boundaries and what people felt guilty for doing or being have evolved and are accepted as common practice today. Add the equation regarding where a person is in their lifecycle and it all adds up to the fact that people and society both change and with them, the concepts of good and bad, right and wrong, accepted and unacceptable."

I paused for a moment and then headed west in traffic and added, "we all seem to be the most liberal when we are young and grow more conservative as we age. Where we start and where we end is really up to us." I hoped this was the right answer.

Amy replied. "But aren't you curious to try new and different things?"

I answered. "To a point, yes, but then no."

"Don't you have fantasies?"

"Some" I replied.

"Tell me!" she countered.

I retorted. "If I tell you my fantasies, then they're not mine anymore."

I'll tell you mine" she answered.

"Then they're not yours anymore" I retorted. I was afraid that hers would be things I really didn't want to hear, even though my prurient interests were certainly piqued … a threesome, bondage, sex toys, who knows what. I almost slapped myself across the face for what I was thinking and wondering if they were her fantasies or mine.

Instead, I drew the conversation back on track. "When you told me that there was a nude beach, my thoughts were 'oh my God' as my Minnie Point values came into play. When we got here and I saw you wearing so little, I was a bit shocked and somewhat dismayed, because it went against the way I was brought up. Then, I noticed that Rodney and Ann were indifferent and, as we walked the beach and played in the water, I realized, I had been wrong…totally wrong. What I saw today were people enjoying themselves, non-judgmental of others and all the titillation was gone. Life isn't about fitting into a mold. It's about creating your own shape and you have done that."

Amy was beginning to relax as I continued. "You are so good and innocent in so many, many ways. There are people out there who will treat you poorly simply because of who you are. They will look at the color of your skin and shake their heads…simply because you are a different shade of brown. They will be envious because of the wealth your family has worked so hard to acquire. They will look at you and wonder why in hell you ended up with me. They will judge me because of the color of my skin. They will judge me because of the wealth of your family. And, they will judge the two of us because we are in love and they can't understand how it can be. Other than our love for each other, all the others shall pass. If people find out about your secret, so what? Some will snicker and yet, in their minds, they will wonder what it was like ... and some will imagine what it would be like if they were liberated enough, brave enough and strong enough to let themselves be free."

I drove and added. "Today has been a perfect day for me, my dear, in many, many ways. I joined a very special flying club, of which I believe there are very few members. I purchased a token-of-my-esteem for the best thing that has ever happened in my life. I got to see a whole bunch of naked people and realized that it wasn't nearly as erotic as I thought it would be and learned something about the woman I love…that she knows more about herself than I ever thought possible ... exploring her world and realizing her bounds, and above all else, she has chosen me above every other person on earth to live with, love with and cherish for the rest of our lives. How can I believe that this day was anything less than perfect? How could I possibly be upset, angry or hurt? How can I do anything more than love you Amelia Marie Williams, more today than yesterday and I sincerely, profoundly, completely, believe less than I will love you tomorrow."

We were driving towards Marigot and Amy pointed to the street just west of the super market and Papa Dan's pizza that Amy said was as good as Paisan's. The tears had stopped and Miss Amelia had calmed down as a slight smile of relief came back. Her emotions were beginning to settle down.

"That's my girl." I said as I took my thumb and wiped the tears from her cheeks as she turned her head into my hand. As we waited to turn left, she leaned across the console and we kissed as her heart stopped pounding. It's incredible how a chance meeting and a few words can open an entirely different chapter in a person's life that they hoped was sealed forever. Yet, I sincerely believe, there was relief on her part, as the short duration of pain washed away a continuation of fear.

We stopped at the subdivision security gate and I looked at her and said, "By the way, I do like your itsy, bitsy, teeny, weeny, bikini!" Finally, she had a satisfied grin splashed across her face as the tip of her tongue seductively slid across her upper lip and she responded, "It's the most conservative one I've got." Gulp!

Amy provided the four-digit security code that I punched it into the gate keypad and we went up the winding road to the top of the hill. The road seemed almost vertical as we zigzagged our way towards the clouds. I thought to myself how difficult it would be to drive in snow and went…'duh!' I shared my stupidity with Amy and that got a chuckle.

The view at the top was simply amazing. We could see Anguilla and St. Barths and the ocean and watched what looked like rain squalls out at sea, along with the sailboats and para-sailors down on Orient Beach. It was surreal! Only a few minutes before, we had been participants and now we were simply spectators to those frolicking in this thing called life. In between, one more thread in the tapestry of our existence together was woven in place…a string that was a vibrant color and multi-hued, containing thoughts and emotions with elocutions of acceptance, support, understanding, compassion, dedication and commitment spliced together, as they should be, to create the foundation of our bond to each other. We were at the top of the world and I understood why the house, the beach and the island could be so narcotizing. My God, there was peace, surrounded by beauty and tranquility, enveloped in a blanket of love.

When we got out of the car, Amy grasped my hand and said in a confident tone, "You, my dear, are so right. We all need to learn who we are. From learning, we need to set our own bounds physically, mentally and emotionally. I have established mine and will not, cannot, nor ever intend, to allow anyone, or any social mores or opinions, determine what is right or wrong, good or bad for me again. To share myself with another person who cared for me and shared her tenderness, was not wrong. To share myself with the man who has shown me that he truly loves me and with whom I want to be a wife, mother and, if God allows, a parent, I know that is what I truly want."

Amy continued "There are feelings and thoughts that will probably never, ever be again and yet I have made a choice and the choice is you. There are no regrets. There is no turning back! There are no second thoughts because every feeling I have had, every sensation I have felt, every thought that has permeated my brain have been eclipsed ten times…a thousand times over by the thoughts, feelings and sensations you have provided. It's called love and my dear, I am truly, profoundly, incredibly in love with you!"

We stood next to the car and kissed…a deep passionate kiss, that summarized all that had been said. As we walked away from the car, the crunch of the crushed driveway stone beneath my feet reminded me that I was back to reality and above all else, I was truly in love.

The House on the Hill: The house-on-the-hill was a huge, very contemporary, white, three-story villa with a flat roof with lots and lots of glass that encompassed the entire top of the hill. Amelia took me on the outside tour first while still wandering around, oblivious to her attired brevity, which I admit, I was getting used to. The yard was filled with cactus and there was a private pool with a huge patio and shrubs around it. Amelia had been right. There was complete privacy, as if that mattered anymore.

Near the pool, I pulled her close and kissed her deeply again. It was the most passionate kiss I believe we had ever participated in. As we stood emotionally enmeshed in each other, my hand slid up her back and I untied the string of her bikini top. It was my way of simply saying "yes". Amy's head pulled back and she looked deeply into my eyes and said. "Well Mr. Terrill, I don't mind if you do," completely forgetting that Rodney and Ann were in the house. As reality struck, we caught our mutual breath and encompassed our urgencies as Amy reconciled her toplessness out of respect to our guests. Whew!

While the outside of the house was spectacular, it really didn't do justice to the interior. The center of the house consisted of an enormous great room that soared three stories high with huge glass windows around the top and the side facing the ocean encompassing a massive stone fireplace that had a trickling waterfall and reflecting pond in front of the mantel and a large, slow-moving, white ceiling fan in the center. The entire east wall consisted of a media center with shelves filled with books surrounding what had to be an eighty -inch TV. On the table next to the sofa was a black book. I looked at the title. "The Holy Bible"... and smiled.

Ann and Rodney had resided in the guest suite that was on the second floor of the west wing of the house. It was angled so that their view overlooked Anguilla and the ocean. Their suite held a huge, glass -walled bedroom, walk-in closet, bathroom, outdoor shower and personal sundeck. Their side included the interior stairway that led from the great room as they were still packing when we arrived trying to cram two weeks' worth of love, laughter and memories into the suitcases they brought with them.

Below the guest suite was the kitchen with white cupboards, walls and tile floors with tan granite counter tops and gourmet everything including Wolf and Subzero appliances The Duke had shipped in from Madison. Complimenting the motif was every type of small appliance and knife you could imagine … all of which had hardly ever been used. There was a long table with a bowl of fresh fruit and flowers and a bar stocked with wine and liquor between the kitchen and the great room where Amelia said few people ever seemed to eat.

Next to the kitchen was a narrow door with one of those built-in combination-locks you find on the front door of houses. Amy punched in a code and opened it to show me The Duke's personal wine closet filled with a rare and I assumed, very expensive collection of his favorites. Amy put her arms around my neck and looked into my eyes. "Next time we come, we can have a special bottle of wine after each time we make love. Do you think daddy will mind if we try to empty his closet?"

We walked back into the great room and Amy pointed to the bridge across the back of the house that led from the outside wall of the guest suite and then to Mr. and Mrs. Williams' private apartment. Amy told me the apartment somewhat matched the guest suite with a larger walk-in closet, sundeck and small pool. She said that her mom and dad didn't like people in their bedroom and so we honored their wishes and the tour didn't go there.

As we entered Amelia's first -floor apartment reality slammed in when I saw photos of her during those first days of recovery. She had certainly come a very long way! The drawn cheeks, eyes circled in darkness, and bald head that marked her battle, were all there. The word Survivor on her shoulder took on a profoundly stronger meaning. Day-by-day, step-by-step, she had advanced, never complaining, never giving up, simply willing herself stronger and stronger and stronger. What a brave soul!

Amelia picked up one of the photos and said, "these are my reminders of how lucky I have been. People tell me to put the pictures away. I keep them here to make sure I **never** forget to thank God **every day** for giving me another chance at life. Above all else, I learned one thing…cherish the moments, as you never know how many more there will be!" The moment was ours and what had transpired in the previous twenty minutes was stored in our private vault of memories, never to be opened unless Amy wanted them to be.

The house tour had done us both good and we were returning to our normal selves … Amy … intelligent, inquisitive, and sensitive, without the negative emotions that had wrought so many tears and me, well, just good old me. Amy pulled open the sliding door and we went back out on the veranda. She noted that this was where she sat for so many days, alone and sad, hoping, wondering, praying, simply to stay alive. This was where her nightmares subsided as her profound will to live brought forth the miracle that we all take for granted … good health, from which springs forth happiness. Amy had already taught me that without health, you have nothing. Take away your health and everything else becomes secondary, distant, insignificant! Houses, cars, airplanes, clothes, money! They all mean so little if you don't have your own wellbeing.

My mind was whirling in so many directions. My fiancée had openly expressed her pleasure with another woman and admitted there were no regrets. She'd indicated I was the one for her, for whom she was willing to give up former inclinations, trepidations, thoughts, feelings and intentions she once enjoyed. Yet she also inferred that if it was the right person, at the right time, in the right place and under the right circumstances, she could easily have another relationship like the one with Sydney, but only if our love had withered and we were no more. I felt challenged and yet honored and glad and quite honestly, somewhat relieved, but also somewhat curious, which I left at that.

We stood by the infinity pool and I looked at her and said, "I don't know what it's like to run naked on the beach. I don't know what the ocean feels like unencumbered. I do know that I love you. I can't promise you the softness or gentleness that you had before. I am open to learning more and promise you that I will try to meet those feelings and give you the freedom and liberty to be what you want to be, to feel what you need to feel and to live a life devoid of regrets of what could have been. If it's your desire to run naked on the beach, we will do so together. If it's your desire to relive memories of swimming unencumbered in the ocean that, too, can be the case...together! If you feel most comfortable wearing nothing, that too will be a part of our existence. Marriage is about acceptance and I pledge to you my acceptance of you for whom you are, what you are and your way of life. In return, all I ask is that you accept me for being me, a little different, a little more conservative, a little more traditional than you … someone willing to meet you here in this wonderful world, in a way I never knew existed."

Our erogenous "urgency" dissipated as I gently placed my hand on her stomach and looked even deeper into her eyes that caught her by surprise as I said, "Someday, I hope and pray our babies will come out of here and will be blessed with good health and the freedom to choose who they are, unrestricted by society or someone else's values … willing to grow in all directions that will allow them to simply achieve one goal ... to be happy. I will do my best, Mrs. Terrill, to live up to your memories and give you the freedom you desire."

We showered together in her outdoor enclave. The water cascading on my body felt good as it washed away the last vestiges of her sadness. I washed Amy's hair as I had done when she broke her ankle and took the bar of soap and massaged every inch of her body to take away any remnants of pain still within her heart. I watched a soft, gentle smile of pleasure slowly make its way across her face as I knelt before her and looked at the small rose tattoo and thought of Great Grandfather and how he once said that love was like a rose whose petals needed to open slowly. As the water ricocheted off Amy and cascaded down upon me, I slowly pulled her into me and kissed her abdomen. I looked up and asked…"Have I told you lately that I loved you?"

Amy opened her eyes and tilted her head down and looked straight into my soul, replying in very serious, measured tone "Yes, my love, you have told me! But, more important, you've shown me from the bottom of your heart, as well."

I stood and we were embracing when reality struck as Rodney politely announced over the shower wall that Uncle Frank was on his way. Time was of the neigh and we quickly dried off. I slid back into the clothes I wore on the flight down as Amelia opened the closet, still filled with her clothes, and slid her naked body into a pair of jeans and black tee shirt. Her serious nature had gone asunder as she cocked her head and, looking at me with a big, sultry grin, scrunched up her nose and giggled as she ran her hands across her chest saying…"oh my, I think I forgot to put something on." With that, her hands slid down and she hooked her thumbs in the front belt loops of her jeans and continued in her devilish whisper, "I don't want you to forget what's waiting for you when we get home".

Oh my God!

Time had stood still at the House-On-The-Hill, waiting, waiting, waiting for the little girl to come home and fill it with love and laughter. She had returned! She had returned! She had returned!

The Big Announcement: We emerged and Rodney and Ann were all packed and it was time to go. Uncle Frank drove us back to the airport in the Range Rover where Dennis, Beth and Miss Amelia II were waiting. We drove out on the tarmac and Uncle Frank gave us all a big hug and invited us back as he slid my morning's purchase into Amelia's hand.

We climbed aboard Amelia II as Beth and Dennis put the luggage in the hold, pulled up the stairs and started the engines. I looked back and the bed was gone. In its place, four more chairs…a little smaller, but with a conference table between. As we took off, I looked down at the beautiful island and then at St. Barths and Anguilla vowing to come back, as we headed back to reality.

When we were at cruising altitude, Dennis came back and told us the flight plan. We were scheduled to arrive in Madison at 11:00 PM. We would need to clear customs in Miami that normally didn't take long. In a little over 18 hours I would have left Madison, gone to St. Martin, joined a very special club, bought an engagement ring, walked on the beach with my fiancée, been introduced to what was her former female 'friend' who made me elicit some profound inner feelings, learned more about my now-official fiancée and was finally bringing my best friend and his bride home from their honeymoon. Incredible!

As we sat making small talk, Amelia smiled her bashful smile and looked at Rodney and Ann and said…"We have an announcement to make…"

Ann's hands went to her mouth…

"We're getting married," as Amelia dropped her left hand for both to admire the morning's purchase.

I looked at the ring and almost choked. Aunt Julia and Uncle Frank had done the old switcheroo! Instead of the two-carat stone Amy and I had picked out, there was this big honker perched on Amy's left hand. When we got home and had it insured, the carat weight came back at nearly five with a large companion stone on each side.

Miss Amelia looked at me with her deep brown eyes and simply smiled, not only with her lips, but with her eyes and heart and I knew that she had what she wanted…a testimony of my love for her. I had paid what I could and provided my personal pride and dignity. Her aunt and uncle had taken care of the rest as their expression of love for their niece and all that she meant to them. What could I say? What should I say? Except, to look back into her eyes and smile, slightly shaking my head, letting her know that I loved her as much as she did me.

"Oh my God, the ring is gorgeous!" Ann countered. Rodney's eyes caught mine and we both just smiled.

Amy looked down at it, then at me and then at Rodney and Ann and said…"I have another wonderful piece of the puzzle of my life. Family, friends and love! Thank you!" A small tear trickled slowly down her cheek that she caught with her tongue and wiped upon her lips. There was a moment of pristine silence as we all basked in the glory of acceptance and then everyone smiled and hugged. We were friends … someone who knows everything about you and still likes you.

After the normal chit chat and wedding excitement, we paired off and I brought Rodney up to date on all that had happened in Madison while they were gone…the casino, the marketing, the loyalty cards, KissAss, social media, Iowa County, the lobbyist, Great Grandfather and the book. I asked his opinion about working with the other nations and having one unified lobbyist instead of individual ones. I asked if he thought the same thing could happen to replace KissAss. He pointed out that the lobbying thing would work, but we needed to remember we were still in competition for the entertainment dollar with the other nations. He made a good point.

I looked at the wall clock and mentioned the Packers were on and wondered what the score was. Amelia went to the cockpit and asked Dennis to put the game on the video boards. I thought the monitors were just for videos or to show us what the pilots saw. Dennis set the station and Rodney and I watched the second half of the game as the Packers played the Bears as we flew seven miles above the earth at over 600 miles per hour. I just shook my head in disbelief.

The girls went in back so they could talk girl talk. Rodney noted…"nice ring!" I just shrugged my shoulders with a somewhat embarrassed look on my face. A farm kid from Waldwick, Wisconsin, riding around in a private jet with his new fiancé who was wearing an engagement ring that cost more than his dad's last tractor wasn't what had been expected.

The resident expert was jocular and pointed out to me that "our brains work all the time from the moment we're born…until we fall in love" as his infectious chortle coincided with a big bear-paw hand grasping my shoulder with affection. It was a smile of acceptance! A smile of appreciation! A smile of brotherly love! He truly was my big brother and I his little brother as our moment, our instance, our sharing of joy, right then and there, was something I will never forget.

As the moment passed and reality returned, Rodney looked at me with a sly smile and raised eyebrows. "No tan lines," he snickered.

I gave him a mischievous grin. "At the pool?"

I was shocked when Rodney replied, "and out on Miss Amelia III…then on Orient Beach."

"Oh my God!"

We arrived as planned at Truax Field with the Jeep warmed up and waiting for us. We thanked Dennis and Beth and took the newlyweds to the cottage and got back to the condo just before the very end of an incredible day. We crawled into bed and I kissed my now-official, fiancée good night as she held me and wouldn't let go. We looked long and deep in each other's eyes as our breaths melded into one. Our hearts beat a symphony of love and acceptance. I thought of the words of Great Grandfather. "Don't judge another and they will not judge you."

As we lay there I thought, "If people in America had been as open about differences as what I saw today, there never would have been the Indian holocaust. If they accepted each other and welcomed differences like I saw today, instead of demonizing them, half the social problems in America wouldn't exist". This glorious day had opened my eyes and let me see that I had lived in a sequestered world. What people do and with whom they do it should be their business and no one else's as long as it doesn't hurt anyone else.

I can only hope that Amelia and I won't be judged by what we are instead of who we are. I'm certain there have been instances when her mom and dad were ostracized and criticized and yet they have survived. Talk is cheap! I was certain that those judgment days were still in front of us, but I simply did not care. The strength of two is much greater than the strength of one. Going to St. Martin had shown me that it can work, but it would take effort on Amelia and my part simply to show people they are wrong, by our looks, by our actions and by our love for each other.

I looked into Amelia's eyes and she in mine and we both closed them with smiles in our heart...we were one! Amelia curled up next to me and said "I love you" and fell into a deep, deep sleep with a contented smile on her face. Her hand was in mine, still wearing the beautiful ring that had been my gift to her and her to me. God, I love this woman.

The Hearing: Dad's cheese took a few days to prepare, mail and deliver. The Duke called and asked for dad's phone number. He wanted to thank him personally for the gifts. Dad called me afterwards and said they talked about the forest and why it meant so much. They talked of Amelia and me and why we meant so much to all of them. They talked of their families and, once again, why being a father meant so much to both of them. Two guys on different ends of the spectrum were bonding. It was cool.

Court was initially set for Friday, October 6th. Instead, the Judge asked for a written summary from which he would decide. Iowa County indicated that its position was that the land had not been properly transferred and therefore remained in the hands of the Terrill family.

Amy and Charlie wrote the requested brief that included proof that, not only the documents were submitted and in proper form, but all transactions abided, federal, state and Iowa County law and had been received and recorded as such. Based on that contention, Charlie then expounded upon the legal relationship between Tribes, States, and the Federal Government. It's a little long, but the judged needed to be remined of the rights of Native Americans as it applied to Eminent Domain issues.

Here's what Amy and Charlie submitted: "In order to be successful in negotiating with Native Americans, it is important for all State, County and Local governing bodies to recognize and appreciate the sovereignty of the Tribes, the nature of the relationship between the Tribes and the States, the relationship between the Tribes and Congress and the role of the United States Department of Interior Bureau of Indian Affairs (BIA) before acting. For over 50 years, Presidents have issued executive orders to reinforce the relationship and fundamental principles contemplated for Federal agencies concerning the American Indian. An excerpt from the most recent order (Executive Order 13175 of November 6, 2000) follows:

"Sec. 2. Fundamental Principles. In formulating or implementing policies that have tribal implications, agencies shall be guided by the following fundamental principles: 'The United States has a unique legal relationship with Indian tribal governments as set forth in the Constitution of the United States, treaties, statutes, Executive Orders, and court decisions. Since the formation of the Union, the United States has recognized Indian tribes as domestic dependent nations under its protection. The Federal Government has enacted numerous statutes and promulgated numerous regulations that establish and define a trust relationship with Indian tribes.'

"The Ho-Chunk nation, is protected under the law of the United States, in accordance with treaties, statutes, Executive Orders, and judicial decisions that has recognized the right of Indian tribes to self-government. As domestic dependent nations, Indian tribes exercise inherent sovereign powers over their members and territory. The United States continues to work with Indian tribes on a government-to-government basis to address issues concerning Indian tribal self-government, tribal trust resources, and Indian tribal treaty and other rights."

"The United States recognizes the right of Indian tribes to self-government and supports tribal sovereignty and self-determination. 'As domestic dependent nations, Indian Tribes are not subordinate to State governments. The State of Montana's legislative definition of the nature of the Tribe-State relationship as follows: Tribal governments are not subordinate to state governments and are not bound by state laws is apropos."

Iowa County countered that the land had not been in Indian ownership for nearly two-hundred years and therefore was not protected by the laws or rulings in effect. Amelia found out that precedence was set when the Badger Army Ammunition Plant south of Baraboo, Wisconsin was built on a three-thousand-acre piece of land and used during World War II, and then both the Korean and Vietnam Wars as the site of the largest munitions factory in the world.

In 1948 the property was being decommissioned and transferred outside federal ownership. The Ho-Chunk nation successfully argued that the land formerly was part of the ceded territory from 1837 when their ancestors gave up right of occupancy. However, the Ho-Chunk argued that, once the United States government was done using the land, it should have been returned back to the Nation. After a long precedent-setting battle, the Ho-Chunk nation was awarded the land through a process called "Public Benefit Conveyance."

Charlie continued, "With rare exceptions, a state has jurisdiction within a reservation only to the extent that Congress has delegated specific authority to it or in situations in which neither federal nor tribal law preempt state law. When there is no reservation, as is the case with the Ho-Chunk, then each piece of land could be left to consideration in times of disagreement. Tribes, however, are subordinate to Congress and for many governmental activities require approval from the Secretary of the Interior or lower ranking officials in the Bureau of Indian Affairs (BIA)."

"The BIA has responsibility for the administration and management of the 55.7 million acres of land held in trust by the United States for American Indians, Indian Tribes, and Alaska Natives. There are 561 federally recognized Tribal governments in the United States. Developing forestlands, leasing assets on these lands, directing agricultural programs, protecting water and land rights, developing and maintaining infrastructure and economic development are all part of BIA's scope of responsibility. As such, the BIA has a direct and important role in the acquisition of easements over Native American lands for transportation projects including ten acres in Iowa, County, Wisconsin."

"There's always a federal dimension to consider in formal state-tribal interactions. Tribal governments are subordinate to Congress. In many arenas of governance, including economic development, environmental regulation, and law enforcement, tribal authorities require authorization, appropriations, and approval from the Secretary of the Interior or lower-ranking officials of the Interior Department's Bureau of Indian Affairs (BIA)."

"The acquisitions of easements over Native American trust lands are subject to the regulations issued by BIA in 25 CFR 169. These regulations cover all types of easements including those required for State and local highways. At its core, the process for acquiring an easement over Native American Lands for a transportation project is not that different from the process utilized to obtain property not held in trust, including land for public parks."

"Both cases require the following primary steps:

- Surveying land identified for potential acquisition.
- Identifying ownerships.
- Identifying land requirements.
- Performing an appraisal.
- Reviewing and approving the appraisal.
- Conducting and concluding negotiations."

"The main difference, when lands are held in trust for Native Americans, is that the recourse to use eminent domain is not available, except in rare instances and then only through Federal courts. This ruling, places an emphasis on resolving and negotiating all settlements with Tribes and individuals who are holding an interest in the trust lands that are required for highway or other improvements."

"Within 25 CFR Part 169, the provisions related to obtaining a highway easement clearly state that obtaining easements over Indian lands requires the prior written consent of the Tribe and owners of such lands. This applies to securing permission to survey and for the specific terms and conditions of use required for the proposed project which has not been secured."

"Before any trust land consents (allotted or Tribal) can be negotiated, an appraisal must be completed for all parcels requested in the right-of-way application. Certified appraisers, approved by the BIA Regional Appraisal Office, must prepare the appraisal. Once completed, the BIA Regional Appraiser must review and approve the appraisal prior to the initiation of negotiations which has not been completed."

"The negotiation process varies slightly based on whether the Tribe owns the parcel or whether the parcel is an allotment to an individual. The State negotiates with representatives of the Tribe, with the outcome of the negotiations subject to approval by the Tribal government. While this process varies between different Tribal governments, most Tribal governments have an established process for acquiring right-of-way across Tribal trust land. Following these procedures, the State and the Tribe will negotiate an acceptable compensation. Then, the Tribal Council usually approves all of the Tribal right-of-way parcels for the entire project by resolution. Often this resolution will authorize the Tribal chairperson to approve the final documents on behalf of the Tribal government. The Ho-Chunk nation has not and will not approve such transaction."

The brief continued. "When the land is owned by an individual, following approval of the appraisals by BIA, the State will negotiate owner consent forms with the individual allotted landowners and secure owner consents for each of the parcels. Usually, on allotted fractional interest parcels, the State will contact the owners with substantial interests personally, in this case Mr. Terrill and the Ho-Chunk nation, and contact small interest owners via certified mail."

"After securing consents on all parcels from the allottees and/or from the Tribal government, the State submits a package of documentation to the BIA Superintendent. The documents submitted generally include the consent forms with a right-of-way strip map and a right-of-way Grant of Easement form for the entire project. Additional documentation may be required at the discretion of the BIA Superintendent. If everything is in order, the superintendent, will approve the right-of-way Grant of Easement for the transportation project. Following approval by the BIA Superintendent, the State must deposit the total dollar amount for the project right-of-way with the BIA. The BIA will then distribute the funds to the Tribe and individual allottees in accordance with internal BIA procedures."

Obviously, this is not about right of ways and yet Charlie felt that it was applicable as it showed the levels of involvement Iowa County would need to be willing to traverse to acquire ten acres of land. The summary regarding eminent domain applicable to highways was mailed certified, with signature required. Within seven days, signature was received and the judge had the argument in his hands. Charlie said he felt we had a good chance that this would end the fight, but also felt that there could be a challenge. He was right. It was challenged.

Charlie laid the groundwork, letting Iowa County know that there were multiple steps that needed to be done and that it would involve the federal government. He knew that the argument would be that the process was begun before the Quitclaim deeds were filed and that they were done only to impede or stop foreclosure. This was just the first step and why we held off with Project Frisco.

Jump Around: I knew there was no need, but it was my turn to reciprocate with Amelia's dad, The Badgers were playing Michigan at home and I had two tickets. I asked Amelia if it would be cool for me to ask her dad to go to the game with just me. No skybox, but reality. The Duke thought that would be fun. Amelia's mom came to town and the girls went to West Towne shopping. The Duke brought a replacement for the crotch rocket, a new Mercedes GL450 for Amy and winter. He said that the Audi would go back to the dealership and Amy could pick out a new one in the spring. We drove Jeepers Creepers to the game, parked on Spring Street and ate brats with friends who were tailgating. I introduced the Duke as Mr. Williams and he seemed to fit right in with a bunch of twenty-somethings who were too old for college, but too young for life. We walked into Camp Randall and sat in section R with the grad students. The seats were on the goal line and probably the worst the Duke had ever endured, or anyway since he was a student at the University.

I was in my Badger garb of red-and-white striped overalls and crazy hat and we watched the game together. I had slipped two pints of Jack Daniels in and we drank whisky and coke and screamed our heads off. When the fourth quarter began, we joined every other nut job in the stadium for the Badger tradition called "jump around" where 80,000 fans stand up and start jumping up and down to the song, 'Jump Around' by a group called The House of Pain. The Duke was laughing and giggling so hard I thought he was going to wet his pants, (but then after a couple pints of whiskey and coke who wouldn't?). When the Badgers scored with two minutes left, to seal the victory, the Duke high-fived me and everyone around him with a great big, shit-eating grin on his face.

We were both somewhat "loose" when the game ended and were heading back to the Jeep when The Duke suggested we go down on Regent Street and have a last one to celebrate the victory. We went down to the College Keg and one led to two and then three and I called Amelia and told her that her dad and I were somewhat blasted. I thought she would be pissed. Instead she told me to take a taxi home and we would get the car later. The Duke wanted to keep partying, but I thought it was getting out of hand and Ubered it. With all the traffic, we never found the Uber guy and so we walked down Regent, up West Main, south on Broom and to the condo. The walk did us good in several ways better known as sobriety.

By the time we got back to the condo we were fine, but the ladies decreed that we needed to get some food in our stomachs. Paisan's it was! All the way next door, where I demanded that, as my guest, I would pay the bill. The Duke was happy. He had a real day with his future son-in-law and loved being one of the guys. No hassles. No pressures and no politics. The people around us at the game had no idea who the screaming old guy was and The Duke was loving it.

We ate a shrimp and pineapple pizza and Mrs. Williams drove home as Amelia and I settled in.

"My dad had a great time today," Amelia said with a smile. "I've never seen him let his guard down that way."

"You and your mom weren't pissed that we had one too many were you?"

"At first I think mom was concerned until you got home and she saw two little boys laughing and giggling and obviously enjoying each other's company. Dad doesn't relax very often and boy he did today and mom really appreciated it. I don't think he's laughed that hard since Derrick died."

Whew!

The following Saturday was proclaimed to be our day of rest as we did nothing except walk around the Capitol Square for what is billed as the world's largest Farmer's Market with 180 stalls where you can buy fresh flowers, vegetables, bakery, crafts and lots and lots and lots of cheese. One stall had over 60 different types. We bought some flowers, vegetables and bakery, but no cheese. It seems that growing up on the stuff didn't thrill me enough to have to buy even more. The skies were turning grey and it was already fall. Amelia wanted a fire in the fireplace and so I turned on the gas logs. We had settled in and were a couple. The next Friday was time for Amelia's monthly bloodletting and so we knew that the week would need to be reserved in many ways. It's amazing how quickly you adjust to people, schedules and things. People found the view from the condo incredible, but after a few months, you hardly paid any attention to it. Sad but true.

Monday, I was working in what had become our study when the phone rang from downstairs. It was some delivery guy who said I needed to sign for a package. I had no idea what it was and went down and was served by Iowa County. I called Charlie and he said not to worry. It was all procedural. I didn't care. It still scared the crap out of me. We were progressing on all seven of the Gannt charts and deadlines were being met. I sent an email to the ladies in Black River Falls telling them that I thought I would have the book completed within 30 days and to let the Chief know. Things were running so smooth that I never heard from him while Rodney and Ann were settling in as husband and wife.

The First Trial: Charlie called and we had a conference call with Mr. Raskin. The county had denied our writ of dismissal and was plowing forward. They just wouldn't give up! They lost on the change of ownership battle because we had followed all aspects of the law and did so to the "T". We lost because the cases Charlie quoted, other than the Baraboo Range, all dealt with easements for highways and not for parks. The core argument was that the land was sacred because of the saving of the life of Rodney's great, great grandmother.

We went to plan "B" and began making the local media aware that the case was moving forward. Amelia's dad pulled some strings and we had person-to-person contacts with newspaper, radio and television reporters who we began keeping in the loop. Each reporter was provided a dossier of the history of the land, copies of the Quitclaim deeds and the public records of the county meeting. In building a file, they had the information they needed to write stories when it was appropriate.

For the trial, Amelia had done her homework and Charlie diligently prepared. This wasn't just about ten acres of farmland in Waldwick, Wisconsin. It was about the entire concept of the rights of Native Americans and all Americans who had their land taken from them time-after-time-after-time because they did not have the resources to fight back.

Iowa County's argument was plain and simple. The ten acres were not sacred because no one was either killed or buried there. Per the written testimony of George the First, as the County so adroitly pointed out, there was no proof that if he had not come on the scene Rodney's great, great, great grandmother would have actually been assaulted or killed. I guess a naked fourteen-year-old girl being held down by one man while another was about to mount her, wasn't proof enough. I wonder what their opinion would have been if the records said white instead of Indian girl. Therefore, because the lands were not sacred and had never been developed, it was the right of the county to "improve" the land for all to use. I could go into all the gibberish, but that's the gist of it.

Charlie on the other hand, took a different tact. It was his position that the land was sacred and should then be protected and here is what he said, "Your honor, at great expense to my clients, we have proven and it has been declared that the joint tenancy agreement between Mr. George Terrill and the Ho-Chunk Nation is a legally-binding agreement and is in effect. In so doing, the County has stated that they do not consider the land sacred and have done so with no proof other than their own opinion and the belief that someone needs to be buried on the land to make it qualify for consideration. From this, it is our belief that the question before you today is the definition of "sacred ground" as presented by those representing Iowa County or those representing the Indigenous Peoples of America and what legally determines its origin."

"As I look to you, your honor and ask what faith you are and then at anyone of a different faith, the differences may be minor or they may be great. There are over 4,5000 different recognized religions in the world, each of them, believing that they are the true faith. Yet, we accept these different religions based on the fact that the First Amendment of the Constitution allows for freedom of religion as a right of all citizens. The Constitution does <u>not</u> say freedom of religion, unless you disagree with the basic tenants of the Masons, upon which our laws were first written."

"We are here today because some men in Iowa County, Wisconsin cannot accept that spiritual land does not need to reflect the taking of a life and can, in fact, reflect the saving of a life to make it holy."

"As I am certain, you are aware this is not a new condition for indigenous people. From the beginning, men have tried to take advantage of the Indians in many different ways, including what we believe in. Most obviously it has been in the aspect of the land and not respecting the earth the way our culture and our ancestors have. I ask you, your honor, to allow me to read some of the passages that address, in much more eloquent terms than I could, our faith and why, the land under consideration is sacred to us."

The judge nodded in agreement as Charlie provided documents and read along. "Chief Seattle was from the Suquamish Tribe in what became the state of Washington. A prominent figure among his people, he pursued a path of accommodation to white settlers, forming a personal relationship with many settlers to the point that the city of Seattle was named after him. Chief Seattle, in a widely publicized speech from the 1850's, argued in favor of ecological responsibility and respect of Native Americans' land rights. However, what he actually said has been lost through translation and rewriting. Chief Seattle talked in the spiritual sense of the land in direct relationship to the abuse that the White Man had exerted on the land."

The judge's facial expression was already telling me that he didn't care.

"Sitting Bull was a Hunkpapa Lakota Chief and holy man who led his people during years of resistance to United States government policies who laid down one of the underlying concepts of Native American religion when he said that the Earth is not ours, not theirs, not anybody's to own. He didn't understand the concept of having someone own land. It was his belief and understanding that the Earth owns us. 'We are part of the earth, and the earth cannot be owned, we are just simply here to use its resources and return it to the way it was before we used it.' Sitting Bull relates our actions to the earth's natural disasters of destruction. "That nation is like a spring fed river that overruns its banks and destroys all who are in its path."

I thought what Charlie was saying made a point, but the judge sat expressionless.

"In the 1930's stories of 'The land of the Spotted Eagle', by Luther Standing Bear, were written. In these stories, Standing

Bear spoke of the dehumanization of the Indian and referred to the land and the Indian as being one. Standing Bear made many analogies of the land and the Indian being together on a higher level. He explains how the White Man does not understand the Indian and therefore does not understand the true America. And if that goal cannot be reached then the White Man can never understand the true America."

"Your honor; in all three cases the Indians spoke of ownership and the abuse put upon the land. In common, most Indians believe that all land has a spiritual aspect to it and we believe that few white men, except those like Mr. Terrill, will ever be able to be one with the earth. This is because the White Man does not understand the earth and does not respect the holy grounds of the dead or the fruits that the earth has offered to him, but rather walks all over these offerings."

"The ten acres that are at stake are sacred lands because, on those lands, a young woman's life was saved by a white man and his sons. A young Indian woman, who, through all the peril of the time she lived saw over 90% of her people killed, gave birth to three children, one of whom gave birth to the Ninety-four, year old war veteran currently residing in Wisconsin Dells, whose son gave his life for America in the Viet Nam War; whose grandson currently employs over 7,500 people of all races here in Wisconsin; whose great grandson sits in this room today. The young Indian woman was saved by the great-great-great-great-great of the young man sitting next to me."

"While some people might infer that mentioning such an act is simply to save some woods and could not be corroborated, the specific act is mentioned in the journal that has been submitted to you as proof of it's happening. While we cannot cross-examine the author, who has been deceased for nearly 150 years. The fact that his hand-written journal is chronological and not redacted should suffice to allow the writing to be considered testimony."

"The first question then becomes, Isn't, saving a life as sacred as giving one? If you concur, then the following arguments support our belief that the land should remain in trust for perpetuity. While we are in a court of law and respect the laws of our country, I would like to share some of the rulings that are applicable to sacred grounds."

Again, the judge nodded in the affirmative, but seemed bored as Charlie added, "The Recognition of Native American sacred sites in the United States can be described as "specific, discrete, narrowly delineated location on Federal land that is identified by an Indian tribe, or Indian individual determined to be an appropriately authoritative representative of an Indian religion, as sacred by virtue of its established religious significance to, or ceremonial use by, an Indian religion". The sacred places are believed to "have their own 'spiritual properties and significance.' Ultimately, indigenous peoples who practice their religion at a particular site can hold a special and sacred attachment to that land."

"The Religion Clauses of the First Amendment assert that the United States Congress must separate church and state. The struggle to gain legal rights over the Glen Cove burial grounds in California is one among many disputes between Indigenous groups and the federal government over sacred lands which have been ruled in the favor of indigenous people."

"As a member of the United Nations, The United States agreed to abide by the rules governing that body including the Declaration on the Rights of Indigenous Peoples that was adopted in 2007 that emphasizes the right of indigenous peoples and includes the protection of sacred sites and their religious practices. Articles 11, 12, and 25 of the Declaration specifically address these rights."

Old McDonald rose to his feet in a bilious manner. "Your honor, do we really need to listen to all of this?"

The judge stared at the attorney and politely said, "Yes we do!" Ahh! Liberal Madison!

"Your honor, with the court's permission, to save valuable time, I would like to provide pertinent articles and rulings have been provided to the prosecutor for discovery I would like to summarize them."

"You may" the judge responded. "As long as all documents have been previously submitted."

"Your honor, in the event any of the following documents have not been recorded as received, I invite counsel to duly note our oversight and we will submit it as evidence at that time."

"Counselor, any objection?" the judge asked McDonald.

"No objection, your honor."

"Proceed."

Amy provided copies to McDonald and the judge as Charlie continued. "Article 11 of the Declaration states: Indigenous peoples have the right to practice and revitalize their cultural traditions and customs. This includes the right to maintain, protect and develop the past, present and future manifestations of their cultures, such as archaeological and historical sites, artifacts, designs, ceremonies, technologies and visual and performing arts and literature."

"Article 12 of the Declaration States: Indigenous peoples have the right to manifest, practice, develop and teach their spiritual and religious traditions, customs and ceremonies; the right to maintain, protect, and have access in privacy to their religious and cultural sites; the right to the use and control of their ceremonial objects; and the right to the repatriation of their human remains. States shall seek to enable the access and/or repatriation of ceremonial objects and human remains In their possession through fair, transparent and effective mechanisms developed in conjunction with indigenous peoples concerned."

Amelia had done her job as Charlie continued. "Article 25 of the Declaration states: Indigenous peoples have the right to maintain and strengthen their distinctive spiritual relationship with their traditionally owned or otherwise occupied and used lands, territories, waters and coastal seas and other resources and to uphold their responsibilities to future generations in this regard."

Charlie came back to the table and faced the judge as he continued. "Through the past 250 years, indigenous peoples in the United States have argued that they have the right to protect sacred sites on the grounds of religious freedom. The Religion Clauses of the First Amendment have been two main documents discussed in the dispute of sacred sites protection."

Slowly, Charlie made his way forward until he stood right before the judge and looked him in the eye. "The Free Exercise Clause and the Establishment Clause prevents the United States federal government from establishing a religion by emphasizing the separation of church and state. However, the basis of the Establishment Clauses causes a problem with regards to the protection of religious practices of religious liberties by the federal government."

"While the Religious Clause may put limits on the actions of the federal government with regards to sacred sites protection, Article Six of United States Constitution requires Congress to treat 'Indian affairs as a unique area of federal concern. Any legal relationship between both parties is treated with special consideration which is based on the belief that indigenous peoples became dependent on the United States government after their land was taken from them."

Charlie was at it again, giving both McDonald and the judge more paper..."The American Indian Freedom and Restoration Act, or the American Indian Religious Freedom Act (AIRF), was passed by Congress in 1978. The act was passed to recognize indigenous people's religious practices by not limiting access to sacred sites. AIRF also obliges federal agencies to administer laws to 'evaluate their policies in consultation' with indigenous groups to assure that their religious practices are protected."

Charlie turned to McDonald and said. "The Religious Freedom Restoration Act prohibits the federal government from restricting or burdening a person's exercise of religion. Under this act, a plaintiff can present a case by showing that the federal government's actions burden his ability to exercise his religion. Still, although the law is not a procedural law and protects the free exercise of minority religion, it does not protect religious activities conflicting with government's land use."

Amy slid another document to both the judge and McDonald as Charlie continued. "The National Environmental Policy Act (NEPA) is a national policy that promotes better environmental conditions by preventing the government from taking actions that damage the environment. This Act also relates to the sacred sites protection because it promotes and encourages a "harmonious" relationship between humans and the environment."

"The National Historic Preservation Act (NHPA) is also a procedural law that implements "a program for preservation of historic properties across the United States for reasons including the ongoing loss and alteration of properties important to the nation's heritage and to orient the American people to their cultural and historical foundations".

Charlie continued…"Finally, on May 24, 1996, President Bill Clinton issued Executive Order 13007. Under this order, executive branch agencies are required to: "accommodate access to and ceremonial use of Indian sacred sites by religious practitioners and avoid adversely affecting the physical integrity of such sites". This order holds management of Federal lands of taking the appropriate procedures to ensure that Indigenous people's governments are involved in actions involving sacred sites."

"The question before you, your honor is whether Iowa County, Wisconsin has the power and the authority to override the Constitution of the United States, The United Nations and the American Freedom Act, the American Indian Freedom and

Restoration Act, The Religious Freedom Restoration Act, the National Historical Preservation Act and Executive Order 13007 and be allowed to secure sacred land to build a parking lot and porta-potty."

Charlie took a deep breath and sat down. The judge looked at both parties and indicated that he would have a ruling in ten days.

Ten days later, the judge ruled in favor of Iowa County based on their argument that no one had actually been harmed on the land and therefore it was not sacred, regardless of the "feelings" of those who had a vested interest in maintaining it for themselves.

I went to tell grandfather but he already knew. He told me not to give up. "Warriors win wars even though they lose battles". He said.

Christmas: It was nearly Christmas and Amelia and I went out and bought our first tree together. We made chains of red and green construction paper and popped popcorn and put it on strings and put on applied sets of twinkle lights. We wanted an old-fashioned Christmas that took time and trouble and it looked cute in the living room corner with Lake Monona behind it. I had no idea what to give her. The weather was cold and it was planned that we would spend Christmas Eve in Milwaukee and Christmas day in Waldwick. Then, I got an idea. Her parents had never been to Waldwick. Why not have them come and we could all go together? Tommie was back with Heather and was going to her house and so it made sense to combine the festivities.

Before asking Amelia's parents, I called mom and she thought it was a great idea. She asked dad and he said he really enjoyed his time with Mr. Williams. We called Amelia's mom with the suggestion and she countered that we come to Milwaukee for Christmas Eve and then go to Waldwick on Christmas day. Peace in the valley. We agreed.

The Sunday before Christmas we got together with Rodney and Ann and exchanged gifts. Rodney and Ann gave us a beautiful photo taken from the house in St. Martin. We gave them the first copy of "Hocak" which is the official Ho-Chunk name. I signed the inside...."To my Big Brother and Best Friend...Little Spirit." Now Rodney and Ann had both the manuscript and the printed version to which Amy drew up a document stating they were the rightful owners of all that was written in both.

Amelia and I made a journey to the Dells to visit Great Grandfather. The wreath was in place above the fireplace and instead of being in his room, Great Grandfather was in the dining room. As we walked in, his head came up and there was a huge smile on his face. "Little Spirit you are here and so is Amelia".

We sat and talked and filled him in on life and I handed him a present. I had asked our new ad agency for a favor and they had the entire Hocak book recorded onto a disc. We gave Great

Grandfather a CD player with embossed buttons so that he could hit start and stop. We added headphones so that he could hear what was being said. We turned on the machine and a big smile came to his face. "Little Spirit, this is the nicest gift anyone has ever given me, other than love and friendship". We turned off the player and then let him practice before we left. It was then that Amelia suggested we give copies of the book to the members of the media so that they could listen to the story of all that had happened. Brilliant!

On the way home, I called the agency and asked that 20 additional copies be made. I told them I would email the addresses to them that afternoon.

Christmas Eve afternoon, we drove to Milwaukee and went out to dinner with the Williams to the Executive Club that the Duke belonged to. I'll bet the huge Christmas tree in the lobby cost $5,000. We went back to the William's house and gave them our present…a professional photograph of the two of us. Mrs. Williams had tears in her eyes. Mom and dad Williams were being a bit coy and I didn't understand why.

"Son," Mr. Williams began. "You have become a member of our family who is loved and trusted and above all else respected. As a member of our family, we want you to share in our joy and also our bounty" as he handed me a small box. I opened it up and it was a set of keys. "Come with me" dad Williams beckoned as we all went out in the garage and I saw a duplicate of Uncle Frank's Range Rover. There it sat…black with tan leather interior.

"Oh my God, it's mine?"

"All yours"

I was incredulous.

"You said it was what you loved." Amelia added.

"But you shouldn't have."

Mr. Williams just smiled. "Uncle Frank's got the diesel. You have the 5.0-liter, supercharged V8. You have to promise me, you'll be careful. My crew says it will do zero-to-sixty in just over five seconds".

"Oh my God!" As you can see, my communication skills fall to zero when overwhelmed!

We went back in the house and I gave Amelia her present. It was a set of poems I had written for her, along with twenty pages summarizing all that we had done and what my feelings for her were. I had it bound and the title was "In the Beginning" and it started with a photo of Amelia Earhart and then the Lockheed 10E.

"In the beginning it was you and I
Then your life and my life became our life
Filled with the happiness of today
And anticipation of our tomorrow!"

So that she wouldn't need to leave the original behind, I made a copy for Amelia's parents and presented it to them as well, outlining how much Amelia meant to me and how happy I was that she came into my life. There were hugs and kisses all around.

I said goodbye to Jeepers Creepers the Second, knowing where he was going...crunch! We left Milwaukee in my new Rover at around 8:00 Christmas morning with Amelia's dad behind us driving a new Chevy Silverado. We quickly stopped at the condo, dropped off the Rover and headed towards Waldwick in the truck. Mr. Williams wanted to ask my dad what he thought of his new toy.

We all went to church and got to the house a little after noon. Nothing ever seemed to change except maybe the number of gray hairs on my parent's heads. The Christmas tree was where it always was and looked simply great. As always, mom was sentimental about Christmas.

There was about six inches of snow on the ground and dad said he had a surprise for everyone. One of the neighbors showed up with a horse-drawn cutter that would hold six people and we went for an old-fashioned sleigh ride into the forest. We were all bundled up beneath quilts and stopped and all got out. Dad took the lead and showed Mr. and Mrs. Williams where Skunk Hollow School had been and then we walked up the little creek to where the water gurgled out from beneath the limestone. I held Amelia's hand and she squeezed mine when we crossed our special place.

Mr. and Mrs. Williams were taken aback by the beauty and the solemnity of the grounds and I think they finally realized why we were fighting so hard for so little. Dad reached down and filled a small metal cup and handed it to Amelia's father who slowly drank the cold, clear, spring water. Mr. Williams smiled and shook his head in an affirmative manner, for he too felt the majesty of purity and innocence.

The Duke was now in communion with us as he breathed deeply and closed his eyes in respect. It was a moment of reverence for all that had transpired as dad filled the cup again and passed it to Amelia's mother who took a sip and became immersed in our feelings. All that had been! All there was! All that would follow was now intertwined between the six of us. The communion of faith in honor, innocence and dignity had been shared for today, tomorrow and always! Amelia's parents had become what we had been, believers that the land was profoundly sacred…sanctified, purified and above reproach.

We paused as Mr. Williams said. "This is one of the nicest Christmas gifts, we've ever received." as he wiped a tear from his right eye. "A cup of water, filled with love!" he whispered. Amelia's mother nodded in agreement as her soft smile concurred with the thoughts and emotions of the man who meant so much to her. A man who had promised her the world and delivered! Tough on the outside, but kind and gentle, sensitive and decent within!

As we were walking back to the cutter, I saw him, the buck. I motioned to everyone to stop and stand still indicating what lie ahead. The buck looked at us and nodded his head and stood for a moment as if to say "thank you" for the fight we were taking. As we slowly continued, the buck did not move. He stood and watched as we climbed back into the cutter and headed for home. Even the horses seemed at ease. "That was running deer," I mentioned above the sounds of the sleigh bells. "Great Grandfather already knows that we were here and his heart will be filled with joy." I don't think anyone but Amelia believed me, but she knew it was true.

Mom cooked a turkey with all the trimmings and talked with Mrs. Williams in the kitchen. Dad took The Duke on a tour of the milking parlor. Amelia and I sat by the fireplace and simply looked at each other and smiled. I kissed her and wished her a Merry Christmas. She said my book was the nicest gift she had ever received.

After dinner, we headed for home and invited mom and dad Williams in to see our tree. They stayed but for a moment and then headed for Milwaukee. I think they thought the tree was neat in that it had taken so long to decorate where everything on it besides the lights had been put together by the two of us. Christmas night we were alone…just the two of us and that was nice. We started a fire in the fireplace and listened to Christmas music. You need a night like that every now and then.

The Final Battle: Iowa County's condemnation procedures were implemented on December 26th. Gee, what a wonderful Christmas present from Iowa County! It was time to let the dogs loose...woof! woof! Because condemnation had been implemented, we needed to sue the County to stop the process and appeal.

Charlie pointed out that because Iowa County had been so successful in the three proceeding actions, it was his belief they would think the appeal would be a slam dunk in their favor and would present an abbreviated or "short case" when it came to their presentation. Charlie explained that this was because their entire argument had already been presented and would be researched by the judge's legal aides before the trial began.

Charlie and Amelia, on the other hand, had some surprises. First, Charlie moved for a jury trial and it was awarded over the objections of the Iowa County Attorney. Charlie and Amelia were also going to come fully prepared to show the jury just what all had transpired. Court was set for February 11th which was exactly what Charlie wanted...a brief period so that the County wouldn't have time to prepare defenses against Charlie's presentation.

Based on the 5th and 14th Amendments to the Constitution, all evidence had to be shared and so Charlie provided the basic research that was compiled knowing that Iowa County would think that it was superfluous and not prepare any arguments against his strategy. In the final tactical move, Charlie motioned that, because the Ho-Chunk were involved, the case be moved from Dodgeville to Federal Court in Madison. Again, Charlie's request was honored. Charlie then asked for a live feed for all TV stations. It was denied. In the end, the case was being presented before a jury, in a federal court, in Madison and what had been long odds against us winning became a great deal shorter.

With Charlie's approval, Project Frisco was implemented in early January...First, there was a bus tour of the land with the media in hand. We picked the media up and took them to Waldwick so they could see the land first-hand while they listened to the book. When we got there, all four Madison TV stations had their remote trucks waiting. We set up a tent and fed them Cornish pasty while providing media guides along with access to all transcripts and special secured sections on our website that allowed for more in-depth information. Amazingly, every major station in Madison and the newspaper sent representatives. I guess Wilco, our new agency, had called VP's at all the media and discussed the upcoming advertising budget and how Miss Amelia Williams was working on the case as she was engaged to one of the plaintiffs.

Second, we were working with our new lobbyist who was representing all Indian Nations in Wisconsin who took it upon themselves to remind the State Representative from our district that his lack of involvement would result in really negative pressure in the upcoming election. The lobbyist also contacted the governor and the issue of eminent domain in Wisconsin was put on the agenda for discussion in the legislature concerning citizen rights by following the rulings in the State of Michigan.

Third, my dad got all the members of the co-op to sign a petition that was published in both the Mineral Point and Dodgeville papers and then in the Madison newspapers stating that taking the land was an example of government intervention where it didn't need to be.

Finally, members of the Ho-Chunk nation began picketing the Iowa County Courthouse and handing out pamphlets telling the history of the land, how it had been taken and how it could happen to anyone.

With so much attention, the national media picked up the story and feeds intended for Madison television were being sent to all four major networks plus MSNBC, CNN and USA Today. Our website was updated daily with information and the Iowa County Courthouse was getting over 100 calls per day from people complaining about their heavy-handed way of treating farmers and Native Americans. The County Commissioner was interviewed and it didn't go very well for him. The Hocak tape was released on Amazon.com and was being played in bits and pieces all over the country.

It was time to go to court in the Robert M. La Follette Sr. Post Office Building. The courtroom was packed with demonstrators out front on M.L. King Drive and media trucks everywhere. The judge seemed surprised as he looked around the capacious courtroom and saw representatives of all the Native American nations situated in Wisconsin in traditional garb, along with one Mr. and Mrs. Rodney Whitehorse, Rodney's mother and father with Mr. and Mrs. Douglas Williams and Mr. and Mrs. George Terrill III, filling the row.

We needed to be careful there wasn't overkill and so Charlie took it slow during the pre-trial explanations and did his best to subdue his contempt for the lawyers representing Iowa County. All evidence was submitted that was on our website and we made it through the examinations and cross-examinations of first the jury and then the witnesses. All had gone well and was pretty mundane and it was time for the closing arguments.

Representing the defendant, or Iowa County, F. Peterson McDonald, County Attorney, began. As I looked at this gentleman, who was a retired lawyer from Dodgeville, all I could think of was the song Old McDonald had a farm...e-i-e-i-oh that kept playing over and over and over in my head. Old McDonald had seen more than his share of good food over the years and his belly hung over his belt. His tie was crooked, but to his credit, there were no soup stains on it. His coat was somewhat wrinkled and he was sweating profusely even though it was cool in the courtroom. Nervous sweat, I surmised. I looked down at his shoes and, if they had ever been polished, it was a long time ago. It was then that I noticed that he had on one black and one navy blue sock. I kept it to myself, but had a chuckle.

Charlie had been right, Old McDonald would summarize what Eminent Domain was with the explanation predicated on the taxed valuations of the land, as a fair and equitable price was offered prior to condemnation. His was short and sweet, just as Charlie had anticipated. I requested and received a copy of old McDonald's statement and instead of me saying what he said…here it is from one end of the horse. I'll let you decided which end you think it came from.

"Ladies and gentlemen of the jury, as citizens of the State of Wisconsin and the United States of America, you are provided with certain unalienable rights specifically outlined in the Constitution of this great land. Our forefathers set out to not only create certain individual rights and liberties but also those for the good of **all** citizens. In so doing, it was our forefather's intent to ensure that the rights of a few did not demean the rights of many and this has included public use of private lands for the good of all. While many good citizens have understood the rationale behind "the good of all", others believe that their individual rights supersede those of others. Again, our forefathers understood this possibility and, within the framework of the US Constitution, provide a method of equity by which matters such as those before you today can be fairly and equitably resolved."

"I speak, obviously, of the concept of eminent domain… the power to take private property out of the hands of a few individuals for public use by state, municipal, county or even private persons or corporations authorized to exercise functions of public character, following the payment of compensation to the owner of that property."

"The ten-acre parcel in question today has remained fallow and unproductive for over 200 years. It is unimproved. Nothing has been done to the land to the point that fallen trees and brush litter the entire property. Recently, the land was "sold" to the Ho-Chunk Nation. The reason provided…as compensation for land purchased by the Terrill family for payment of medical bills while their son was hospitalized".

With this, Old McDonald, shook his head. "While 10 acres might seem like a great deal of land, it represents less than two-tenths of one percent of the land owned by the Terrill family. Two-tenths of one percent!"

"In many instances, private citizens, who have held fallow land and who have no intent to develop it themselves have seen the transfer of ownership to a governing body as a logical way in which land can be preserved for future generations. However, a few individuals resist the logic and refuse the intent of public good. Once again, our forefathers examined this possibility and added the Fifth Amendment to the United States Constitution dealing with the legal and equitable condemnation of lands through judicial proceedings. Added to this, the Fourteenth Amendment to the Constitution makes the federal guarantee of just compensation applicable to the states. Beyond this, all state governments except North Carolina, which gains power through statute, derive power to initiate condemnation proceedings from their state constitutions in all states, including Wisconsin."

"As you can see, the laws of the land and those of the State of Wisconsin that protect you, also provide for the exercise of eminent domain which, in today's case, has been done in accordance with all state and federal laws and there has been no valid point made by the plaintiff that challenges the law, the method of action or the rationale behind the actions taken, for the good of the citizens of Iowa County and the State of Wisconsin."

Old McDonald spread his hands as if to show compassion. "The intent of Iowa County is not to destroy the land, but to open it so that **all** residents and visitors have the opportunity to enjoy its beauty and tranquility while cleaning up the refuse that has been allowed to accumulate for all these years. Preliminary designs indicate that only one-half acre will be cleared for improvements such as parking and restrooms with the remaining nine-and-one-half acres, once cleaned up, left for all to enjoy."

"We are here today because the Ho-Chunk Nation, instead of agreeing to fair value compensation of $15,000 per acre for undeveloped land, has exercised their right of due process in a court of law. Normally, these proceedings take place before an independent judge. However, the Ho-Chunk Nation has elected, which, again is their right, to leave it up to twelve of their peers, namely, you, the jury. This case and those like it are not easy decisions and any case of eminent domain is both a time consuming and challenging area for the courts throughout the country."

"You have heard the testimony of the Terrill family and the Ho-Chunk Nation. You have listened as the Terrill's read from a journal purported to have been written by their great-great-great-great-great grandfather regarding events and activities on the land in question. You have listened to tales of how their ancestors saved the life of an Indian girl and about a one-room school that existed...for public good...for over 100 years. You have seen how, in order to evade the laws of our country, the Terrill family "sold" the land to the Ho-Chunk nation in anticipation of condemnation."

Old McDonald slowly shook his head. "We believe that in the proceedings you have been witness to, we have, beyond any reasonable doubt, satisfied the four elements set forth in the Fifth Amendment...First, the land was private property...Second, the land is being removed from private ownership...Third, the land in question will be put to public use...Fourth, fair and equitable compensation has been offered."

"Without referencing multiple legal decisions that have repeatedly set precedent in favor of our position and taking up both your, and the courts valuable time, I would like to summarize the following..."

For dramatic effect…Old McDonald, took a breath and cleared his throat…"Actions by the Iowa County parks department in terms of plans for the ten-acre parcel have been done with the full knowledge of all parties in attendance today. By re-zoning the land from agriculture to public use, the action has **not** constituted a takeover of the land without formal notification with the Ho-Chunk Nation or the Terrill's. The desire to develop the land is because the land has remained unproductive for nearly 200 years. Finally, legally, the State can exercise its authority and does have the right to control the use of the property with or without either the Ho-Chunk or Terrill's approval and we are here today as a gesture of cooperation, and in good faith, to show our intent to abide by the plans indicated for the parcel in question for the public's good."

"As you can see, and contrary to what the esteemed counselor will try to show otherwise, we have met all criteria needed for resolution and request your approval for condemnation and remittance of the sum of $150,000 as fair and equitable payment for the land in question."

With that Old McDonald returned to his table, looked at the entire jury one last time, took a long drink of water and sat down.

Charlie stood and took his time, looking first at the judge and then slowly walking down the entire row of jurors making eye contact with each of them. Charlie had come prepared in many ways. First, he was dressed in a black pinstripe suit with a white shirt and multi-color necktie. His black hair was streaked with grey and pulled back into a medium-length pony tail while his black boots shined. Charlie looked good and his socks did match, while being not too flashy and respecting where he was…in federal court.

It was time for Charlie's final statement that I also I received a copy from the court reporter as she punched the little keys on her machine. Here is what Charlie had to say.

"Thank you, ladies-and-gentlemen, for your time and attention. While Mr. McDonald is quite right in his outline of the Amendments to the Constitution and the rights of the government to acquire private property for public good, there are several points that he has failed to point out. As you can see, the courts tend to emphasize the rights of the property owner but, as has been the case here today, there is rarely a discussion of the methodology of how this entire matter takes place or what happens when the land is legally owned by a different nation."

"Counselor McDonald has done an excellent job of outlining the rights of the government. Let me outline the rights of the Terrill's and the Ho-Chunk Nation and anyone whose land has been condemned by the government, including you."

With that Charlie pointed towards the jury for effect raising his index finger. "First and foremost, the Terrill family sold 50% ownership of the land to the Ho-Chunk nation for what was considered a fair and equitable price based on the land's history, events and circumstances that transpired. Legal transfer of the property through use of a Quick Claim Deed had been submitted but had not been processed by the Iowa County recorder. We cannot determine what caused the delay but can assure you that all documentation was complete and received and was signed for by the Register. In so doing, half ownership of the land was transferred to the Ho-Chunk Nation who then legally placed the land in trust for the benefit of all citizens including those of the Ho-Chunk Nation."

Charlie stopped and added. "The Terrill family and the Ho-Chunk Nation and any party, including you, have the right to due process during condemnation. Both parties were supposed to be notified in a timely manner and given a reasonable opportunity to be heard on the issues of whether the use, for which the property was to be expropriated, is public in nature and the compensation just."

"Due process considerations mandate that both the Terrills and the Ho-Chunk Nation including you, receive an opportunity to present evidence and confront or cross-examine witnesses. Both parties also have the automatic right to appeal before the bulldozers arrive and destroy 200 years of memories, which is why we are here today. Finally, a condemnation judgment or order must be recorded, which it was, but only in the Terrill's name and not that of the Ho-Chunk nation."

"I could go into all kinds of legal speak and fill you in on this law or that law, but I, Like Attorney McDonald, would like to save precious time for all of you. Let's look at what happened?"

Following the lead of McDonald, Charlie shook his head as if in disbelief. "First, someone, somewhere, decided, either by themselves or in a committee, that this specific parcel of land is desperately needed. As it was in this case, rarely do these discussions include the owner or ever consider of any emotional or historical values applied to the property. In this case, there was no communication whatsoever."

"Second, Iowa County did not appear to take into consideration what the need was. Less than five miles from the property exists a similar park that is rarely used. How do we know about the use of the nearby park? The Terrill family and the Ho-Chunk Nation positioned a motion sensitive camera on a tree adjacent to the existing park and did so by leasing the tree from the Fitzsimmons family per the receipt submitted in the court documents you have seen. The camera audited park-use for a three-month period that coincided with the time from condemnation and the beginning of this trial. Three summer months, when people would be outdoors and using parks!"

"For privacy rights, we blanked out all license plates and facial images on non-employees. How much was the existing park used in the three most popular months of the year? Only 18 vehicles entered the parking lot in the entire period of time. Of these eighteen vehicles, six were county park vehicles sent to empty trash and clean the restroom and six were county law enforcement officers. This means that in three months, during peak season, in an existing park, less than five miles from the proposed new park, only six…that's right, six vehicles entered the parking area. That's one car **every other week.** One car and Iowa county wants to spend over a quarter of a million dollars in acquisition and development costs to add another park."

Charlie opened his palms as if incredulous. "Second. As was the case with the Terrill family and subsequently the Ho-Chunk nation, none were unaware of any decision by the Iowa County parks commission to simply take the land until the Terrill family received notice and were informed that they needed to bring the matter to litigation, simply because their property was deemed necessary for public use."

"While the government has salaried legal employees such as Mr. McDonald who are paid from funds collected in the form of property taxes from those who own the land, families like the Terrill family are required to hire an attorney to defend what is already theirs. If you have ever needed an attorney, you know that this is not an inexpensive venture. As an example, here in Madison, the average cost for an attorney is about $ 400 per hour and a case such as this can easily cost $25,000 to $50,000 to simply defend what is already yours." The jury shook their heads.

Charlie shook his head as if in dismay and added, "Most families look at the legal costs of defending what is already theirs and simply give up. They can't afford the costs of a lawyer and the realization that government resources are virtually limitless as their lawyers are paid employees whose salaries come from the taxes paid by the family and their neighbors who are fighting to keep what is legally theirs."

McDonald objected as speculation! The judge over-ruled as Charlie continued, "Mr. McDonald talked about fair market value which is commonly defined as the price that reasonably could have resulted from negotiations between an owner, who was willing to sell the land, and a purchaser who wanted to buy it. Someone, somewhere determined $15,000 per acre. This is for tillable farmland. On the land in question, there are over 100 mature oak trees, which if cut and milled would generate over $500,000 in revenue. Beyond that, what value do we place on memories? What value do we place on emotions? What value do we place on generations who have toiled the adjacent land and made sacrifices elsewhere so that the land in question could remain unspoiled?"

Charlie was pacing in front of the jury box, catching each juror in the eye as he talked, making them feel as if he was talking only to them. "As you can quickly see, the deck is stacked against those whose land belongs to them. Throughout the United States there is a backlash to recent eminent domain decisions. People are dismayed to learn that their government has the power to force landowners to surrender their property so that a new owner can utilize the land for a different, arguably better purpose. This shockwave of vulnerability extends to landowners and legislatures from all political spectra because most people don't think it will ever happen to them. Honestly, it's really hard to find a group within the United States that is not outraged by recent eminent domain developments when they hear about them, except, perhaps, American Indians which is the reason why I am here today. As was the case at Standing Rock, South Dakota, Native American's have drawn a line in the land and are now saying, enough is simply enough."

Charlie paused for a moment, walked back to his desk and took a sip of water not only to quench his thirst, but allow him to change gears and make his point. "I am not here to speak of the past, but only give you a perspective on all that has happened so that you understand why 10 acres means so much to our nation. I do so, not to sway your judgment regarding the issue in front of you, but to provide a perspective regarding all that has happened and why we are defending the property as diligently as we are."

"Objection! Immaterial!"

"Overruled!"

Charlie continued without even looking at McDonald. "As you are aware from the proceedings, the land in question was sold and deeded by the Terrill family as co-owners to the Ho-Chunk Nation. As you know, the transfer of title for the land was disputed by the Iowa County Court. Subsequent to that decision, the land was condemned and we, as fellow litigant, have elected to issue a reverse condemnation suit which is the matter before you today."

Charlie moved to the center of the juror's box and rested his hands on the railing. "Now let's look at what was the reason for the transfer of half ownership? Not to escape taxation! The land remains on the tax rolls. Not to thwart condemnation! Even though the Ho-Chunk nation is recognized as such, it too honors the laws of the U.S. Constitution. The reason is that this land is sacred to both the Terrills and the Ho-Chunk people and, by sharing ownership, the intent is simply placing the land in the hands of those whose forefathers came before them. The question then becomes, what does it mean to be sacred?"

"For many Indians, the entire world is full of sacred purpose and being. Our faith and that of our forefathers placed value on all living things and anything that helped sustain life. But even within such contexts, there are certain, especially important, places where the creator or spirit beings brought people into existence, and the world into order. These are the places to be revered, remembered and continually honored and such are the ten acres under consideration."

Charlie stepped back as if to talk to all of the jurors at one time. "Faith in sacred land was taken for granted by Native Americans before colonization. As settlers pushed northward, westward and southward, many Indian peoples were removed from their sacred origins and forced to live in new territories, away from their most sacred places. The tribes did what they could under the circumstances. Tribal communities often gathered their sacred bundles, moved to their newly assigned locations, and continued to seek protection of the creator through ceremonies and prayers. Even as they continued to be separated from their ancient locales, sometimes by hundreds of years and hundreds of miles, they continued to honor those points of origin and understand their attachments to them."

Shaking his head, Charlie continued. "Today, many U.S. tribal communities do not control their most sacred places. In many cases, the geographical displacement has been so arbitrary and calamitous as to render mere remembrance meaningless. As settlers lived and died, they were buried in family plots such as the one on the Terrill farm, until the family plots became illegal and then family member were interred in cemeteries such as those in Mineral Point where the Terrill family ancestors have been buried since the late 1800's. I sincerely do not believe we would be here today if there was a cemetery on the ten acres of land under discussion and yet, the question arises, does someone need to be buried on a plot of land to make it sacred?"

With his palms raised again as if in disbelief. "The federal officials, who are supposed to assist in these matters, are often of little help. In many instances, not because they don't want to, but simply because they just don't understand. They may produce treaties and reservation assignments, but they don't appreciate the spiritual geography of the land and its relation to the people. If a tribe's most sacred spaces happen to remain on their reservation, then the tribes have access to their preservation. Sadly, most sacred sites are not located directly on reservations. As a result, Indian Nations have a difficult time gaining access to and protecting them. The difficulties of the Lakota and Cheyenne to protect the Black Hills and Bear Butte are well known examples."

Charlie was working the group and doing a masterful job. Casually, he crossed his arms in front of him and cocked his head. "What happens when there is no reservation, as is the case with the Ho-Chunk, caused by the repeated forced moves or the sacred places are far away from reservations? Legal cases to protect sacred mountains have resulted in concessions of minuscule areas in which Indians can pray. Though the American Indian Freedom of Religion Act requires government officials and agencies to respect tribal sacred spaces, they do not offer enforcement capabilities."

Charlie's hands fell to his side and a slight smile came across his face as if there was a revelation. "A new and promising movement, however, may be afoot. Lately, various nonprofit land-conservancy organizations have used federal and state laws to buy land and put it into conservancy trust and Indian tribes have organized and joined such conservancies such as the Native American Land Conservancy. These groups have also used existing laws to remove sacred places from the market, while preserving plants and animals, such as leaving fallen trees and brush in its natural state as on the Terrill land."

"To us, this is an ideal arrangement. These sacred places are protected but their nature is not revealed. Rather than being under tribal control, the conservancy trust land is controlled by tribal, state and federal agencies and groups seeking to preserve its original condition. The whole approach promises a means for providing protection for the most spiritual and unprotected places in the country."

Charlie looked at me and spoke. "The Terrill family has shared the story of their family through the generations and their love for this specific piece of property they have left untouched as a symbol of gratitude for those who came before them. Now, I would like to share with you the reasons that we, members of the Ho-Chunk Nation, are defending the land."

Charlie turned back towards the jury. "For centuries, American Indians have seen their lands taken by federal and state governments without consent, and at times, without compensation. Some Indian land takings have fallen squarely within the exercise of eminent domain powers, but takings have routinely occurred under other theories that provide no legal remedy."

"Objection misleading!"

"Overruled!" The judge was getting pissed.

"In both situations, the underlying rationale for the taking was the belief that Indians were not using the land as 'efficiently' as another owner would. In short, the "public good" necessitated the taking of land from the Indians, so the land could be redistributed to others who would make better use of it. From these experiences, American Indians have long been confronted with the reality that no matter what legal interest anyone holds in property, those ownership interests are always subject to divestiture by the government, whether tribal, state, or federal."

Charlie walked to the end of the jury box and stood so that the jurors were at an angle and he was looking at the judge. "There are interesting parallels to be drawn from the American Indian experience in land takings and the rationale provided by Mr. McDonald today. Your decision will either agree with how … historically … federal actions divested American Indians of vast land holdings using much of the same logic or you will make a statement against the theoretical framework of today's eminent domain debate that allows governing bodies to take land away from those who have owned it and have emotional reasons for its preservation and maintenance."

"As the litigant, we agree that, as American citizens who abide by the Constitution of the United States, the federal government has constitutional authority to seize private lands for public good provided the landowner is equitably compensated and there is a legitimate need. We also agree that the various states within the federal union also have the right to exercise the power of eminent domain pursuant to state constitutional provisions. However, the point of contention is **what determines public good**?"

Charlie walked halfway down the jury box, but never took his eyes off the judge. "The power of eminent domain can be traced back to Roman law and was a well-established concept long before the American Revolution. However, with the advent of the United States, there was a change in terms of how people viewed the power of the sovereign against the individual's right to the ownership of property, particularly land, and with this change, the expectation of individual rights to property increased significantly."

As he stopped, Charlie turned his back on the jury and looked squarely at McDonald. "It is argued today that eminent domain powers, particularly the public use doctrine, which has evolved in recent years, has been severely abused, with all types of governing bodies having a newly recognized power to take private lands for redistribution to other private parties. Critics suggest that present eminent domain powers are inconsistent both textually and ideologically with what the fathers of our nation had as their intent."

Charlie spun on his heels and faced the jury. "Although the outcomes of recent court decisions might suggest an expansion of eminent domain powers, a review of prior cases reveals that courts have historically deferred to the legislative and executive policy determinations in what are called 'takings cases'. Very rarely have federal courts sided with landowners."

Charlie stopped, came back to the table and took another drink. "Condemnation of privately-owned lands for uses such as water projects, roadways, parks and recreation areas, hospitals, and military bases are seldom challenged. However, once the government takes the land, there is absolutely no requirement or guarantee the government must use the land for what is was condemned for, or even that citizens have access to the taken land.

A good example can be found in Kenosha County, here in Wisconsin, where land was taken through eminent domain to build an air defense fighter base for the Chicago and Milwaukee areas. It was conceived in the early 1950s and construction began shortly thereafter. Families were uprooted and farms destroyed. Construction had barely begun when the base was transferred to the Strategic Air Command who considered it obsolete as it had become apparent to Air Force officials that the base would be rather redundant with installations nearby and the project was abandoned in 1959. Was the land returned to its original owners? No! The land was sold to private developers who made a fortune by creating an industrial park."

Charlie paused to let his words sink in. "Imagine living in your parents or Grandparents home that they dreamed about, saved and sacrificed for and having some politician decide that it would make a great addition to a parking lot for the park your ancestors donated to the city. You can say "no" and the condemnation procedure can begin. In the end, your legal fees to simply defend your right to live in the home you own could be more than the value of the house and so, you are forced to leave, only to watch the house demolished and asphalt placed where your family once lived."

I saw the eyes of one lady juror widen as she shook her head no. "While we think only of government use, there are hundreds, if not thousands of instances where land was taken and given to private corporations…those with connections, if you know what I mean."

"As an example, many of the first eminent domain cases involved taking land to make way for railroads. In these cases, the federal government subsequently granted ownership to the railway corporation who then sold the land at enormous profits and the good of themselves. Critics of recent cases argue that the courts have taken the public use requirement almost out of existence by allowing private land to be awarded to other private individuals with more money, more political clout and expertise than those who were the victims of the action."

I looked at Amelia and winked. Charlie was on a roll as he continued. "Attorney McDonald brought up the 14th Amendment and has a good point as it is the primary reason for legal battle. Not all people have bad intent, nor are most members of government out for themselves. These are reasonable situations to which most people agree. Property owners do not expect an absolute right to refuse when there is a logical need for the good of all. Moreover, when a legitimate public purpose exists, most property owners do not expect to keep their homes. No matter how unpleasant it may be for them, few would expect to prevail in litigation that argues a property taken for a needed road, flood control or hospital. For this reason, most claims are challenged on grounds of inadequate compensation."

"When railroad companies became new owners of taken land, there was VERY little public outcry because it primarily happened in isolated instances and remote areas. Other types of taking claims have also gone seemingly unnoticed by mainstream Americans, despite the large number of people that were impacted. One such category of takings that has failed to enrage mainstream Americans is the taking of lands considered slums or "blighted" areas."

Charlie walked back and stood directly in front of the jury. "Litigation of the "blight" cases began in the 1950s and increased in number with the advent of urban renewal projects. Blight cases involve condemnation of land where public use is the removal of undesirable or unhealthy living conditions. Yet, rarely are these cases initiated for the purpose of actually protecting the unfortunate residents from uninhabitable conditions or improving their standard of living. Instead, private corporations, working in collaboration with state, federal, and local governments in urban renewal programs, are waiting in the wings to redevelop the land."

Shaking his head, Charlie continued. "One such area was right here in Madison, Wisconsin and was located in a triangular shaped neighborhood bounded by the 700 block of West Washington Avenue, Park and Regent Streets. Locally called "The Green Bush, or "The Bush" the triangle area was populated by Italian-Americans, African-Americans and those of the Jewish faith. The Bush was filled with people who grew up together, lived together, respected each other and wanted nothing more than a better life for their children. Someone, somewhere decided that the Bush was a blighted area and had to go. Many families didn't want to move and businesses didn't want to relocate and so condemnation proceedings took place. Houses were torn down. Families separated and neighbors scattered. The Italians settled in an area called Burr Oaks with different schools and different neighbors. African-Americans settled in an area south of Murphy's or Wingra Creek called Hell's Half Acre. In a matter of months, segregation replaced integration. Families who had lived next to each other, respected each other and understood each other became strangers, all in the name of blight."

Charlie shook his head, came back to the table and took another long drink of water. I hoped he had a big bladder.

Turning back to the jury, he continued. "It didn't happen just here in Madison but all over America. By definition, "blight" is a highly subjective term which easily leads to expansive interpretations. Condemnation of property may meet the public use requirement when it is taken for any number of reasons, including building dilapidation, deterioration, age, inadequate ventilation, population overcrowding, arrested economic development, traffic congestion; or where the area is conducive to ill health, juvenile delinquency, or high crime rates. In many states, condemnation proceedings may commence as soon as an urban renewal plan has been adopted through a local resolution declaring the need to acquire real property to execute the plan. Challenging these takings has proven difficult.

Condemnation for the redevelopment of blighted areas has been repeatedly declared a sufficient public use to validate the taking, even though the condemned land ultimately goes to private entities."

Charlie turned and looked at Old McDonald for a moment before returning his vision to the jurors. "Attorney McDonald spoke of blight and public use of the land. However, blight cases allow governments to take private land and redistribute to another private entity on the grounds that it is in the public's best interest simply because the people are poor or can't afford to maintain their houses. In many cases, these eminent domain actions have resulted in state-sanctioned condemnation where the government transfers private property to other private parties who then build new houses, apartments or even businesses on the land."

Slowly, Charlie made his way to the juror's box and rested both of his hands on the oak railing, leaning forward as if to tell them a secret. "In the blight cases, perhaps the average middle-class American failed to identify with the mostly low-income communities that had been displaced who couldn't afford to 'fight City Hall'. Some of these cases did end up in the Supreme Court. One of the most famous eminent domain cases that has set precedent for nearly 50 years, is legally referred to Kelo vs. City of New London, Connecticut, but is known by most simply by the word Kelo."

"The petitioners in the Kelo neighborhood lived in a "regular" neighborhood, much like the Green Bush area here in Madison. These weren't transients. In fact, one resident was born in her home in 1918 and lived in New London her entire life. The targeted neighborhood was part of an urban renewal plan. However, this neighborhood differed from the typical blight situation because it was neither run-down nor crime ridden. Nevertheless, the community in Kelo was considered a "distressed municipality" based on its economic condition and high unemployment rate."

"Eminent Domain was applied when a private non-profit entity began assisting the local government with economic development planning and, incredibly Pfizer Corporation announced plans to build a research facility in the area. In the end the families of Kelo lost. They lost their homes. They lost their neighbors. They lost their friends."

Charlie stepped back to encompass all of the jurors once again and let his message sink in as he continued. "Many states have proposed legislation or initiated studies on restrictions to their eminent domain. In 2004 the Michigan Supreme Court held the use of eminent domain, like that used in Kelo, as unconstitutional in their state. At least seven other states had laws in opposition to Kelo when the case was decided. In Michigan, like many other states, the legislature is considering constitutional amendments, despite Kelo having no effect in the state, because people, like you, do not want to rely on a Court ruling that can be overturned."

"The Kelo decision was not a departure from precedent in eminent domain law. Instead, Kelo simply affirmed a long history of judicial deference to policy decisions of state and federal legislatures as it applied to Native Americans. Kelo is most important because… for the first time it extended the same feelings of vulnerability to mainstream America that have long permeated other groups of people including most minorities."

Charlie put his hand to his chin as if pondering a thought. "Perhaps the trust of private property owners has likely been misplaced all along. When resources are limited, federal and state governments have always determined one land use to be superior to another. These policy decisions have long resulted in taking of land from inefficient use, followed by transfers of property interests, to the most efficient user. Now that land resources are depleting, mainstream Americans are finally being affected. Where was the outrage when American Indian lands were taken to make way for new settlers, or when inner-city apartment buildings were taken for office buildings and parking garages? Is it the perceived abundance of lands in the United States has given a false sense of security to mainstream American landowners? What if the expectations of individual property ownership, which are rooted deeply in the American way of life, have been flawed from the start? Perhaps the owners should have always expected their land could be taken away from them by legal force simply to make way for what someone else perceives to be a better use. As you can see, it affects everyone, including you" as Charlie pointed at the jury foreman for emphasis.

Again, another Old McDonald objection but based on speculation this time! Again, another objection over-ruled! "e-i-e-i-o."

Charlie paused for a moment to show his displeasure with McDonald. "Now let's look at why we are all here today. First, there is a latent perspective on taking land that allegedly distinguishes the United States from the rest of the world. Within America, there is the high priority placed on individual rights, the most sacred of which are property rights. The irony of this belief is that it is told, and whole-heartedly believed, by the very people whose individual ownership interests necessarily originated from the dispossession of another land owner, the American Indian."

Now Charlie was pacing. All eyes followed his every move. "The history of federal Indian policy is replete with examples of land taken from one owner and redistributed to another who will presumably make better use of the land. In some areas of the United States, every single tract of land was previously owned by a tribal government or individual tribal citizen. The reason these lands are now owned by non-Indians is simple ... the United States Government took lands from the Indians and redistributed them to non-Indians. The present owners, resting on a very short chain of title, are often the same people who profess the "un-Americanism" of current takings law. While takings of Indian land are innumerable and immeasurable, I am taking the liberty, with the court's permission of detailing just four examples of federal action involving all three branches of the government that lead to the dispossession of Indian lands to make way of non-Indian ownership."

"Objection – Hearsay!"

"Overruled!"

Now Charlie was burrowing in! "Why am I doing this? Why are we fighting so hard? Because, the similarities between these actions and the present-day eminent domain debate you are witnessing are stunning. Each scenario involves the same set of events.

First, a governmental taking property. Second, doing so without the consent of the owner. Third, simply doing so on the BELIEF that the present owner is not using the land efficiently. Fourth, the redistribution of lands to a different party that the government **believes** will put the land to presumptively better use."

Charlie continued, "When Europeans first arrived in the Western hemisphere they discovered a pre-existing property owner, namely, the Native Americans. Although Europeans viewed Indians as inferior non-Christians, they were still considered owners of the land, per international law, that recognized that Indians had property interests that could not simply be ignored."

"In the 1760s, the British Crown affirmed land could not be claimed without Indian consent before or after a just war against them and these continued to dominate discourse...that Indian peoples had both property rights and the power of a sovereign in their land. They also noted Indian lands could only be acquired with tribal consent or after a just war against them and acquisition of Indian lands was solely a governmental matter, not to be left to individual colonists."

"For example, the European powers did not simply declare themselves owners of the lands. They negotiated land transactions with tribal leaders. In the Land Grant from the Ottawa and Chippewa of May 15, 1786, the tribe conveyed lands to the British Crown. Through the practice of treaty-making, the United States recognized Indian land and resource rights in traditional lands. In that Land Grant **if**, the Indian Chiefs, **with consent of their nations**, conveyed lands to European powers using the following language: "given, granted, enfeoffed, alienated & confirmed & by these presents do give, grant & enfeoff, alien & confirm unto His Majesty George the Third, King of Great Britain, France & Ireland ... a certain tract or parcel of Land.""

"While the words are different, this is the same type of language used to convey property interest in our deeds today. Without going into even further detail, International Law's 'discovery doctrine' governed the relations between European powers and allowed them to recognize and acquire Indian lands. Moreover, early treaties between European powers and Indian tribes reflected the belief Indians owned the land. European powers were grantees who acquired their property through treaty negotiations in exchange for valuable consideration. The very terms of these treaties recognized the Indians, as the grantor, who had the power to cede, transfer, or convey their lands and as such, as those included in the numerous treaties between the Native American nations and the United States Government.""

"When one power succeeded a previous sovereign, as did the United States after the American Revolution, title or ownership to all lands within the boundaries claimed did **not** automatically pass to the new sovereign. To the contrary, a successor-in-interest sovereign merely obtained the right, to the exclusion of other European powers, to purchase or otherwise acquire lands from the Indians. Yet, the doctrine of discovery merely governed the relationships between competing European sovereigns. Lands could either be purchased or acquired, as the spoils of a "just war. However, it was impermissible, under international law, for a European power or the US government to simply declare ownership over Indian lands without the consent or knowledge of the Indian nation."

"The United States operated under this international approach early on. Along came the Declaration of Independence and the Revolutionary War and the new United States continued to recognize Indian ownership of lands, even entering into treaties to obtain some of it. Sadly, the leaders of the Old World found no difficulty in convincing themselves they made ample compensation to the inhabitants of the new, by bestowing on them civilization and Christianity, in exchange for unlimited independence. In the establishment of these relations, the rights of the original inhabitants were, in no instance, entirely disregarded; but were necessarily and to a considerable extent, impeded, impaired and sadly, impinged upon."

"The issue kept coming to the forefront and cases would be heard in the Supreme Court. Reference to an 1823 case of Johnson v. McIntosh, U.S., the determination was…'Indians were admitted to be the rightful occupants of the soil, with a legal as well as just claim to retain possession of it, and to use it according to their own discretion.'

Two of the jurors shook their heads 'no'. All of Amy's hours of research were being chronologically outlined in a logical manner that everyone seemed to understand as Charlie continued…"Unfortunately, when asked to determine the status of disputed land, the U.S. Supreme Court transformed, and ultimately diminished the property interests of all Indian tribes. Rather than recognizing tribes, as the original owners of the lands, therefore had the power to grant land to an individual or another sovereign, the Court simply reclassified the tribe's original property interest. The Supreme Court ruled the only property interest held by tribes was a right of occupancy, which was subject to transfer only by the federal government. The

Court's action, though not an exercise of eminent domain, nonetheless constituted a taking of what is called a property interest. By judicial action, the federal government took a property interest away from the original owner by simply declaring the original owner never held absolute title in the first place. The Supreme Court never mentioned that both grantees, the individuals and the United States, clearly thought the Indian grantors had the full power to convey title. Simply put, the Court refused to recognize the tribe ever owned a full property interest. In other words, the Indians had no right to the land that was theirs, simply because of their way or life."

"The Court's decision in McIntosh, while devastating to Indians, also violated international law, which the US had agreed to abide by. To justify the departure from precedent, the Court rationalized the 1778 Treaty with the Delaware Indians, where the Delaware Nation, one of hundreds of different Native American nations, promised to allow American troops to develop a base camp on Delaware lands during the American Revolution and the Court used this as the basis for their decision against all Native Americans."

"The Treaty of August 19, 1825, commonly called the "Treaty of Prairie des Chiens" or "Prairie du Chien," was the result of continuous warfare among the nations of the Upper Mississippi region. The warring tribes were assembled at Prairie des Chiens and a treaty was entered into establishing boundaries among them in an attempt to remove the cause of their hostilities. The preamble of the treaty clearly bears this out."

Charlie stopped and picked up a piece of paper. I was spellbound. 'The United States of America has seen, with much regret, wars that have, for many years, been carried on between the different tribes who were parties to the treaty. In order, therefore, to promote peace among these tribes and to establish boundaries among them and thereby to remove all causes of future difficulty, the United States has invited the different tribes who were parties to the treaty to assemble together, and in a spirit of mutual conciliation, to accomplish these objects.

Charlie looked up and continued. "Thus, it can be seen that the purpose of the treaty was to promote peace by establishing boundaries among the tribes and thereby to remove all causes of future difficulty. In establishing boundaries, the United States government established recognition of ownership of the land and therefore recognized property rights … by Native Americans.'

Charlie continued looking at the jurors. "We believe that this happened because our ancestors were inexperienced and did not understand the laws that were placed upon them similar to the Miranda decision regarding a person's rights if they get arrested. However, the decimation of land ownership didn't stop in 1800's."

"In 1937, the Shoshone Nation attempted to recover damages for appropriation of lands where the United States took land from them for settlement of another Indian tribe. They argued the jurisdictional act was an exercise of eminent domain based on the language that the final decree of the court 'shall be in full settlement of all damages, if any, committed by the Government of the United States and shall annul and cancel all claim, right, and title of the Shoshone Indians in and to such money, lands, or other property."

"The Supreme Court stated it was not eminent domain, because it did not require the Shoshone to sue at all. Moreover, the failure to sue or prosecute the suit left liabilities as they were, before the act was passed. The Supreme Court then said 'The sovereign power is not exercised to extinguished titles or other interests against the will of tribal occupants by force of eminent domain.' In doing so, the Supreme Court recognized its own power to take Indian property interests without just compensation simply by refusing to recognize the land belonged to Indians."

Charlie picked up another page that Amy had prepared and said, "It wasn't only in the somewhat distant past that the government participated in eminent domain without due cause. In

1991, Justice Thurgood Marshall, the first African-American Supreme Court Justice wrote, 'We will not enter into the controversy, whether agriculturists, merchants, and manufacturers, have a right, on abstract principles, to expel hunters from the territory they possess, or to contract their limits. But the tribes of Indians inhabiting this country were fierce savages...whose subsistence was drawn chiefly from the forest. To leave them in possession of their country was to leave the country a wilderness.'"

The jury sat and shook their heads. Charlie was driving his point home as he added. "Several scholars have pointed out that Justice Marshall's stereotypical view of all Indian land uses and all Indians in general, was not supported by the evidence. Many tribes, particularly the eastern tribes, that would have had the most contact with colonial United States, were farming societies with elaborate property law systems. Nonetheless, the Court's perception, whether disingenuous or not, that Indians' land uses were less efficient and therefore inferior to non-Indians' land uses, served as partial justification for dispossession."

"The McIntosh decision paved the way for westward expansion by making it easier for the federal government to acquire Indian lands and redistribute those lands to non-Indian settlers. 'Indian title' was minimized or removed simply by judicial interpretation to nothing more than a fight of occupancy, which could be determined by the federal government without tribal consent. From these decisions, the chain of title for most lands in the United States began with the elimination of Indian title, followed by the redistribution of the land from the federal government to a non-Indian individual with no approval or adequate compensation."

"Although original Indian title after McIntosh was considered merely a right of occupancy, full Indian ownership in lands was affirmatively recognized by the federal government in many of the treaties the government negotiated with different nations. When lands guaranteed by treaty were subsequently taken by the federal government, tribes were entitled to compensation based on the value of the land at the time of the taking. Some tribes received fair compensation. Sadly, just like Madison's Green Bush neighborhood, compensation didn't soften the effect, from the tribal perspective, of the repeated actions of the federal government to invoke the McIntosh decision for the white man's benefit.

"Andrew Jackson's Indian Removal Act of 1830 codified the federal policy of relocating Indians to less desirable lands in the west to make way for non-Indian settlement. 'The president was given the power to remove Indians west of the Mississippi River "as he may judge necessary.' Making the case for Indian removal, President Andrew Jackson noted that non-Indians had long pressured tribes to retreat to other lands. President Jackson promised this type of dispossession would not happen again.

Again Amy handed Charlie a piece of paper and Charlie read, "Jackson wrote, 'The pledge of the United States has been given by Congress that the country destined for the residence of this people shall be **forever** secured and guaranteed to them. A country west of Missouri and Arkansas has been assigned to them, into which the white settlements are not to be pushed. A barrier has thus been raised for their protection against the encroachment of our citizens.' Needless to say, that promise didn't last very long."

Even old McDonald was paying rapt attention. It was like watching a great football game where one team had outstanding players and the other outstanding coaches as Charlie rolled on…"The most famous story of dispossession of Indian lands is the 1838 Cherokee Trail of Tears which was a forced removal of the Cherokee people from their lands in the southeastern United States to lands within present-day northeastern Oklahoma. The Cherokee owned 40,000 acres of Tennessee Valley farmland, 22,000 cattle, 7,200 horses, wagons, sawmills and a large number of slaves and lived in what would have been considered traditional log and wood homes. Members of the Cherokee Nation, none of whom was an elected chief, signed the Treaty of New Echota in 1835 by which they sold all eastern lands for five million dollars, plus seven million acres of land in the west, with an option to purchase another eight million acres for $500,000."

"Under the terms of the agreement, the Cherokee were to leave by the spring of 1838. About 7,000 Cherokees moved west, but the remainder refused to give up their land, homes and possessions as they had not been compensated at all. In response, some 7,000 US troops arrested 18,000 Cherokees, holding them in stockades, like cattle, during the summer when dysentery and fever killed thousands. Imagine, giving up your home and all your belongings and fenced in like cattle! Isn't this what World War II was all about?"

"Objection - Inflammatory!" McDonald literally hollered.

"Sustained!" The judge replied.

Charlie had taken one extra step but made his point. Words and images could not be erased from the minds of the jury and everyone knew it.

Charlie continued. "During the winter of 1838-39, the Cherokees were allowed to organize their own march to the new lands, promised to them 'forever'. Thirteen different parties set out on the six-month trip covering twelve-hundred miles of which nearly 4,000 died along the way. So much for eminent domain!"

"Objection - Inflammatory!"

"Sustained! Counselor, please refrain further speculations"

Charlie nodded and toned his oratory down one notch. He had made his emotional point and now it was time to move into the final phase of his argument…the personal consequences of all that had transpired.

"The Cherokee story is just one of literally thousands of tribes being relocated to new lands to make way for non-Indian settlements. The Ho-Chunk nation was forced to relocate eleven times. Eleven times! Moved and moved and moved until there was no specific land left for our nation to call home."

Charlie walked over and literally turned his back on the jury and faced McDonald again. Watching "Law and Order Episodes" while I was in the half way house, I had never seen a lawyer turn his back on a jury before, but Charlie continued. "Once Indian removal became federal policy, it was simply not an option for tribes to retain their homelands. Instead, tribes could voluntarily sell their land to the federal government via treaty or be forcibly removed without compensation.

In this context, tribes faced a similar decision as the landowners in Kelo. They could voluntarily accept the offers made for purchase of their lands, or the lands would be taken by the government. The difference of course, is that there were no judicial remedies available to the tribes should they decline the offer of purchase. The federal Indian removal policy was fortified by the military's physical seizure of homes and ouster of individual objectors."

Charlie turned again and looked at the jury. "After the tribes were forced to relocate to new lands, new treaties, once again recognized Indian property ownership in the lands. Typically, the tribal government was recognized as being the beneficial owner, sometimes in an absolute way. The tribal government controlled the land use of individual tribal citizens and internal property transactions were governed by tribal law."

Slowly he made his way over to the railing the separated the jury from the rest of us and lowered his voice. "Many tribes held their lands with common ownership, shared by all on their reservations where non-Indian ownership of lands was prohibited. It was the preference of the federal government that the tribal government, not individual Indians, owned the land."

"If further land cessions were acquired from the Indians, it was much easier for the US Government to have a single transaction with the tribal government, than to recognize, as a matter of federal law, individual Indians had property rights. Moreover, where tribal law unequivocally recognized and protected individual property interests, the federal government ignored them. In a few short decades, the federal government began making deals with tribal governments for more land from one tribe to make room for the forced relocation of yet another."

"The continued need for Indian land for non-Indian settlement necessitated yet another new federal Indian policy called the General Allotment Act of 1887. One of the reasons for the new policy was, once again, the inefficiency of Indian land use. Indians were viewed as making inefficient use of their land because they allegedly did not promote or permit individual ownership of land as the US government had instructed them to do."

"Tribes in areas such as the Great Plains and the Pacific Northwest, who primarily relied on hunting and fishing, recognized individual property rights. Tribal recognition of individual property rights became even more entrenched as their land became scarce within the confines of small reservation boundaries. The proponents of the allotment thought it was in the best interest of the tribes to abandon all forms of common ownership in favor of individual property rights. It was believed, or at least stated, that common tribal ownership was stagnating any chance for economic or social development in Indian country."

Charlie stepped back and continued. "The federal allotment policy was firmly rooted in the notion farming and other agricultural pursuits were the best uses for land. The thought was common lands should be divided into individual parcels so the individual Indian could become a farmer with the incentive to work harder and make the most profit from the land. The policy, of course, ignored that many individual Indians had been farmers for many generations and those Indian farmers owned, under tribal law, lands they had already improved."

Charlie was on the move again, for emphasis and to overcome any tedium as he made his way to the empty witness stand and paused for a moment before squarely looking at the judge.

The federal government ordered all tribal lands to be allotted to individual Indians, with or without the consent of the tribes or the individual Indians. In order to document the transaction, the federal government typically took lands out of the ownership of the tribal government and redistributed those lands as the United States saw fit. As a procedural matter, this transaction was sometimes completed by forcing the tribal government to deed lands directly to individual Indians, and in these instances, the United States, as the middleman, was not a party to the actual transaction."

With that statement, Charlie turned and once again faced the jurors and was shaking his head. "The tribal governments were never compensated for the loss of ownership, even when the transactions violated express treaty guarantees. The federal action of allotting lands without tribal consent, a complete violation of treaty guarantees, was once again, unsuccessfully challenged in the federal courts. Furthermore, the tribal governments were not entitled to compensation because the transaction was viewed ... not as taking land ... but as an appropriate exercise of federal administrative power of tribal property, even though the tribe had formal deeds to the land."

Now Charlie had his eyes focused on the American flag behind the judge as if lost in its design and meaning. "In effect, the action of Congress was an exercise of such power, where the mere change in the form of investment of Indian tribal property, made all Indians wards of the United States government. Today, those of us who are descendants must presume that Congress acted in good faith in the dealings with our forefathers and the legislative branch of the government exercised its best judgment in their assumptions."

Charlie had the entire speech memorized and choreographed using people and images to enforce and enhance his statement. "Prior to allotment, only the federal government could acquire Indian lands. After allotment, Indian lands could be acquired through private transactions like any other piece of land. The land transactions that followed almost always resulted in the land passing, once and for all, to non-Indians."

Again, Charlie walked to the front of the jury box and faced the twelve members as head cocked his head to one side. "As part of the allotment process, tribal lands were divided into individual parcels and conveyed to individual Indians. If there were any remaining lands within a tribe's territory after the allotments were redistributed to individual tribal citizens, the "surplus" lands were deeded to white settlers as homesteads. These lands were deemed **"surplus"** because it was presumed the tribe did not need the land, or implicitly, that the tribe would not make good use of the lands."

"Decisions were not contemplated." Charlie said as he held out his hands and shrugged his shoulders. "It was simply believed that there were other people who could make better use of the land: the white settlers, who the federal government had previously promised to keep away from Indian land.

Shaking his head and then looking down at the floor, Charlie quietly continued. "Sadly, the allotment of tribal lands eventually led to the loss of most of the land that was still under tribal control by the end of the late 1800's. Ninety percent, I repeat, ninety percent of the land owned by Indians at the time of European contact had already been taken before the allotment process ever began."

Charlie looked up and added. "The loss of land continued, and the erosion increased, following allotment. One reason for rapid loss was that, once the lands were parceled out to individuals, those lands were no longer under the protection of either the federal or tribal governments. Individual lands were open to liens and could also be acquired by eminent domain or by adverse possession, which happens when people don't pay bills or taxes. You can see what happened. You make people wards of the government, put them on unproductive land and make them poor and then, when they simply can't pay their taxes, take away the land they live on."

Charlie walked to the far end of the jury box and looked directly at the man in the back row. "White homesteaders acquired sixty -million acres of the Indian land through this federally sanctioned program. Although tribes received some compensation for the surplus lands, their consent was irrelevant. The tribes were required to cede their lands to the United States. The surplus lands were typically returned to the public domain and homestead deeds to non-Indian private landowners followed."

Charlie slid his hand down the smooth oak railing and stepped to the woman to the left of the last juror. "The redistribution of surplus lands provides the best analogy from the many examples in federal Indian law to the current eminent domain debate because of the Kelo decision. The surplus lands example clearly involves the governmental taking property over the landowner's objection for the purpose of redistributing those lands. In the Kelo context, the legislative determination deemed commercial and economic development land use as superior to individual residential property. The surplus lands, though a less deliberative process, presumed non-Indian settlement would lead to more efficient land use than continued Indian ownership."

"Today, the allotted lands that remain under Indian control are highly divided, or fractionalized as it is called, with multiple co-owners sharing the same parcel of land that had been deeded to a common ancestor. The allotment process, that provided for disposal of surplus lands did not provide for subsequent generations: 'The lands were not, of course, surplus. The formula used consisted of 160 acres for the head of the family, eighty acres for older children and wives, and forty acres for minor children, but did not look even five years down the road.

Conventional wisdom presumed that allotment would be the end of the Indian 'problem' and there would eventually be no more Indians or Indian tribes. The allotment process would prepare the Indians for ultimate United States citizenship and full inclusion into the American melting pot. When that did not happen, the practical problems with allotment were quickly revealed, and those problems are exasperated with each passing generation. As an example, if an adult man were capable of supporting his family on 160 acres, did that mean that his eighteen-year-old son could do so on eighty acres, and a decade later his twelve-year-old, now twenty-two, on forty acres?'

Charlie took another step as he looked at juror number three in the back row. All eyes were upon him. "For all Americans, when an original property owner dies, their property interest passes to their heirs. If there is no will, it is equally divided by all their children. With Native Americans and the laws passed, with each generation, the number of co-owners increases, yet the tribal land base was never allowed to expand because it was locked into a finite number of parcels."

Charlie stepped back without looking and stood in front of McDonald's table blocking McDonald's view of the jury. "Simple math shows you what happens. As the number of co-owners increase, the share of each co-owner is diminished, and the more difficult it becomes to make efficient use of the land. Obviously, if one of the requirements to stave off government intervention is efficient use of the land, the proposition that it continues to be divided does nothing more than increase the probability that the land with fall into such a conundrum."

"There are multiple examples that illustrate the problem of fractionated ownership in Indian country, but the most famous description follows: Tract 1305 is 40 acres and produces $1,080 in income annually. It is valued at $8,000. It has 439 owners, one-third of whom receive less than $.05...that five cents...in annual rent and two-thirds of whom receive less than one dollar. The common denominator used to compute fractional interests in the property is 3,394,923,840,000 that three trillion! The smallest heir receives **one cent** every 177 years. The administrative costs of handling this tract are estimated by the Bureau of Indian Affairs at $17,560 PER YEAR! You wonder why there is up to 80% unemployment on reservations".

"Objection - Misleading!" McDonald demanded.

"Over ruled!" the judge replied, once again totally entrenched in the history lesson Charlie Birdsong was sharing.

Charlie moved in front of the judge and quietly assuaged his honor as he continued on. "Congress recognized that highly fractionated allotments precluded any meaningful economic development in Indian country. The allotment process that was premised on maximizing the efficiency of Indian land use has rendered most Indian land useless. In attempt to address this situation, Congress passed the Indian Lands Consolidation Act, which included a forced provision where small fractional property interests, such as the example above, would revert to the tribal government. The forced provision only applied to lands that had an economic yield of less than one-hundred dollars per year. Unfortunately, when challenged by individual Indian property owners, the U.S. Supreme Court struck down the Lands Consolidation Act as unconstitutional under the 14th Amendment as taking of individual property without equitable compensation, which, obviously, opened the doors for even more attempts at selling off the land."

Charlie walked back in front of the jury. "In response, Congress amended the ILCA by extending the time period over which economic viability of the subject lands would be gauged. Congress's second pass at change was also stricken by the Supreme Court and on the same grounds. Yet, another amendment has been enacted in hopes of reducing fractionated property interests. Many Indian people, like their non-Indian counterparts, die intestate, or without a will, which makes it even more complicated."

"The Act had good intent in that it sought to take some property interest and redistribute those lands back to the tribal government, so that tribal lands could be consolidated towards increased efficiency. Rather than have the federal government pass this type of law for redistribution of land, perhaps an exercise of tribal eminent domain power would be the best avenue to address arrested economic development in tribal communities."

Charlie's was making eye contact with each juror and continued. "As you can see, eminent domain has been an issue since the beginning of America. I have outlined the situation with our ancestors so that you have a better understanding of why we have been so diligent in defending our right to this small, sacred property.

Charlie stopped for a moment as if in reflection, looking down at the floor and then up at the ceiling and the at the jury. "This was a land that our ancestors lived on, loved on and valued. It is where our families began and specifically, where, had it not been for the honor, decency and dignity of the Terrill family, members of our nation, simply would not exist."

"Who are these people you ask?" Charlie turned towards those in the seats. "The Native American man seated in the last row" as Charlie pointed towards Rodney, "was educated at Cornell University where he graduated Magna Cum Laude and first in his class. He has dedicated his life to the betterment of the members of the Ho-Chunk nation. His father, sitting next to him is CEO of the Ho-Chunk nation. He oversees the financial aspects of the nation and focuses on using its revenue for social programs including health, education and counseling to allow members of the nation and those who are in need, regardless of race, throughout Wisconsin, to better themselves. His grandfather, gave his life in Viet Nam by throwing himself on a land mine so that others could live and was posthumously awarded the Congressional Medal of Honor, and his great grandfather, who is 94 years old and currently resides in an assisted living center that is owned and operated by the Ho-Chunk nation in Wisconsin Dells, where 50% of the residents are non-Indian people, who have been given the chance to live out their lives in dignity and do so for free. Without the Terrill's and their ancestors, **none** of these people would be here today."

Charlie spun on his heels and walked back to the railing, taking a long pause for effect. "In conclusion, I am speaking about ten acres of land located in Iowa County, Wisconsin. Ten acres, that's all…three acres smaller than the State Capitol grounds, two blocks away. Yet these ten acres hold spiritual significance to the rightful owners. While I speak specifically of the Ho-Chunk and what we have attempted, it must be noted that tribal nations are diverse in their history, culture, language, and legal traditions and yet, like you, they have been citizens of the United States, who have been rewarded by the integrity of the laws of our country. Also, like you, they are subject to the decisions made by that government…both good and bad."

"The point here is whether Iowa County has the right for eminent domain on the land in question. My worthy opponent has pointed out that the laws of Native Americans concerning land preceded the laws of the United States. It goes without saying that it is impossible to declare a "traditional" tribal viewpoint on whether tribal governments, prior to contact with Europeans, exercised the power of eminent domain or some equivalent. Additionally, it goes without saying that Indians had a system of law for determining property rights prior to the day Columbus arrived on North American shores. It is also inconceivable that the millions of people that populated the continent prior to European contact were aimlessly moving about with no norms, customs, or laws. As Justice Marshall said…prior to contact with

Europeans, Indians recognized property rights, made conveyances of land, regulated trade, and exercised the full gamut of jurisdiction. But did they exercise the power of eminent domain, or an equivalent sovereign power, at that time? No one really knows!"

Throughout my explanation, I have spoken generally of tribes or nations as if they were one and yet each nation had its own laws and its own rules just as each State within the United States does as well. Because of this, you cannot and we cannot make blanket statements that are applicable to all nations, just as we cannot make assertions regarding laws that folks are supposed to abide by. As an example, Wisconsin, Michigan, Indiana, Minnesota and Iowa require you to slow down in construction zone when there are workers present. However, in Illinois, the law states that you must abide by the lower speed limit at all times. As you can see both laws regulate speed limits but with different rules. The exact thing can be said for tribal laws today and yesterday. Those nations that truly practiced common ownership of lands, of which they have long been accused, exercised the highest form of governmental power. The permanent exclusion of private rights for the good of all citizens embodied a public use doctrine that far exceeds the current eminent domain model. The tribal government, through the people, pre-determined that all lands be used for the public good, and there was no room for the recognition of private individual rights. However, it is doubtful that many tribes practiced common ownership in the purest form. The tribal government either owned the land or they exercised rights over specific territories which are documented by the conflicts that were occurring between tribes prior to European contact and thereafter, in order to establish safety, security and supremacy for their people."

Charlie paused again. It was time to bring it all home! "The Constitution of the United States recognizes Native American Nations as **independent nations** who are provided by and protected by the exact same words that protect and provide for each of us as American citizens including freedom of speech, freedom of religion, freedom to bear arms and the freedom to own land…freedoms you and I take for granted every single day upon which our government, our society and our beliefs are founded and upon which we all function."

Charlie looked down at the floor and then at the flag. "I am but a common man and yet, I think it is very clear that the Constitution neither speaks of Native Americans as states or foreign states, but sadly, just as what they were considered to be, Indian tribes…an anomaly, unknown to the rules and bonds which addressed the structure of the United States and its institutions of the time. My ancestors were people, where sadly, the laws of our nation regarded them as nothing more than wandering hordes, held together only by ties of blood and habit, having neither laws or government, beyond what is required in a savage state. And yet, these were humans. People who married, had children and wanted nothing more than to live in peace so that their children and their children's children and their descendants could enjoy the fruits of their labor, accept and appreciate the beauty and sanctity of their culture and honor those who had come before them."

There was sadness in Charlie's voice as he continued. "The myth of "wandering hordes" of people attaching no value to property is one that was told by non-Indians seeking to seize Indian land or otherwise disregard Indian claims. Contrary to the prevailing myths, most tribes here in Wisconsin had some form of recognized private ownership of the land including the Ho-Chunk, Menominee, Mesquakee, Winnebago, Sauk, Potawatomi, Oneida and Illini Nations who **ALL** had laws that protected individual property and private rights to a greater extent than the Constitution of United States or their European predecessors."

Shaking his head, Charlie continued. "We are **<u>not</u>** here today to discuss the actions of our forefathers or what was right and wrong 200 years ago. We **are here** to consider and decide the merit the State of Wisconsin and the County of Iowa have in taking sacred land…land that remains a primeval forest…clean and pure, populated only by memories, thereby keeping it pristine for those with whom the land has been protected and nurtured for nearly 200 years."

"Over the years, American Indian people have come to view property rights differently from their non-Indian counterparts, but perhaps your decision will bring the two groups a little closer together."

Charlie was drilling down and you could sense his passion growing. The jury sat mesmerized. "Indian people have known for some time that the right to own land is far from absolute. The notion that the government can take land at any time is a foundation of the American Indian experience. The inquiry as to what is in the best interest of the "public" is an exceedingly broad question. American Indian people have watched their lands transferred to other individuals for centuries. Are you and other mainstream American families coming to realize what American Indians have known for generations? Eminent domain, and similar theories of land allocation, are rarely discussed when land resources are abundant. But when competing interests eye a particular tract of land, a hierarchy of preferred land uses emerges. And **YOU**, members of the jury, will more than likely lose".

McDonald attempted to stand to object, but the judge raised his hand and the attorney sat back down. Charlie was now stooped as if there was a heavy burden on his shoulders as he continued. "In order to save their own land, the Terrill family elected to participate in these proceedings, which have placed both emotional and financial burdens not faced by the opposition. When you retire today to make your decision, should you vote in favor of Iowa County, the Terrill family will lose sacred land that has been in their family's possession for nearly 200 years and before was that of my ancestors. The Terrill family will lose land that saw them save the life of a little girl who, had she not been saved, four people in this room would not exist. If, on the other hand, you vote to sustain ownership with the Terrill family, Mr. McDonald will simply return to Dodgeville, go home to his wife and children or grandchildren and tomorrow, the government of Iowa County will discontinue plans for a park that it appears few will ever use."

Charlie stood erect. "Mr. Terrill returned this land to its original owner's and, per his own determination, has been fairly compensated for it…the sum of twenty dollars. In so doing, the Terrill family has willingly acquiesced control for the good of those who preceded them. They have done so with just **one intent**…to ensure that the sanctity of this sacred land remains forever. There are **no signs** that say keep out. There are **no signs** that say no trespassing. There are **no signs** impeding those willing to honor the purity of the land from stepping forth on hallowed ground. To add port-a-potties and a parking lot that might be used by a **few people** per year will violate the integrity of those who persevered to sustain the land's purity for many generations. Don't we have enough parks? Don't we have enough dumpsters? Don't we have enough places available for people to go so that we don't have to take this small, pure, parcel of land that holds so many sacred memories for the families who are its neighbors and allow them the dignity of their heritage?"

Charlie took a deep breath and wiped a tear from his right eye. "The families gathered here today are only present because of what happened on that land. They are sharing today because of yesterday. Please, do not allow the government to strip away one more set of memories, one more set of dignities, one more set of purity from our world. Thank you!"

I looked at the clock and it read exactly noon. There wasn't a word spoken. The jury sat there in stunned silence. They had been given a diplomatic history lesson and in so doing, shown that they too could be on our side of the table someday.

There was total silence as the judge adjourned the jury and we all stood as he exited the room.

I took a deep breath and looked at Big Brother. We all had tears in our eyes.

Charlie whispered "I did my best. Now it is up to them" nodding towards the now-empty jury box "but I've got to pee!"

Rodney gave Charlie a big hug. The Chief stood and quietly walked out the back door. Mom and Dad Williams came forward and dad Williams gave me a hug.

My dad came forward with tears in his eyes. "You were right son. You were right."

"Now what?" I asked.

"We wait." Charlie responded.

"How long?" I asked.

"You never know." Charlie added.

The Madison Club: The Chief told Rodney that all of us should meet at the Madison Club, which was across the street from the courthouse and next to the Hilton. I later learned that the Chief was the first American Indian ever to gain membership to this exclusive club of lawyers, businessmen and politicians.

All of us walked across the street and in through the front door. You could tell by the depth of the carpet that the place was exclusive. The hostess guided us to a private room and we entered to see the Chief standing with his back to us, looking out the window at the beautiful State Capitol dome. Slowly he turned and stared at us all. There were tears on his cheeks. He knew that what could be done had been done, what could be said had been said and what could be felt had been felt. He was proud of all of us and the effort that had been given in the name of justice.

The waiters came all dressed in white shirts and bowties and took our orders. Water and iced tea! No alcohol! Food was served as we sat anxiously awaiting, not knowing how long we would be required to sit. It had only been two hours and yet it seemed like an eternity. As the dishes were being cleared, Charlie's phone rang. "We're needed, they have reached a decision."

We all let out a gasp and headed for the door. The silence of each one's thoughts smothered the city noise as we headed back across the street and into the courtroom. We all took our respective places as if we had never left. The clerk appeared and the jury was admitted. The clerk then announced that we should all rise. With that, we did, with me holding the back of my chair for support.

"Have you reached a verdict?" The judge inquired.

"We have", the jury foreman announced.

With that the bailiff took a piece of paper from the foreman and handed it to the judge.

"What say you?" the bailiff asked.

The foreman looked at the judge and then at Old McDonald and then at Charlie. I thought I was going to die. "We, the jury, find in favor of the litigant."

WE WON! WE WON! WE WON! The land was to remain our land. My respite would remain forever as it had been, filled with the dignity of purity and joy of knowing that my children and their children and even theirs would have a place to go and find tranquility and peace.

We all hugged and shook hands. My eyes met Amelia's then Ann's and Rodney's and we all turned to Charlie and smiled. Charlie reached across the aisle and shook hands with Mr. McDonald who was filling his briefcase with papers that no longer had any merit.

Everyone knew where I had to go. I had to drive to the Dells and tell Great Grandfather the good news. I kissed Amelia goodbye. My hands were shaking as I stuck the key in the Rover's ignition and headed out East Washington Avenue. I turned north on Stoughton Road and headed for the interstate with a huge smile on my face. We Won! "Great Grandfather will be so proud of Little Spirit."

My mind was a whirling dervish as I passed the rest area and the place where I got to drive the Batmobile. As the Interstate narrowed with 90-94 heading towards the Dells and 39 towards Wausau, my mind slipped back into all that had happened and how much I had learned. I was proud of all that had transpired and the fact that I sincerely felt I had gone from being a smart-ass college kid, to a man who sincerely cared about others. So many people had entered my life and changed so much. So many people had allowed me to see goodness and generosity and I could hardly wait to thank Great Grandfather for his wisdom and allowing me to be a part of so many lives and honoring me by allowing their story to be told through me.

It wasn't long until I was at the Dells exit and I headed straight for the assisted living center. I parked my car and walked through the front door. The front desk was empty. I thought it was odd because it was nearly dinner time. I walked down the hall to Great Grandfather's room and looked at his rocking chair. It too was empty. Perhaps he was in the bathroom, but the light was off. Perhaps at dinner? It was then that Marge came in behind me and I turned and saw the look in her eyes.

"He left us." she said.

"Oh no." I replied as I crumpled into his rocking chair.

"I came in this morning and he said that today he was going on a long journey. He said that the Great Spirit was calling him home and that he was looking forward to seeing his family and those who had come before him. I thought it was just an old man talking. He asked me to get a paper and pen as he wanted me to write you a note. I did as he asked and here is the letter he had me write to you." I sat upon the cedar chest and carefully opened his letter.

My Dear Friend:

My time has come to go and be with my family and those who came before me. I could not go without telling you one last time that you will always be within my heart. Do not grieve for me as all my wishes have come true.

You, Little Spirit, are the chosen one. You have been selected to carry on now that I am gone. At first the voices will be soft and you will not understand. As the years pass like waves upon the shore, the messages will become louder within your heart and you will understand. As the chosen one, you will speak for those who came before you and I know that you will tell the truth and be honorable. That is why my heart is filled with joy.

Do not think that we will never meet again. Someday, a long time from now, I will look in your eyes and see the young boy who became a man before me. I will smile and we will walk through eternity together.

Until that day, I will always be with you and when you visit the forest, I will be amongst the trees whispering to you, not of melancholy, but of bravery, for you truly are a warrior for what is right and what is good.

So, Little Spirit, I must go. As I depart, the cedar box upon which you sat and what is in it is yours forever. Cherish it. Honor it. Defend it. Keep it close to your heart.

Great Grandfather

Tears were streaming down my face. My friend, my dear, dear friend who taught me so much was gone.

Marge added. "He called me just after lunch and I came in. He was sitting in his rocker with the quilt upon his lap. He asked me to take his hand and thanked me for my love and kindness."

"But, he never got to know". I whispered.

"He knew." Marge said. "He knew. He said his work was done. Then he simply slipped away, but the smile remained upon his face even when he was gone. I called the Chief and told him and he said he already knew, for the spirits had spoken."

With that, I stood and opened the cedar chest and my breath was taken away. I peered down and it was there…still soft, still white…the bear skin that had changed the Terrill world. On top were the two eagle feathers intended for me, Little Spirit.

The Waldwick Series: The ten-book series spans nearly 200 years and are independent yet intertwined in several ways including, characters, location and thematic objectives that examine current social issues from different perspectives. Regardless of the time period or the characters in question, the core component - judging people by who they are instead, of what they are, remains paramount.

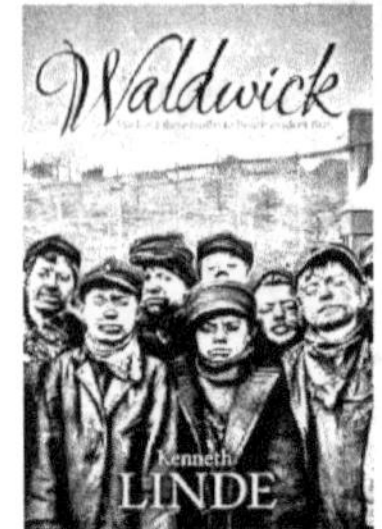

Waldwick addresses the subject of physical, social, economic and political oppression in the 1800's. Set in Cornwall, England, Virginia and Southwestern Wisconsin, *Waldwick* frankly discusses what one family was willing to do to overcome oppression, as told through the eyes of the narrator, George Terrill. *Waldwick* then summarizes what happens when the oppression is removed and opportunity arises. Integrated into the story line are actual events and people and how the main characters are affected by their existence and their interaction with these people and events. Above all else, *Waldwick* is a love story … love of the land, love of one another and the love of freedom, woven in a tapestry of acceptance, tolerance and justice. *Award Winner*

War of My Brothers examines America of the early 20th century and how and why it changed as seen through the eyes of Hank Terrill, great grandson of George Terrill from the original Waldwick. Ride along as Hank witnesses World War I, the Spanish Flu, the 19th Amendment, that gave women the right to vote, the Great Depression, World War II, Korean War and Viet Nam and how life changed, people changed and those who govern changed, as well. Experience the traumas of life and the joys of the living as you thank God that it didn't happen to you.

The King of Hearts has been reviewed as *"ambitious, extensively researched and deeply engrossing"*…a story that traces the actual Terrill family through 60 generations as it learns the consequence of wealth, power and prestige over 700 years only to have it all collapse around them. Using a blend of magic realism, lyrical prose and imagery *The King of Hearts* weaves a complex tapestry of a family's history from 65 BCE through sixty generations. Beneath it all, the book is about friendship and the deep, mutual bond between people based on trust, support, and genuine connection that goes beyond just companionship—it's about understanding, loyalty, and being there for each other through life's ups and downs.

Little Spirit Based in contemporary Wisconsin, *Little Spirit* examines the concept of eminent domain and the taking of land and dignity, first from the Indian's perspective and then today, as seen through the eyes of George Terrill IV a descendant of the original George Terrill. Using flashbacks through a 94-year-old, blind, Ho- Chunk Indian elder, named Great Grandfather, George learns about the feelings and challenges of the Ho-Chunk nation and the taking of their land and also how contemporary America hasn't changed that much in terms of citizen rights.

Driftless revisits George and his wife fifteen years into their marriage. Reflecting on the challenges they face when their marriage becomes mundane while examining the profound question of which is worse… having nothing or everything. As the mystery of the Forest is revealed *Driftless* examines the consequence of technology and the power of special interest groups to control the status-quo for their financial gain, while addressing the issue of individual rights in time of personal need, where the one thing all people have in common is … time!

The Hayflick Limit addresses the challenges of parenthood, while discussing a person's rights to live and die. When affected by an incurable malady the question becomes *"Would you choose five-to-seven years of normal mental acuity, at which time you would abruptly expire, or risk everything and allow for the slow, gradual decline with hope that a different, longer-lasting cure might come along?" The Hayflick Limit* addresses the role of government in establishing the validity of the Hippocratic Oath?

Let Go examines the consequence of bullying as Melia Terrill is affected by the verbal onslaught and her commitment to the only friend who has shown her the beauty of acceptance for who she is. The books examines the perks and perils of extreme wealth, the solitude of loneliness and frustration of achieving one's goals only to realize that all dreams can become nightmares when one risks everything for perhaps nothing as it delves into thoughts, emotions, joys, sorrow and consequences of being a captive of one's own past and fleeting fame.

Survivor…How Death Saved My Life looks at the consequence of an altered set of priorities and how it can take a near-death experience to "right the ship". Totally immobilized for six days, George Terrill examines his life and it's mistakes and vows, if he survives, to make things right. *Survivor* addresses the psychology of fear, the challenges of being told you have less than a 5% chance of living three hours and what you think about when you sincerely believe you're going to die.

Greed is a thought-provoking literary tale of ambition gone awry, exposing how the pursuit of wealth can fracture family relationships. This intense novel, explores the intricacies of human nature and the pursuit of meaning. It serves as a critique of modern society's obsession with wealth and status that challenges readers to reconsider what success truly means, making this book not just an exhilarating journey but a profound reflection on the human condition.

And/Or Using Newton's Third Law as a lens to explore relationships where every action sets off a chain reaction, *And/Or* journeys in ways no one can predict or control while asking difficult questions about resilience, identity, and redemption. As such, it ponders deep philosophical reflections and existential questions by drawing sharp connections between science and human nature, asking such profound questions as…Is it possible for a person to truly recover from betrayal? Can love survive after it's been broken? And when one loses everything, what's left? *And/Or* is a gripping, thought-provoking read that will linger long after the final page.

Disclaimer: This book is a work of fiction. Some of the events detailed herein are true and have been faithfully rendered as researched by the author, to the best of his abilities. The information contained in this book is intended to provide helpful and informative material on the subjects and events addressed and written as an interpretation of his learning. It does not guarantee accuracy or social integrity and has been written for the purpose of education and entertainment.

The author is a descendant of miners from Cornwall. There is a town called Mineral Point, Wisconsin where his childhood was filled with magical moments and marvelous memories. There is a village called Waldwick that remains nearby and is the birthplace of the author's grandmother and mother. There are many Terrill's living in the area who are the author's relatives and he hopes and prays that he has done the family name justice by what he has written for they, along with the American Indians, are the kindred spirit upon which our country was created. There is no reality to the names used as they are all of consequence.

Today, the Ho-Chunk nation is a vibrant and positive segment of Wisconsin lore and society. The people represented within are all part of the author's imagination and the sum of his interaction with this wonderful group of people who smile often, laugh easily and are proud of their heritage.

If the tale he weaves meets your fancy and your interest is piqued, the author highly recommends visiting Madison, Wisconsin and the wonderful area to the southwest, as well as Wisconsin Dells. The scenery is spectacular and is only exceeded by the honor, dignity and warmth of the people who reside there.

This book along with others in the Waldwick Series was written as a tribute to his grandmother who was a Terrill and from whom, the author learned the value of integrity and honesty and the joy of acceptance that only comes from an open heart and a profound sense of decency that she emanated with each breath and also to the Native Americans who gave so much so and got so little so that we might all call this great land "home".